THE THEORY OF
EXPERIENTIAL EDUCATION

EDITED

BY

RICHARD J. KRAFT
University of Colorado
Professor of Education

AND

MITCHELL SAKOFS

Association for Experiential Education
Box 249—CU
Boulder, CO 80309

ISBN # 0-929361-00-8

PREFACE

The Association for Experiential Education is committed to furthering experience-based learning in a culture that is increasingly "information rich, but experience poor." A growing body of evidence, including the reports of five different national commissions, indicates the need to incorporate direct experience in education. The AEE's mission is:

1)   to empower individuals by helping them assume
     responsibility for their own learning and personal
     development, and to contribute to the quality
     of life in their communities;
2)   to promote definition, application, and evaluation
     of experiential learning; and
3)   to support and guide Association members and other
     practitioners in their efforts to develop experiential
     learning within human service programs.

The Association is an international network of individuals, schools, and other educational organizations which share a common interest in and commitment to experience-based teaching and learning. The AEE was incorporated as a not-for-profit organization in 1977 and offers both individual and institutional memberships.

The articles found in this anthology were originally published in the Journal of Experiential Education, the official publication of the Association. Special thanks are due the editors of the Journal for their careful selection and editing of the original manuscripts. Dan Madden (1978-79), Anne Wasko (1980-81), Pamela Wood (1982),and Peggy Walker Stevens (1983-Present)

Among the benefits of membership in the Association for Experiential Education are the following: A subscription to the Journal of Experiential Education; a membership handbook; reduced rates at the annual conference; reduced rates on the Jobs Clearing House; a membership directory; consultant network· network resource assistance; and reduced rates on Association books and other publications. Interested persons should write to the AEE at Box 249-CU, Boulder, CO 80309.

The initial article in this anthology, Towards a Theory of Experiential Learning, was adapted from a paper produced under contract with the National Technical Institute for the Deaf.

TABLE OF CONTENTS

A CALL TO ACTION AND REFLECTION

by Richard J. Kraft

E.F. Schumacher, a patron saint of the environmental and experiential education movements, stated:

> When the available 'spiritual' is not filled by some higher motivations then it will necessarily be filled by something lower—by the small, mean, calculating attitude to life which is rationalized in the economic calculus.

Experiential education is at a critical turning point, in which the temptations to meet budgets, sell ourselves to the corporate elites of this world, meet the narcissistic desires of the rich, or reprogram insensitive governmental and educational bureaucracies, threaten to undo the profound commitments of founding fathers such as Kurt Hahn, who saw among the ends of experiential learning; service to one's neighbor, the cause of international peace, and the development of morally responsible men and women. We are threatened on the one hand by our inability to penetrate in any long-term or in-depth way the educational, welfare and penal bureaucracies with whom we work, while on the other hand, we find ourselves increasingly caught up in what Jacques Ellul calls technique, any complex of standardized means for attaining a predetermined result. The temptation at a crisis time is to further refine our technique, so that we can guarantee life changing experiences to those suffering mid-life crises, greater profits to managers who raft down rivers with their employees, or lower recividism rates to prison officials seeking a quick fix for the failures of the system.

Almost 50 years ago, George Counts wrote his provocative essay, "Dare the Schools Build a New Social Order," founding the reconstructionist philosophy of education, and challenging educators for decades to come with a vision of a just, moral and responsible society. Experiential education, as it is practiced by members of AEE and similar groups, is one of the last inheritors of Count's vision, but one fears that the flame of idealism is flickering as we face the problems and temptations listed above. Have we lowered our sights and begun to use only the economic calculus of which Schumacher speaks in deciding the direction for the future of experiential learning?

A major problem has been a lack of understanding of our historical roots. Experiential education did not spring full blown out of the Second World War and the need for British seamen to be prepared to face disaster by being placed in challenge or stress situations. As James Coleman so cogently pointed out on these pages 3 years ago, experiential learning preceded the use of symbolic media, assimilating information, and the direct memory-to-memory transfer of information by millions of years. Through an unbroken line of formal and non-formal educational programs, experiential learning was passed on from parents to children, from master to apprentice, through the centuries of unrecorded and recorded history, right up to the present day realization on the part of many educational institutions of the validity of on-the-job training, vocational programs, medical internships, and a host of other experiential learning settings, too numerous to mention. A difficulty that many of us in the "adventure-based" wing of the movement have, however, is our inability to see our connectedness to the broad spectrum of experiential learning, not only historically, but in the contemporary United States. The FIPSIE Study on Internships, The Council for the Advancement of Experiential Learning, ACTION, The National Center on Volunteerism, and national centers on vocational education, career education and numerous other organizations are involved in promoting experiential learning for children and adults, and it would

1

behoove us to recognize our common heritage and goals, and not just emphasize our differences.

If we lack a sense of history, an equally prevailing problem is the cry that we have no theoretical base. Attempts at definition have proven difficult, and many of us await a John Dewey or Jean Piaget to provide the legitimation we so desperately seek in the academic, corporate and governmental worlds in which we work. Alas, after years of waiting, no messiah has come to lead us out of our wilderness. Perhaps it is because our theoretical roots, like our honorable history, are there to be claimed. The empirical tradition of Aristotle is as much ours as it is that of men of science. Aristotle stated, "Men of experience succeed even better than those who have theory without experience," a phrase which could serve well as the motto of AEE over two millenia later. Descartes and Mill upheld the tradition during the Enlightenment, and in the past century, American pragmatism through Peirce, James and Dewey provided both the philosophical and educational roots for much of what goes under the guise of experiential education today.

This connection with pragmatism has led many of us to see the contemporary roots of the experiential education movement in that of the progressives of the 1930s, of which Dewey and Counts were leading lights. One has only to listen to members of the moral majority to know that certain people in this group believe that progressive education and John Dewey in particular, are at the root of our problems of juvenile delinquency, teenage pregnancies, and massive illiteracy. The judgment is unfair by any reading of history, but it has led many, even in the experiential education movement, to seek comfort in such phrases as rugged individualism, management by objectives, back to the basics, and phrases which do more justice to B.F. Skinner and Ronald Reagen than to our true historical and philosophical roots. The goals of the progressives paralleled those of Kurt Hahn mentioned earlier, and perhaps it is time that we as experiential educators claimed our indebtedness to them and truly laid hold of their educational and societal vision.

The progressive vision was a social vision, and Dewey would bridle at the extreme individualism of many of today's experiential educators, who appear to emphasize the individual, the mystical experience of the mountaintop and the narcissistic pleasures of the wilderness, rather than the arduous task of building a just and democratic social order. Our heritage, however, is not just from the progressives, as we can find parts of our roots in the writings of Maria Montessori, the practice of the British Infant Schools, the action

learnings of the Peace Corps and VISTA, and the humane vision of the open/alternative education movement, to name but a few movements that have contributed to our theoretical and practical base.

Even if we have no Dewey or Piaget to claim as our own prophet, both these giants of educational thought have contributed mightily to our theoretical underpinnings. We would not be the first educational movement to be eclectics in our philosophy of education and learning theory, and will no doubt not be the last. Dewey's belief that all "genuine education comes about through experience," led him to advocate the use of a wide variety of educational settings, a thought much in keeping with experiential educators of all persuasions. It is recent research on Piaget's stages of development, however, that provides perhaps our strongest research base for a defense and expansion of experiential learning modes. In his original research, Piaget found that children moved from concrete operational thought to formal or abstract operational thought at around the age of eleven. This finding tended to justify the use of symbolic media, lectures, "book learning," and other traditional modes in the classrooms of this and other countries. Recent research by Epstein, however, has found that large percentages of junior and senior high school students are not yet capable of formal/abstract thought, and that many adults never reach Piaget's formal operational stage. This is not to conclude that such persons are condemned to a life without learning, but to indicate that formal and non-formal educational agencies and institutions must begin to take a serious look at what experiential education has to offer, when it comes to learning through concrete or experiential modes.

A recent research project which I conducted for the National Technical Institute for the Deaf (NTID), brought home once again the critical nature of experience, not just for deaf persons, but for all people. Even an adult cannot think abstractly without an appropriate experiential base. As educators we must begin with concrete, action oriented contexts in presenting concepts or ideas, and only later move to more internalized modes, from objects to symbols of objects, and from motor action to speech. As experiential educators we have known that this progression is the most efficacious for a large percentage of learners, but now we have the research to back it up. We must not be hesitant in claiming these findings to justify our approaches to the teaching/learning process.

If we lack an historical sense or an understanding of our theoretical roots, a final problem is a missing sense of purpose, or for lack of a better word, a driving ideology. One is always hesitant to plead for idealogical commitment, as most of us find the driving force behind the ideologies of Muslim Fundamentalism or Soviet Bureaucratic Communism to be abhorrent, but there can be no question that experiential education today lacks the moral imperatives of its founders such as Kurt Hahn, or the deep commitment to a just and democartic society of John Dewey and the Progressive Education Society. What is it that will motivate experiential educators in the last two decades of the twentieth century? Will it be profit margins, programmed rituals in the wilderness, the search for the best technique, or will we move beyond these superficial and at times destructive goals and into seeking, as did our founders and intellectual precursors, a more just society, a peaceful world, a world free from hunger, and other goals which demand that we adopt an ideological posture and begin to do battle with those aspects of our societies which prevent the achievement of these goals.

Paulo Friere warns us that liberation is a praxis, and that both action and reflection are necessary to bring about meaningful change. Too often we have been guilty of reflecting on the needs of our world, while sitting on the mountaintop, but have not been moved to action on our return to the city. We have lost the meaningful service ethic, to which we were called by our founders, so that service activities at the end of many of our programs become nothing more than picking up litter, rather than a call to commitment and action to deal with poverty, ignorance or disease in our communities and around the world. Is service to the corporate giants of American society, service in the sense to which Kurt Hahn called us? I think not. Only as we gain a sense of being the "loyal opposition" to governments, bureaucracies, educational and penal institutions, and business corporations, will we perhaps regain a small portion of our eternal souls, and fill the spiritual space, of which Schumacher was speaking, with higher motivations.

Richard Kraft, Ph.D, is a professor of education, Division of Social and Multicultural Foundations and director of the Experiential Education Program at the University of Colorado at Boulder, Colorado.

HISTORICAL FOUNDATIONS

TOWARDS A THEORY OF EXPERIENTIAL LEARNING

By

Richard J. Kraft

I. INTRODUCTION

Experiential education is not something new. In fact, one must agree with James Coleman that the growth in experiential education in the 1970's and 80's appears to be a "throwback", an anachronism," as experiential learning has always been with us and what is new, by standards of the millions of years during which persons have been on this earth, is

> ...educating   through assimilating information, education through being taught via a symbolic medium, learning by being given the distilled experience of others, direct memory-to-memory transfer of information. (Coleman, p. 6)

It is the overwhelming dominance of this "new" type of education with its emphasis upon vicarious experience that has led to the reintroduction of experiential learning in recent years. Non-formal and informal education are related concepts which have entered the lexicon of education to describe the educational process which occurs in settings outside the formal schools.

The experiential education movement can trace its roots back to Rousseau's Emile or to the Progressive Movement of the 1930's in this country, but the immediate reasons for the reanalysis of the role of experience in learning comes from the failure of contemporary schooling to meet the needs of large portions of the youth. The percentage of failures, drop-outs, push-outs, and alienated youth varies from community to community, but those percentages are significant enough, particularly in the large urban centers, to prompt educators to take a serious look at what they are doing.

Every major national study of the problems of youth, adolescents and the secondary schools and universities in the 1970's made similar recommendations concerning the need for experiential modes of learning for most, if not all youth, in the last quarter of the twentieth century. The International Commission on the Development of Education in 1972, issued a UNESCO report calling for lifelong integration of education, work and leisure, with students leaving and returning to their studies without penalty at any time. Distinctions between in-school and out-of-school education should be eliminated, and abillity to do a job, not a credential, should be the criteria for hiring. Programs at all levels should combine theoretical, technological, practical, and manual skills, with a good balance between theoretical studies and practical work. Lastly, education must become self-education. (Faure)

The National Commission on the Reform of Secondary Education, led by B. Frank Brown saw the secondary schools on the verge of collapse in the large cities in 1973. Little has happened since that time to change the prognosis. Among the Commission's recommendations relating to experiential education were: The curriculum should concentrate on students' needs and interests and should include on-site experiences in the working life of the community; and students should be permitted alternate paths to graduation including independent programs involving credit for action learning. (Brown, et.al)

The President's Science Advisory Committee, chaired by James S. Coleman in 1974, reported on the societal changes which have led to the need for greater experiential learning environments, and then recommended the following actions: offer a greater range of experiences within the school structure; alternate school and work; and encourage business and industry to create roles and provide training for youth. (Coleman, President's Commission)

The National Panel on High Schools

and Adolescent Education out of U.S.O.E. in 1974 echoed the recommendations of the other panels, calling for structural and conceptual change to get away from schooling as only that which occurs in a classroom with a teacher talking to a group of students. Among its many recommendations are those related to experiential learning: respect for individual differences; the integration of schools and the broader community; preparation of students for family and work roles; and youth participation in decision-making in the society. (Martin, et. al.)

Perhaps the most far reaching, radical, and experientially oriented report is the Phi Delta Kappa Task Force on The New Secondary Education. The Task Force was chaired by Maurice Gibbons, father of the American Walkabout concept, so that it is little wonder that the report has a strong experiential bias. Among its many recommendations and prepositions are the following: an appropriate set of alternatives to school must be sought; current schooling does not demonstrate any superiority over other possible systems of educating the adolescent; the current system resists change; current school contradicts the nature and demands of human growth and development; formal studies are more powerful when combined with concrete experiences and challenging productive activities; students need to learn from more adults and each other, not just teachers; schooling should involve gradual transitions into adult situations, issues, tasks, and responsibilities; students need to learn to select, design, implement and manage their own learning; students trained to experience and direct their own sensory, emotional, and mental functions will be better able to achieve self-understanding and self-directed learning, and self-development; and schools and communities must have much more interaction; Gibbons and the staff conclude their report with the theory and practice of the New Secondary Education. These will be dealt with later in this paper, as they include some of the more important aspects of an experiential learning environment. The years 1983 and 1984 became the Years of Educational Reform in the United States. During those two years there were literally hundreds of reports at the

local, state and national levels. Unlike the Reports of the 1970's, referred to above, most of the Educational Reforms of the 1980's called for a return to the basics. Ignoring the fact that the "crisis" in education is due to the old ways in which we have been doing things, and not to "progressive" ideas which have never been implemented, many of the state and national reports call on us to return to the way we imagine things used to be. President Reagan's Commission Report, titled A Nation At Risk, was perhaps the most myopic of all the national reports.

Experiential education faired much better in the book, High School, by Ernest Boyer of the Carnegie Commission, in which he called for a Service Learning requirement for all high school students, closer transitions to the world of work, and greater flexibility in teaching styles. A Place Called School by John Goodlad advocated less "teacher talk," and more hands-on experiences. While it is too early to say whether the "Basics" or "experiential" modes will prevail in the late 1980's, the battle has been joined, much as it was in the 1930's by John Dewey.

II. THE PROBLEM OF DEFINITION

One of the major problems of the experiential education movement has been its inability to agree upon a definition. This makes the task of finding the philosophical, psychological and other underpinnings of the emerging discipline that much more difficult. Morris Keeton, Executive Director of the Cooperative Assessment of Experiential Learning (CAEL), defines it as that which "occurs outside of classroom," (Keeton, 5) perhaps the broadest possible definition, while others say that it is "learning by doing." Larry McClure and his colleagues at the Northwest Regional Educational Laboratory say that experience-based programs are characterized by seven kinds of learning: "Learning how to learn; Learning about life; Learning about careers; Learning about themselves; Learning to be responsible; Learning about others; and Learning by doing; (McClure, et.al.) Those who come from the outdoor/adventure based education movement define experiential education more in line with what occurs in those settings, emphasizing such aspects as challenge and stress.

Experiential education as it is coming to be known in the 1980's has its roots in a wide diversity of settings and movements; among which are: progressive education, holistic education, vocational education, career education, clinical training, internships, apprenticeships, alternative education, adventure programming, character training, developmental theory, child and adult stage theory, and moral and ethical development to name but a few of the more important sources.

At this point in the paper, we shall not attempt to define experiential education or learning, but rather move into a discussion of the roots from which the above mentioned movements draw. Through an analysis of a wide variety of theoreticians in philosophy, psychology, sociology, and anthropology, it is the intention of this paper to draw towards not only a conceptual base upon which the movement can build, but also to more carefully define the parameters of the emergent discipline and come closer to a definition. Where one looks for insights, of course, prejudices the direction of the final closure which we hope to reach, and it is only fair to the reader to state at the outset that the search is towards those theorists who see experience as liberating the individual and the society, rather than towards those who would use it as a perpetuator of the status quo, or to provide a docile and trained work force for business, industry or government.

III. THE PHILOSOPHICAL FOUNDATIONS OF EXPERIENTIAL LEARNING

It is difficult to come up with a coherent philosophy of experiential learning as few philosophers have addressed the problem at any length. Dewey's Experience and Education comes closest to providing a philosophy on which experiential educators can work, but Dewey would be the first to claim that much more needs to be said on the issue. Since experiential education is a new field of study. It is not surprising that its philosophical underpinnings should come from a variety of individuals and schools of thought. The approach taken in this section of the paper, as with other sections will be to give a brief quote from a particular philosopher and some explanation of how it relates to the building of a philosophy of experiential education and learning. The debate over epistemology, or the theory of knowledge, goes back in the history of philosophy to the Greeks, with Plato and Aristotle representing the two basic positions of rationalism and empiricism. The debate has continued to the present day and forms the basis for many of the arguments between experiential educators and those who would have us maintain the more formal school system.

A. Plato and Aristotle

Socrates: It seems that so long as we are alive, we shall continue closest to knowledge if we avoid as much as we can all contact and association with the body, except when they are absolutely necessary, and instead of allowing ourselves to become infected with its nature, purify ourselves from it until God himself gives us deliverance. In this way, by keeping ourselves uncontaminated by the follies of the body, we shall probably reach the company of others like ourselves and gain direct knowledge of all that is pure and uncontaminated--that is presumably, of truth. (Plato, 4)

All men by nature desire to know. An indication of this is the delight we take in our senses; for even apart from their usefulness they are loved for themselves.....With a view to action, experience seems in no respect inferior to art, and men of experience succeed even better than those who have theory without experience. (Aristotle, 689-690)

In these two quotes, Plato and Aristotle

set the stage for the philosopher's answer to the question, how can we know? and the educator's question, how can we best learn or teach? Plato questions whether we can "know" anything through our senses, a position which has led the rationalists to claim that knowledge comes through the reasoning processes, not through our senses. Aristotle, on the other hand, became the father of science and knowing through our senses and experiences.

Some twenty-four hundred years after their death, the debate still rages between the anti-empirical rationalism of Plato and the empiricism of Aristotle. It is perhaps obvious that "knowledge or truth" comes to the learner both through rational and empirical means, but in the debates over educational practice, it becomes a question of emphasis, with experiential educators taking their cue from Aristotleian metaphysics and decrying the (lack of experience on the part of young people today, who spend thirteen to twenty or more years in a formal school setting mastering theories which are often unrelated to the "real" world for which that education is supposedly preparing them.) Science and language laboratories, vocational education and a variety of other things have entered the formal schooling process, taking their cue from Aristotle's emphasis upon the empirical, but there can be little doubt that much, if not most of formal schooling in the twentieth century has a rational base.

B. Descartes and Locke

> Thus as our senses deceive us at times, I was ready to suppose that nothing was at all the way our senses represented them to be...Since this truth, I think, therefore I am (or exist), was so firm and assured that all the most extravagant suppositions of the skeptics were unable to shake it, I judged that I could safely accept it as the first principle of the philosophy I was seeking. (Descartes, 24)

> Whence has it all the materials of reason and knowledge? To this I answer, in one word, from experience. In that all our knowledge is founded, and from that it ultimately derives itself...Experience here must teach me what reason cannot: (Locke, 89, 339)

Descartes and Hume carried on the Platonic rational ideal, while Locke and Nietzsche, spoke out for the empirical, experiential ideal in their philosophical treatises. Formal schooling had become highly rational in its orientation throughout the Dark Ages and even up until the nineteenth century, so that the philosophic debates of the period tended to have little effect on practice in the schools. Schools, from primary through universities had become institutions which were separated from the societies for which they were supposedly preparing the young and were given over the lectures, recitations, and deductive forms of thinking. In the nineteenth century, the pressures of modern society were being brought to bear on the universities of the time, so that first in Germany, and later in England and the United States, "practical" forms of education such as engineering, agriculture and architecture were added to the curriculum. Practice in the liberal arts, however, still tended to be rational and theoretical, with few connections to experiential modes of learning.

C. John Stuart Mill

> ...Whatever we do for ourselves, and whatever is done for us by others, for the express purpose of bringing us somewhat nearer to the perfection of our nature; it does more: in its largest acceptation, it comprehends even the indirect effects produced on character and on the human faculties, by things of which the direct purposes are quite different; by laws, by forms of government, by the industrial arts, by modes of social life; nay, even by physical facts not dependent on human will; by climate, soil, and local position. Whatever helps to shape the human being--to make the individual what he is, or hinder him from being what he is not--is part of his education. (Mill, 333)

John Stuart Mill, the great British philospher, was highly trained in the traditional, formal sense of the word, but recognized the importance of the experiential, non-formal aspects of his own learning, and wrote at some length on experiential ways of learning a foreign language (by living in the country), or learning many other subjects by reading and studying on one's own, rather than through formal instruction. In his own Autobiography he differentiated between his formal education and that which he gained through "self-education." (Houle, 27)

D. Peirce and James

It appears, then, that the rule for attaining the third grade of clearness of apprehension is as follows: Consider what effects, which might conceivably have practical bearings, we conceive the object of our conception to have. Then, our conception of these effects is the whole of our conception of the object. (Peirce, 124)

...theories are instruments that we employ in order to solve problems in our experience... a theory or belief is true, the pragmatists answer that it has been verified and found to deal successfully with experience... James opposed the traditional philosophical view that the truth of ideas is a property independent of human experience. (Popkin, 172-173)

As precursors to Dewey, Peirce and James have had a profound, if indirect effect on the practice of education in the United States and throughout the world. The quote from Peirce above is the famous "pragmatic maxim" encouraging us to subject all ideas to the test of the empirical method. "Experience" for Peirce is the combination of ideas interacting dynamically with the external world and the senses, a more comprehensive view than that taken by either the rationalists or the traditional empiricists. As the quote from Popkin about James' thinking indicates, the pragmatists do not ignore theorizing or

rational inquiry, but rather subject all theory to the crucible of experience to test its "cash value." James shared the general American distrust of purely theoretical or intellectual activity and kept asking the question, what difference does it make?

E. John Dewey

I assume that amid all uncertainties there is one permanent frame of reference: namely the organic connection between education and personal experience; or, some kind of empirical and experimental philosophy. (Dewey 25)

With this quote, Dewey places himself and the pragmatists squarely in the camp of the empiricists, and ties that tradition of philosophy to education in society. Whereas other philosophers spoke primarily of theory, Dewey, in his Experience and Education speaks eloquently of a philosophy which directly impacts what occurs in the school or other learning settings. Dewey, unlike many of his followers in the Progressive Education Movement, or even an occasional voice in the current Experiential Education Movement, does not equate experience and education.

The belief that all genuine education comes about through experience does not mean that all experiences are genuinely or equally educative...some experiences are mis-educative... any that has the effect of arresting or distorting the growth of further experience...engenders callousness...produces lack of sensitivity and of responsiveness...Everything depends upon the quality of the experience which is had. (Dewey, 25-26)

A proper understanding of the miseducative nature of some experience is critical for not just an understanding of Dewey, but also so that experiential educators do not fall into the same traps which destroyed the Progressive Education Movement in the 1930's. This is not to say that one cannot learn from any and all experiences, but Dewey warns us that unless the principles of continuity and interaction are carefully considered, an experience can all too easily be miseducative. By continuity, Dewey is referring to an experiential continuum. Growth, or growing as developing, physically, intellectually and morally, is one exemplification of his principle of continuity. It is growth in a positive direction, however, and it is here that ethics or values enter the picture. Space does not permit a discussion of Dewey's ethics, here. Suffice it to say, the growth through any experience must create the conditions for further growth, according to Dewey, or it is miseducative.

Dewey reemphasizes that experience does not take place strictly within the individual learner, but has an active side which changes the objective conditions under which experiences are had. This led Dewey to warn educators:

> Above all they should know how to utilize the surrounding, physical and social, that exist so as to extract from them all they have to contribute to building up experiences that are worthwhile... the teacher should become intimately acquainted with the conditions of the local community, physical, historical, economic, occupational, etc., in order to utilize them as educational resources. (Dewey, 40)

Dewey's second criteria of experience, interaction, assigns equal weight to both factors in experience-objective and external or subjective and internal conditions. Experiences always involve a transaction between the individual and what constitutes his environment at any given moment, whether that be the child in the classroom, the apprentice in the shop, or the climber on the mountain. Continuity and interaction are characterized by Dewey as the longitudinal and lateral aspects of experience. Dewey juxtaposes traditional education with experience-based education in his initial chapter.

> To imposition from above is opposed expression and cultivation of individuality; to external discipline is opposed free activity; to learning from texts

and teachers, learning through experience; to acquisition of isolated skills and techniques by drill, is opposed acquisition of them as means of attaining ends which make direct vital appeal; to preparation for a more or less remote future is opposed making the most of the opportunities of present life; to static aims and materials is opposed acquaintance with a changing world. (Dewey, 20)

Although other educators have made similar comparisons, as will be shown in later sections of this paper, Dewey's listing provides a good starting point for any definition of experiential learning. Some key aspects of Dewey's definition might be paraphrased in 1980 as: Individual learner involvement in what is to be learned; learning through experiences inside and outside the classroom, and not just from teachers; learning through experiences immediately relevant to the learner; living in the present and not just preparing for the future; and finally, preparation for a changing world. It is presumptuous to attempt to cover Dewey in a few short three pages, so the reader is referred back to Experience and Education, Democracy and Education, and Experience and Nature for a more detailed discussion of the philosophical roots of Dewey's educational ideas.

Dewey concludes Experience and Education with a chapter titled, "Experience-The Means and Goal of Education," and argues that:

> Education in order to accomplish its ends both for the individual learner and for the society must be based upon experience--which is always the actual life-experience of some individual... The educational system must move one way or another, either backward to the intellectual and moral standards of a pre-scientific age or forward to ever greater utilization of scientific method in development of the possibilities of growing, expanding experience... There is no discipline to the tests of intelligent development and direction. (Dewey, 89-90)

[Dewey would bridle at the extreme individualism of many of today's experiential educators, who appear to emphasize the individual, almost mystical experience, of the mountaintop, as opposed to the building of a more democratic society, one of Dewey's continuing themes.] He would also scorn those who see experience, whether a field trip, wilderness camp, or apprenticeship, as the "easy" way of teaching and learning. Rigor and discipline in the "new", "progressive" education were constant themes of Dewey's, as he had observed the fruits of the almost whimsical progressive education movement, and the lack of effect it had on the educational mainstream of American schools. Experiential educators of the 1980's would do well to read American educational history, so as not to fall into the same traps.

F. Mao Tse-Tung

> All genuine knowledge originates in
> direct experience...human knowledge
> can in no way be separated from
> practice...practice is higher than
> (theoretical) knowledge...Whoever
> wants to know a thing has no way of
> doing so except by coming into
> contact with it, that is, by living,
> (practicing) in its environment...
> practice, knowledge, again practice,
> and again knowledge...such is the
> dialectical-materialist theory of
> the unity of knowing and doing.
> (Mao, 8, 7, 20)

With the death of Mao, the Chinese have repudiated many of Mao's political and educational ideas, and without question have downgraded the importance of the experiential, from where it was during the Cultural Revolution of 1966-76. Even with "revisionists" or "traditionalists" now in power, the educational system still contains many elements of experiential learning. Production of goods for sale still continues in most primary and secondary schools, city children still spend time in the countryside during harvesting season helping the farmers, and May 7 Cadre Schools still train the bureaucratic elites in simple, rural settings. Although the universities have returned to a more competitive,

selective, and traditional mode, July 21 Worker's Universities and Polytechnic Institutes continue the experiential tradition of the Cultural Revolution.

Mao's works were written only one year prior to Dewey's influential book, Experience and Education. But while few of Dewey's ideas were put into widespread practice, Mao dramatically influenced not only the education of one-fourth of the world's people in China, but established a model and theory of experiential learning which has been copied, at least in part, by numerous Third World countries. It is interesting to note that a Brazilian, Paulo Friere and a Chinese, Mao Tse-Tung, have had perhaps the greatest practical effect on experiential modes of learning, while world renowned philosophers such as Dewey, languish on the book shelves, or serve as the source of discussion among educational theorists, but seldom find their way into educational practice in the U.S.

It is this writer's opinion that the cause for this is the dichotomizing of education and politics which occurs in the United States and most other Western nations. This is not to say that education is not political, but rather that education is primarily seen as a promoter of the status quo and a passing on of a cultural heritage, and the vicarious, symbolic modes of traditional educational practice are more conducive to producing a passive citizenry. Friere' exile from Brazil and the adoption of his methods by revolutionary regimes, along with the changes wrought in China during the educational experiments of the Cultural Revolution, point to the likely conclusion that experiential learning can and does have a "liberating" effect on its participants, and can lead to profound personal and societal change.

G. Paulo Friere

> Liberation is a praxis: the action
> and reflection of men upon their
> world in order to transform
> it...When a word is deprived of its
> dimension of action, reflection
> automatically suffers as well; and
> the word is changed into idle
> chatter, into verbalism, into an
> alienated and alienating

"blah"...On the other hand, if action is emphasized exclusively, to the detriment of reflection, the word is converted into activism... Men are not built in silence, but in word, in work, in action-reflection. (Friere, 66, 75-76)

Paulo Friere is a Brazilian educational philosopher, who has had perhaps the greatest effect on educational practice throughout the world during the past decade, and his thought, as excerpted above, makes extensive use of the dialectic of action and reflection as the two inescapable aspects of any true or liberating education. He makes a strong case that contemporary education is given over to what he calls a banking concept of education, in which the teacher makes deposits on the brains of the students. This is the alienating verbalism of which he speaks above. On the other side of the coin, however, he condemns those educators who would be involved in actions, strictly for their own sake, as many of the educational and political movements of the sixties and seventies were, as this is meaningless activism.

While traditional education as we know it today is, without question, caught on the verbalism horn of Friere's Dialectic, experiential education is all too often caught in meaningless action which neither liberates the individual nor changes the society in which those individuals find themselves. Friere's educational theory is not politically neutral, but rather seeks to change the world, through the learners' participating in their own Liberation and education. It is cooperative, non-manipulative, dialogic, active, and reflective education.

The educational philosophy of Friere, brings again to the forefront of educational thinking the necessity of the cognitive, the rational, the reflective as we find it in traditional, vicarious education as practiced in the schools, while at the same time pointing to the need for active learning outside the classroom, which change the personal and social realities of the learner.

H. Robert Pirsig

The real cycle you're working on is a cycle called yourself. The machine that appears to be "out there" and the person that appears to be "in here" are not two separate things. (Pirsig, 319

In his influential book, Zen and the Art of Motorcycle Maintenance, Robert Pirsig helps to define experiential learning in the way in which we would like to approach it in this paper. Experiential learning is more than traditional vocational education programs, internships and other settings familiar to generations of American educators. The differences are ones of means and ends, process and product, behaviorally defined goals and serendipitous learnings. While traditional "experiential" programs see the "repair of the cycle," as the goal, end, or purpose of the activity, experiential educators in the new mode, see the cycle as but one of the many vehicles for helping the learner not only in cycle repair," but also to gain insight into oneself, to approach learning as something intrinsic to the learner and not imposed by external sources, and to go beyond the traditional goals of learning a skill and go to the very heart of the rational/scientific method.

The example of the motorcycle was specifically chosen, as most of the new breed of experiential educators see the wilderness, American subcultures, and traditional, non-mechanical trades as their source of inspiration for experiential learning. Rather than fall into such a trap, one should take seriously another quote from Pirsig as we define and theorize about experiential learning throughout this brief paper.

The Buddha, the Godhead, resides quite as comfortably in the circuits of a digital computer or the gears of a cycle transmission as he does at the top of a mountain or in the petals of a flower. (Pirsig, 18)

Those who are unacquainted with experiential education, particularly as it has been defined and practiced by those persons in the Association for Experiential Education (AEE), may not see the need for Pirsig's caution, but to do justice to breadth and depth of the experiential learning process, it is necessary to state that experiential learning as it is being discussed in this paper is not just Outward Bound, adventure-based education, outdoor education, Foxfire, or apprenticeships in boat building or blacksmithing, but rather includes all those environments in which the learner is actively involved in his or her own learning, and is not just a passive recipient of the knowledge of the teacher.

I. Kurt Hahn

No discussion of the theory of experiential education would be complete without some recognition being given to Kurt Hahn, the founder of the Outward Bound movement in Great Britain during World War II. Hahn lashed out at his native German education as setting tasks which bear little relation to the age and stage of development of children, nor in keeping with their interests. He saw most reforms as artificial, leading to little or no meaningful change in the system or in the classroom climate. One of his constant themes was the need for an attractive environment for learning to take place. For political reasons he was compelled to emigrate to Great Britian, and it was there that his concepts of "rescue" and "internationalism" bore fruit in such schools as Salem and Gordonstoun, and later in the Outward Bound Schools. (Rohrs)

Hahn saw service to one's neighbor and in the cause of peace as major aspects of any educational program, and service has continued as part of the Outward Bound movement, since that time, although perhaps downgraded in importance in the American schools in recent years. Hahn saw adventure as a critical activity for youth, and one which was missing in most modern societies. It was to lead to a sense and wonder and astonishment, qualities so lacking among contemporary youth.

Hahn saw the morally responsible man, not the scholar or artist, as the ideal for his school. Justice was to be sought, and the schooling process which taught only the basic skills was only doing a small part of its task. (MacArthur, 8) Hahn's ideas had a strongly religious, Christian base to them, but the institutions he founded have continued on in a more secular mode, while continuing to provide adventure and service and to seek a more just world.

IV. THE PSYCHOLOGICAL FOUNDATIONS OF EXPERIENTIAL EDUCATION

This second major section on the theory of experiential learning will draw from a variety of sources including the major schools of psychology; Freudian, Behavioral, Humanistic and Transpersonal, in addition to educational pscyhology and learning theory. As with the section on the philosophical foundations, no pretense is made that all possible sources have been tapped, or that significant depth is to be found on any of the various sources from which experiential learning draws its insights. Experiential education has no well developed psychology or learning theory, so that once again its foundations are eclectic and are only now being explored. Of the various schools of psychological thought, experiential education has been most closely allied to the humanists, with Rogers and Maslow, in particular, having a profound impact on many practitioners. In recent years, however, with experiential programming for delinquents, dropouts, handicapped, and other special populations, insights from behavioral psychology have been making ever greater inroads. Finally, a growing number of experiential educators have been exploring insights from transpersonal psychology, as they relate to the individuals' relationship with the cosmos and the environment. Through yoga, Transcendental and other forms of meditation, and other "spiritual" sources, experiential educators have been attempting to stretch the boundaries of human potential.

Before discussing concepts from the basic schools of psychology and how they relate to experiential learning, we shall turn our attention to basic research on learning theory and developmental psychology, as this appears to one of the most promising areas upon which experiential education can base its

theory. Of the various developmental and
learning theorists, the most promising
appears to be that of Jean Piaget.

A. Jean Piaget

STAGES IN THE MASTERY OF OPERATIONS

AGE LEVEL	DESTINATION	PRINCIPAL FEATURES
0 - 2	Acquiring Sensorimotor Control	Extensive trial-and-error. Movements develop bodily control and eye-hand coordination. The perceptual field is organized into objects.
2-	Extracting concepts from experience.	Words heard are associated with objects. Concepts are formed for recurring experiences.
4-	Intuitive use of concepts.	Direct perceptual comparisons are accurate. Associated concepts are confused. Complex situations are reacted to as unanalyzable. WHOLES: Conclusions are based on superficial impressions.
7-	Concrete operational thought.	Comparisions requiring one to hold information in mind are accurate, if the information is presented concretely. Operations can be imagined and results anticipated. Adjustment by reversal leads to an exact result. Associated concepts are distinguished one can be changed while the other stays fixed.
11-	Formal operational thought.	Operations among symbols or abstract ideas can be carried out in the mind. A complete array of logical possibilities can be comprehended. Accurate comparisons and deductions can be made from information not concretely presented. (Cronbach, 336)

16

One of the most critical questions in psycholinguists is; are thought and speech inseparable? Watson, the behaviorist, answered strongly in the affirmative, holding that thought processes were but motor habits of the larynx. Piaget is strongly in opposition to the behaviorist tradition on this critical point, holding that cognitive development proceeds on its own, generally followed by linguistic development and finding reflection in a child's language, but that language in itself does not bring about cognitive growth. Piaget's critical point for experiential educators is that intellect grows through interaction with things and people in the child's or adult's environment. Although Piaget locates each stage on an age scale, there are no abrupt transitions, and a learner may be at a formal operation stage in one concept and at an intuitive or concrete operational stage in another. Intellectual development consists of the mastery of one concept after another, through pertinent experience.

Piaget, Inhelder and other Piagetian experimenters have shown that the "lattice" or "lens" which organizes a child's perceptual world is not necessarily language, but rather is developed through the "actions of the child on the environment." (Inhelder, 163) Furth, through his research with deaf children, provides some of the strongest backing for this position. Furth's research points to the conclusion that deaf children are not drastically different from hearing children in intellectual performance, and that they follow the same basic Piagetian stages, though at times at a slower rate. Slobin's statement is of extreme importance to experiential educators and deaf educators alike:

> It is quite likely, though, that this occasional slowness may be due not so much to specific lack of language as to general lack of experience, given the sort of environment in which many deaf children are raised. (Slobin, 116)

Even an adult cannot think abstractly without a base of experience. Intellectual development consists of the mastery of one concept after another,

though pertinent experience.

The implications of Piagetian thought for the practice of education in general and of experiential education specifically are numerous. We shall only point out some of the more obvious and important ones here. His research on stages provides strong justification for the use of the most concrete and action oriented context possible in presenting concepts or ideas, moving progressively to more internalized modes, from objects to symbols of objects from motor action to speech. Experiential educators at all levels have known this intuitively, but the practice of schooling has too often been to introduce the symbolic at too early an age, or too early in the learning process in the lives of adults who generally function at the stage of formal operational thought.

Piaget also emphasizes that in "genuine learning" the child or adult regulates his or her own activities, decides what needs to be learned, sets the pace and selects certain kinds of activities. This self-direction, though not always part of experiential learning environments, has become a critical aspect of many of them. Interest is another concept which comes through in Piaget. Learners learn best that in which they are interested.

Perhaps this is an obvious statement, but one which traditional education all too often forgets. Piaget warns against superficial learning through rote memorization. Free time in which students, be they small children, adolescents or adults is important in the educational setting, so that students can find things out for themselves and discover things on their own. Direct training is not ignored by Piaget, however, as research indicates that children make more rapid progress towards operational thought when given direct training.

B. James S. Coleman

While James S. Coleman is a sociologist by training, he has written one of the best comparisons between "Experiential and Classroom Learning." In fact, one might say that he has become to contemporary experiential education, what John Dewey was to Progressive Education. Coleman gives classroom learning the title of "information assimilation," and carefully points out that most of the learning that takes place in class learning, "proceeds through acting (or in some cases, seeing another act), and then experiencing or observing the consequences of action." (Coleman, Experiential Learning, 50)

Coleman outlines the steps followed in both types of learning.

Information Assimilation Process:
Steps in Learning

1. Receiving Information: Information is transmitted through a symbolic medium...lecture, book...General Principles...Commit information to memory.
2. Assimilating and organizing information so that the general principle is understood...learned the meaning of the information...lead to understanding a generalization.
3. Being able to infer a particular application from the general principle...implies some cognitive abilities.
4. Moving from the cognitive and symbol-processing sphere to the sphere of action...knowledge gained is actually applied. (Coleman, 50-51)

Coleman goes on to point out that experiential learning proceeds in almost a reverse sequence, and does not use a symbolic medium for transmitting information, as the information is generated through the sequence of steps itself.

Experiential Learning Process:
Steps to Learning

1. Carry out an action in a particular instance and see the effects of that action.
2. Understanding these effects in a particular instance...has learned the consequences of the action...and how to act to obtain his goals in this particular circumstance.
3. Understanding the general principle under which the particular instance falls...it does not imply an ability to express the principle in a symbolic medium (words)...only the ability to see a connection between the actions and effects over a range of circumstances.
4. When the general principle is understood, the last step is its application through action in a new circumstance...the actor anticipates the effect of the action. (Coleman, 52-52)

Coleman suggests that schools use both learning processes, but that they seldom raise the issue of appropriate mix of the two approaches to learning. Since school is the institution in society designed to pass on the cultural heritage, it is not unexpected that information assimilation is the dominant mode of learning, as it can reduce the time and effort needed to learn something new. The wheel need not be reinvented with each generation. Coleman agrees with Bruner that structure is needed to tie together otherwise disparate facts, but goes on to say that information assimilation through symbolic media is not the only or necessarily the best way of doing so.

Information assimilation is also highly dependent on the symbolic medium of language.

"The first step requires the ability to understand the language, to assimilate information that uses that language as a medium. The second and third steps require processing of information that still lies in the form of words...Thus there is the cost to the compression of experience through language, a cost that lies in incompletely understood language, defects in chains of associations that words may bring, defects in processing of information stored in the form of words and their associations. Indeed, this process of learning depends on prior learning of a complex system of symbols." (Coleman, 55)

Persons who have learned the symbolic medium poorly, who are still too young to have learned it well, and the culturally disadvantaged in linguistic and verbal skills, are groups to whom Coleman points as having difficulty with the information assimilation mode of learning. It is in the second and third steps of applying what is learned, that the information assimilation model usually breaks down, as even students who have mastered the symbolic medium, are all too often unable to translate the learnings into concrete sequences of action.

A third difficulty with the information assimilation model is its dependence upon artificial or extrinsic motivation. This is due to the fact that the action (the intrinsic motivation) comes at the end of the learning sequence, thus grades and other external motivations must be supplied to motivate the learner.

Experiential learning on the other hand is a time consuming process because it involves "actions sufficiently repeated and in enough circumstances to allow the development of a generalization from experience." (Coleman, 56) Ideally it uses no symbolic medium and consequences follow actions immediately. In practice, however, this is not always true, as consequences may take months (as in the birth of a baby), to follow specific actions. When consequences do follow in an observable period of time, experiential learning provides a direct guide for further action. There is no hurdle from a symbolic medium to action. Coleman suggests that this bypassing of the symbolic medium may account for the inability of some learners to show on paper and pencil tests, that they have learned the information, even though their behavior may evidence the knowledge.

Motivation is intrinsic in this mode of learning, as action occurs at the beginning of the sequence, and if the learner is to gain his ends through the action, he must learn the necessary information to guide that action. The third step, that of generalizing from particular experiences, is the weakest link in the experiential learning process, but this difficulty appears in information assimilation processes also.

Finally, experiential learning appears to be etched more deeply and permanently on the brain of the learner,

as all learning can be associated with concrete actions and events, not just abstract symbols or general principles.

C. Jerome Bruner

One of the most influential learning theorists in the past two decades is Harvard psychologist Jerome Bruner. Bruner points to two other modes of representation besides linguistic representation. A primitive, but useful mode, is through action or through "doing". Some things are better learned or demonstrated by doing. Such "outdoor" or "adventure-based" activities as knot tying, rock climbing, river rafting, or any number of other skills must be "done" to be learned. Bruner calls this form of cognitive organization "enactive representation", and defines it as a process of representing past events through motor responses. Iconic representation, such as language, is the third form. As children mature through their developmental stages, they are increasingly able to use symbolic representation to integrate their experience. (Mathis, 198)

In his highly influential book, Toward A Theory of Instruction, Bruner makes the case that children are innately curious and are capable of learning far more at a much earlier age than had been traditionally thought. Education, for Bruner, is the process of reorganizing experience, and the emphasis in learning should be on the process not the product. Students are participants in the learning process, not receptacles into which knowledge is to be poured. He emphasizes the intrinsic rewards of learning, rather than placing the emphasis upon extrinsic rewards and punishments as do behaviorists. Finally, his theory of instruction emphasizes inquiry and discovery, and attempts to use problem-solving methods, rather than more traditional lecture, recitation, and rote memorization approaches. (Bruner)

Although Bruners' theories of instruction have had more influence on the classroom behavior of teachers than it has on out-of-school experiential approaches, there can be no denying its applicability to such settings. Experiential educators seek to enable

19

students to use whatever environment they find themselves in and to learn skills, understandings or concepts, and such educators strongly agree with Bruner's emphasis upon process rather than product. Student choice and participation in structuring the learning environment is critical to any successful experiential learning environment and is closely related to the intrinisc rewards which characterize such learning experiences. Although many experiential learning programs have skill development aspects to them, which are highly structured for reasons of safety, be it an auto repair shop or rock climbing, most have moved strongly towards Bruner's emphasis upon the need for discovery and problem solving as critical aspects if any "true" learning is to take place.

As Bruner's influence has waned in the classroom during an era of "back to the basics", his theories are being proven in countless other settings.

D. Maria Montessori

"The environment should contain means of auto-education." This basic principle of Maria Montessori can be restated that the child educates him or herself. Montessori developed her methods in protest to schools which followed the needs of the adult, not the child or the learner. Montessori took as her basic method to impose nothing, but to create a school environment in which the child can "do-and-think" for himself. Children learn through their own developing mastery of experiences. (Montessori, 1972)

Although these basic insights were developed for use with pre-school and elementary age children, they have been adopted by experiential educators in a variety of ways, for use with adolescents and adults. Montessori's emphasis upon the learner rather than the teacher, is crucial to an understanding of the experiential method, as is her emphasis upon the creation of, or use of the environment, as a learning tool. Whether one is in the wilderness, in a workshop, or utilizing the city as a school, the environment itself becomes a teacher, and learner "discovers", "does" and "thinks" about that which is to be learned from the experiences in that environment.

Another insight to be gained from Montessori is the developmental stages she set in the mastery of experiences. Whether it is the step-by-step procedures of safety in a mountain climbing exercise or the writing skills needed to carry out cultural journalism, experiential education emphasizes the need to master certain skills before moving on to higher stages.

E. Insights From Freudian Psychology: Freud and Neill

Despite the fact that A.S. Neill, one of the most influential educators of the past thirty years, was deeply influenced by Freud in his writing of Summerhill and in his educational practice at that particular institution, his influence and that of Freudians in general has not been of a direct nature, but more in the subtle ways in which schools and teachers work with children.

Unlike behaviorists and humanists, leading Freudians have not written extensively on education, although much has been written about the related field of child rearing.

Although Neill cannot speak for all Freudian psychologists or eduators, most would probably agree with his insight that the aim of life is to find happiness, and that the traditional school systems do little but prepare students for a sick society through their drudgery. (Neill) Sexuality and psychological and biological determinism are major themes of Neill and Freud, with an emphasis on the need for non-repressive sexual experiences for children and adolescents, and a recognition of biological readiness which must precede any internally motivated learning. The role of the unconscious in human behavior is a primary concept of Freudian pscyhology, and a variety of educators, such as Richard Jones, in his Fantasy and Feeling in Education have made the case that creative potential can be unleashed in all students if we can but tap the unconscious.

Freud's discussion of the id, ego and superego have been translated in recent years by Berne and others into the concepts of parent, adult and child in Transactional Analysis, with the id corresponding to the child, the ego to the adult and the superego to the parent. (James and Jongeward) Numerous classes in Transactional Analysis have been conducted for teachers, and the concepts are now being taught even to pre-school children.

Experiential educators have written little or nothing about the role of Freudian psychology in the movement, but most share Neill's abhorrence for the "drudgery" of the traditional school classroom and would share his enthusiasm for the joy of learning, when the motivation comes from within the student. They also owe him a great debt for stating the most extreme case for change in the public school, so that educators who now seek even minimal changes are not looked upon as such educational heretics.

The movement has also sought less repressive environments for students, an idea perhaps traceable to Freud and his discussions of repression and its causes. Although most experiential educators would not see themselves as deterministic in their viewpoints as many Freudians, they nevertheless owe a debt for the insights gained about human behavior and motivation.

F. Insights from Behavioral Psychology

Behavioral psychology has had a deep and long-lasting impact on American education. In fact, one could make the case that it dominates the American educational scene today, through such related programs as behavioral objectives, competency-based education, reward and punishment schemes for learning and discipline, and a host of related aspects. Although most experiential educators, at least of the adventure-based variety, reject the label of behaviorists, there can be no denying behaviorism's impact on many aspects of experiential learning.

One initial impact has been to "clarify" what one is doing. Instead of accepting testimonials from participants in experiential programs, behaviorists have insisted that goals be stated in measurable terms, and that programs be more carefully planned when clear objectives have been written. Where experiential educators have trouble with the behavioral objectives movement is in the serendipitous aspects of the learning experience which cannot always be programmed, and in the emphasis upon process which sometimes precludes exactitude in stating learning outcomes. Behaviorists would deny that these are drawbacks to stating clear objectives, but they are accused in turn by humanists and others of reductionist thinking, and teaching only that which can be predetermined and measured, things hardly in keeping with what most experiential educators see as their educational task.

The accountability movement, coming out of behaviorism, has also had an impact on experiential educators. No longer can educators "do their own thing," be it in the classroom or elsewhere, without being responsible to the taxpayer, parents, students and others for the learning experiences they have designed. While this has forced a cutback in some types of learning environments, it has also forced traditional and experiential educators to define for their publics, what it is they are doing and whether it was "worth the time, money and effort."

Reinforcement, or the idea that it is a consequence of an action that makes that action more likely to be repeated is another basic concept of behaviorism. The intrinsic/extrinsic distinction is based on whether the behavior is reinforcing itself or whether it is reinforcing because of subsequent rewards that are not an integral part of the behavior. Experiential educators are likely to claim a much greater use of intrinsic rewards through such things as pride of achievement, joy of learning, aesthetic or physical pleasure, than would most traditional educators, who are more likely to use grades or other extrinsic stimuli to promote appropriate behavior or learnings. The same could be said of classification of reinforcements as positive or negative. Experiential educators see themselves as using primarily positive rewards, leading to recurrence of positive behavior, while holding that traditional education uses too many negative reinforcers to motivate and control students. A final categorization of reinforcement is self-administered, social (from someone else), and impersonal. Experiential educators like to claim that their reinforcers are more of the self-administered variety, but particularly in some of the more recent programs dealing with delinquent youth and special or handicapped populations, there would have to be a recognition of social reinforcement, as the populations are not participating of their own accord.

Some of the rules of reinforcement are:

Choose an appropriate reinforcement. The reinforcement should come after the behavior. The reinforcement should come as soon after the behavior as possible. Many small rewards work better than a few big ones, especially for shaping. (Roberts, 137)

Experiential educators have for many years recognized the validity of these principles, through the use of environments which provide rapid, appropriate reinforcement for the learner. This is true whether the reinforcer is a paycheck for a paid internship or falling off a cliff, because a knot was tied improperly. Rather than having to "wait until one grows up," or "seeing the relevance of what I am teaching you several years from now," experiential education is geared to giving immediate and appropriate feedback to the learner.

It can be concluded that there is no way not to use behavior modification, and that what behaviorism has contributed to the experiential education movement is a greater sense of accountability, a push for clarity of goals, and a better understanding of the role that reinforcement plays in the learning process.

G. Insights from Humanistic Psychology.

If Freudians can be characterized as counselors attempting to cure the pupil, the behaviorists as engineers, structuring the appropriate reinforcements, then humanists could be seen as facilitators of learning, helping students to achieve their highest potential. As with Freudian and

Behavioral pscyhology, it is difficult to characterize a whole field, but there are certain themes which come out, particularly from Carl Rogers and Abraham Maslow, the two humanistic psychologists, who have written and spoken extensively on the role of their perspectives for education. As stated earlier, experiential educators have tended to see themselves as being based most firmly in this camp of psychologists, but as has also been shown in earlier sections, they have not been uninfluenced by other perspectives. The following chart summarizes many of the perspectives in which the humanists see themselves differing from more traditional, subject-centered schools, classrooms and teachers.

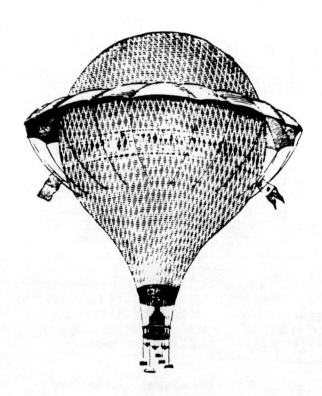

Tradition, Subject-Center Schools	Contemporary, Student-Centered, Humanistic Schools
1. Teacher controls all aspects of learning.	1. Learning environment is cooperative developed by parents, students and teacher.
2. Facts dominate the curriculum.	2. Discovery, inquiry, and meaning are more important than discrete facts.
3. Rigidity.	3. Flexibility.
4. All students do the same time.	4. Individualized education and varying the program to meet the needs of each child.
5. Isolation from society.	5. Integration with the society.
6. Sterile environment.	6. Creative environment.
7. Emphasis on permanence and tradition.	7. Emphasis upon change and the future.
8. Product.	8. Process.
9. Control and constraint.	9. Freedom.
10. External discipline.	10. Internal discipline.
11. Authority.	11. Self-actualization.
12. Subject-centered.	12. Person-centered.
13. Emphasis on teaching.	13. Emphasis on learning.
14. Competition.	14. Cooperation.
15. Only the best succeed.	15. Everyone succeeds.
16. Group works at same rate.	16. Individualized rates.
17. Learn only from teacher.	17. Learn from fellow students.
18. All education in the school.	18. Education in many environments.
19. Adults are responsible.	19. Children are responsible.
20. Children perceived as untrustworthy.	20. Children perceived as trustworthy.
21. Intolerance of ambiguity.	21. Tolerance of ambiguity.
22. Controlling.	22. Freeing.

(Van Scotter, 275)

H. Abraham Maslow

Maslow held that human nature had been sold short by Freudian and Behaviorist psychological theories, with their attempts at being objective, detached and value free. Humanists or Third Force Psychologists, as Maslow called them, reject this perspective and seek to help persons discover ultimate ends and values. They reject the Freudian conception of instincts in favor of a conception of basic needs, Maslow's hierarchy of needs being the most explicit humanist outline. Maslow saw the goal of education as not just satisfying the lower need of persons: hunger, sex, etc., but to reach the highest levels of need, namely, "self-actualization." Maslow stated that Freud's error was seeing the unconscious as an undesirable evil, and not as a place from which creativity, joy, happiness, and goodness could also come. Maslow emphasized the "love for, awareness of, and reverence of the body," as paths to lead persons to peak experiences. (Maslow, 1968) He saw traditional schooling as "collecting associations, conditionings, habits, or modes of action...as if these were possessions which the learner accumulates." (Maslow, Fall 1968) Teachers are active in this paradigm and the pupil is the passive one to be shaped and taught through an indoctrination process. The values, goals and ends of the learner are ignored. Maslow states that "The experiences in which we uncover our intrinsic selves are apt to be unique moments that persons discover their true identify, not the traditional learning situations in schools. The teacher in Maslow's conception is the "Taoist helper and is receptive rather than instrusive." (Maslow, Fall 1968)

I. Carl Rogers

Carl Rogers reflects most of the same perspectives as Maslow, emphasizing the higher needs of persons, the role of the teacher as facilitator, the involvement of the student in the selection of what is to be learned, and that the teacher cannot really teach anything, but only that a learner can learn, for his or her own intrinsic reasons.

In addition to many of the same themes as Maslow, Rogers emphasized the dearth of creativity which pervades our schools and culture, and that our educational system turns out conformists and stereotypes whose education is "completed," rather than producing freely creative and original thinkers. In order to be creative, Rogers emphasizes the need for "Openness to experience: Extensionality." Persons who are open to experience, lack rigidity and permeability of boundaries in concepts, beliefs, perceptions, and hypotheses. They are able to tolerate ambiguity and deal with conflicting information without forcing closure.

Another major theme of Rogers is the locus of evaluation, which he sees as internally, rather than externally located. The critique, judgment, and evaluation of any given activity comes from within the person, not from others. Acceptance of self and others, empathic behavior towards other beings, and psychological and emotional freedom are other themes which come through in many of Rogers' writings. (Rogers, 1969)

It is not too difficult to see why most experiential educators look to humanist psychologists for their direction, as so many of their themes are parallel. The emphasis upon the learner rather than the teacher, with the learner participating in all aspects of structuring the learning situation and in evaluation of what is learned is one such theme. William Glasser, the founder and leading proponent of Reality Therapy, could be considered to be within the Humanistic Psychology movement, even though some of his ideas come from the Behaviorists. His emphasis upon "success experiences" for children in his book Schools Without Failure, has also become an important component of most experiential learning situations. Challenge must be there, but the challenge must not be so difficult that the student cannot succeed. Humanistic pscyhology's emphasis upon internal motivation and evaluation are also echoed in the literature and practice of experiential education, as is the role of the adult or teacher, who is seen as a peer teacher or facilitator of discovery, rather than as the source of knowledge.

The process orientation of the humanists coincides nicely with most of the emphasis in experiential learning, particularly in those situations in which end goals have not been clearly specified, but rather are open to whereever the learner wishes to take it.

A high percentage of the research on various experiential programs has been done in the area of self-concept, rather than in cognitive domain. This is in keeping with the humanist's emphasis upon the affective development of the learner, and although neither experiential educators nor humanist psychologists would deny the role of the cognitive or intellectual development of the learner, they both tend to strongly emphasize physical and emotional growth.

Much more could be written about the relationship of these areas, but suffice it to say that much of the impetus for experiential education has come from humanistic psychologists and their followers in and out of the public schools.

J. Insights from Transpersonal Psychology

Over the past decade, transpersonal psychology has become a "Fourth Force" in the field of pscyhology, and while its impact on education has been limited, experiential educators have been among the first to adopt and adapt some of its ideas. The following chart summarizes many of its basic positions, and the movements which are part of it.

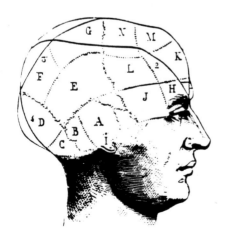

METHODS OF SELF DEVELOPMENT: PERSONAL AND TRANSPERSONAL

Methods of Experience		Methods of Development
Title	Description	
PERSONAL:		
1. Physical	The five senses.	Sensory awareness, dance, diet, sport, massage, exercise, Rolfing, Polarity therapy, Hatha Yoga, Alexander technique.
2. Emotional	Love, anger, sadness, joy, etc.	Psychotherapy, music, art, I.A., play therapy, bioenergetic, encounter, psychodrama, gestalt, co-counseling.
3. Mental	Intellect, discursive thinking	Empirical research, scholarly research, math, language, philosophy.
4. Personal intergrative	Capacity for fulfillment in outer life, the world.	Psychoanalysis, psychosynthesis. Existential therapy, direct decision therapy, behavior modifications.
5. Intuitional	Empathy, vague ESP, imagery.	Spontaneous imagery, visualization, analytic psychology, guided fantasy, dream analysis, self-hypnosis.
6. Psychic	Para-psychological phenomena.	Bio-feedback training, Scientology, psychedelics, directed meditation, yoga, psychic training, astrology, tarot.
7. Mystical	Experience of Universal Oneness, Unity.	Dance, asceticism, prayer, Bhakti yoga, Quiet meditation, mediation in action.
8. Personal/ Transpersonal Integrative.	Simultaneous experience of all dimensions.	Ariea Training, Gurdjeiff method, Zen Analytic Psychology, Psychosynthesis, Yoga, Sufism, Buddhism.

One cannot claim that a signficant number of experiential educators have become deeply involved with transpersonal psychology, but several practitioners of adventure-based programs have, in recent years, moved beyond river running and mountain climbing and into the use of a variety of new techniques to help the learner delve much deeper into him/herself. In a sense, adventure-based educators have found that there is more to life than the mountaineering or human relations skills which have been so emphasized in the past, and are seeking to move on to new levels of awareness. This has led to several religiously-based programs being founded, while others make use of yoga, meditation, fasting, and other "transpersonal" techniques to help learners. Perhaps Thoreau's oft-quoted passage from Walden, summarizes this longing best.

> I want to live deep and suck out all the marrow of life, to live so sturdily and spartanlike as to put to rout all that was not life, to drive life into a corner, and reduce it to its lowest terms, and if it proved to be mean, why then to get the whole and genuine meanness of it, and publish its meanness to the world; and if it were sublime, to know it by experience, and be able to give a true account of it in my next excursion. (Thoreau, 91)

The wilderness, the workshop, and the experiences of everyday life have been found to be powerful environments for learning, but the transpersonal psychologists suggest, not without evidence, that once the skills and abilities have been learned to master those environments, spiritual voids still exist for many persons, and these can only be filled by going deeper into the human being and outward into the cosmos for answers.

K. Insights from Developmental Change Theory.

In this section we shall concentrate on the insights of a variety of developmentalists, who deal with develomental stages in both children and adults on a wide variety of dimensions, including: moral and ethical development, intellectual development, interpersonal and cognitive styles, and ego or character types.

The adult stages have been documented in the popular book, Passages by Gail Sheehy, based on the research of Levinson and Gould. The transitional periods in the late teens and late twenties, as well as the "mid-life crisis" of the late thirties and early forties have captured the attention of many experiential educators as times particularly appropriate for challenging experiences, to help the adult come to grips with a new stage or period in their lives. This has been shown in a variety of studies on Outward Bound and similar adventure-based programs, where it has been found that many adults participated in such activities to come to grips with a particularly vexing problem or concern in their professional and/or personal lives. The challenge activities were seen as a motivator to help deal with the issues, and as evidence that change is possible, "even in an adult."

Arthur Chickering in his article in the book, Experiential Learning has done as excellent job of summarizing in chart form, what a variety of developmental pscyhologists have written about child and adult stages in ego development, moral and ethical development, interpersonal style and intellectual development. In stage theory, development is seen as a series of hierarchical stages, each of which builds on and includes the earlier stages. Movement is not automatic through normal growth processes, but rather is moved along through person-environment interactions, or in other words, through the experiences of the individual. Some of the most widely read stage development work is that of Lawrence Kohlberg, whose basic ideas are reflected in several of the appendices.

Experiential educators have in recent years been attracted to Kohlberg's ideas in structuring settings in which children and adults are confronted with experiences, which help to move the learner up Kohlberg's scale from obedience to external controls towards internal, principled autonomy. Kohlberg has attempted to connect his theory with that of Piaget's, so that moral and ethical development and intellectual development can grow at the same time.

Competence in interpersonal relationships and interpersonal style is another major category that stage theorists have written about and researched. The appropriateness of childhood or adolescent behavior for a mature adult is one way of conceiving the problem of interpersonal competence. Experiential educators have long held that when children and young people are placed in settings outside the schools where they must interact with adults other than their teachers, appropriate interpersonal styles and competent adult behavior are much more likely to result than if they continue in the isolation of their peer groups.

Much more could be said about the applicability of experiential learning in these critical areas, and the reader is encouraged to carefully study the for ways in which such learning promotes moral, intellectual and interpersonal development.

Erik H. Erikson

One of the most important developmental psychologists speaking to the needs of adolescents and adult learners is Erik Erikson. Erikson bemoans the "imbalance between passive stimulation and active outlet" in the pleasures that are sanctioned for young people today. He sees the youth of today substituting passivity for adventure and activity and this leading to the nearly inevitable explosion in delinquent behavior. Erikson is perhaps the best known for his eight developmental stages, though he cautions that the healthy personality must reconquer each of the negative traits, so that with each crisis, under favorable conditions, the positive traits outbalance the negative, and each reintegration builds strength

for the next crisis. The Eight Stages in the Life Cycle of Man, are:

  I. Infancy: Trust vs. Mistrust
 II. Early Childhood: Autnomy vs. Shame and Doubt
III. Play Age: Initiative vs. Guilt
 IV. School Age: Industry vs. Inferiority
  V. Adolescence: Identity vs. Identity Diffusion
 VI. Young Adulthood: Intimacy vs. Isolation
VII. Adulthood: Generativity vs. Isolation
VIII. Senescence: Integrity vs. Disgust   (Erickson)

Experiential education speaks to many aspects of each of the eight stages in the life cycle, recognizing as does Erikson, that there must be a constant reintegration of each of the positive traits throughout our lives. Trust in oneself, one's peers and one's environment have become a cornerstone of most experiential education programs, with adventure programs even naming some of their intiative games, "trust walks" and "trust falls." Autonomy, intiative, and industry are also critical components of most experiential learning programs, while experiential educators accuse the traditional school settings of promoting Erikson's negative traits of Shame and Doubt, Guilt, and Inferiority, through severe competition and guaranteed failure.

The later stages of Erikson's life cycle also are seen as critical parts of most experiential learning programs. Numerous research studies on the effects adventure programs for youth, speak to their role in helping the adolescent develop a positive identity, and in recent years countless experiential programs have been developed for delinquent youth suffering from what Erikson calls "Identity diffusion," or a negative identity based on what society or parents, do not want him to be. Erikson's final stages of Intimacy, Generativity, and Integrity are often found as basic goals of experiential programs and the literature is filled with personal testimonials, if not statistical evidence, that learning in the experiential mode promotes these qualities.

V. ANTHROPOLOGICAL FOUNDATIONS OF EXPERIENTIAL LEARNING

In recent years, adventure-based experiential educators, along with Maurice Gibbons and his Phi Delta Kappa Task Force, have looked to anthropology for insights into experiential learning and the role it should or could play in the educational process.

One of the most used concepts is that of "ritual," or what the anthropologists define as a continuum of events which together create a process experience for the individual. The three stages of this process are: Separation, Transition, and Incorporation. Anne Ketchin, Anthropology Ph.D. and adventured-based educator defines these three processes as follows:

> Separation: Abrupt separation
> from everyday life and
> familiar places and
> things...and relationships.
> The group, or person, often
> enters an entirely new
> social and physical
> environment.
> Transition: The transition
> through these new experi-
> ences usually takes on a
> dream-like quality, referred
> to as "liminal." Although
> "reality" is back in every-
> day life, the present
> situation becomes "more
> real than real". If there
> is a group, the members
> become close, and mutually
> reinforcing.
> Incorporation: Incorporation
> back into everyday life is a
> very important stage, receiving
> a lot of attention   in most
> societies.
> (Ketchin, 1-2)

Other criteria for ritual mentioned by Ketchin are status and role reversals;   status leveling, the abruptness and rapidity of separation, the use of drama,   the use of metaphor, the presence of stresses (social and/or physical),   isolation, symbolic challenges, and a kind of knowledge to be gained. Ketchin's   dissertation is

an attempt to apply these   concepts of ritual to women in Outward Bound perhaps the best known of the adventure-based experiential education programs. It is not hard to see how Outward Bound and similar programs have become modern day rituals.

The isolated group in a wilderness area develops a new sense of identity, with strong in-group feelings of support for the members of the group. Highly successful persons in the "real" world, suddenly find that they are no longer necessarily the best or even capable of coping in the new environment. New criteria of success are placed on the participants, and most programs place them in a series of stressful situations. The mountains, rivers, oceans, rocks, marathons, etc...all become a metaphor for life in the outside world, and new symbols replace those which were left behind.

Even non-adventure based experiential programs contain contain certain   aspects of ritual. The student going out on a work-study assignment is separated   from the most of his or her peers, who   remain in the "womb" of the school, is   rewarded for his or her ability to "do" the real life tasks, rather than perform on pencil and paper tests, is placed   under new varieties of stress, and gains   a new or different kind of knowledge than is usually to be found in the classroom.

Maurice Gibbons

Maurice Gibbons is not an anthropolgist, but his article titled, "Walkabout: Searching for the Right Passage from Childhood and School" in the May, 1974, Phi Delta Kappan borrowed extensively from anthropological concepts, and has had an increasingly important effect on the nature of secondary education in this country. Gibbons theme was taken from the Australian film by the same name in which an aborigine child spends six months on the rite of passage in the deserts of Australia. Children from the city are also in the desert at the same time, but are lost, helpless and exhausted/Gibbons draws the parallels between the city children's inability to cope, with the similar inabilities of many American youth to function in adult society upon completion of secondary school. The skills on the one hand are those of survival, life and death, while on the other they are pencil and paper tests far removed from survival in the "real world." Isolation and the need to trust one's inner and spiritual resources is contrasts with the crowd experience of secondary education in this country.

Gibbons went on to propose in the article that American young people could benefit from a Walkabout characterized by real, not vicarious or simulated experiences, and that students would be asked to meet five basic challenges: Adventure, Creativity, Service, Practical Skill, and Logical Inquiry. The article and subsequent Walkabout association have led to experimental programs in many secondary schools throughout the U.S., implementing various aspects of Gibbons' ideas.

VI. TOWARDS A DEFINITION OF EXPERI-
ENTIAL LEARNING

In this final section on the theory of experiential learning, we shall draw materials and ideas from a wide range of sources in an attempt to define more closely what we mean by experiential learning. Chickering defines it as:

> learning which occurs when changes in judgments, feelings, knowledge or skills result for a particular person from living through an event or events...Experiential learning may also result from an encounter group or an exam, discussion or demonstration, work or play, travel or sitting on a stump. (Chickering, 63)

The appeal of Chickering's definition is its emphasis upon change, and the breadth of the definition which recognizes that experiential learning can occur in the classroom a well as in the wilderness.

From the outdoor, adventure-based group of experiential educators come other definitions. The necessary characteristics of the Outward Bound process have been defined by Vic Walsh, Director of the Pacific Crest Outward Bound School and by Gerald Golins,

Director of Colorado Outward Bound School. The experiences must be:

1. Organized...problems are intended to be planned, programmed, and managed...problem solving tasks, not all experience is necessarily educative...
2. Incremental...problems are introduced incrementally in terms of their complexity and consequence...
3. Concrete...problems are concrete, i.e., recognizable as problems limited in time and space...
4. Manageable...problems can be solved with the use of common sense and the application of basic skills which have been taught (incrementally).
5. Consequential...tasks have real consequences not vicarious ramifications.
6. Holistic...problems are holistic, that is, their solution requires the fullest complement of an individual's mental, emotional, and physical resources. (Walsh and Golins, 7-9)

Walsh and Golins also describe the learner, the physical environment, and the social environment, which go to make up the "Outward Bound Process." In a final chart they lay out the various steps in the process, and summarize it into the following statement: "The learner is placed into a unique physical environment and into a unique social environment, then is given a characteristic set of problem-solving tasks, which lead to a state of adaptive dissonance, to which he adapts by mastery, which recognizes the meaning and direction of the learner's experience." (Walsh and Golins, 16) A similar definition has been drawn up by Bob MacArthur for use with his Leadership Program at Dartmouth College. "The learner is placed into a demanding situation which necessitates mastery of new skills, which are followed immediately by responsible, challenging action, demanding application of new skills, coupled with an opportunity for critical analysis and reflection, which ultimately reorganizes the meaning and direction of the learner's life experience." (MacArthur, 11)

James Kielsmeier of the Center for Youth Development at the University of Minnesota, lists the following aspects of experiential learning as critical to any definition: An emphasis on process rather than program; how to learn rather than content acquisition; internal learner motivation as opposed to imposed learning; value forming experience- not sterile learning; intergroup, cooperative learning versus isolated, competitive approaches, and the use of discovery, inquiry, problem solving, hands-on, high intensity, and active reflection in all experiential learning situations. (Kielsmeier)

The National Commission on Resources for Youth lists the important ingredients for learning by service programs as: filling genuine needs of adolescents and of society; providing a real challenge to students; an opportunity for guided selection on the service experience; providing participants with a sense of community; contributing to the knowledge that adolescents need regarding career options open to them; the program must be both structured and flexible; and allowing young people to exercise adult responsibility and permitting them to actively participate in decision-making and governance of the project. (National Commission on Resources for Youth)

Project Exploration's suggested elements of an experiential learning model are quite inclusive and include the following elements: a sense of adventure, unpredictability, drama and suspense; a sense of organizational understanding and commitment; a high level of expectation; a success orientation in which growth is supported and encouraged and in which the positive is emphasized; an atmosphere supported and encouraged and in which the positive is emphasized; an atmosphere of mutual support; a sense of enjoyment; group problem solving; the integration of group and individual challenges; environments beyond the regular school classroom; a merging of intellectual, social, physical and emotional learning and development; a significant amount of cognitive work related to the experience; a combination of active involvement with moments of personal and group reflection and evaluation; and finally, continued emphasis on the basic skills of reading, writing, mathematics and verbal communication. (Project Exploration)

It is Maurice Gibbons and the Phi Delta Kappa Task Force in The New Secondary Education that have done the most extensive and detailed analysis of the theory and practice of experiential learning. They list a variety of elements which go to make up a quality secondary education, most of which closely parallel those aspects of experiential learning dealt with throughout this paper. The following is an abbreviated list of significant experiential program elements.

> Education is a lifelong, continuous process providing the experiences, environments, relationships, challenges, and guidance individuals need to maximize their opportunities for growth in each period of personal transformation, to prepare for the changes demanded by each period of transition, and to cultivate the ability to negotiate the demands of changing circumstances in the society in which they live. (Gibbons, 91-92)

The influence of Levinson's and Gould's research, referred to earlier, is evident in this part of the program definition, as is the emphasis on change, which was such an important part of Dewey's philosophy.

> The purpose of education is to assist individuals to create a learning lifestyle with a developmental perspective, based upon the discovery and continuing refinement of each person's unique capacity for personal growth, relationships with others, and functional competence. (Gibbons, 95)

The emphasis in this program element reflects many of the ideas from the humanistic psychologists and from such learning theorists as Bruner. Developmental perspectives are also pointed to as critical, with insights from Piaget and Erikson being likely sources for such insight.

> ...programs should cultivate such transformations as independence and responsibility in behavior and

the formulation of a sense of identity based on competence...apply their knowledge and talent in useful work and jobs, to act cooperatively with many, and to form loving, mutual, and lasting relationships with a few...programs also should prepare students to negotiate unprogrammed events in actual circumstances so that they will be able to cope with reality...(Gibbons, 96-97)

Numerous theorists have spoken of the need for experiential programs to better teach independence and responsibility. The ability to cope with unplanned events is a critical component of not only outdoor, adventure-based experiential programs, but also many work-oriented activities. The application of knowledge, not the useless verbalism which Friere condemns, is also a critical part of any experiential learning environment.

...learning situations should give full attention to personal and interpersonal as well as academic content. The treatment of content in each domain should be as concerned with intense firsthand experiences and challenging productive activities as with relevant theoretical studies. (Gibbons, 100)

In order to prepare students for transformation, transitions and societal change, Gibbons and his colleagues hold that the classroom is too narrow an environment and that the learner must deal more directly with personal and social issues through concrete experiences. The academic domain is important, but so are the personal and social or interpersonal domains.

Learning is a cycle that includes "the sensory input of concrete experience, the process of theoretical studies and the output of productive activities." (Gibbons, 102) Experience is the raw material which stimulates curiosity and interest, but experience and study are not enough, as they must lead to productive activity in the world.

...education should be organized to teach students to develop and implement their own personal programs, to develop programs in cooperation with others, and to pursue appropriate programs designed for this. In this process teachers should be organizers of suitable experiences, environments, and personnel as well as programs of study, and they should be competent in methods of guiding individual development, training groups in interpersonal relationships, and teaching the skills of academic mastery. (Gibbons, 104)

This element of an experiential program emphasizes the role of the student in developing programs, not without the help of teachers and other adults, but in keeping with their own need and interests. It also calls on teachers to play the role of trainer, counselor, and guide in the personal, interpersonal and academic domains, and not just the dominant instructor of today.

The practical outworkings of the model call for a Junior Segment (Junior High School), consisting of eight centers in which students would spend up to two months: The Center for the Fine, Applied and Performing Arts; Wilderness School; The Local Bureau of Investigation; Workshop in Practical Activities, The Institute of Advanced Studies, The Humanities Center and Life Skills Laboratory, The Center for the Study of the World, and finally the School of Guided Self-Education. The Senior Segment would consist of eight challenges: physical/psychological challenge, creativity challenge, service challenge, investigation challenge, practical skill challenge, work-experience challenge, academic challenge, and extension program. (Gibbons, 117-122)

We shall not burden the reader here with a final, all-inclusive definition of experiential learning, but suggest that the elements for such a definition can be found in the theoretical discussions which preceded this section, and in the practical program elements reviewed in this section on definition. The programs observed and evaluated by this writer, and the massive study by Diane Hedin dealt with in the next section, both lead to the inescapable conclusion made by the Brazilian educational philosopher, Paulo Freire, that action without reflection is mere activism and creates unauthentic forms of existence, while reflection without action becomes mere verbalism, idle chatter, or an alienated and alienating blah. (Friere, 75-76) It is a challenge to traditional education to escape the meaningless verbalism into which it has fallen, and for experiential educators to beware of the trap of meaningless activism, or mis-educative experience as Dewey has called it.

VII. RESEARCH AND EVALUATION IN EXPERIENTIAL LEARNING

Since the dominant focus of this paper is the theory of experiential education, this section on research and evaluation may appear to be rather cursory, but our purpose here is not to give a complete review of all research on experiential learning, or to design all the possible evaluative strategies. Rather, following a brief summary of some of the critical research in the field, some strategies for conducting evaluations in experiential learning environments will be outlined. The research in vocational education and internship/apprenticeship settings will not be dealt with in this review, as this has been done elsewhere, but rather the concentration here will be on the outdoor adventure, volunteer service, and related experiential programs, to which most of the theory section of the paper was dedication.

Diane Hedin, perhaps the leading experiential education researcher, concludes in a recent article that

"There is relatively little 'hard' evidence about the impact of such programs on student participants. Little effort has been made to test sytematically the assumptions underlying the recommendations or to investigate empirically which specific forms of experiential programs may be most effective in realizing the hypothesized benefits." (Hedin, 3)

This author's search of the literature confirms Hedin's judgment, that there is little 'hard' evidence. The literature is filled with testimonials, journals, case studies and other data indicating the positive effects of experiential learning on child, adolescent and adult participants, but very few experimental or even quasi-experimental research projects have been conducted. There are a variety of reasons for this lack of data, not the least of which was referred to earlier, namely, that experiential educators have allied themselves much more closely with humanistic psychologists than they have with the behaviorists. This has led to a great many more 'soft' research designs involving participants filling out surveys or keeping journals, and has been confined primarily to "self-concept" research, rather than data concerning cognitive or intellectual development. This does not mean, however, that the research is insignificant or irrelevant, only that it is limited in its scope and applicability. One of the major difficulties of experiential education research is the problem of finding appropriate assessment tools. Since many programs do not have explicitly stated academic, cognitive or intellectual goals, the use of traditional test scores is limited. This does not mean, however, that such programs have not or should not be evaluated on their effects in these critical areas. In addition to a lack of appropriate instruments, there is some question as to the validity of many pencil and paper tests when applied to experiential settings, where the objectives often deal with things more difficult to measure than the usual cognitive objectives of the classroom. Because outcomes are elusive in most experiential settings, Hedin used a variety of techniques to obtain data, including: paper and pencil tests, systematic observations of parents, teachers, and community supervisors; student journals and writing samples; case studies of individual students and programs, and several unobtrusive measures. This use of a wide variety of approaches and types of instruments and measures appears to be the most satisfactory approach, in order to avoid the criticism leveled at most of the research in the area, where the reliability and validity of the instruments and procedures is constantly called into question.

Arnold Shore, in 1977, compiled over 80 studies which had been conducted over the years on the effects of Outward Bound. He concluded the research literature on Outward Bound is weak, due to the lack of rigor imposed on many of the studies, and methodological weaknesses in research design. (Shore, 1977) His own summarization, however, can be criticized for not stating explicitly his own criteria for judging the research. The Reference Volume by Shore, however is an excellent starting place for persons wishing to gain an overview of the research literature on outdoor adventure programs. Robert Godfrey reviewed a long list of studies on outdoor-adventure programming and found evidence of positive growth on a wide variety of factors: positive self image, social functioning, stability of personality, control of personal fate, changes in values and personality, tolerance of others and self-confidence. studies also indicated growth in positive attitudes towards parents and peers, improved race relations, an improved sense of the value of education, increased desire to go to college, and a lessening of positive attitudes towards regular school and classroom settings. (Godfrey)

Hedin's evaluation has been refereed to earlier in this section and is probably the most thorough and extensive evaluation of experiential programs to date. Thirty programs in independent, public and parochial schools and over 4,000 students were part of the analysis. There was near unanimity in the initial studies on the basic features about what is learned in experiential settings, and these twenty-four items with their percentage responses are included here, as they clearly indicate what participants in such programs believe to be the fundamental characteristics of the experiential learning environment.

In addition to finding out what students say they learn in experiential settings, the authors also used instruments to assess social, psychological and intellectual growth. It is the comprehensive nature of this research effort which makes it stand out from the vast majority of other attempts at finding out what happens to participants in experiential settings. Among the scales used or developed for the study were: Personal and Social Responsibility Scale, Semantic Differential on Adults, Career Exploration, Community Problem Inventory, Rosenberg Self-Esteem Scale, the Janis-Field Feeling of Social Inadequacy Scale and a Problem Solving Inventory.

Among the many findings on this massive study are: students entered into more relationships with adults and experience more positive attitudes towards them; students developed more responsible attitudes and behaviors; community participation is more highly valued by experiential learners; active involvement in careers leads to more positive attitudes towards careers; self-concept and self-esteem in relation to others was positively affected in the large majority of programs; in general there was a significant movement upward in empathy and complexity by students; no single practice or set of practices guarantees effectiveness for all students; the strongest factor influencing constructive change was the existence of a seminar in which students could reflect on their experiences; and the most effective programs lasted at least one semester or 18 weeks. The following chart indicates the characteristics of experiential learning considered most important.

CHARACTERISTICS OF EXPERIENTIAL LEARNING

RANKINGS IN EXPERIENTIAL PROGRAMS	RANK	RANKINGS IN CETA PROGRAMS
Had Adult Responsibilities	(1)	Was Given Clear Direction
Made Important Decisions	(2)	Did Things Myself
Did Things Myself	(3)	Had Variety of Tasks
Free to Develop and Use Own	(4)	Got Help When I Needed It
Felt I Made A Contribution	(5)	Had Variety of Tasks
Free to Explore Own Interests	(6)	Was Appreciated For Good Work
Discussed My Experiences With Teachers	(7)	Had Challenging Tasks
Discussed With Family/Friends	(8)	Felt I Made A Contribution
Given Clear Directions	(9)	Used My Own Ideas
Adults Took Interest In Me	(10)	Developed A Personal Relationship

BIBLIOGRAPHY

Action, National Student Volunteer Program. _Evaluating Service-Learning Programs: A Guide For Program Coordinators._ Washington, D.C.: Action Pamphlet No. 4300.7, 1978.

Aristotle. _The Basic Works Of Aristotle._ Edited by Richard McKeon. New York: Random House Press, 1948.

Boyer, Ernest L. _High School: A Report on Secondary Education in America._ New York: Harper & Row, 1983.

Brown, B. Frank, et.al. _The Reform of Secondary Education._ New York: McGraw-Hill, 1973.

Bruner, J.S. _Toward a Theory of Instruction_. New York: Norton, 1966.

Chickering, Arthur. "Developmental Change as a Major Outcome." in Morris Keeton, _Experiential Learning_. San Francisco: Jossey-Bass Publishers, 1976.

Coleman, James S. et. al. _Youth: Transition to Adulthood_. (Report of the Panel on Youth of the President's Science Advisory Committee.) Chicago: The University of Chicago Press, 1974.

Cronbach, Lee J. _Educational Psychology_. New York: Harcourt, Brace and World, Inc., 1963.

Descartes. _Discourse on Method_.

Dewey, John. _Experience and Education_. New York: Collier Books, 1938.

Dewey, John. _Experience and Nature_. LaSalle: Open Court Publications, 1971.

Erikson, Erik H. _Childhood and Society_ 2nd Rev. Ed. New York: W.W. Norton and Co., 1963.

Faure, Edgar, et. al. _Learning To Be: The World of Education Today and Tomorrow_. Paris, UNESCO, 1972.

Friere, Paulo. _Pedagogy of the Oppressed_. New York: The Seabury Press, 1973.

Furth, Hans G. _Deafness and Learning: A Psychosocial Approach_. Belmont, California: Wadsworth Publishing Company, Inc. 1973.

Furth, Hans G. _Thinking Without Language: Psychological Implications of Deafness_. New York: The Free Press, 1966.

Gardner, William. _Learning and Behavior Characteristics of Exceptional Children and Youth: A Humanistic Behavioral Approach_. Boston: Allyn and Bacon, Inc., 1977.

Gibbons, Maurice. "Walkabout: Searching for the Right Passage from Childhood and School." _Phi Delta Kappan_. May, 1974, 594-602.

Gibbons, Maurice, et. al. _The Secondary Education_. (Report of the Phi Delta Kappa Task Force) Bloomington: Phi Delta Kappa, 1976.

Godfrey, Robert. "A Review of Research and Evaluation Literature on Outward Bound and Related Education Programs." A paper presented to the Conference on Experiential Education at Estes Park, Colorado, October, 1974.

Goodlad, John I. _A Place Called School: Prospects for the Future_. New York: McGraw-Hill, 1983.

Hedin, Diane. "Evaluating Experiential Learning", _Change_, (1980), 2-9.

Hedin, Diane and Dan Conrad. "Johnny Says He Is Learning Through Experience," _The Journal of Experiential Education_. Vol. 2, No. 1 (Spring, 1979), 42-47.

Houle, Cyril. "Deep Traditions of Experiential Learning," in _Experiential Learning_. Morris Keeton, Editor. San Francisco, Jossey-Bass Publishers, 1976.

House, Ernest R. "Assumptions Underlying Evaluation Models," _Educational Research_. (March, 1978), 4-12.

Hume, David. _A Treatise of Human Nature_. Oxford: Oxford University Press, 1978.

Inhelder, E. M. Bovet, H. Sinclair, and C.D. Smock. "On Cognitive Development." _American Psychologist_. 1966, 21, 160-164.

James, Muriel, and Dorothy Jongeward. _Born to Win_. Reading: Mass.: Addison-Wesley Publishing Company, 1973.

Jones, Richard M. _Fantasy and Feeling in Education_. New York: Harper and Row, 1968.

Keeton, Morris T. "Credentials for a

Learning Society," in Experiential Learning. Morris Keeton, Editor. San Francisco: Jossey-Bass Publishers, 1976.

Ketchin, Anne. "Women Out of Bounds: An Essay," Dissertation in anthropology at the University of Colorado, 1980.

Kielsmeier, James. "Toward an Operational Definition of Experiential Education." A paper from the University of Colorado and the American Youth Foundations.

Levine, Edna Simon. The Psychology of Deafness. New York: Columbia University Press, 1980.

Locke, John. An Essay Concerning Human Understanding. Edited by A.D. Woozley. New York: The New American Library, 1964.

MacArthur, Robert. "Leadership Handbook." A mimeographed booklet from Dartmouth college.

Mao Tse Tung. "On Practice," Four Essays On Philosophy. Peking: Foreign Language Press, 1968.

Martin, John Henry, et. al. Report of the National Panel on High Schools and Adolescent Education. Washington, D.C.: USOE, 1974.

Maslow, Abraham. "Music Education and Peak Experience," Music Educators Journal, 54, No. 6 (1968), 72-75, 163-171.

Maslow, Abraham H. "Some Educational Implications of Humanistic Psychologies," Harvard Education Review, 38, No. 4 (Fall, 1968), 685-696.

Mathis, B. Claude, John W. Cotton, and Lee Sechrest. Psychological Foundations of Education: Learning and Teaching. New York: Academic Press, 1970.

McWaters, Barry. "An Outline of Transpersonal Psychology: Its Meaning and Revelance for Education," in Thomas B. Roberts, Four Psychologies Applied to Education. New York: John Wiley and Sons, 1975.

Metfessel, Newton S. and William B. Michael. "A Paradigm Involving Multiple Criterion Measures for the Effectiveness of School Programs," in Blaine R. Worthen and James R. Sanders, Educational Evaluation: Theory and Practice. Belmont, California: Wadsworth Publishing Company, Inc., 1973.

Mill, J.S. Dissertations and Discussions. Vol. IV. New York: Henry Holt, 1874.

Montessori, Maria. Spontaneous Activity. New York: Schocken Books, 1972.

National Commission on Excellence in Education, A Nation at Risk: The Imperative For Educational Reform, Washington, D.C.: Government Printing Office, 1983.

National Commission on Resources for Youth. "Ingredients for Successful Learning by Serving Programs," a mimeographed paper.

Neill, A.S. Summerhill: A Radical Approach to Child Rearing. New York: Hart Publishing Company, 1960.

Nietzsche, Friedrich. Schopenhauer as Educator. New York: Hart Publishing Company, 1960.

Peirce, Charles S. "How to Make Our Ideas Clear," Charles S. Peirce: Selected Writings. Edited by Philip Wiener. New York: Dover Publications, 1958.

Pirsig, Robert M. Zen and the Art of Motorcycle Maintenance: An Inquiry Into Values. New York: Bantam Books, 1974.

Plato. Plato: The Collected Dialogues. Edited by Edith Hamilton and Huntington Cairns, Princeton: University Press, 1969.

Popkin, Richard H. and Avrum Stroll. Philosophy Made Simple. New York: Doubleday and Company, Inc., 1956.

Project Exploration. "Elements of an
    Exploration Curriculum." A document
    presented at the Association of
    Experiential Education Conference
    in St. Louis, 1978.

Rogers, Carl. Freedom to Learn.
    Columbus, Ohio: Charles E. Merrill,
    1969.

Rohrs, Hermann. "The Educational
    Thought of Kurt Hahn." Kurt Hahn.
    London: Routledge & Kegan Paul,
    Ltd., 1970.

Roberts, Thomas. Four Psychologies
    Applied To Education. New York:
    John Wiley and Sons, 1975.

Walsh, Victor and Gerald Golins, "The
    Exploration of the Outward Bound
    Process," A mimeographed paper
    available from Colorado Outward
    Bound.

Watson, Thomas J. The Education of
    Hearing-Handicapped Children.
    Springfield, Illinois: Charles C.
    Thomas, Publisher, 1967.

Whitehead, Alfred North. Process and
    Reality. Edited by David Griffin
    and Donald Sherburne. (Corrected
    Edition) New York: The Free Press,
    1978.

Whitehead, Alfred North. Science and
    the Modern World. New York: The
    Free Press, 1967.

Sketch of a Moving Spirit: Kurt Hahn

by Thomas James

The historical antecedents for Kurt Hahn's ideas can still be traced in the philosophy of the Colorado Outward Bound School.

Someone said once that Kurt Hahn was the "moving spirit" of Outward Bound when it began in Britain during World War II. Imported to the United States two decades later, Outward Bound, in turn, became a moving spirit of the experiential education movement. Now history has left the man behind--Hahn died nearly a decade ago--but his ideals are as ubiquitous in experiential education as is neoclassical architecture in Washington, D.C. What was once innovation has become assumption, shaping and defining our vision. To ask about Hahn's ideals today is really to ask about ourselves as teachers and learners, whether in Outward Bound, in other experiential programs or in the mainstream of American education. The answers we find should help us to understand, among other things, the meaning of our careers as educators. Work from the dream outward, Carl Jung once said. If we use history to probe the core of idealism that sustains much of experiential education as we practice it, we cannot help but encounter the man who founded Outward Bound in 1941.

"Moving Spirit" is a better designation than "Founder". What Kurt Hahn caused to happen was larger than the program he created to prevent men from dying in lifeboats when their ships were sunk by German U-boats in the North Atlantic. It was larger than the educational methods he applied to solve the problem at hand. It was, above all, a renewal of social vision.

Not a hero himself, Hahn infused others with a sense of heroic quest. He was an educator--the word comes from Latin roots meaning "to lead out." As a leader, he left enough unsaid that the people working with him were able to add their vision to the common pursuit. In each of the schools with which he was associated, not to

Thomas James, formerly Editor of **COMPACT** magazine and Associate Director of Communications at the Education Commission of the States, lives in Denver and writes about education, politics and the outdoors. He has a one-year grant this year to write a book about the history and philosophy of the Colorado Outward Bound School, where he first published this article as a School issue paper.

mention the smaller programs he brought into being through the years, there was always, in the minds of those who were close to him, a sensation of having within their grasp a unifying aspiration with the power to strengthen individuals and transform social life. Kurt Hahn instilled a pervasive culture of aspiration that remains the essence of Outward Bound and a crucial part of experiential education to this day.

From where did this culture of aspiration come? What went into it that made it so compelling?

We might begin to address these questions by looking for the origins of Outward Bound in 1913 instead of 1941. In the summer of 1913, as an Oxford student vacationing with a friend in Scotland, recuperating from a lingering illness, a result of the sunstroke he had suffered a few years before, Kurt Hahn outlined his idea for a school based on principles set forth in Plato's **Republic**. This was without doubt an audacious, some would say foolish, act of the imagination. Hahn believed that the most extremely utopian conception of society ever formulated should be applied, purely and simply, to create a school in the modern world. He was twenty-eight-years old and had never run a school, nor even taught in one. The ideal school he imagined never came into being, but it exerted a profound influence on all his subsequent efforts as an educator and statesman. He launched Salem School, in Germany, in 1920; Gordonstoun School, in Scotland, in 1934; Outward Bound, in Wales, in 1941; and Atlantic College, in England, in 1962.

The main point is worth repeating. Though the youthful fantasy of a Platonic school never came into being, its influence crops up everywhere in the institutions he built and in the people he drew to his cause. In **English Progressive Schools**, Robert Skidelsky analyzes Hahn's debt to Plato as follows:

Plato was a political reformer who sought to recall the Athenians to the old civic virtues eroded, as he saw it, by democratic enthusiasm and soft living. His aim was to educate a class of leaders in a "healthy pasture" remote from the corrupting environment, whose task it would be to regenerate society.

39

Hahn must have been haunted by similar visions of decay as, inspired by these ideas, he drew up a plan in 1913 for a school modeled on Platonic principles. The war that broke out a year later and ended in the collapse of Germany was to give them a new urgency: to convert what might have re-mained a purely academic speculation into an active campaign for social and political regeneration.

It takes little digging to find precisely the same intentions in the founding of Outward Bound in 1941. Men were dying in lifeboats; the English nation despaired of its strength and will to face the coming onslaught of the

---

"Always Bringing Out The Best In People"

by John S. Holden

Kurt Hahn was visiting our house in 1968 when Lyndon Johnson announced that he would not run for President again. At almost the same time we heard of the tragedy of Martin Luther King. We watched the riots on television. Hahn was there when I took a phone call from one of our students who was doing volunteer work for the Southern Christian Leadership Conference in Washington. Here was "Whitey" in the Black stronghold. His description was far more graphic than what we were able to see on television. The conversation was cut off when the boy said he couldn't stand the tear gas any more.

In spite of this graphic warning, Hahn left our house the next day for Los Angeles. He went right to the Watts area to confer with a black man who had organized the youth there to carry out projects in their neighborhoods to make better living conditions for themselves and their families. He wasn't afraid of the Watts riots.

Except for the lifelong sunstroke affliction that kept him out of bright sunlight, Hahn had the greatest courage both physical and mental. He wasn't afraid of jogging in the dark along the road during an April thaw when he visited us. He wasn't bothered by the fall he experienced on the way back to the house--just embarrassed and wanting a clothes brush to remove the mud from his suit. He always jogged in the dark, and that was neither the first nor the last fall he lived through.

He showed us another example of his courage one time when he was guiding us around Gordonstoun School in Scotland. We came to the watchtower manned by the boys every time there was a storm at sea. I think he was eighty-one years old at the time, and all his life he had been afflicted with unusual clumsiness. He called himself a physical illiterate. Nevertheless, he had to lead us up the steel ladder into the tower. I stayed close below him as he fumbled and almost slipped on his way up. The trip down was even more hair-raising.

John S. Holden is an educational consultant . He is a Lifetime Trustee of the Colorado Outward Bound School and a former Headmaster of the Rocky Mountain School in Carbondale, Colorado.

At times I couldn't help thinking that this was the most unlikely man to have started the Outward Bound Movement. But, as I listened to his talk about Salem, about Gordonstoun, about Atlantic College and about Outward Bound, I realized that he was always moving in the same direction, always bringing out the best in people, always stretching himself to the limit and always demanding that same stretch in the people working with him.

The last time I saw him was in Cambridge, Massachusetts, after he had returned from Watts. He was full of optimism and hope, uplifted from his meeting with the black man who had calmed multitudes in the California ghettos by giving young people something that they could be proud of doing. Hahn was full of plans to bring together from all over the world the leaders of mountain rescue, Red Cross, water safety, firemen and ski patrols. Prince Phillip was to foot the bill for this great conclave, which actually did take place in England the following year. Behind this was the theory: teach them to save lives and they'll never be willing to kill.

Kurt Hahn told us one of his favorite stories once as we were leaving the chapel at Gordonstoun. Prince Phillip, who had attended as a student, never returned to his old school until long after World War II when he was already very famous, married to Princess Elizabeth, soon to be Queen of England. Of course, there was great excitement. All the staff and his old teachers gathered around him as he toured the grounds. Suddenly, the Prince disappeared. There was speculation about where he had gone. To the chapel? To his old stand at the watchtower? When Prince Phillip returned, he smiled and said he had gone to see if the pigpen he had built in his student days was still there.

I'm glad we knew Kurt Hahn personally. He made it quite clear to us that the physical aspects of Outward Bound were secondary to the really important things. In his talk he brought out the thinking part, the serving part, the spiritual part. As a warden of the Eskdale Outward Bound School put it, the aim was to arm students "against the enemies--fear, defeatism, apathy, selfishness. It was thus as much a moral as a practical training". Hahn was disgusted with any article or movie that didn't emphasize this more subtle and more important part of human kind.

Nazis. Twenty-one years later, the founders of the Colorado Outward Bound School raised similar concerns about the character of Americans. It had been reported that an alarming percentage of American prisoners of war in Korea had collaborated with the enemy. Americans were overweight, deluged by material goods and technology; the young were seen to be increasingly apathetic and often violently self-centered. In that year, 1962, Outward Bound took a hundred boys into the mountains and tried to teach them something about self-discovery. The purpose of the school could easily have been stated in the Platonic terms used by Hahn in 1921 to describe the purpose of Salem School: "to train citizens who would not shirk from leadership and who could, if called upon, make independent decisions, put right action before expediency and the common cause before personal ambition."

The Colorado Outward Bound School was not started to teach people how to live in the mountains. The idea was to use the mountains as a classroom to produce better people, to build character, to instill that intensity of individual and collective aspiration on which the entire society depends for its survival. Kurt Hahn summarized the school's idealism when he said that the goal was to ensure "the survival of an enterprising curiosity, an undefeatable spirit, tenacity in pursuit, readiness for sensible self-denial, and, above all, compassion". Another summary appeared in an article published in 1962 by the school's founding president, F. Charles Froelicher:

> Without self-discovery, a person may still have self-confidence, but it is a self-confidence built on ignorance and it melts in the face of heavy burdens. Self-discovery is the end product of a great challenge mastered, when the mind commands the body to do the seemingly impossible, when strength and courage are summoned to extraordinary limits for the sake of something outside the self--a principle, an onerous task, another human life.

Outward Bound places unusual emphasis on physical challenge, not as an end in itself, but as an instrument for training the will to strive for mastery. There is also the insistent use of action, instead of states of mind, to describe the reality of the individual. Education is tied unequivocally to experience, to what one does and not so much to one's attitudes and opinions. A thread running from Plato through Hahn and through Outward Bound is the responsibility of individuals to make their personal goals consonant with social necessity. Not only is the part subordinated to the whole, but the part cannot even understand its own identity, its relations and its responsibility, until it has grasped the nature of the whole. This explains the connection between self-discovery and self-sacrifice in Froelicher's statement, and it also shows where Hahn parted company with

many others in the English Progressive School Movement who saw his stance as threatening to individual freedom. Having stood up to Hitler before being exiled from Nazi Germany in 1933, Hahn believed in individual freedom, but he believed that students should be impelled into experiences that would teach them the bonds of social life necessary to protect such freedom. He took from Plato the idea that a human being cannot achieve perfection without becoming part of a perfect society--that is, without creating social harmony to sustain the harmonious life of the individual. This is the overall structure of the argument in the **Republic**, and it is also the most important lesson of an Outward Bound course, the lesson without which personal development is of questionable value. In a small group,

---

Having stood up to Hilter before being exiled from Nazi Germany in 1933, Hahn believed in individual freedom, but he believed that students should be impelled into experiences that would teach them the bonds of social life necessary to protect such freedom.

---

the patrol, and in a "healthy pasture" away from the degenerate ways of the world, the individual student comes to grips with what must be done to create a just society, within which a human being might aspire to perfection. Here is the true, unadvertised peak climb of an Outward Bound course. An inner transformation precedes outward conquest. This is why Hahn placed compassion above all other values of Outward Bound, for it among all emotions is capable of reconciling individual strength with collective need.

The prospect of wholeness, the possibility, at least, of human life becoming an equilibrium sustained by harmony and balance, is what makes this form of education even thinkable. Skidelsky again offers a lucid analysis of the source of Hahn's thinking:

> The second idea which Hahn assimilated was Plato's notion that the principle of perfection was harmony and balance. The perfection of the body, he held, depends upon a harmony of its elements...Virtue (the health of the soul) is the harmony or balance between the various faculties of the psyche: reason, the appetites, and spirit. Virtue in the state is the harmony between its functional elements: thinkers, soldiers, and artisans. The same principle can be extended indefinitely-- to relations between men, relations between states, and so on.

This passage sheds some light on Hahn's interest in giving his students experiences that would complement their strengths and weaknesses. In his speeches he said he wanted to turn introverts inside out and extroverts outside in. He wanted the poor to help the rich break their "enervating sense of privilege" and the rich to help the poor in building a true "aristocracy of talent". The schools he founded sent bookworms to the playing field and jocks to the reading room. He did not produce outstanding athletes, but his students exhibited consistently high levels of fitness, accomplishment and social spirit. He said he valued mastery in the sphere of one's weakness over performance in the sphere of one's strength. To carry forward into Outward Bound today, the program is not meant to turn out virtuosos in any sense. Hahn would have liked what the Colorado staff call "ruthless compassion", the breaking of strong students by forcing them to keep a slow pace with the weaker members of the group. He would also have been happy with the not quite so ruthless encouragement of the weaker members to press beyond their limits.

Hahn would have liked what the Colorado staff call "ruthless compassion", the breaking of strong students by forcing them to keep a slow pace with the weaker members of the group. He would also have been happy with the not quite so ruthless encouragement of the weaker members to press beyond their limits.

If the miniature society that results is full of conflict, as is often the case in an Outward Bound patrol of widely differing abilities, we may find solace in the words of H.L. Brereton, Hahn's Director of Studies at Gordonstoun. In his book called **Gordonstoun**, Brereton accepts the life of aspiration, of struggling for a goal that always lies beyond the grasp of the society striving for it. He recommends that we follow Plato's use of a "fluid definition" of where we are in relation to the ideal form. Conflict is valuable, both for the group and for the individual, because "out of the inevitable conflict we can avoid complacent but narrow successes and reach after an elusive but much broader achievement". Brereton goes on: "It is the nature of a society trying to develop wholeness that it should be a sort of active debate, or even conflict. Plato demands that we accept complexity and the conflicts which result from it, not as avoidable evil, but as a necessary condition of health."

In a very real sense, Outward Bound and other experiential education programs are still trying to answer the questions posed by Socrates in the **Republic**: "What are we to do?...Where shall we discover a disposition that is at once gentle and great-spirited? ...What, then, is our education?" Brereton speaks for all of us when he says, "We must seek to make the tough compassionate and the timid enterprising." He shows how this view, coming from Hahn, stands next to other educational priorities:

Hahn, in his broadcast talk just after Gordonstoun was opened in 1934, said that there were three views of education, which he called the Ionian, the Spartan, and the Platonic. The first believes that the individual ought to be nurtured and humored regardless of the interests of the community. According to the second, the individual may and should be neglected for the benefit of the State. The third, the Platonic view, believes that any nation is a slovenly guardian of its own interests if it does not do all it can to make the individual citizen discover his own powers. And it further believes that the individual becomes a cripple from his or her own point of view if he or she is not qualified by education to serve the community.

The preceding paragraphs only scratch the surface of Plato's influence on Hahn. They do not begin to record his debt to other thinkers--Rousseau, Goethe, Max Weber, William James, to name a few of the major ones--whose ideas reach Outward Bound and experiential education in one form or another through Hahn. William James, for example, in "The Moral Equivalent of War", asked if it is not possible in time of peace to build the kind of social spirit and productivity one takes for granted in time of war. Hahn saw Outward Bound as an answer to that question. Goethe wrote of an education that would need to occur in a place apart, a "Pedagogical Province", so that individuals could be strengthened and given skills to survive, individually and collectively, in the debilitating environment of human society as we know it. This has much in common with Plato's notion of a "healthy pasture", and it is the *sine qua non* of most adventure programs operating in the outdoors.

Like any idealist in education, Hahn was profoundly indebted to Rousseau, both for the idea that awakening an individual's collective concern is the key to healthy personal development, and also for Rousseau's assumption that Nature is an educator in its own right, more akin to the true nature of a human being than is the society that humans have built for themselves. Hahn also drew heavily from the experience of the English school movement at the beginning of this century. But his genius was in applying ideas to emphasize the interdependence of the community as a whole, rather than a disproportionate excellence of some of its parts. A man of aphorisms more than of systematic theory, of aspiration more than of exact analysis, he lived out the aphorism of another great educator, Pestalozzi, who said "to reach a worthy goal is better than to propound much wisdom."

If Hahn had only been an idealist, if he had not applied his ideals to the humdrum of educational programs--including Outward Bound--then we might be better off leaving him to his rest. As it is, however, his practical concerns are still concerns of Outward Bound and of experiential education.

First, for instance, Hahn asked his students to pledge themselves to a "training plan" that established personal goals and a code of responsibility. Outward Bound instructors make a similar appeal to their students today, though not in the detailed terms used by Hahn at Salem and Gordonstoun, and it is a crucial aspect of the Outward Bound experience. It is no exaggeration to say that the individual commitment of the student, the expressed desire to accomplish a worthy goal by means of the course, becomes, in effect, the moral basis of the community. It becomes the foundation both of compassion and of achievement, and it is, in addition, the ultimate source of value for the Outward Bound pin and certificate. These are not mere objects. At best, they come to represent the energy and determination that have been invested in them all along by students. They signify the pledge, the willingness to press beyond limits, the membership each student earns in a community of seekers. There are times when everyone wants to turn away from it all, just blast away from the cajoling of instructors and other students, but comes back because of the persistent lure of that self-imposed challenge, and the dishonor of withdrawing from it. The pledge imposes a necessary code of responsibility on people who have grown accustomed to a far different set of rules in our time. If the program taps previously undiscovered resources of courage and mutual support in the face of crisis among its students, even in what appear to be trivial situations like cooking a meal or getting up at an early hour, at least it will have opened the door to the revitalization of social life that Hahn had in mind. It will have started its students thinking about living up to an aspiration they have come to realize is possible.

A second concern that Hahn incorporated into all his educational programs had to do with compressing time. From Salem onward he woke his students early, exercised them, controlled their activities. Even their time to relax and their time to be alone were strictly regulated. As one writer has pointed out cynically, every molder of character wants to control as much of the environment as possible. But on the positive side, this form of education, if it is handled sensitively to foster growth instead of merely to control, can be remarkably effective in leading students out of apathy and self-indulgence. The conflict that arises can be dealt with constructively, so that it causes both the individual and

the group to confront what must be done to meet collective goals without trampling on the rights of the individual. Any discussion of freedom that ignores this conflict has little basis in reality. Every Outward Bound instructor--indeed, every educator--has probably asked at one time or another: "Is it necessary to make such an incursion into the personal domain of students, their private world of choice and motivation and meaning, in order to give them a learning experience?" When they ask this, they are in effect arguing with Kurt Hahn, and

---

There are times when everyone wants to turn away from it all, just blast away from the cajoling of instructors and other students, but comes back because of the persistent lure of that self-imposed challenge, and the dishonor of withdrawing from it.

Hahn's answer would be: "Yes, but if it is done gently and with a caring spirit, it will not be such an incursion after all." The structuring of time is a critical factor in influencing behavior. To slow Outward Bound down, to shift its focus from action to sensibility and individual well-being apart from the needs of the group, would be to leave out an element ("**impelled** into experience") that Hahn saw as essential to the program.

Third, a centrally important element that Hahn brought to Outward Bound was adventure--with all the risk it entails. He believed that education should cultivate a passion for life and that this can be accomplished only through experience, a shared sense of moment in the journey toward an exciting goal. Mountaineering and sailing were integral parts of his program at Gordonstoun, and he made space in all his programs for student initiative--an expedition, a project, a sailing voyage. Hahn welcomed powerful emotions, such as awe, fear, exultant triumph. Part of his lifelong aspiration, part of the "whole" he sought through programs like Outward Bound, was that the experience accessible to any human being, at any level of ability, could be charged with joy and wonder in the doing. But the corollary is that he saw adventure in a social perspective, as an event of community life and not a private thrill. The adventure of the individual is always mediated to some extent by the values and needs of the group. This is why, almost forty years after the program was founded, Outward Bound retains an unusual world-view among the outdoor programs that have sprung up around it. Everyone touts adventure nowadays, but in Outward Bound the adventurer must still break down and learn to serve his companions. The experience is individual; the pledge and the challenge are individual; the achievement necessarily belongs to all. Hahn saw his schools as a "countervailing force" against the declining values of the world at large. Perhaps, among outdoor programs, Outward Bound is a countervailing force against narcissism and self-centered virtuosity.

As one writer has pointed out cynically, every molder of character wants to control as much of the environment as possible. But on the positive side, this form of education, if it is handled sensitively to foster growth instead of merely to control, can be remarkably effective in leading students out of apathy and self-indulgence.

Fourth, Hahn understood the educational value of working with small groups of students. He probably took this idea from military organization as it came into the youth movements of the late 19th century, especially the Scouting movement of Lord Baden-Powell in England. Oddly enough, military jargon persists in Outward Bound to this day in terms such as patrol, resupply, debriefing and reconnaissance. Hahn saw small groups as a way to develop the natural leadership abilities he thought were present in most people, but were suppressed by the dependency, passivity and bureaucratic impersonality of modern life. Such groups place heavy social pressures on individual initiative, yet at the same time they require it absolutely. Small groups require tremendous amounts of energy to reach the consensus necessary to meet objectives. In a wilderness environment, effective group dynamics are paramount to survival; they rank in importance with technical skills. Natural leaders emerge when the group must solve real problems instead of playing games with an unnatural reward system. A genuine community begins to appear on a small scale—at least the possibility is there. If it happens, each of the separate selves may glimpse an aspiration worth fighting for back home. At its worst, the small group is a troublesome obstacle to the fine experience any wilderness has to offer; but at its best, it opens a new dimension not acessible to solitary escapists, no matter how intense their devotion to the outdoors.

The fifth concern, which could be seen as encompassing all the rest, was Hahn's dedication to community service. It is possible to make a case that the Outward Bound concept was born when the headmaster of Gordonstoun looked around him during the 1930's and saw that the boys in Hopeman Village, near the school, were in terrible physical condition and that they fell into delinquent ways as soon as they reached puberty. Hahn believed the school should serve the community around

it, so he allowed a few of his boys to go out on a project to teach the kids how to take care of themselves. The project grew, along with many other service projects he set up, ranging from craftsmanship to landscaping to rescue service. By the time he started developing a program to help sailors acquire the fortitude to survive in lifeboats at sea, Kurt Hahn already had an extensive outreach program from his school, including sailboats, mountaineering gear, tools and other paraphernalia. As Hahn saw it, the link between individual and school depended for its meaning upon the link between school and society. The notion came into Outward Bound in the form of rescue service, and it has since been applied to diverse needs in communities and the natural environment.

These are a few of the ideas that Kurt Hahn brought to Outward Bound and to experiential education. Perhaps another writer would spend more time enumerating the man's limitations. I believe I have done enough by depicting Hahn's aspiration in a way that is true to the scale in which he envisioned it. Much more could be said about him that would be relevant to American education today. For example, his practice of hiring people who disagreed with him, and then challenging them to challenge him, is a tradition that ought to be perpetuated, even when the resulting conflict is painful. A more thorough inquiry into Hahn's life would undoubtedly turn up other treasures. But such an inquiry would eventually miss the point. The point is that he started Outward Bound with an immense aspiration that gave meaning to the program far beyond the needs being addressed at the time. The task facing Outward Bound and experiential education is to retrace some of that aspiration in the minds of all who come into contact with the programs. If this is done, other elements will fit readily within the whole. Instructional objectives, systems, models, policies, procedures, formats, evaluation schemes--all can play a part, alongside the irreplaceable devotion of staff, once we have come to terms with the essential nature of our business. All are a hollow shell without that recognition.

The staff of experiential education programs enter each course with a large store of technical skill and, in the outdoors, wilderness experience behind them. No student will ever see it all, but it helps to define their world throughout the course. In the same way, the social vision of staff can help to bring a world of dignity and compassion into being, if they are gentle and high-spirited enough. Each course, each student, each moment is an opportunity to use the mountains and other experiential "classrooms" to find the only mountain really worth climbing. This may sound wildly idealistic, but it is not out of keeping with the origins of Outward Bound or with the aims of experiential education. It is the tacit code that unifies and justifies the endeavors of all of us.

THE LONG CONVERSATION: TRACING THE ROOTS OF THE PAST

Experiential education has a rich and long past that is often not recognized. By explaining this past, it is hoped that current practitioners can avoid some of the pitfalls of their predecessors.

by Albert Adams and Sherrod Reynolds

INTRODUCTION

Experiential education is heir to a rich history of progressive thinking and writing. In examining these ancestral artifacts, some striking similarities to modern practice appear, while once prominant features seem to have been distorted or lost completely. Weaving the tapestry of past and present together is the refrain of openness to experience and change; a refrain which occasioned Joseph Featherstone to remark in a recent interview that "the conversation is a long conversation.", Pausing to listen to progressive forefathers engaging in this dialogue may provide experiential educators with the kind of historical perspective that helps clarify future directions.

The awareness of a need to seek out common roots is a growing concern, as evidenced by the proliferation of articles on the subject in past issues of the "Journal of Experiential Education." It is the purpose of this paper to continue the exploration of historical and philosophical influences and to examine what relevance the progressive perspective has for modern experiential educators.

One of the strongest warnings heard through the pages of the history of the Progressive Education Association — the formal organization of the movement — is the need for a clearly articulated statement of identity. Without such a stance, the paradox of pluralism threatens to dissipate the energy of the whole into scattered efforts. In the larger context of the educational community, the Association for Experiential Education remains on the fringes, relatively invisible and often misunderstood. Ultimately, the Association may or may not aspire to a leadership role in the arena of educational reform, accepting the burden and social responsibility a progressive inheritance implies. But the end result of critical reflection is not the issue.

The issue for modern educators is to be open to the

discoveries to be made along the way, leading toward a more thoughtful understanding of what the A.E.E. is and who it serves. Joseph Featherstone also noted that "reform movements are notoriously a-historical."[2] The propensity to reinvent the wheel is not irrevocable, however. Building the wheel of experience-based learning was a task not only attempted, but impressively accomplished by progressive pioneers. Collectively, the thrust and impact of their efforts is called the progressive education movement.

Throughout the life cycle of the progressive movement three central themes emerge: the pluralism that characterized its followers, initially breathing life into the movement but ultimately contributing to its demise; the profound nature of the issues and seminal thinking which sprang from the movement; and the practically based model which the movement established for theory building and testing by practitioners. Until its later years, the progressive education movement promoted an atmosphere which fostered ongoing, intense, and introspective dialogue — a yeasty prototype for professional growth today. As a result, its history draws a poignant, well-documented picture of innovation and reform in education through both its successes and its failures.

HISTORICAL OVERVIEW

Lawrence Cremin wrote the definitive work on the progressive education movement: "The Transformation of the School." In his introduction, Cremin asks whether the movement is "quite as dead as its critic believe, or are the reports of its demise, in the words of Mark Twain, 'very much exaggerated'?"[3] Pronounced dead in 1957, the Progressive Education Association's collapse supported the critic's claim. But a distinction must be made between P.E.A. and what is commonly referred to as the "progressive education movement," an extension of the larger progressive movement in America. Predating the founding of the P.E.A. by at least three decades, the movement, and its basic concepts, endure into the present.

The progressive education movement emerged in the 1870s as a response to the advent of universal education, or "common schools" as they were called. After an uneven beginning, the schools ran head long into mass industrialization and were found sadly unprepared to cope with the new demands made on them, creating a situation ripe for progressive reformists. During the 1880s and 1890s, the movement attracted the attention and energies of recognized intellectuals, became a force behind the thrust for manual training in schools, and supported a growing number of comprehensive progressive schools that were being established.

The years immediately preceding World War I were the zenith of the movement. Progressive schools grew in number and were of high quality, resulting in a dynamic impact on the larger educational community. Enthusiasm and idealism ran high among progressive educators, creating a healthy spririt of comradery. The 1920s witnessed r   the influence of a less experienced "new   " of followers, but also the responding fragmentation of the thrust of the movement's energy. Dewey recognized the corruption of important progressive prinicples and warned against the aimlessness and dangerous permissiveness of the notion of the "child centered school."[4] It is ironic that this early divisive period gave birth to the Progressive Education Association in 1919.

The Depression spurred a reversal of the laissez-faire, child-oriented trend, and it was the social reformers who spoke most authoritatively for the movement in the decade leading up to World War II. Following the War, the country's conservative mood discouraged the support of progressive ideals. It was not until the turbulent years of the 1960s that these ideals resurfaced, taking a variety of new shapes and forms. Today's experiential educators stand among those who have the opportunity to recapture a sense of the vitality and the substance of this legacy. Unwinding the threads of experiential heritage suggests not only an opportunity, but an obligation to come to grips with familial issues.

THE PROGRESSIVE MOVEMENT IN EDUCATION

As is often the case with reform movements, the progressive movement consistently found it more expedient to state what it was against rather than to define what it was for. Given the critical stance of progressive proponents, it was not surprising that

progressive ideals were catapulted into public view by Joseph Rice's sensational expose of public schools. In 1892, Rice published a series of articles based on visits to 1,200 classrooms in 36 cities which charged that "schools and teachers 'dehumanized, immobilized and atomized the children."[5] Rallying around the excitement produced by such criticism, the movement attracted a motley coalition of enthusiastic supporters. It was clear, however, that more than negative criticism was needed to launch an effective movement. As Dewey was to point out later, "there is always the danger in a new movement that, in rejecting the aims and methods of that which it would supplant, it may develop its principles negatively rather than positively and constructively."[6] Building a forward looking, positive identity proved to be one of the movement's most elusive tasks. Not only the quest for such an identity, but also the process employed in searching for it contributed to the movement's high level of professional exploration and interchange. Establishing a firm identity was made more difficult by the number of diverse directions the movement was supporting simultaneously. For example, an early disagreement concerned the nature of progressive schools: should schools be liberal and comprehensive in nature or should they be committed to manual traning objectives? Advocates for both arguments claimed the progressive banner.

Attempts to present and preserve a cohesive, unifed front were also sorely tried by the abortive efforts of misguided imitators. Cremin, on several occasions, refers to vulnerable aspects of the progressive education movement which could be too easily "caricatured" by its detractors. Two specific examples of this tendency are the "bohemians" of the 1920s, and the overzealous reformers of the '30s. Coupled with the general misuse of Dewey's ideas, these weak spots soon festered and spread, infecting the entire movement.

The 1920s were "fat" times, allowing the bohemians the luxury of their lifestyle. Following what had become a popular educational trend, this new generation of progressive educators retained some of the form but little of the substance which had been the hallmark of the movement prior to the first World War. Fascination with the arts in general and with Freud in particular became the vogue for the intellectual avant-garde, and social reformism was virtually eclipsed by the rhetoric of child-centered pedagogy.[8] Caricatured by the student asking, "Do we have to do what we want to, again?"[9] the image of progressive education suffered in public opinion. While patently unfair to the many good progressive schools and teachers of the day, there was sufficient basis-in-fact to make a lasting impression, resulting in the devaluation of what earnest progressives were striving for.

Although social reformism enjoyed a resurgence in the 1930s, its proponents failed to recognize that they were hopelessly out of step with the rest of the country by the end of the decade. As the nation tried to prepare for a second war while still struggling under the suffocating weight of the Depression, the prevailing mood was anything but progressive. The progressives became increasingly isolated and their rhetoric more defensive, encouraging the satiric edge of the cartoonist's pen — this time sketching them as "the radical pedagogues using the school to subvert the American way of life."[10] Considering the patriotic fervor of the times, this charge proved to be seriously debilitating.

The difficulty and abstruse nature of Dewey's writing created an additional opportunity for distortion which is directly relevant to the present. Cremin noted that "Dewey frequently used words like 'experience', or 'growth'. . . to connote so much that they could be borrowed by others to mean almost anything."[11] Such terms are notoriously over-used and little understood by their populizers and detractors alike. Manual educators frequently claim Dewey's statements on experience to support their ideas on education, but Dewey himself was strongly opposed to education restricted to manual education. Child-centered advocates cite Dewey's comments on organic growth, but Dewey argued against education which did not stretch the child beyond his or her existing interests.

In contrast to the distortions and caricatures of progressive ideals are the inspiring examples of the effectiveness of progressive methods when applied skillfully. Progressive educators repeatedly claimed that their approach to learning produced happier, better educated, more well-rounded individuals. The ambitious Eight-Year Study verified this assertion unequivocally. Begun in 1932, the Study initially identified several progressive secondary schools and stimulated the creation of progressive programs in others. It then monitored the development of nearly 1,500 matched pairs of students, taking one from a traditional setting and one from a progressive situation, throughout their high school and college careers. Traditional entrance requirements were waived by participating colleges and universities for the students from progressive schools. For the survey, students were chosen from 13 public schools, 17 independent schools, and attended 200 different colleges. Results of the study not only vindicated the efficacy of the full range of progressive programs, but also demonstrated that the graduates of the most experimental programs fared the best of all.

Reported in five volumes under the title, "Adventure in American Education," the study was also subjected to an independent review by an esteemed committee from the American Association of Colleges. They con-cluded in part that: "It looks as if the stimulus and the initiative which the less conventional approach to secondary school education affords sends on to college better human material than we have obtained in the past."[12] Unfortunately, the timing of the release of these results could hardly have been worse in terms of their potential import for the cause of progressive education. Released in 1942, the report was lost in the overwhelming concentration on the war effort. By the time the dust had settled, the progressives had lost their audience altogether. The Eight-Year Study remains both a largely ignored and untapped tribute to the effectiveness of well-conceived and executed progressive education.

PHILOSOPHICAL BACKGROUND: THEORY AND PRACTICE

The purpose of unravelling the threads of thought woven into experiential education is to strive for a clearer understanding of the movement's philosophical origins. Having joined in the "long conversation," it should be instructive to reflect on how central themes have been integrated, altered, discarded, or augmented by modern interpretation.

A dominant motif running through much of the progressive literature is the school's essential bonding to the ideal of democracy. This a peculiarly American theme born in the last century's 25 year struggle for, and eventual realization of, free public schools. In championing the universal school movement, Horace Mann "poured into his vision of universal education a boundless faith in the perfectability of human life and institutions."[13] Schools were to be the panacea for society's ills, the "great equalizer" of social classes, and the instrument that would shape the destiny of America. There was a clear perception of the dynamic relationship between freedom, self-government, and universal education. Social harmony, a key element in maintaining a democracy comprised of such a diverse constituency, was a primary goal of popular education.

A second major thread in progressive thinking is Romanticism as defined by Jean-Jacques Rousseau. Rousseau, in "Emile," advances three central themes: the destructive influence of modernization and "progress," the quest for a dynamic mediation of reason and emotion as an ideal of growth, and the search for a "countermodern" way to consciously institutionalize the "natural" in politics, family life, and education.[14] He incorporates the basic romantic notions of unity: reuniting man with himself, man with nature, and man with his fellow men in a mutual striving for the common good. Rousseau believed in man's innate goodness, but thought him ill equipped to understand the corrupting influence of "modernity." While often impractical and extreme, his ideas offer a provocative perspective on the education of children toward becoming autonomous, dignified human beings. The realization of a true democracy could only be achieved through the development of such a "genuine personality." A dedicated progressive, Rousseau describes in "Emile" how each stage of instruction is carefully adapted to the child's developing needs. The essential place of experience is exalted, and the value of learning through a process of trial and error is recognized. In many ways, Rousseau is the originator of progressive education's most cherished ideals.

In pre-Civil War America, these threads were gathered up by the New England Transcendentalists and were permanently woven into the popular American consciousness. Romanticism as portrayed by Rousseau can be defined in terms of human nature espoused by seventeenth and eighteenth century science's quest for a fuller vision of humanity that would encompass autonomy, value, and the creative capacity of the imagination to renew itself.[15] Emerson, Thoreau, Channing, Parker and others projected a Romanticism based in moral idealism, drawing from the influence of Unitarian beliefs. They were critical of the form of democracy that demanded conformity to depersonalizing custom and a consequent sacrifice of "self-reliance." Identifying with the concept of the godlike nature of the human spirit and the authority of the individual conscience, they recognized a respect for the significance of every facet of human experience within the organic whole of existence. Embracing an intuitive, mystic, idealistic, and eternally optimistic view of life, these thinkers captured the American imagination.

Described by Featherstone as "high Romatics," in reference to their attempt to balance reason and feeling, these individuals had a profound influence on progressive educators. Taking the anti-formalist position that knowledge is fluid and expounding on it, they claimed that humans exist in a world of changing reality. Changing reality provides the most stimulating condition for creativity, the highest form of human endeavor, in that it presents humans with the challenge of uncertainty. Implicit in this attitude is a commitment to the "open-ness to further experience that is the democratic and Romantic value of values."[16]

'Changing reality' is an apt description of America moving into the end of the nineteenth century in the wake of expanding industrialization. The country seethed with the ferment of rapid change, population growth due to large-scale immigration, and an impressive flowering of new thinking and ideas. Darwin's theory of evolution presented a fundamental challenge to the dominant idealism of the age. Pragmatism emerged, expounded by Charles Peirce and William

James, stating that methaphysical questions could be resolved by tying ideas to operations, actions, and consequences in order to comprehend meanings. A new spirit of social consciousness spread across the land, manifesting itself most dramatically in settlement houses. Settlement workers aimed for the humanizing of industrial civilization, and education was their instrument for social reform. Psychology of child developmen was wedded to pedagogy, exerting a profound and enduring influence. The developmental view of education built on the approach first advanced by Rousseau in "Emile," focusing on "child-centered schools whose curriculum would be tailored to a larger view of nature, growth, and development of children."[18] Such a focus was to become a centerpiece in the progressive movement, eventually displacing the social reformists.

It was during this period that John Dewey stepped onto the educational stage, bringing with him the belief that "education is the fundamental method of social progress and reform."[19] Dewey has had an important influence on present-day experiential educators, and for that reason bears close scrutiny. A pragmatic focus led him to develop his so-called "experiential theory of education" based on the scientific method of inquiry. His is a doctrine of experience, but experience within fairly specific restrictions. "No experience is educative that does not tend both to knowledge of more facts and a more orderly arrangement of them. It is not true that organization is a principle foreign to experience. Otherwise experience would be so dispersive as to be chaotic."[20] Building his ideas of child development around observation of a child's native impulses, Dewey outlined four phases of development: the social desire to **communicate** and share through language; the **constructive** impulse to do or make things, beginning with play and moving to shaping raw materials; the more advanced desire to **investigate** and experiment; and finally, a refinement of sharing and construction in **expression**. The story of the developing curriculum was seen as the continuous attempt to meet and utilize these urges toward expression and creative effort. Incorporated into the scientific method of inquiry, these native impulses became the basis for a process of investigation and reflection applied to many aspects of education.

All of these ideas circled around the central concept of "experience." The question of how to define experience occupied Dewey frequently, and he made many attempts to clarify his meaning, with only moderate success. Not all experience could be considered "worthwhile"; experience must function as a moving force toward more fruitful and creative subsequent experiences. The teacher must utilize the physical and social environments in order to build up worthwhile experiences within a meaningful context. The proposed experience must stretch the child, yet remain within the range of his capacity. Every experience should arouse in the learner an active quest for information and for the production of new ideas, which provide grounds for further experience, presenting new problems.[21]

In "The Dewey School" Mayhew and Edwards describe how Dewey's theories of education functioned in practice during his tenure there as principal. This account provides a fine example of a progressive school in action, offering a richly detailed description of every aspect of school life over a period of years. Emphasizing child-centered education at the Dewey School meant that students' interests were tapped as a point of arrival. Too many progressive schools tended to dwell on the child's interests in the present, resulting in a stagnant learning situation which failed to stretch the child or expand his interests. School life embraced progressive ideals, offering an integrated curriculum in which subjects were taught through the medium of work or around central themes. Experience, in Dewey's terms, was explicit in teaching methods, lead through the paces of the scientific method. To his credit, Dewey-the-Headmaster conscientiously adhered to his own principles by constantly re-evaluating his theories in the light of their feasibility in practice, and actively encouraging his teachers to do likewise. Much of his later writing shows clear evidence of this close contact with day-to-day schooling.

Dewey's school is but one of many fine examples of progressive theory put into practice during the first two decades of the twentieth century. Constituting a rich legacy of adventure and discovery in education, these tales are far too voluminous to cover in the modest scope of this paper. It is possible, however, to briefly discuss some of the dominant elements in these schools in order to provide some sense of the direction and scope of "progressive education".

Col. Frances Parker, whom Dewey called the father of progressive education, declared that his purpose in the Cook County Normal School was "to move the child to the center of the educational process and to interrelate the several subjects of the curriculum in such a way as to enhance their meaning for the child."[22] This kind of sentiment was characteristic of progressive educators. For the most part, these schools were child-centered, stressing learning through free activity and direct experience, introducing the study of skills as a means to attaining direct ends, incorporating an interdisciplinary approach to curriculum, using the natural environment extensively, emphasizing the integration of the arts into all aspects of school life, and seeing education as a process of living, rather than a preparation for future adult responsibilities.

Caroline Pratt, founder of the City and Country School in New York City, expressed her view of the function of schools in this way: "It seemed to me that a school's greatest value must be to turn out human beings who could think effectively and work constructively, who could in time make a better world than this for living in."[23] Taking a more child-centered position, Marietta Johnson spoke of her Organic School in holistic terms, its aim being, "to minister to the health of the body, develop the finest mental grasp, and preserve the sincerity and unselfconsciousness of the emotional life."[24]

Inherent in the goals expressed by Mrs. Johnson is an underlying belief in the value of human dignity. Everyone in the school environment was treated with deference and respect. Children were expected to behave towards each other and adults with this same consideration. At every age level students were given a great deal of responsibility in the ongoing life of the school, thereby gaining an appreciation of the community and their role in it. Internal control rather than external discipline was stressed as a means of developing citizenship, tolerance, and understanding of others.

Teachers saw themselves not only as instructors, but also as researchers into progressive methods of pedagogy. As noted by educational historian Vito Perrone, they were self conscious "students of teaching", employing close observation and detailed record keeping as a means of determining children's interests and designing curriculum. Serving a dual purpose, this approach not only built integrity into the development of child-centered curriculum, but also provided a vehicle for teachers to constantly test their hypotheses in practice. A great deal of individual judgment was involved in deciding which attitudes were conducive to continued growth and which were not. Close observation coupled with a sympathetic understanding of what the individual child was thinking and feeling was required. Finding teachers with the openness and commitment to become serious students of teaching was both a problem and a challenge.

At Shady Hill School, Katherine Taylor's solution to this problem was a rigorous apprentice training program which addressed the need for teachers to be students of **learning** before becoming "students of teaching." The more experienced teachers worked with new faculty, helping to provide the essential link of continuity. Taylor's program had a rejuvenating effect on her regular faculty and served to advance the strong tradition of teacher development in progressive schools.

The role of 'teacher' in progressive education has always been ambiguous, ranging in interpretation from a hands-off laissez-faire approach to a one-on-one individualized relationship. Dewey spoke forcefully of the responsibility of the teacher within the democractic structure of a progressive classroom: "It is the business of the educator to see what direction an experience is heading. There is no point in his being more mature if, instead of using his greater insight to help organize the conditions of the experience of the immature, he throws away his insight. Failure to take the moving force of an experience into account so as to judge and direct it on the ground of what it is moving into means disloyalty to the principle of experience itself."[25] Predictably, the best progressive educators developed an inner sense of how to balance the various elements of their role, but communicating that ability proved difficult, if not impossible. Once outside of the traditional mode, teachers were forced to find new ways of relating to their students, often relying on intuition and the best working models they could find. Not all who attempted this juggling act were successful.

The uncertainty of developing a new role as a teacher should strike a familiar note in experiential educators. Many of the goals and aspirations, the struggles and disappointments, the successes and failures of progressive forebearers mirror present experience. There is real value in returning to the source of these efforts. Participating in the vivid accounts of early progressive work is a little like returning to the ancestral home and discovering that you share your name with an ancient relative who, by all indications, was very much like you in many ways. Tapping these educational odesseys provides a touchstone, a source of renewal and reaffirmation. The authors commend the attached bibliography, with an earnest invitation to join in the "long conversation."

A COMPARISON

In contrasting progressive ideal with modern practice, it is instructive to turn to James Coleman's model of the four phases of the experiential process and compare them to Dewey's scientific method of inquiry, which he used to shape experience.

Dewey's process begins from a point of uncertainty in the face of a new problem and proceeds through the following steps:

1) recognizing existing conditions and tentatively interpreting them
2) surveying all available material concerning the problem to help clarify and define the situation
3) formulating a hypothesis
4) testing the hypothesis in action
5) studying the effects of the action and generalizing the results (which should lead to new problems)[26]

Coleman's phases are as follows:

1) action, and observation of the consequences of action
2) understanding of the consequences in the particular case at hand
3) generalization to the overarching principle by correct anticipation of the consequences of the next similar action[27]

Coleman's model begins with "action" while Dewey's method originates out of a state of uncertainty which takes the form of active reflection. In a sense, Dewey's method anticipates and prepares for the experience while Coleman's phases are based on a reaction to an experience. Dewey also stresses the cognitive and critical aspect of the experience while Coleman emphasizes understanding what actually took place and generalizing that to a larger principle, essentially ignoring other sources of information or the context in which the experience took place. On the other hand, Coleman allows for serendipity, for the inclusion of life experience of the type that Morris Keeton discusses in *Experiential Learning,* for the unplanned element of experience that does not mandate subsequent action. Dewey's scientific method seems restive and highly directed in contrast. Immediate, physical action is implied in Coleman's phases, suggesting a flexible, short-term exposure unfettered by institutional restrictions. Dewey's method lends itself to a more structured, long-term situation which a career of schooling provides.

The distinctions between Coleman and Dewey point to a major difference between the experiential education movement and the progressive educational movement. Dewey's explicit emphasis on the cognitive/reflective aspect of experience as opposed to Coleman's more action oriented model is symbolic of the larger manifestations of the two movements. However, it must be pointed out that these meanderings through the progressive pages of history and thought are neither meant to tell the exclusive story, nor to suggest that experiential education has no other roots. The goal is to recognize and acknowledge the significant parallels between the two movements and to hear whatever lessons are offered. The fact that progressive education has faded into a quarter of a century of relative obscurity, and that its Association suffered an ignominious death does not, in itself, portend disaster for experiential education of the A.E.E. Rather than view the reasons for progressive education's demise as prophetic, the authors choose to see them as provocative. We think they are worth consideration by those who call themselves experiential educators, specifically those involved in the Association for Experiential Education. Lawrence Cremin offers eight factors which he considers destructive causal elements in the downfall of the progressive movement. We offer them here as warnings from the past.

PLURALISM: The persistent lack of a unified identity rendered the Progressive Education Association both amorphous and vulnerable. Because of its disparate constituency, it seldom bore any resemblance to a bona fide movement after its early years. In a last desperate attempt to survive, the P.E.A. narrowed its identity drastically, and inadvisably, and renamed itself Life Adjustment Education, which only hastened its decline.

DISTORTION: The eclectic make-up of progressive education meant that anyone could call his/her program "progressive," no matter how superficial the rendition might be. The non-specific definition of the word "progressive" only exacerbated this weakness while encouraging harmful caricatures.

NEGATIVISM: A protest is not a program. Progressive education was plagued throughout its history by a strand of thought which fed its nihilistic image. This was especially true during the difficult period of the 1930s.

DEMANDS ON TEACHERS: Child-centered and integrated approaches required much more energy, ingenuity, close observation, and resources than traditional methods. "In the hands of first-rate instructors, the innovators worked wonders; in the hands of too many average teachers however, they lead to chaos." For all teachers, the demands of progressive teaching were exhausting.

GENERAL ACCEPTANCE: One of the major prices of success was that progressive ideas were integrated into the educational mainstream. Even when they were not bastardized, they became associated with the status quo. The public schools of the 1980s reflect many more vestiges of progressive education than most people would suspect.

SWING TO CONSERVATISM: Since the progressive education movement had risen on the coat tails of the larger Progressive Movement, its currency could only be devalued as conservatism captured the spotlight of the political arena in the late 1940s.

PROFESSIONALIZATION: The call for higher esteem for teachers and increased political power ultimately separated the movement from its grass roots support.

OUT OF STEP WITH THE TIMES: The relentless march of time had little respect for what had become "conventional wisdom." Progressive education kept its appointment with obsolesence in the late 1940s.

CONCLUSION

In looking at present day experiential education programs, it is evident that they have retained what Ed Yoemans, an historian of the progressive movement, fondly refers to as the "adventure, romance, and life in community" reminiscent of the early Romantics. But the corresponding emphasis on academic rigor and an integrated approach to the arts in many instances has been minimized or eliminated. Not only is there no longer an implicit belief in the validity of education for social reform, but in fact, many experiential programs function completely independent of schools. While a strong commitment to developing the powers of the individual persist, the broader goal of upholding a democratic society through the education of future citizens has faded into cynical disillusionment.

Given the state of public schools today and our generation's distinctly different perspective on American society, there are valid reasons for these departures from traditionally progressive goals. As experiential educators, we are responding to a new set of problems in a more complicated age, an age that has put us largely outside of traditional schooling. Being on the fringes of mainstream education means, among other things, that we are constantly in jeopardy of being pushed out altogether. By establishing a strong sense of past, we not only strengthen our position in the present, but also command a powerful lens through which to view the future.

The "long conversation" did not begin with us and it certainly will not end with us. What contribution we ultimately make to it depends on our ability to respond meaningfully to the needs of our times. With our help, the A.E.E. has the potential to galvanize the scattered energies surrounding experience-based learning into a movement of substance and focus; a movement that can learn from the mistakes of its predecessor. Bringing an awareness of historical roots to the effort pulls the threads of our various heritage taut in the warp of our mission. By throwing the shuttle into this larger design, we marry present dreams with past realities and joining in a cause that is still worth fighting for.

Albert Adams is a Ph.D. aspirant in educational administration, planning and social policy at the Harvard Graduate School of Education.

Sherrod Reynolds is a former staff member with the Foxfire Fund, Inc. and is currently working on a M.A. degree at the Harvard Graduate School of Education.

FOOTNOTES

[1] Featherstone, Joseph. Interview. Harvard Graduate School of Education. 12/80.
[2] ibid.
[3] Cremin, Lawrence. The Transformation of the School, p. viii.
[4] Dewey, John. Dewey on Education, p.10.
[5] Kraft, Richard. Foundations of Education: Social Perspectives, p.20.
[6] Dewey, John. Experience and Education, p.20.
[7] Cremin, op. cit. p. 93.
[8] ibid. p. 181.
[9] Kraft, op. cit. p.23.
[10] Cremin, op cit. p.8.
[11] ibid. p.237.
[12] Yeomans, Ed. Independent School Bulletin. "Adventures in American Education". p.17.
[13] Cremin. op. cit. p.8.
[14] Featherstone, Joseph. Daedalus. "Rousseau and Modernity". p.192.
[15] ibid. p.195.
[16] Featherstone. Interview.
[17] Cremin. op. cit. p.60.
[18] ibid. p.103.
[19] Dewey. Dewey on Education, p.30.
[20] Dewey. Experience and Education. p.82.
[21] ibid. p.79.
[22] Cremin. op. cit.
[23] Pratt, Caroline. I Learn From Children, p.25.
[24] Johnson, Marietta. "What is Organic Education?" p.149.
[25] Dewey. Experience and Education. p.38.
[26] Mayhew & Edwards. The Dewey School. p. 320.
[27] Coleman, James. "Differences Between Experiential and Classroom Learning".
[28] Cremin. op. cit. pp.348-149.

BIBLIOGRAPHY

Addams, Jane	Democracy and Social Ethics. 1902
Blow, Susan	Symbolic Education. 1894
Cole, Natalie	The Arts in The Classroom. 1940
Clapp, Elsie	Schools in Action. 1939
Cremin, Lawrence	The Transformation of the School. 1964
DeLima, Agnes	Democracy's High School. 1941
	The Little Red Schoolhouse. 1942
Dewey, Evelyn	New Schools for Old, 1919
Dewey, John	Dewey on Education: Selections, 1959
	Experience and Education, 1938
	The Child and The Curriculum, 1902
Hooper, J.W.	Three Score and Ten: In Retrospect, 1900
Johnson, Marietta	Thirty Years With An Idea, 1930
Lewis, Mary	Adventure With Children, 1928
Mayhew, Katherine & Edwards, Anna	The Dewey School, 1936
Mearns, Hugh	Creative Youth and Creative Power, 1925
Mitchell, Lucy Sprague	Young Geographers, 1934
	Our Children and Our Schools, 1950
Naumberg, Margaret	The Children and The World, 1928
Ocutt, Hiram	Reminiscences of School Life: An Autobiography, 1898
Olson, Alice	From Woodstoves to Astronauts: An Autobiography, 1977
Page, David	Theory and Practice of Teachers, 1847
Parker, Frances W.	Notes of Talks on Teaching, 1883
	Talks on Pedagogy, 1894
Partridge, Lelia	The Quincy Method Illustrated, 1885
Pratt, Caroline	I Learn From Children, 1948
	Experimental Practice in the City and Country School, 1924
Rotzel, Grace	The School in Rose Valley, 1971
Rousculp, Charles	Chalk Dust on my Shoulder, 1969
Sarton, Mary	I Knew a Phoenix, 1959
Smith, Eugene	Education Moves Ahead, 1924
Smith, Lydia	Activity and Experience, 1976
Washburn, Carleton	A Survey of The Winnetka Public Schools. 1926
Weber, Julia	Country School Diary, 1946
Winsor, Charles H.	Experimental Schools Revisited, 1973
Yoemans, Ed	The Shady Hill School: The First Fifty Years. 1969
Young, Ella Young	Isolation in the School, 1902

Excerpts from the First Kurt Hahn Address

Given by Joe Nolds, October, 1983 at the annual AEE Conference

On Kurt Hahn, John Dewey, and William James

Kurt Hahn saw decline in the West — and spoke of the decline in fitness through the increase in spectator sports, spectatoritis. This was before the era of television. He spoke of the decline in craftsmanship, man's alienation from his work given the monotony of assembly line industrialization. There was the decline in concentration, given the increased use of drugs, and this was before the decade of the sixties. Above all there was a decline in **compassion.**

This is the diagnosis. The prognosis we know well: adventure training to develop fitness. Not just physical fitness, but the psychological toughness that goes with it, — resilience and resolve. Crafts and the arts are to nurture aesthetic sensitivity, but also to foster pride in one's creativity, the defining of oneself through one's works. And finally service — Samaritan service to instill compassion.

This part of Hahn's thought is well

Joe Nold, former director of the Colorado Outward Bound School, currently teaches at the United World College of the American West and directs a student volunteer village development project in India for the Round Square Conference Schools.

documented. But I repeat it not only for emphasis but to point out the difference in intellectual perspective from the great American experiential educator, John Dewey. Hahn's formative life experiences were World War I, the dreadful slaughter and rending of the fabric of European civilization. It is a disaster that cast a depressive pall over European life and thought for two generations. The war was followed by the collapse of Imperial Germany, and then the face of democratic Germany, the rise of Hitler and Nazi barbarism, and the Holocaust. Hahn was a Jew and was left, perhaps, with the guilt so many surviving Jews experience. So "decline" was not merely malaise, or mid-life crisis, but was a deeply rooted existential response to his life experience. He viewed the world broodingly, deeply conscious of man's capacity for evil, a Jew's sense of sin and guilt — but also of redemption. Indeed Hahn distrusted the intellectual community, seeing how easily they were cowed by Hitler. He was witness to their failure to resist. To him the purpose of education is moral, moral and social. Indeed, with Hahn education is a form of redemption.

How different from Dewey. We tend to seek the commonalities between Hahn and Dewey. The differences are more significant. Dewey has a totally different intellectual perspective and view of human nature. Dewey comes out of the American experience (the naivete of the American experience our European colleagues would add) with the optimism, the progressivism, the sense of success in America, the belief in infinite perfectability. Dewey has a belief in democracy — its inherent strength and goodness — and to him education is the pillar and cornerstone of a free and democratic people. "Democracy and Education" is Dewey's educational testament.

These are two divergent streams of thought that underpin experiential education, or at least experiential education as espoused by the AEE. I do not know if Hahn ever read Dewey. He makes no mention of him. Certainly Dewey never read Hahn, for Hahn never wrote much, and he does not read well. But both did read William James. The pragmatism of William James is central to Dewey's thought. The essay James wrote "On the Moral Equivalent of War" was central to Hahn's educational practice. James points out that aggression is deeply rooted in human nature, imprinted in our genes and lodged in the very marrow of our bones, and that man will always respond to the call of the bugle, and take up the banner of war, because he is drawn to the excitement, to the adrenalin rush. He craves the exhileration. The pacifist solution will never be successful, the peace will never be secure until mankind finds a substitute, a moral equivalent for war, that stirs his loyalty and galvanizes his energy that draws on his need for daring and excitement. James saw the answer in hard physical labor of a risk taking kind, work in the mines, on the fishing boats in winter; he called for a conscription of youth in service of the needy. This idea inspired the CCC (Civilian Conservation Corps of the 1930's) the forerunner of Job Corps, and the Peace Corps in the 1960's. It also inspired Hahn. This was language he understood, and he incorporated it into his educational thought and practice.

On Questions Outward Bound Has Faced In The Past 22 Years

Do you force all students through the Outward Bound mold or do you design and program that meets the needs of students?

The questions became pressing ones as we were challenged to take more inner city youth. In the late sixties, cities were burning — Newark, Detroit, Watts — and Outward Bound was seen as a way of keeping the cities cool. Funded by federal grants under the War on Poverty, large numbers arrived on the mountainside with cigarettes, knives, and drugs; ill informed, unfit and unprepared for the rigors of the course. While some did not succeed, surprising numbers did. British instructors, many from a working class background and speaking in broad overseas accents were particularly effective with their direct, no nonsense approach. Somehow they were not seen as "white honkies," a part of the white establishment. But most of all, it forced us to look at the interaction between instructor and student, student and student, and the group process more closely; to examine our assumptions about fitness standards and question what a student was really gaining from the experience. What is the difference between an adventure and an ordeal? Most of all the approach became more client-centered, and the Outward Bount mystique had to be bent to accommodate new mores.

Is Outward Bound the custodian of a program or the steward of an idea?

Greg Farrell was the first to insist that the idea of Outward Bound was greater than the Outward Bound organization; that Outward Bound had an opportunity, indeed a responsibility, to apply its technology to new circumstances, to adapt to the urban setting. "What is the moral equivalent of the mountain in the city?" Farrell was director of the War on Poverty community action program in Trenton, New Jersey. He put himself through the Outward Bound program and then sent others: teachers, parole officers, youth workers, street gang leaders, and when they returned he helped them set up their own programs.

The idea caught on. Outward Bound as an organization began to see itself in a new light. In quick seccession, adaptive programs sprang up in the late sixties. The Massachusetts Division of Youth Services set up "Homeward Bound" on Cape Cod, and the Job Corps Centre in Collbran, Colorado, where Murray Durst was director, contracted Outward Bound instructors to develop a program. Prescott College and Dartmouth College both set up programs developed around Outward Bound concepts, and high schools in Denver adapted experiential-based curriculum.

There was much experimentation. Sometimes too much. And, of course, there were skeptics. Within Outward Bound we called adaptive programs "Mainstream." "The only streams I know all run downhill," was the way one crusty trustee expressed his concern.

On the dangers of being "Hooked" on adventure.

It is easy to be hooked on adventure. We have a distorted view of Hahn's vision, given the Outward Bound bias. Hahn valued the adventure ethic for the qualities of character it nurtured: self-reliance, self-sufficiency, endurance in the face of hardship, resilience. But he also harboured an underlying suspicion of Outward Bound. He was concerned lest it become a toughness cult or a haven for the wilderness freak, the social drop-out. Hahn was particularly concerned with the development of responsibility, personal responsibility and social responsibility, and above all of compassion. He spoke most resoundingly of Samaritan service. The mature Hahn institutions have followed this lead. The Round Square Conference Schools, founded by Kurt Hahn or those influenced by him, sponsor a student volunteer village development project in India, building schools in Himalayan villages. The United World College of the American West, in New Mexico, one of six of the Hahn-inspired colleges around the world, requires two afternoons of service training a week. Service is the core of the activities program. All students are trained in basic wilderness skills so the whole college can be called upon for mountain search and rescue. At least half the students are involved in some aspect of community service: working with handicapped and retarded children, visiting old age homes, organizing community clean-up campaigns, assisting in day care centers. At Pearson College, the United World College of the Pacific in British Columbia, marine biology students taught deaf and dumb students scuba diving, who in turn taught them a sign language shorthand that has become the standard language of underwater communication. It is no longer necessary to surface to give instructions. Schools wishing to be serious about service as a program requirement have proven precedents. "There is the need to be needed," says Alec Dickson, the founder of VSO (Voluntary Service Overseas) the model and precedent for the Peace Corps. Hahn's answer to the alienation of youth is to "help them overcome the misery of unimportance."

PROGRESSIVE EDUCATION IN THE 1980s

by Albert M. Adams II

Some of the recent high school reports--particularly the Department of Education's A NATION AT RISK--obscure or ignore the complexities of teaching and learning in the 1980s by calling for an enshrinement of "business as usual." As Theodore Sizer recently noted, these studies share several uninspired themes: 1) a myopic reverence for "the basics," echoing both the subject matter and the pedagogy prescribed by the Committee of Ten in 1893; 2) a conviction that the main goal of education is to drive the American economy; 3) a determination that adults should once again take charge of schools by limiting student choice and enfranchisement; 4) a belief in a top-down reform model emanating from state governments; 5) a notion that a school's performance can and should be judged exclusively by quantitative measures; 6) an assumption that schools cost too much and that the nation's resources for supporting education are finite. The more useful themes from these studies, Sizer notes, are: 1) the promotion of diversity rather than standardization among schools, and 2) the conclusion that the pivotal concern for secondary education in coming years will be the ability to attract and retain first-rate teachers.

Sizer also notes the relative silence of such studies regarding more enlightened perspectives: 1) to make an intrinsic, in addition to a utilitarian, case for education in our society; 2) to assess curricular substance rather than simply time elapsed; 3) to stress the interconnectedness of education with a broad social context; 4) to reinforce the school's role in moral and ethical development; 5) to acknowledge the complexities and implications of growing up in America today. And he points to a significant shift in the language of discourse pervading these studies--with qualities like "responsiveness," "adaptation," and "support" being replaced by "beef up," "toughen up," and "stiffen" the academic program; the latter terms, of course, being from Marine boot camp.

Vito Perrone--at the 1983 Conference on Progressive Education held at Miquon School, Miquon, Pennsylvania--underscored the obligation of contemporary progressive schools to reject notions of a "quick fix" for America's schools:

> In light of the current circumstances educationally--and one could certainly find corresponding examples beyond education--it may appear anomalous to be celebrating as we are the visions of those who began the still flowering progressive schools represented at this conference. Those who poured their lives into these schools wanted, as you know, settings in which children and their growth, their natural interests, curiosity, and creativity were primary places that developed, as Grace Rotzel noted, "all of the native capacities of each child" instead of just teaching reading, writing, and the gathering of facts. Those who sacrificed to construct a base for these schools even talked unabashedly about wanting for children a world in which "cooperation, human understanding, democratic practice--citizenship writ broadly--and peace" were dominant

56

themes. And they characteristically saw the schools as being central to the fulfillment of such a world. While such visions may seem on the surface a bit out of place--even contradictory--in this current manifestation of a technocratic and conservative America, they remain critical, part of the important legacy that each of us here needs to keep alive, the base for a continuing and necessary progressive outline of education.

As important as it is for today's progressive educators to reaffirm their historical roots, Diane Ravitch, in THE TROUBLED CRUSADE, echoes a warning commonly attributed to Joe Segar, Director of the Shady Hill School: "The problem with pioneers is that they tend to become settlers." Referring to the demise of the Progressive Education Association in 1955, Ravitch says:

It died for several reasons, but largely of old age. With all their talk of being forward-looking and future-oriented, in reality the spokesmen for the movement had become keepers of the sacred texts, defending ideas and practices of the past, ignorant of the emerging issues in American life and education. For all the talk of linking school to society, progressives failed to assert leadership on the already explosive racial issue and remained blind to the social implications of their separation of children into academic, general, and vocational curricula. As society and global conditions changed, they did not: the need for international understanding might have been reason to stress the teaching of foreign languages; the mobility and rootlessness of postwar society might have been reason to stress the teaching of history; the persistence of international tension might have been reason to stress the teaching of the history and literature of other cultures; the rapidity of technological change might have been reason to emphasize science and mathematics; the widespread concern about the plight of the individual in mass society might have been reason to elevate the teaching of literature; instead, they continued to talk on about the needs of youth in a way that reflected their insulation from events and their habitual, unthinking dependency on their own tradition and authority.

Progressive education in the 1980s, then, cannot be thought of nostalgically as a set of doctrines. Rather, it must be viewed as a set of fundamental questions for educators to use as guides, probes, and measuring sticks: What are the aims of education, given the wide range of young people's individual and collective needs? How do these aims translate into the pillars upon which schools are built? Given these aims and foundations, what should we teach and how should we teach it? These are timeless questions which endure expressly because they elicit updated answers for our times.

Nor can modern-day progressives allow themselves--because of their small numbers and their passionate commitments--to be viewed as elitist. In fact, several recent high school studies, cut from different cloth than A

NATION AT RISK, demonstrate that progressives are in good company these days.

For instance, in THE GOOD HIGH SCHOOL, Sara Lawrence Lightfoot captures a richness, complexity, and diversity among exemplary schools which defy simplistic characterizations. Likewise John Goodlad (A PLACE CALLED SCHOOL), based on his eight-year investigation and careful analysis of the inner workings of a thousand classrooms, calls for a major overhaul--not mere tinkering--of our schools, and pulls no punches in asking the fundamental questions. And elements of Mortimer Adler's PAEDEIA PROPOSAL sound like echoes of Dewey: 1) his commitment to democratic education through the elimation of tracking (The late Steven K. Bailey of the Harvard Graduate School of Education was fond of saying, "There are two kinds of people in the world--those who believe there are two kinds of people in the world, and those who don't.); 2) his discussion of different kinds of knowing and seeing; 3) his insistence on a balanced variety of teaching methods--didactic, Socratic, coaching (coincidentally responding to John Goodlad's observation that in most schools most teachers do most of the talking).

Ernest Boyer, President of the Carnegie Foundation for the Advancement of Teaching, also adds grist to the progressive mill through HIGH SCHOOL: A REPORT ON SECONDARY EDUCATION IN AMERICA. Boyer and his distinguished panel not only pose the most fundamental questions about schools, but they also advance a bold agenda for action. Among the notable "progressive" elements of that agenda are: 1) the need to clarify and to articulate schools' goals ("Such goals should focus on the mastery of language, on a core of common learning, on preparation for work and further education, and on community and civic service." [p. 301]; 2) a single track for all students, combined with "elective clusters" in the junior and senior years; 3) a service requirement and broad opportunities to become engaged in social and civic obligations; 4) use of a variety of teaching styles; 5) greater flexibility in class schedules; 6) increased use of community resources in the curriculum; 7) the principal as the key educator (in independent school parlance, the headmaster); 8) multiple connections among all levels of schools and between these levels and business/industry.

Similarly, Theodore Sizer (HORACE'S DILEMMA) challenges what he calls the "regularities" of today's high schools: 1) age grading, which ignores the reality that people learn at varying rates and at different times; 2) the goal of time spent in school and "on task" which overshadows the goal of proficiency; 3) the concepts of "giving an education" and "taking classes," based on the assumption that teachers, rather than students, are the key workers in schools; 4) the centrality of the traditional disciplines, which devalues the arts, fails to reflect real life and emphasizes "covering" subject matter rather than learning how to learn; 5) the primacy of the Carnegie Unit daily schedule which severely limits the possibilities for employing, or even dreaming about, innovative learning approaches. Noting the intimate interconnection of these "regularities," Sizer sympathetically quotes Seymore Sarason (SCHOOLING IN AMERICA: SALVATION AND SCAPEGOAT): "Unless you change everything, nothing will change."

While none of these enlightened commentators on high schools is an avowed "progressive," each, in the mode of past and present responsible progressives, is searching for clues to the creation of good schools. They do so by insisting on answers to fundamental questions about human development, learning, and teaching. It is not enough to demonstrate that a bona fide niche exists for progressive educators in the 1980s. Rather, like our predecessors, we today have an obligation to continually assess the limitations of conventional wisdom and to insist that young people's learning not be circumscribed by outmoded principles or be left to chance.

Adele Simmons, President of Hampshire College, recently noted that we can expect the current debate over schools and schooling to hold the nation's attention for only another twelve to eighteen months. Theodore Sizer also acknowledges the cyclical nature of the nation's historical long conversation about education.

It is important then to recognize that A NATION AT RISK is not the definitive statement to chart the course for the next school cycle. Other hopeful and compelling voices are now emerging. The voice of progressives should be in the forefront of mounting a challenge to dangerously narrow, technocratic formulations about schools of today and tomorrow. My recent address to Cambridge School parents represents one attempt to define the needs of adolescents today and to shape appropriate responses to those needs.

Unlike most conventional schools whose hopes for young people are circumscribed by an inflexible schedule and, too often, a static vision of teaching, a good progressive school has an opportunity, and even an obligation, to build its curriculum around the individual developmental needs of its students. Such a commitment to address all strands of young people's development--physical, cognitive, aesthetic, emotional, and moral--results in a starburst of learning objectives and teaching methods.

One absolute associated with progressivism is innovative teaching which grows deliberately and systematically out of an understanding of adolescence and what it means to approach adulthood in the 1980s. What, then, are the learning needs of young people and what skills and qualities are we not willing to leave to chance in our students' development?

I have chosen five overlapping lenses through which to consider these questions. The first lens is that of individual learning styles. While many students come to a progressive school already highly motivated, others are already disaffected. They may well be skeptical about claims that learning can be fun--or even engaging. We know that young people do not develop at a standard rate, that they exhibit a wide variety of skills, preferred learning styles and perspectives on their place in the world. It is clear that people are more likely to take risks--to expose their inadequacies in order to grow--if they first feel successful because their strengths are being valued and rewarded. Most students are accustomed to passive approaches to learning where they view teachers as managers and information disseminators. Some, indeed, are well on their way to becoming "terminal" learners believing that legitimate learning can occur only within school walls and that knowledge is some kind of a mystery which can be unlocked and deciphered only by specialists.

59

Progressive education means prescribing individual academic programs according to students' strengths and weaknesses. It necessitates measuring and rewarding achievements in a variety of ways, whereby performance and product take many different forms, and all disciplines have equal status.

Adolescence, the second lens, is actually a twentieth-century phenomenon. We come from a time in the last eighty years or so when children entered adulthood directly. There were many reasons, portrayed effectively by Charles Dickens, for society to eschew that model. Now we have created an extended rite of passage for young people--in the form of school, which has become a kind of enforced holding pattern extending to age 22 and beyond for many young people.

Society thereby provides two messages for adolescents: they have no meaningful role in society while they are going through this evolutionary phase, and it is only after they successfully negotiate the long road which we call adolescence that they will experience "real" life. The implicit message about school, then, is that it can represent no more than preparation for life which, it seems, robs it of much of its vitality.

At the turn of the century, writes James Coleman, a sociologist at the University of Chicago, children were "experience-rich and information-poor." Given that angle of vision, he said it made good sense that schools, as they began to grow in the early twentieth century, should be geared toward disseminating information. He contrasted that state with the present in which our children are "information-rich and experience-poor." This does not necessarily mean that they know how to deal with the barrage of information available to them. From this, Coleman built arguments for what has come to be called experiential education--education outside the four walls of the classroom.

Similarly, Maurice Gibbons, in his book, THE NEW SECONDARY EDUCATION, addresses the importance of having students learn in a variety of ways, using the community as a resource, for example, and being engaged productively in the world around them. And, in fact, he suggests a concept best described as a post-industrial version of the aboriginal walkabout--a rite of passage where high school seniors would spend six months to a year out in the community applying the skills they had learned culminating in a ritualistic welcome into the adult world.

Given such a perspective on adolescence, it is not by chance that most progressive schools value school service and community service opportunities in which students can make meaningful contributions, or that internships in many settings are encouraged. Indeed, progressive educators constantly look for opportunties for students to apply what they have learned, and they exploit as many outside resources as possible--both by bringing them into the school and by going out to them. Finally, there is a continual search for ways to make the measures of success real rather than abstract.

The third lens is, quite simply, the most fundamental of the basics. We hear, these days, a lot about "back to basics," referring, of course, to reading, writing, and arithmetic. While these, obviously, are very crucial skills, there are others which are even more basic. The first deals with self-esteem--much of which is related to developing confidence based on competence. So the traditional definition of basic skills is an integral component of self-esteem. At the same time, a student requires a community where he or she is respected as an individual as a prerequisite to developing self-esteem. Other basics include empathy for others-- interpersonally, nationally, and internationally; learning how to learn, becoming both self-directed and life-long learners; learning how to think--moving beyond the traditional "know how" to the "know why"; learning how to analyze problems and to make informed and reasoned decisions; being adaptable, in the best sense of the word--discerning what one wants or does not want to adapt to. Given the rapid changes in our world, certainly adaptability is important. Strong communication skills and the ability to nurture one's curiosity are also high on the list.

It is not by chance, then, that sensitive and supportive interpersonal relationships are the hallmarks of progressive education or that its credo is not only to tolerate but, in fact, to celebrate individual differences. Neither is it by chance that progressive schools breed self-starters and engage students in intensive rather than fragmented learning; nor that class discussions often transcend the level of facts and concepts to incorporate the level of values; or that students enjoy a legitimate franchise in the decision-making process campus-wide. Progressive education, then, ideally produces graduates with self-direction, self-discipline, creativity, and resourcefulness.

The fourth lens deals with preparing students to be effective adults. Douglas Heath, a psychologist at Haverford, says in his article "Teaching for Adult Effectiveness" that "it is the rare faculty which has self-consciously sought to identify the qualities that will be required to live in the unpredictable world of the twenty-first century." He cites one school which did this, along with its three top priorities: compassion, self-confidence, and adaptability. He goes on to say, "It is an even rarer faculty that deliberately seeks to educate for such qualities and then has the courage to assess whether it is successful or not." And among those who have done so, there is a growing conviction that "a priority goal should be to empower youth to become more adaptable, self-educating, autonomous learners."

In Heath's 15-year longitudinal study on males who, by most standards, would be considered stereotypically successful and effective American men, happy in their jobs, their family lives, and high in personal satisfaction, the most important finding was that the psychological maturity of a youth and then later of an adult, was the most powerful predictor of subsequent effectiveness. "A highly effective adult must be an adaptable person who can achieve a satisfying balance between the demands of his own needs and the various roles he plays," Heath says. He describes the major attributes of the "self-educating person": possessing a self-concept that he is growing and can continue to grow and learn, and has confidence in his capacity to adapt; and having a curiosity about his world that spurs him to explore and to learn. A third attribute is an openness to learning from both his peers and teachers: "A defensive youth, whether manifested in hypersensitivity to criticism or in passive negativism, is not educable," Heath says. And finally, the basic academic skills are crucial blocks for self-education.

Progressive education does not leave the acquisition of these various qualities and skills to chance as do most conventional schools but, rather, features them in the forefront of curriculum planning and interactions with young people.

The fifth lens relates to the central question of what it means to be growing up in 1984. Who hasn't heard the litany related to young people feeling set adrift in the 1980s? We know a lot but we need to know much more about families in flux, about the decline of many of our social institutions, shifting values, and the shrinking economic pie, about a redefinition of work and leisure and the impact of the media--to name only some of the components and complexities of life in the eighties. We also know a good deal about the precocious nature of adolescents today. Many of us are incredulous when our children do things at age 12 or 14 that we would never have thought of doing before 18. We also hear talk of "super baby." It is sad to see parents of pre-schoolers vying to get their youngsters into the "right" pre-school and, in fact, doing so for some good reasons--knowing that the pre-school where their child is enrolled may determine later opportunities. There are even third graders who are already anxious about what their SAT scores are going to be when that time comes. Too often children in today's society are being pushed toward sharpening their elbows as they rush toward a shrinking and, in many aspects, hollow-looking pie. As we think about lost innocence and disappearing childhood we, of course, cannot avoid considering the situation in our world today--not totally unlike the world's other generations have found--except, perhaps, for the threat of a nuclear holocaust.

It is not an easy time to be growing up. If you listen to the music of this generation, if you consider break-dancing or some of the costumes our high school students wear, you see not only the normal conflict of generations, but other elements which are exceedingly disturbing. Too often, there is a sense of helplessness and hopelessness on the part of young people.

It is clear that business-as-usual as portrayed on the national educational scene is not sufficient for nurturing today's teenagers toward effective adulthood. Progressive educators have known for over seventy years that we need to base curriculum on young people's needs. As educators, ours is a broad and a lofty mission and we do, in fact, expect our graduates to become effective adults. We expect them to acquire the knowledge, the skills, and the confidence to shape their world into a sane and satisfying one. At the same time, we want them to know the unfettered joy of childhood and the security of knowing that they are both cared about and cared for while they are young.

*****

Albert M. Adams, II, is Headmaster of the Cambridge School, Weston, Massachusetts. This article is based upon his presentation at the NAIS Annual Conference held in New York City in March, 1984.

*****

PHILOSOPHICAL FOUNDATIONS

Babies and Bath Water:
Two Experiential Heresies

by Theodore F. Wichmann

Is the Experiential Education Movement doomed to an early death like its predecessor the Progressive Education Movement? The author argues that heresies evident in the literature of the Experiential Education Movement militate against its survival.

This paper centers on the philosophies of John Dewey and Edward Hall by exploring two heresies that presently limit, and may ultimately threaten the modern Experiential Education Movement. Practically, this movement is defined by an annual conference which began in 1973, the Association for Experiential Education, incorporated in 1977, and the **Journal for Experiential Education**, first printed in 1977. Philosophically, the movement still self-admittedly lacks a "crisp, broadly accepted definition". In the first issue of the Journal, Murray Durst identified certain assumptions about the members of the AEE. He saw them as working within and from without various educational institutions, at all levels, and across many disciplines with a unifying interest in "the nature and process of experience for educational purposes". Furthermore, he viewed the members' perception of their role "to be at the leading edge for educational reform" (1977).

One purpose of this paper is to provide a brief historical perspective that may reveal the subtle suicidal tendencies of the Experiential Education Movement. Although this may seem unduly pessimistic, I can't help but see the parellels between this modern movement and the now dead Progressive (or Experimental) Education Movement: both movements accepting Dewey as mentor; both being highly holistic and multidisciplinary; both seeking learning through experience; both operating largely outside traditional institutions; and neither one well researched. In fact, one of the few scholarly works on Progressive Education served as an epitaph with the following obituary:

Theodore F. Wichmann was a secondary teacher in St. Louis, Missouri for seven years. For the last five years he has worked for Southern Illinois University at Carbondale. He is presently a staff member of the Environmental Center, Division of Continuing Education, where he directs and evaluates experiential education programs. He chairs the AEE professional group, Adventure Alternatives in Corrections, Mental Health and Special Education.

"The death of the Progressive Education Association in 1955 and the passing of its journal, **Progressive Education,** two years later marked the end of an era in American pedagogy. Yet one would scarcely have known it from the pitifully small group of mourners at both funerals" (Cremin, 1964). I somehow cannot avoid the image of this as handwriting on the wall. In order to survive, experiential education must help both the individual learner and the culture, of which it is a part, to grow and evolve.

The credibility of the school is its tradition. The credibility of innovative experiential learning must be its demonstrated effectiveness in promoting the survival and growth of the individual. As with the American Progressivism Movement, many modern programs and practitioners have often interpreted experiential education as "learning by doing". In our enthusiasm for developing alternatives to traditional schooling,

> One purpose of this paper is to provide a brief historical perspective that may reveal the subtle suicidal tendencies of the Experiential Education Movement.

we have overlooked the fact that experience can be noneducative or even miseducative. In our rush to innovate, many of us have thrown out the babies of experiential education philosophy with the bath water of traditional pedagogy. The philosophy and theories born in the work of Rousseau, Pestalozzi, James, Dewey and Piaget should be nutured rather than discarded or ignored. These educators refused to resort to the popular experiential euphemism that if you have to ask the question, you won't understand the answer. Rather, they each dared to ask the question that Dewey phrased: "What is the place and meaning of subject-matter and of organization within experience?" (1938, p. 20).

As learning promotes the survival and growth of the individual, educational reform must contribute to the evolution of the culture. As with Progressive Education, many modern programs and practitioners have often interpreted educational reform as improvisational reforming by doing. We are all too acutely aware that traditional education's primary function has been to transmit and maintain culture, and, in so doing, has been "the principal instrument for setting limits on the enterprise of mind" (Bruner, 1962). However, in developing alternatives to traditional education, we have sometimes merely scrambled the internalized cultural program that is mind. We have thrown out the babies of cultural insight with the bath water of educational bureaucracy, with all its violations of cultural norms that limit the development of self. We must dare to ask what is the place and meaning of experiential education within the culture?

Forty Years of Either-Ors

Forty years ago John Dewey (1938) began **Experience and Education** by observing that educators had been formulating their instructional theories in terms of "Either-Ors". More importantly, he deplored the fact that the Progressive Education Movement, which had recruited Dewey as symbolic father, had not progressed past a philosophy of rejection. Progressivism represented a radical reaction against three primary learning assumptions of traditional education: 1) subject matter and proper conduct from the past are imposed upon students, 2) books are the representatives of this past, and 3) teachers transmit this subject matter and enforce rules of conduct. Thus, the basic learning tenets of progressive education were: 1) to ignore organized subject matter, 2) to emphasize the present and the future to the exclusion of the past, and 3) to view any form of direction by adults as an invasion of individual freedom. Dewey saw that these negatively based principles were vague and inadequate guides for conducting and managing education.

Progressivism also represented a radical reaction against the following cultural assumptions, which Edward Hall (1977) saw as implicit in traditional education: 1) the dominant WASP culture is imposed upon cross-cultural or ethnic groups that are segregated through homogeneous groupings, 2) time schedules and spatial ordering are sacred and rule everything, 3) bureaucracies are real and organization is placed above everything else, and 4) winning and losing are not necessarily dependent upon the context of the subject matter or the real world. Thus, the basic cultural tenets of progressive education were: 1) ethnic minority groups were generally not included or were integrated through heterogeneous grouping with no concern for cross-cultural differences, 2) time schedules and spatial

ordering were ignored, 3) organization was placed below everything else and bureaucracies were considered unreal, and 4) winning and losing were de-emphasized, but not necessarily made dependent upon context. Traditional schools were not developing enterprising minds, but were producing good citizens who could maintain a culture that is extremely linear, monochronic and low context. Unfortunately, it is a culture that is not able to adapt to the future shock of rapid technological change. The Progressivists, of course, realized this, but in their haste to react, failed to actualize Dewey's dream of an education that "is the fundamental method of social progress and reform" (1929). In fact, at the end of the Progressive era, American education found itself in a quandary, surrounded by pseudo reforms.

In developing alternatives to traditional education we have sometimes merely scrambled the internalized cultural program that is mind. We have thrown out the babies of cultural insight with the bath water of educational bureaucracy, with all its violations of cultural norms that limit the development of self.

Levin (1975) recently attempted to resolve this quandary by legally defining the goals of education by identifying a set of broad societal expectations. He described the following four major mandates for education: 1) to certify the achievement of technical competence, 2) to develop physical, emotional and intellectual skills and abilities, 3) to generate social integration among individuals and across cultural groups, and 4) to nuture a sense of social responsibility for the consequences of personal and group actions. In spite of Hall's insight and Levin's redefined social mandates for education, we are faced with very similar "Either-Ors", forty years after **Experience and Education**. The opponents have updated their banners to: Competency-Based Education versus Experiential Education.

The Competency-Based Education Movement (CBE) described by Spady (1977) as a bandwagon in search of a definition, appears to be here to stay -- at least until it is renamed and resold as another hot McCarthistic political issue. In spite of vague popular definitions, this movement looks suspiciously like Dewey's "traditional education" of 1938 with its emphasis on subject matter, books, teacher dominance, and a rigid, dinosaurian, cultural structure. Likewise, the Experiential Education Movement resembles the

Progressive Education Movement in that its present impetus comes from a negative reaction to traditional education and those forces that support CBE. It is interesting to note that both of these movements are highly unidimensional in relation to Levin's societal expectations. CBE is concerned with the certification of students' achievement of technical skills, while the Experiential Education Movement is limited to the development of physical, emotional and intellectual skills, and abilities. Neither has done more than pay verbal homage to social integration and social responsibility.

There is little hope for reformation of education or society through the CBE Movement. It is highly static, self-perpetuating and reactionary. In its popular "back to basics" or "3 r's" form, it in fact represents the traditional American education thought of the past 100 years. On the other hand, the Experiential Education Movement presents the same promise for educational and social reform as did the Progressive Education Movement. Its advocates are innovative and dynamic and appear to be more concerned with learning and reform than with institutional self-perpetuation. However, this potential is limited by its continuing self-conscious, over-reaction to traditional education. This self-consciousness has restricted multidimensional, holistic approaches and produced an obvious reluctance among experiential educators to risk philosophical and

---

CBE is concerned with the certification of students' achievement of technical skills, while the Experiential Education Movement is limited to the development of physical, emotional and intellectual skills, and abilities. Neither has done more than pay verbal homage to social integration and social responsibility.

---

theoretical exploration. Most have been content to criticize traditional education and to limit affirmative positions to vague generalities and mystical metaphors. This has created a dangerous philosophical vacuum between the "Either" and the "Or".

The Learning By Doing Heresy

The paradox of the Experiential Education Movement is that its strengths are sometimes also its weaknesses. An educator's personal discovery of the charismatic power of an educative experience can make an unquestioning convert of him or her. A small group of secondary teachers, for example, shared an intense

Outward Bound course in which they collectively overcame various exciting challenges and very real physical and psychological stress. They all felt emotionally reborn at the end of the course. They felt they had changed and had increased their self-awareness and self-confidence. They knew it worked. However, in trying to adapt the model to their own traditional school, the educators were unable to explain to their administrators why such an experience was educational. The experience was never examined from an historical or theoretical perspective, for that would have seemed to decrease the mystery and the importance of the educators' own experience. If one of these teachers explores the possibilities of taking Mohammed to the proverbial mountain, he or she will find that most experiential programs exist as alternatives well outside the educational mainstream. Money, security and training opportunities are scarce. This has caused practitioners and programs to constantly struggle for survival. This struggle has stimulated innovation and excellence in some cases, while also creating high staff turnover and a paucity of life long careers in experiential education. The educator who does carve out a career niche, within or without traditional education, is likely to become addicted to the process of discovery. He or she may then ignore past knowledge and experience and opt for the self-indulgent joy of reinventing educational wheels. This, of course, limits the advancement of the state of the art to one generation. Each discovery addict begins and ends where his/her predecessor began and ended. Cold turkey treatment involves the revelation that many of the addict's anecdotal, axiomatic "discoveries" are 75-years old and have been found to be theoretically and empirically unsound. All of these paradoxes have, of course, limited the growth and influence of experiential education and have contributed to the development of the "learning-by-doing" heresy and its three syndromes: 1) the blind faith syndrome, 2) the cookbook syndrome, and 3) the process-centered syndrome.

The limited literature of the modern Experiential Education Movement is saturated with examples of the blind faith syndrome. Nold (1977), in "On Defining Experiential Education: John Dewey Revisited" wrote that:

> Some feel about experiential education the way Hemingway felt about making love: Don't talk about it, you'll only ruin the experience. We know it's good because it feels good, and as G.E. Moore, the philosopher said: good is good, and that's the end of the matter. It can only be defined in terms of itself, it has intrinsic worth so there is no other standard to judge it by, it requires no further justification. The values are "self-evident". Let the mountains speak for themselves!

Arnold Shore (1977) attempted to define the Experiential Education Movement in terms of its past and its present. He stated that "..we conceived of something undefined that was larger, but closely related, that is, experiential education. Not unlike the bead game in Hesse's **Magister Ludi,** this central concept can remain undefined with its purpose yet safe to get us beyond ourselves to something which must be grander." Both of these quotes describe a typical attitude within the Experiential Education Movement. There is no reason to ask questions or verbalize answers. You must know intuitively that all experience is good because it is good.

The educator who does carve out a career niche, within or without traditional education, is likely to become addicted to the process of discovery. He or she may then ignore past knowledge and experience and opt for the self-indulgent joy of reinventing educational wheels.

There does exist some support for intuitive knowledge, from Socrates through the present. Of course, the belief in an Inner Truth makes proving any point possible. Whether all experience is good or not from an educational perspective is the focus here and will be further discussed later.

The cookbook syndrome is not as obvious in the literature, but is prevalent among instructors and teachers. Often they must buy a bag of tricks rather than learn the complex magic. They want lists of experiential education activities that work. How does one know if an activity works? It works if the students can do it without losing too much interest. It works if it fills the time slot. It works if it has a reputation for working. Line staff who demonstrate the cookbook syndrome often have little choice. They have received little or no training in experiential education and need "tricks" if they want to survive their apprenticeship. Of course, this is not very different from colleges of education where teachers are trained primarily through memorizing curriculum and compiling related lists of activities called lesson plans. The difference becomes only the nature of the tricks. The traditional educator learns tricks for imposing multiplication tables or grammatical rules on unwilling children, while the experiential educator finds out how long a wilderness solo should be, or what kind of questions and people should be used for interviews by students in his or her cultural journalism class.

Walsh and Golins (1976), Gager (1977) and Greenberg (1978) have all developed process-centered experiential learning theories. These three papers are examples of the process-centered syndrome. Each of these papers describes in detail how the experiential learning process flows, but all avoid any detailed discussion of **what** is to be learned. In terms of Bruner's (1966) framework for a theory of instruction, they have generally included the predisposition to learn and a very general sequence of learning. None of these theories, however, develop an optimal structure of the knowledge to be learned or specify the form and pacing of reinforcement. In our reaction to traditional information transference, we have made process the end rather than the means. There has been little discussion of behavior and knowledge resulting from the experiential learning process. Even more importantly, we have discussed this process as if it were common to all learning and all learners. Should the learning process be identical for enactive, iconic and symbolic learning; or for personality development, language and mathematics? Should it be the same for persons at different levels of biological cognitive development? The same for formal operators as for concrete operators? For learning disabled as well as the gifted? We seem to have become parsimonious in our theorizing by ignoring what has been discovered recently about learning and development and by even avoiding Dewey's questions related to the meaning and organization of subject matter within experience.

The fallacy that is basic to the "learning-by-doing" heresy and that unites each of the three syndromes discussed above, is that experience and education can be directly equated to each other. Dewey stated that, "The belief that all genuine education comes about through experience does not mean that all experiences are genuinely or equally educative" (1938, p. 25). Experience can also be "noneducative" or even "miseducative". A noneducative experience is one that does not promote the growth of further experience. A miseducative experience is one that arrests or distorts the growth of further experience. Furthermore, there is a two-dimensional qualitative difference between educative experiences. There is the short-term quality of the immediate agreeableness or reward and there is the long-term quality in terms of its influence upon later experiences. In its broadest definition, experience includes all stimuli and all response, everything that happens to us and every thought or action we make. We must whittle this down to size. We must carefully decide what to leave in our educational plan, and more importantly, what to omit. Furthermore, we must better understand the nature of experiencing, including the subtle, but all important differences.

Thus, it seems obvious that blind faith, activity cookbooks and even process-centered theories are not only inadequate, but can be miseducative. All three syndromes can limit the growth of further experience for educators and students by avoiding the issue of miseducative experience and by failing to provide complete criteria for determining the relative quality of a situation-specific and learner-specific educative experience. What is needed now is the development of specific theories of experiential learning and instruction based upon a general philosophy of experiential education. As

---

The fallacy that is basic to the "learning-by-doing" heresy is that experience and education can be directly equated to each other.

Dewey wrote, "Unless experience is so conceived that the result is a plan for deciding upon subject matter, upon methods of instruction and discipline, and upon material, equipment and social organization...it is wholly in the air. It is reduced to a form of words which may be emotionally stirring, but for which any other set of words might equally well be substituted unless they indicate operations to be initiated and executed" (1938, p. 28).

The Reforming By Doing Heresy

Why educational reform? Because as learning promotes the survival and growth of the individual, educational reform must contribute to the evolution of the culture. Why cultural evolution? Because the increasingly rapid advance of technology is shocking our culture to its very foundations. Increasing crime, suicide, divorce, child abuse, resource depletion, pollution and nuclear proliferation are symptoms of this shock and of our culture's inability to adapt and control technology. As educators we must not shirk our responsibility to do what we can through our own educational medium to help our culture adapt and evolve. This is, of course, the long-term goal of any education in any culture. Why should the fledgling Experiential Education Movement concern itself with reform? First of all, in terms of its own survival, it must serve a culturally adaptive function. Perhaps more important is the fact that few other educational organizations or institutions are doing it. George Counts' words to the Progressive Education Association's national meeting in 1932 are strangely descriptive of the present situation:

> That the existing school is leading the way to a better social order is a thesis which few informed persons would care to defend. Except as it is forced to fight for its own life during times of depression, its course is too serene and untroubled. Only in the rarest of instances does it wage war on behalf of principle or ideal. Almost everywhere it is in the

grip of conservative forces and is serving the cause of perpetuating ideas and institutions suited to an age that is gone. But there is one movement above the educational horizon which would seem to show promise of genuine and creative leadership. (pp. 2-3)

In 1979, this movement is the Experiential Education Movement.

However, an examination of the programs and philosophies of Experiential Education reveals certain inherent cultural obstructions to effective reform. The first and most obvious problem is the one of cultural homogeneity. Nearly all experiential educators within the movement are white Anglo-Saxon Protestants and Agnostics (WASPA's). There seem to be several reasons for this. One is that most educators from ethnic or minority groups may presently be concerned more with basic needs, such as security, than with such idealistic needs as social reform. Secondly, they may be more concerned with providing educational opportunities for their youthful constituents who are often limited to traditional schooling than are WASPA children. Thirdly, the Experiential Education Movement has demonstrated little or no sensitivity or affirmative action toward involving minority students or educators in their programs or professional activities.

Another problem is that of hidden cultural meanings within both traditional and experiential education. Since this problem is so complex, the discussion here is meant to be only illustrative, not comprehensive. Any educational transaction can be placed along a cultural continuum, from low context to high context. High context transactions depend upon the immediate environment as well as information the receiver has. Low context transactions depend almost totally upon the content of a particular lesson, in order to make up for what is missing in the context. Traditional education is, of course, very low context while Experiential Education is typically high context. The traditional educator is most concerned with the curriculum (content), while the experiential educator is more interested in the environment (context). More importantly, high context communication, in contrast to low context, is efficient and satisfying as long as the communicators are both tuned into the particular contexts involved. If one is not tuned in, the communication is incomplete. Thus, the experiential educator has great difficulty communicating to the traditional educator or bureaucrat what it is they do or want to do. The typical reaction is frustration on both sides.

Another important aspect of the problem of hidden cultural meaning has to do with how time and space are used as organizing frames for activities. Most Americans use what Hall calls "monochronic time" or "M-time" as opposed to "polychronic time" or "P-time." M-time emphasizes time schedules and spatial segmentation. P-time is characterized by several things happening at once with little regard for spatial segmentation. P-time emphasizes the completion of transactions rather than adherence to preset schedules. Traditional education is, of course, very monochronic, while experiential education is ideally polychronic. This makes integration of experiential learning into the school very difficult. It is one thing to end a history lecture at the ringing of the bell and take up where you left off the next day. It is quite another thing to be involved in a powerful learning experience only to have it cut off before completion at the end of 55 minutes. Similarly, most traditional schooling is designed to take place in very small well-defined spaces---classrooms, laboratories, gyms, etc. Realistic experiences do not always lend themselves to such simplistic spatial segmentation.

The first and most obvious problem is the one of cultural homogeneity. Nearly all experiential educators within the movement are white Anglo-Saxon Protestants and Agnostics (WASPA's).

Besides these cultural obstructions to easy integration of experience into traditional schooling, there is the more subtle problem of the experiential educator's own acculturation. He or she is a product of the dominant culture and probably operates most comfortably in low context, monochronic situations with little or no conscious awareness of this fact. Thus, as Hall states, "Given our linear, step-by-step, compartmentalized way of thinking, fostered by the schools and public media, it is impossible for our leaders to consider events comprehensively or to weigh priorities according to a system of common good, all of which can be placed like an unwanted waif on culture's doorstep" (1977, p. 12). These problems of cultural homogeneity and hidden meaning have also limited the growth and influence of experiential education by contributing to the "reforming-by-doing heresy" and its three syndromes: 1) the lollypop syndrome, 2) the missionary syndrome, and 3) the culture-free syndrome.

In order to explain the lollypop syndrome, I have to tell you a simple story from which the lollypop metaphor was derived. This story was told me on several different occasions by various experiential educators. It goes something like this. Unlike most children, there are some who have never experienced a lollypop. If you give these children a lollypop once or several times, they know what lollypops taste like and may even grow fond of them. Then these children go back to their lollypopless world. They will be all the worse for this

experience since they may now want lollypops and not have them. The story teller then goes on to explain that the same is true in relation to providing experiential education for students from ethnic and minority backgrounds. Thus, the experiential educator can return to doing his own thing with his own kind. There is no need for understanding complex cross-cultural differences or for adapting programming to meet minority student's needs.

The experiential educator who does not buy the lollypop metaphor may demonstrate the missionary syndrome. This syndrome is based on the fallacy that mind is not synonymous with culture, but rather is created in the image and likeness of God. Minds which appear to be different than our own must, therefore, be inferior or distorted. This belief frees us to practice what Hall describes as "an unconscious form of cultural imperialism which we impose on others" (1977, p. 206). This syndrome makes educational and cultural reform nearly impossible. We become like the missionaries who left their mother country to avoid religious persecution, only in turn to impose their own beliefs on others in a new land. Because we have left the cultural imperialism of traditional schooling, we feel all the more confident that God is on our side. Although we may have developed innovations in our approach, it is doubtful that we have changed all those practices that are synonymous with culture. We become stagnant with our own self-righteous belief that we are reforming education and society through doing "good works".

The culture-free syndrome is the most subtle and sophisicated of the three syndromes. This syndrome centers around the fallacy that education and culture are two separate entities. We may be aware that mind and culture are related. However, we believe that education that deals with information, thinking and simple forms of behavior can be kept distinct from such things as morals and culture. This makes things much simpler. We can now reform education, and to some extent society, without having to understand the complexities of culture and mind. It becomes just a matter of inserting appropriate experiences or experiential processes into the classroom. The culture-free syndrome was demonstrated recently by an experiential educator who stated, "Because I dream of the day when my nine-year-old son Danny will not have to sit through an entire unit on plants, as he did last month, without a single plant in the classroom. He needs us" (Leiweke, 1975, p. 5). One assumption here seems to be that all Danny was supposed to learn was information about plants. Our linear logic tells us that this is a safe assumption. However, from a more comprehensive point of view, we might perceive that Danny was learning more than just botany. He was also learning how to function in and maintain a low context culture. Another assumption here seems to be that plants in the classroom would have been a significant improvement. How would such changes affect the classroom study of nuclear physics, evolution or elephants? The point is that such changes as plants in the classroom could easily sublimate real educational reform.

The fallacy that is basic to the "reforming-by-doing" heresy and that unites each of the three syndromes discussed above, is that experiential education and educational reform can be directly equated to each other. Hall stated that "Those features of education that are synonymous with culture are very likely to change when the educators start innovating, when they try opened and closed classrooms, permissive and non-permissive discipline, fast and slow tracks, reforming curriculum, and the like. This point is crucial, and its importance is frequently overlooked" (1977, p. 206). Thus, it seems obvious that cultural segregation, cultural imperialism and the fallacy of culture-free education will not effect reform and bring us closer to fulfilling Levin's mandates for social integration and social responsibility. We must begin to see the interrelatedness of education and culture, and begin to understand such cultural features as action chains, situational frames and extensions, and how one uses them. We must reappraise our philosophy and practice in realizing that "denying culture can be as destructive as denying evil. Man must come to terms with both" (Hall, 1977, p. 7). Otherwise the Experiential Education Movement will not contribute to the evolution of the culture, and being useless, will be selected for cultural extinction.

Conclusion

In discussing Progressivism in American education, Cremin (1964) pointed out that "the transformation of the schools" has always been incomplete at best, and often produced inconsistent or contradictory organizational elements. Effective and politically acceptable education programs can be developed only if the historical alternatives are understood within a theoretical framework and subjected to systematic research. In order for the modern Experiential Education Movement to be more successful than Progressivism in surviving the onslaught of reactionary critics, to develop effective educational programs, and to influence traditional education, it must be more than merely reactive. In other words, it must: 1) reexamine its present operations and theories in light of the learning-by-doing and reforming-by-doing fallacies, 2) develop a more sound theoretical framework based upon an understanding of historical and cultural alternatives and philosophies, and 3) provide for the ongoing empirical investigation of subject matter, methodologies, processes and outcomes. In other words, we must work toward reliable criteria for distinguishing between the babies and the bath water.

References

Bruner, J.S. **On Knowing.** Cambridge: The Belknap Press of Harvard University Press, 1962.

Bruner, J.S. **Toward a Theory of Instruction.** Cambridge: The Belknap Press of Harvard University Press, 1966, pp. 39-72.

Counts, G.S. **Dare the School Build a New Social Order?** London: Feffer & Simons, Inc., 1932.

Cremin, L.A. **The Transformation of the School: Progressivism in American Education, 1876-1957.** New York: Random House Vintage Books, 1964.

Dewey, J. **My Pedagogic Creed.** Washington: Progressive Education Association, 1929.

Dewey, J. **Experience and Education.** New York: Collier Books, 1938.

Gager, R. As a Learning Process...It's More Than Just Getting Your Hands Dirty. **Voyageur,** 1977, 1.

Greenberg, E. The Community as a Learning Resource. **The Journal of Experiential Education,** 1978, 1, pp. 22-25.

Hall, E.T. **Beyond Culture.** New York: Anchor Press/Doubleday, 1977.

Leiweke, T. Experiential Education as a Movement. **The Journal of Experiential Education,** 1979, 2, pp. 4-5.

Levin, H.M. Education, Life Chances, and the Courts: The Role of Social Science Evidence. **Law and Contemporary Problems,** 1975, 39, pp. 217-240.

Nold, J.J. On Defining Experiential Education: John Dewey Revisited. **Voyageur,** 1977, 1.

Pipho, C. State Activity Related to Minimal Competency Testing. Unpublished report. Educational Commission of the States, Denver, CO, 1978.

Shore A. and Greenberg, E. Challenging the Past, Present and Future: New Directions in Education. **The Journal of Experiential Education,** 1977, 1, pp. 42-46.

Spady, W.G. Competency Based Education: A Bandwagon in Search of a Definition. **Education Researcher,** 1977, 6, pp. 9-14.

Walsh, V and Golins, G.L. **The Exploration of the Outward Bound Process.** Denver: Colorado Outward Bound School, 1976.

This article is an opportunity to invite reader response the ideas presented in the **Journal.** The Board, believing in the positive effects of controversy within the movement, will continue to print articles that run counter to received opinion and invite your comments on any article printed.

A CRITICAL LOOK: THE PHILOSOPHICAL FOUNDATIONS OF EXPERIENTIAL EDUCATION

To say that we know by experience presupposes an answer to centuries of philosophical debate on the theories of reality and knowledge. Here, an historical overview of these problems is presented.

by April Crosby

I had participated in experiential learning as student and as teacher numerous times, but I was not officially introduced to the concept nor to its many organized schools, camps and activities until very recently. When I did become aware, I approached it in the way consistent with my training — skeptically. I found myself questioning all the assumptions and values of E.E., and I found myself, as some advocates of E.E. would say we all are, unable to really look at it until I had put it into a context that means something to me. In my case this context was philosophical, and I began to look at E.E. as a philosophy of education that would include assumptions and value judgements. I investigated E.E. as a philosophy of education in a long line of such evolving philosophies, and I examined it in light of this line. I found it has a very interesting place in line.

Before I go on I must make some ideas clear. It is important to see that a philosophy of education, or a theory of education, is based on more general beliefs than may appear in the theory. These are the preconceptions or underlying assumptions of a theory, and until they are seen to be the basis of a theory, and accepted, the theory is unfounded. Some are of the school of thought about E.E. that is **activity,** not theory, and second, that nothing should be written about E.E. because it threatens its action-orientation and tends to rigidify it. But even if you only "do" E.E., there are presuppositions you are acting on. What I want to clairfy here is that any theory (or action) of education is based on more general theories of epistemology, and those in turn are based on assumptions about metaphysics.

Epistemology is, roughly, the study of how and what we know. It deals with such questions as whether we know via our sense or our reason, or some combination of the two, and whether we know objects of reason (like higher mathematics, for which there is no action or experiential route) with more certainty than we may know things which we learn through our senses. We might think this because information we get from our senses is sometimes mistaken, as when an object in the far distance appears small when in fact it is large. Epistemology is also concerned with the objects of knowledge: can we know only things which we can tangibly experience, like rocks and tables, or can we know that a non-tangible object, like love, or perhaps God, exists? Some, of course, would say that we have equally reliable experience of God as we do of tables, but for others this claim raises the question of what do we mean by "experience?" Epistemology is a field which examines many of the underlying assumptions which may be made by people working in the field of E.E.

Also, epistemology is concerned with such distinctions as that between "belief" and "knowledge." Do we say we **knew** the world was flat but now we **know** it is round? We might say we "know" the true things and "believe" the things which may be proven false, or the things which aren't available for proof, as some would say of the existence of God. The point I am trying to make here is how epistemology, or ideas about how we might learn about the world, are based on what we feel and think to be the case about that world, and hence, it is based on metaphysics.

Metaphysics is, roughly, the study of the way the world is. Aristotle said it is the study of things which don't change, for the most part. It is investigation into what is real; for instance, Why does time seem to up and slow down? The clock measures objective time while we feel it pass subjectively. Which is real? Is there objectivity at all? Shoud there be? Is it a handy concept for explaining things, or is it a troublesome ideal which gets in the way? What are the organizing principles in the world? Is history headed in a certain direction, toward a specific actualization toward which we progress, as Christians believe we are headed toward the Kingdom of god and Marxists believe we are headed toward a classless society? Or do we go in cycles of reincarnation, as the Hindus say? Are all of these merely subjective human constructs? Does the world change, or is the change an illusion? Is there every novelty in the world? These are some of the issues on metaphysics, and clearly theories about how and what we learn about the world would have to entail cerain things about that world itself. This is what I mean when I say that philosophy of education, or any activity in the field of educaiton, is based on an epistemology, and therefore, on a metaphysic.

What I found when I did investigations about the philosophical underpinnings of E.E. is that those assumptions underlying E.E. are much more reliable than those underlying more traditional theories of education, and I want to explain what I mean by that. One thing it implies is that students educated according to these assumptions are better prepared to deal with the world than are students educated according to traditional epistemologies. I must say one more thing before going on, however, That is that I am aware that not all people who do E.E. agree on what E.E. is, or what a statement of its theory or values would be. What I mean by E.E. is a very general belief: that learning will happen more effectively if the learner is as involved as possible, using as many of his faculties as possible, in the learning; and that this involvement is maximized if the student has something that matters to him at stake. How you get the learner to have something at stake is another issue, and it is, I think, the most controversial question I've encountered in connection with E.E., but I'm not concerned with it here.

Back to the philosophical underpinnings of E.E.; I want to cursorily review the history of the philosphy of education to show how I think E.E. and some of its philosophical assumptions developed, and why I think it is epistemologically sound.

HISTORY

An early theory of education was illustrated by the Sophists, who were teachers in ancient Greece. We think of them as flourishing prior to what we call the golden age of classical Greece, though they were still extant then. These men charged fees for their tutelage, and leading citizens of Athens would pay handsome sums to have their sons taught by them. The teaching consisted primarily of reciting opinions on profound subjects, and helping students to learn to recite these opinions equally pursuasively. Students learned an-

swers to questions such as "What is virtue?" "What is piety?" " What is the nature of the beautiful?", and others. We can call this theory the "pouring theory" of education, because the teachers had the learning which they could pour into the students as if they were vessels. Once the student had the learning, they too could recite definitions and theories on deep subjects.

We can see the epistemological and metaphysical assumptions of this educational practice even more easily if we look at another modern counterpoint: the way the catechism is taught in very orthodox Roman Catholic church schools. There children are given books which pose questions and also give answers. The children learn to recite the specified answers and are said to know their catechism. According to this, we could know that God exists whether or not we have experienced Him, and we know that He, the utmost Reality, does not change. That's why these answers need not change, and why the method of teaching need not change. The children are learning about an unchanging reality, and those who know can tell those who don't yet know the truth about it. Because of the nature of the **object** of knowledge, in this case God (which is a metaphysical principle), the subjectivity of the learner is not relevant. What is true of God is simply true of Him, not true for me but not for you, or true in different ways.

The Sophists also thought that way about the objects of knowledge. Each knew the final word about things which did not need debate. A curious thing is that the Sophists disagreed among themselves, just as our religious leaders might also disagree about what they think is absolute. A father sent his sons to the Sophist with the most prestige, or to the Sophist who would make his son the most influential orator, or, if he were a thinking father, to the Sophist with whom he agreed. In any event, learners were the uninformed who could be filled up with knowledge as if it were soup and one could get it all.

This model of education changed radically with the teacher Socrates (470 - 399 B.C.) He taught by asking questions, not reciting answers, and he asked many questions of the Sophists which they couldn't answer because their opinions couldn't stand up under scrutiny. Socrates was asking about **their** underlying assumptions, and they frequently got confused. There were not used to discussion.

As a teacher, Socrates made two major methodological changes from the Sophists. First, he believed that the students had something to contribute to the learning and he elicited that; second, he believed that the **process** of becoming educated was the important thing, rather than arriving at a final static state and he practiced that. He taught by beginning where the students were and leading them, through discussion, to examine their own ideas. He taught that the educated person was the one who questions all through life; that learning is a life style, and this style he called "tending the soul." These beliefs and practices sound much closer to those of E.E. than do those of the Sophists.

However, according to Plato, who recorded the conversations of Socrates, the true goal of this search for knowledge is knowledge of the Forms (or what we might call essences) and these were Objective Reality. According to Plato, dialectic discussion is the epistemological tool by which we can learn of The Forms, the metaphysical principles of Reality. Plato says in the *"Republic"* that this true knowledge of absolutes is not achievable by most of us because of our limited capacity to learn from dialectic. Most of us are doomed to forever mistake images and the sensible objects around us as the highest Reality. Any learning of which we are capable is gained by reflection on our own beliefs, and this is accomplished best by critical discussion with others. Plato also pointed out, accurately, that most of us are hesitant to have our beliefs and assumptions questioned and therefore learning is usually painful.

Let's look at Plato's epistemological and metaphysical assumptions. Although few students would ever know them, Socrates tried to lead knowledge of the Forms, or absolutes. There was an essence or Form of virtue, and of beauty, and of other less profound things, each of which was a true, perfect and unchanging model of that quality or Thing. The Forms existed, in some sense, and functioned as paradigms.

Why would he arrive at such an idea of absolutes? He saw that all we have available to us through experience are **particular** beautiful things, yet we say that one is more or less beautiful, as if we had some knowledge of an absolute standard of Beauty to which we compare all individual cases. Or, take the idea of a chair. We all know more or less what a chair is, but if you were asked to define it, would you include four legs? Bean bag chairs have no legs at all, and some chairs have three. Would you include that it is used for sitting? If I sit on a table does that make it a chair? Perhaps you would specify that it has to be **intended** for sitting. Well, is a bicycle seat a chair? We can imagine some stopping us by saying, "That's not a chair!" when we start to sit on something which might break. Plato saw that although not many of us can articulate what the essence of "chair" is there **must** be one, because despite differing and changing definitions, we all know what a chair is.

The same is true of Virtue. We may think we know what it is until we are forced to define it. Most likely even if we don't claim to be able to define it, we could recognize particular cases we would call acts of virtue, and cases we would say clearly are not. Plato watched people wrestle with these things and it made him propose that objective absolutes do exist but we are just in very hazy touch with them. We can get closer to the metaphysical realities by the epistemological method of reflective and critical dialogue about our theories. This is accomplished in education by asking students to set forth their ideas which are then examined.

We may call the Socratic philosphy of education the "midwifery theory" because Socrates saw the role of the teacher as that of a midwife: helping give birth to the knowledge which is already within the student. The teacher simply assists with delivery. The goal is persons who can continue to express and examine their own and others' ideas. Socrates saw such constant intellectual exercise as a way of life.

Philosophy of education went through another evolution with Aristotle, (384 - 322 B.C.). In metaphysics, Aristotle rejected Plato's theory of the Forms as Reality because he saw too many problems with trying to defend their existence. Besides, Aristotle's background was as a biologist and he saw the universe in terms of growth and change as a biologist would. Reality as unchanging Forms made no sense to him. He believed that the organizing metaphysical principle was one of change: the world can be explained in terms of things changing from what they **potentially** are to their state of being **actually** realized. For example, acorns always become oak trees, oak trees may become tables, that table may become firewood, or decay into the earth again, etc. Aristotle's Reality was one which took into account change, and the change is from potentially to actuality. The actualization of a thing depends on its species. For example, the full actualization of a colt is a beautifully running horse because it is the highest function of a horse to run. The fully actualized human being, according to Aristotle, is the one who thinks most fully because thinking is the function of the human species peculiar to it only.

At this point we can see how the metaphysical principles of potentiality, actuality, and the change from one to the next would influence education theory. Young men were taught to use the highest function of their species, their cognitive minds, in order to become fully realized humans. This led to obvious trouble with ethical questions. We can see that a man who is most highly developed **mentally** might not be what we think of as a **morally** developed man. Aristotle never solves this dilemma very satisfactorily but he begins to answer with a distinction between "theoretical wisdom" which is the highest function of our minds, and "practical wisdom," which is the highest human potential in the social or moral realm. This is the distinction between "theoria" and "praxis," and Aristotle seems to say that theoria is the higher goal for man.

We can see that by the end of Plato and Aristotle's time, western intellectual thought had developed a twofold bifurcation: the distinction between Reality and the sensible world, and the distinction between theory and practice. In each case, there is an implied value judgment in favor of the former, but for neither philosopher was attainment of highest knowledge readily possible for man. Very few people could truly know the Forms, said Plato; and the life of pure theoria was not possible for man, said Aristotle. Hence, the search for knowledge in its true form was frustrating.

Western intellectual thought, and the philosophy of education with it, thus inherited a problem of the separation between:

Knowing Mind ←——————————→ Knowable Mind
    (subject)   (object)

The object of knowledge may be a substance like the Forms, for Plato; or a process like theoria, for Aristotle. The problem of epistemology and therefore education, becomes: how do we get the knowing mind in touch with its object of knowledge, the world?

The answers to this question fell into two major categories. The Rationalists in the 16th century led by Descartes in France, thought we could only know with certainty those things which we knew through Reason or thinking alone. This meant logic and mathematics were knowable but the sensible world which we know through our senses was suspect. 2+2=4 never changes, he thought, but sensual things do. The other epistemological school, led generally by the Scotsman Hume, said we could rely only on sense data, and that mental operations were only compilations and augmentations of what we gain through our senses. He thought, exactly contrary to Descartes, that knowledge gained through purely mental means was suspect, and it led to such unfounded hypotheses as "God." All knowledge must be based on what is empirically available to our senses. The debate between empiricism and rationalism is the most basic epistemological debate in philosophy, and depending where you stand on this issue, radically influences how you would think education is effectively conducted, and what its proper subjects are.

Let's examine for a minute the problems which would follow from adhering to either a strict rationalism or a strict empiricism. If we believe with Descartes that the information we gain through our senses is unreliable because it is sometimes misleading, then the only knowledge we can have reliably is that gained from using reason only. That limits us to abstract areas such as math and logic and theoretical subjects. We could not even have certain knowledge of our own bodies, as, after all, amputees often "feel" their non-existent limbs. While the knowledge we **can** have may be objectively true, it is not very useful for functioning in this human world. If we can't trust our senses, how could we ever check our knowledge of the external world, or of each other? If I perceive that an object in a dim light is a dark blue, and I want to confirm it so I ask you, the confirmation means little more than my original sense impression. The reason is that if I can't trust my senses, then I can't trust my ears to hear you correctly any more than I can trust my eyes to correctly see the blue. If our senses are unreliable, then checking like this is like buying another copy of the same newspaper to confirm a story. Hence, the predicament which follows from a strict rationalist epistemology is that each individual consciousness is forever locked into itself with no way to verify that the external world (and that includes other people) is really there. Knowledge is limited to fairly useless abstractions.

If, on the other hand, we believe with Hume that knowledge comes from empirical sense data, and all knowledge must be traced back to its empirical evidence for validation, then the mind and what it can know is severely limited in another direction. Hume says we cannot legitimately draw conclusions on the basis of sense data which are not themselves directly evidenced. "God" is not the only concept which immediately goes out the window as unfounded. "Causation" is another one. Hume points out that while we may be able to see billiard ball #1 hit billiard ball #2, and then we see billiard ball #2 move, we never in fact **see** the sensual impression which is "cause." All we **know** is that ball #2 always moves when ball #1 hits it (if ball #2 is not impeded) because that is all we **see**. When we jump to the conclusion that ball #1 **caused** ball #2 to move and from there to the conclusion that causation is an explanation of relationship between events, this is an unfounded mental move. "Causation" is merely mental construct which is made on the basis of habit, not because there is legitimate evidence for the idea. Hence for the empiricists, our knowledge is grossly limited to what Hume called the "blooming, buzzing confusion" of sensual impressions, and any inferences to what causes them or relates them to each other are baseless. We may know our own sense impressions, but we cannot know what it is out there that "causes" them, or orders them.

Before returning to the implications of all this for

education, one more step in the history of epistemology must be discussed. This step is how the German philosopher Kant, in 1787, resolved the rationalist/empiricist debate. Reading Descartes and Hume, Kant saw an impasse. He realized that if we assume that the world is orderly, as both Plato did with his Forms and Aristotle did with his growth model, and if we assume that to gain knowledge of this order the human mind must in some way find and match that objective order, then there was no way we could ever have knowledge. We would have to be outside our own minds to see if what we thought was right about the world was in fact the way the world was.

So Kant saw that the basic approach of expecting the mind to match the world was an impossible premise: it made knowledge impossible. He revolutionized the whole field by supposing instead that the source of order is not in the external world but in the human mind. That is, we order our world in the very process of perceiving it. We cannot use what we perceive unless it is ordered according to certain categories, e.g. space, time, and causation. Kant hypothesized that because of the structure of the human mind we would never receive experience except as already organized by our active, structuring minds. For all we know, the "objective" world may be Hume's "blooming, buzzing confusion" but by the time it is available to us, it is not confused. The point is that any notion of what the objective world is like is of no interest to us and should not be taken as a goal of human knowledge because there is absolutely no way we can get in touch with it. We would have to be gods or at least some consciousness other than humans to see it. The only "objectivity" we can have is knowing that humans all order experience in some of the basic same ways because our minds have the basic same structure. Hence, according to Kant, I cannot imagine experience outside of time and space, and I can count on your not being able to either.

By seeing the mind as the active source of order, rather than some objective unchanging Reality as the order, Kant attempted to solve the problem of certainty. Certainty, Reality, objectivity, etc., all have less rigorous meanings, in a sense. They are reality-for-us, or objectivity-for-us, but that is good enough.

Thanks to Kant, western thought got beyond this epistemological impasse. (There are lots of problems with Kant's work, but those are other issues.) His theory provides room for both reason and experience to function, and gets us out of the disastrous problem of how to get in touch with that which we want to know.

Years later the American, John Dewey (1859-1952) picked up the debate. We can say that he accepted Kant in that the mind is an active, ordering principle, and in that he accepted the world as we experience it rather than seeking some other Reality.

Dewey noted that not only theoretical problems followed from the split between Reality and the sensible world, and from the split between theoria and praxis, but problems of immediate human concern arose because of them also. One problem was that the emphasis on the intellectual or cognitive side of man (especially noted in Aristotle) alienated man from his immediate environment, and also from his emotional, affective self. The emphasis of the rationalists is overly cerebral. Dewey noted that the unavoidable concerns of human beings are not with some abstract and unattainable Reality, but with prosperity and adversity, success and failure, achievement and frustration, good and bad. In other words, humans are more concerned with questions of value than questions of Reality, and any adequate epistemological and educational theory ought to be geared toward knowing values, rather than toward theoretical abstractions.

Dewey saw that the need to achieve **certainty** led western thought to theoretical constructs like that of Plato and Descartes, or to the epistemological impoverishment of Hume. Dewey saw clearly enough to see that the goal of certainty must be rejected as a starting point. Man is first and foremost an active and emotive being, said Dewey, and reflection and concern with knowing is secondary learned behavior. Furthermore, it is learned primarily as a result of uncertain or problematic situations.

Therefore, said Dewey, the metaphysical starting point should not be an abstraction, but experience itself: philosophy should investigate life as humans experience it, not as it might be. We find ourselves in continual transaction with the physical, psychological, mental, spiritual world, and philosophy should be a **systematic investigation into the nature of this experience.** Dewey's systematic investigation led him to see that experience is subject to a pattern: first, it has an immediate, felt, aesthetic quality. Experience is not, at first, reflective, and is not at first replete with the distinctions which reflection bestows upon it. Then, the distinctive qualities **evolve** from the indeterminate, inchoate; and experience **becomes** determinate and meaningful. Finally, experience is often felt to have a consummation, or what might be now called a closure. Dewey saw that the enemy of experience in this sense is not the intellect but the extremes of diffusion or rigidity, either of which would preclude the movement from the felt aesthetic immediacy to reflective meaningfulness. Human life, concluded Dewey, as felt, is a rhythmic movement from events of doubt and conflict to events of integrity and harmony. When humans face the world and want to know about it, the goal is not to find Reality, but to change the problematic to the integrated and consummated.

Starting with this notion of experience as the metaphysical category of what is, changes in epistemology followed. Gaining knowledge was the process of making determinate the indeterminate experience, and the method was the scientific method. The steps are:

1. We find ourselves in a "felt difficulty" and this is the condition for inquiry.

2. We articulate the problem for solution.

3. We form a hypothesis for solution, and deduce the consequences of alternative solutions.

3. We form a hypothesis for solution, and deduce the consequences of alternative solutions.

4. We test the hypothesis: we confirm or disconfirm.

5. We have knowledge: that which is warranted through inquiry, and it becomes incorporated as background for further inquiry.

Hence, "Reality" is not that which matches some abstract objective level of being, but that which gives meaning to inquiry, and that which is repeatedly meaningful in inquiry and experience. This method of inquiry is self-correcting, because if something is incorrect, it will make experience meaningless, not meaningful, and will be found out.

And   "Truth" is not some abstract, objective reality, but rather "that which works" or "that which explains." Knowledge is primarily instrumental for action, not an end-in-itself.

And   "Reason" is not an intuitive light which puts men in touch with certainty and truth, but rather it is a disposition of conduct to foresee consequences of events, and to use what is foreseen in planning and conducting one's affairs.

And   "Mind" refers to an instrumental method of directing change.

For Dewey, the point is to intentionally **use** experience in its dynamic form to divest experience of its indefinite and unintelligible nature, and to bring about consummations in life. The point is to make experience usable.

The difference that Dewey made in metaphysics was to start with experienced world as reality and not to assume some objective Reality which would require God's vision to see. The difference that follows from this for epistemology is that the knowing tools we have, including pure reason and including empirical data from our senses, are both legitimate tools for knowing our world and functioning intelligently in it. The goal of learning is to know about the world as we experience it, and both theory and practice are components in the scientific method for achieving this knowledge.

All of this, which is Dewey's metaphysical and epistemological starting point in experience **as felt**, rather than as objective, leads to a very clear philosophy of education which is, I think, the foundation of what most people call experiential education. In Dewey's philosophy of education, the goal of education is not the right answer, for that might change. The goal is being able to understand and use our experience, and this is achieved by developing the thought processes with which we examine our experience. In this model, the teacher aids the student in developing an approach to his own experience by structuring the student's experience so that he may move from a challenge to a resolution. The educational process is based on the human experience of movement from difficulty to resolution. After resolution comes reflection on the movement so that what is learned may be generalized and used again.

Early in this article I said that the assumptions of experiential education are more reliable than those underlying more traditional theories. By "more reliable" I meant more helpful in understanding our world, and why I conclude this is by now, I hope, clear. In E.E., the learner-involved-in-immediate-experience is the object of knowledge, and the activity in, and reflection on that involvement are the means of knowing. E.E. attempts to blur the distinction between cognitive and affective learning because experience does not come distinguished this way and is not lived this way.

The paradigm of E.E., which I encountered in a model designed by Laura Joplin, has the following elements: challenge, support, "feedback," and "debrief." Dewey's theory of experience begins with a challenge; the "felt difficulty" which must be resolved. It includes support and "feedback" in that the attempts at resolution either work or don't work; they help in making meaning or they increase confusion. For Dewey, "debriefing" consists of reflection on the now-resolved difficulty, and is the process of integrating what was learned in a way which makes future experiences more intelligible.

Experiential educators may or may not be familiar

with Dewey, or with Einstein, Heisenberg, Godel and other thinkers whose hypotheses imply how misconceived is an educational process which aims at objectivity. What they do recognize is that education which teaches tools which can be used regardless of whatever is currently called truth is the more lasting accomplishment. The assumptions of this orientation better fit the world as we know it, and would appear to still fit as that changes.

In looking at E.E. in this way I was able to see that it is not unfounded, nor is it anti-intellectual as some critics charge and as some practitioners hope. The philosophy and practice of E.E. is a development which has a heritage, regardless of whether its advocates know, acknowledge, or value it. On the basis of this examination, one is able to see that E.E. "teachers" are subject to a misconception which faced the Sophists even 2,000 years ago: they thought they knew the truth, and that therefore people should behave accordingly.

April Crosby, Ph.D. is a professor of philosophy at Loretto Heights College in Denver, Colorado.

DEWEY'S PHILOSOPHICAL METHOD AND ITS INFLUENCE ON HIS PHILOSOPHY OF EDUCATION

Although Dewey's educational practices are well known by educators, it must not be forgotten that Dewey was also a technical philosopher. This paper attempts to bridge the gap between Dewey the technical philosopher and Dewey the educator.

by Jasper Hunt, Jr.

INTRODUCTION

The thesis of this paper is that John Dewey developed a philosophical method and that his philosophy of education presupposes this method. I want to show that; given his way of doing philosophy, it would have been impossible for Dewey to have espoused any other philosophy of education than the one he developed.

The paper will proceed by first outlining Dewey's method of philosophy. This will be done by focusing in on two fundamental ideas of his entire philosophy. These are Dewey's attack on any form of philosophical dualism and his category of experience. The final section of the paper will show how Dewey's philosophy of education comes directly from his basic philosophical method.

ATTACK ON DUALISM

As a young graduate student of philosophy at Johns Hopkins University between 1882-1884, Dewey was confronted by a philosophical corpus that seemed to draw its very lifeblood from philosophical dualism.

In epistemology the lines were drawn between the rationalists and the empiricists. On the American philosophical scene this contrast was made evident to Dewey by the diverse views of Chauncy Wright and Charles Peirce. Although both Wright and Peirce were empirical in their methods, they reached different positions, with Wright maintaining a rigid empiricism and Peirce becoming, eventually, more of a rationalist. Dewey was also confronted by William James, who termed himself a radical empiricist but who sought at the same time to defend religious sources of knowledge.

In metaphysics the battle lines were well established between the materialists and the idealists. On the one hand, Dewey was confronted by the philosophy of Ralph Waldo Emerson, who explicitly advocated an idealistic view of metaphysics. Dewey was also familiar with the work of Auguste Comte and his resulting rejection of metaphysics and adoptation of materialism. Dewey quotes Bertrand Russell as an example of the attempt to create dualisms in metaphysics. Russell says that mathematics, "finds a habitation eternally standing, where our ideals are fully satisfied and our best hopes are not thwarted."[1]

It should be pointed out here that Dewey was himself a metaphysical idealist as a young man. Morton White points out that Dewey turned towards Hegelian idealism as a reaction against British empiricism.[2] Indeed, Paul Conkin says that, "Dewey had learned to hate the atomistic sensationalism of British empiricism."[3] But Dewey's exposure to the scientific thought of Chauncy Wright and Charles Peirce led him away from the dominant influence of idealism.

The ultimate dualism Dewey fought was the separation of the human from the natural. Dewey saw this separation as having disastrous results both in epistemology and in metaphysics. In epistemology it resulted in either an empirical skepticism, which said that all man could know truly was his own sensations, or else a rigid scientism, which said that all man could know was the phenomenal world.

In metaphysics dualism resulted in either a denigration of the world of being, in favor of the world of becoming, or the opposite. Dewey's main concern was that these dualisms resulted in an ontological fragmentation, that is a fragmentation of being, with negative results in practical affairs. Dewey refers to the opposites in metaphysics as either total objectivism or else total subjectivism. He was critical of both as evidenced by the following quote: "But philosophical dualism is but a formulated recognition of an impasse in life; an impotence in interaction, inability to make effective transition, limitation of power to regulate and thereby to understand. Capricious pragmatism based on exaltation of personal desire; consolatory estheticism based on capacity for wringing contemplative enjoyment from even the tragedies of the outward spectacle; refugee idealism based on rendering thought omnipotent in the degree in which it is ineffective in concrete affairs; these forms of subjectivisim register an acceptance of whatever obstacles at the time prevent the active participation of the self in the ongoing course of events."[4] This quote shows the stress Dewey laid on the practically bad results of such philosophical dualism as subjectivism or objectivism. Indeed dualism, says Dewey, renders man "impotent."

Dewey refers to philosophical dualism by means of a technical term. He calls the attempt to create dualisms both in epistemology and metaphysics the "fallacy of selective emphasis."[5] This fallacy consists in the efforts of philosophers to take a particular aspect of knowledge or reality and to universalize it to a superior status of reality or knowledge. Dewey illustrates the fallacy of selective emphasis by entering into the metaphysical conflict between being and becoming. Dewey refers to the "precarious" and "stable" aspects of existence.[6] He argues that ever since the days of Heraclitus and Parmenides, metaphysics has tended to focus in on either the world of the precarious or else of the stable at the expense of the reality of the other. Dewey rejects the idea that the world is either in a state of total flux or of total being. The fallacy of selective emphasis is also seen in epistemology by the old conflict between rational and empirical sources of knowledge. He refers to both epistemological systems as falling under the heading of the fallacy of selective emphasis.

THE CATEGORY OF EXPERIENCE

Dewey was not content to simply criticize the prevailing tendency of philosophy to fall into the fallacy of selective emphasis and thereby create dualisms. Dewey saw his major philosophical task as dealing with this fundamental issue and, hopefully, solving it. Dewey does not attempt to solve the problems of dualism by entering into the old dialectical arguments directly. Indeed, he rejects the attempt to enter directly into the conflicts outlined above both in epistemology and in metaphysics. He says, "I know of no route by which dialectical argument can answer such objections. They arise from associations with words and cannot be dealt with argumentatively."[7]

Dewey's resolution to these problems rests in his analysis of experience. The word "experience" is a technical term for Dewey and contains within it the seeds of his entire philosophy. Evidence for this claim can be seen simply be reading the titles of three of his most influential works. These are *Art as Experience, Experience and Nature* and *Experience and Education.*

It is with the category of experience that Dewey enters directly into the conflicts which he inherited philosophically. Dewey terms the method of basing philosophical inquiry upon experience as "empirical naturalism."[8] The empirical naturalist is attempting to make a bridge between the human and the natural, the rational and the empirical, and the material and the idealistic. Dewey wants empirical naturalism to render the old philosophical dualisms obsolete, rather than refute them directly. He simply abandons these terms and approaches philosophy from a new perspective — the perspective of experience.

It is at this point that a critical aspect of Dewey's philosophical method comes into play. In his analysis of experience as the base for philosophical method, Dewey distinguishes between two different but interconnected aspects of all experience. These are the "primary" and "secondary" parts of all experience. These two terms serve as the base by which Dewey later reconciles the dualisms in epistemology and metaphysics. It will also play a pivotal role in his philosophy of education.

Primary experience for Dewey refers to the immediate, tangible, and moving world which presents itself to the senses. Dewey refers to primary experience as "gross, macroscopic, crude."[9] When British empiricism refers to sensation as the basis for all knowledge, they are referring to the primary aspect of experience. Primary experience provides the raw materials from which knowledge can begin. When Dewey refers to his method as empirical naturalism, we see the primary aspect of experience at work. His method begins with the world of primary experience. It is explicitly empirical in its method in that it has as its starting point the world presented to the senses. But Dewey goes on to explain that primary experience is essentially "non cognitive."[10] Primary experience is the starting point in his method but it is not the end point. It is not the stopping point because of its non-cognitive nature. Dewey does begin his entire method on the empirical immediacy presented to man.

Secondary experience (also called reflective exerience) for Dewey refers to what happens after a primary experience is had. Reflective experience takes the "gross, macroscopic, and crude" materials furnished by primary experience and seeks to make it precise, microscopic, and refined. The work of reflective experience is to take the data provided by primary experience and order and arrange it. In effect reflective experience is that part of all experience which temporarily removes itself from the immediacy of empiricism. Secondary experiences, says Dewey, "**explain** the primary objects, they enable us to grasp them with **understanding**, instead of just having sense contact with them.[11]

Dewey illustrates the distinction between primary and secondary experience by looking at the work of the modern scientist. The scientist does not have a series of disconnected sensory experiences. He does not sit and stare steadily at his instruments. In short, the scientist does not rest content with primary experience. The scientist takes the data derived from primary experience and reflects upon it. He removes himself from the immediacy of primary experience and reflects upon the information conveyed by the primary experience. The ultimate goal of the secondary experience in science is to take the data and reflect upon it in such a way as to be able to make predictive statements about future experiences in the form of the hypothesis.

The category of experience in empirical naturalism seeks to unite the primary and the secondary into a single unity. As Dewey says, "What empirical method expects of philosophy is two things: First, that refined methods and products be traced back to their origins in primary experience, in all of its heterogeneity and fullness; so that the needs and problems out of which they arise and which they have to satisfy be acknowledged. Secondly, that the secondary methods and conclusions be brought back to the things of ordinary experience, in all of their coarseness and crudity, for verificaiton."[12]

In the opening section of this paper I argued that the foundation of Dewey's method rested upon his rejection of philosophical dualism and his adaptation of experience as the base for empirical naturalism. I also pointed out that this method had implications both in epistemology and in metaphysics. In epistemology I contrasted the positions of Chauncy Wright and Charles Peirce as immediate precursors of Dewey. Extrapolating from Dewey, we can see how both the fallacy of selective emphasis and the category of experience attempt an answer to the empiricism versus rationalism dialectic. In the primary aspect of experience we see Dewey adopting empiricism and its method of basing knowledge on the senses and on the data provided by the senses. In the idea of reflective experience we see Dewey making room for the method of rationalism. The fallacy of selective emphasis refuses to focus exclusively upon the primary aspect of knowledge. It also refuses to focus exclusively upon the reflective, or

rational, nature of knowledge. In short, by beginning from experience in the first place Dewey avoids the dualisms, while at the same time allowing for the combined roles of empirical and rational knowledge.

There are obvious metaphysical implications in Dewey's epistemological method. I contrasted Ralph Waldo Emerson with Auguste Comte as representing idealism and materialism in the opening section of this paper. Dewey refers to metaphysics "as a statement of the generic traits manifested by existence of all kinds without regard to their differentiation into physical and mental."[13] Later, Dewey also says of metaphysics that "Qualitative individuality and constant relations, contingency and need, movement and arrest are common traits of all existence."[14] The point to be gained here is that metaphysics for Dewey is **not** an attempt to discover some aspect of being, either materialistic or idealistic, and then elevate that aspect to a status of the really real at the expense of the other aspects of reality. Dewey sides neither with Emerson nor with Comte in this matter. Rather, his answer to the really real question rests in his notion of the "generic traits manifested by existence" lying **within** experience. Again, the fallacy of selective emphasis comes into play and saves Dewey from metaphysical dualism. By beginning from experience as the basis for metaphysics, Dewey allows for the reality of both the material and the ideal as "generic" traits within experience. What is ultimately real for Dewey is experience.

PHILOSOPHY OF EDUCATION

Richard Bernstein has argued that the heart of Dewey's philosophical endeavor is to be found in his philosophy of education. Bernstein says that according to Dewey, "All philosophy can be conceived of as the philosophy of education."[15] In keeping with the thesis of this paper that Dewey's philosophy of education presupposes his philosophical method, outlined above; I want to show how the method gives rise to his educational position.

Dewey's attack on dualism in philosophy in general can be seen clearly in his philosophy of education. The opening two sentences in *Experience and Education* make this evident: "Mankind likes to think in terms of extreme opposites. It is given to formulating its beliefs in terms of Either-Ors, between which it recognizes no intermediate possibilities."[16] Dewey connects the epistemological dualism of empiricism and rationalism to educational problems. He says, "Upon the philosophical side, these various dualisms culminate in a sharp demarcation of individual minds from the world, and hence from one another. While the connection of this philosophical position with educational procedure is not so obvious as is that of the points considered in the last three chapters, there are certain educational considerations which correspond to it."[17] On the one hand Dewey was confronted by an educational philosophy that emphasized a purely rationalistic approach to learning. This school maintained that the main goal of education was to inculcate into students the received ideas and facts of the past.[18] This method of education laid great stress on the ability of the student to sit passively and to commit ideas to memory. It tended to devalue initiative and rewarded obedience and docility. Dewey contends that a philosophy of education which is based upon a purely rationalistic epistemology, necessarily presupposes a separation of the mind from the external world. This method saw the goal of education as purely cognitive and not connected or involved with the environment in which mind existed.[19] Methodologically we see the rationalistic school of education taking the secondary, or reflective, aspect of experience and elevating it to an idolatrous position. That is, reflective experience was pursued in and for itself at the expense of primary, or empirical, experience.

We can see that the opposite educational philosophy drawing from Dewey's method would be to elevate the primary aspect of experience to the sole end of education. This would involve taking the purely empirical element in experience and neglecting the reflective element. One of the most common criticisms of the so called "progressive" education derived from Dewey, was, and is, that in reacting against the rationalistic elements so dominant in education, the progressives neglected the role of the reflective. Dewey himself explicitly rejects any idea that education should swing from a purely reflective, rationalistic position to a purely empirical, non-reflective mode.[20] Here he is being consistent with his fallacy of selective emphasis in avoiding creating any dualism in his reaction to the educational system he inherited.

Dewey's answer to educational dualism is drawn directly from his philosophical method. Just as metaphysics and epistemology must begin from experience rather than from dialectical bifurcations, so too must education begin from experience. Dewey rejects any idea that education must be completely based upon primary experience or upon secondary experience. Education, according to Dewey, must be based upon experience, period, which involves both the primary and the secondary. In describing the central role of experience in education Dewey says, "For one has only to call to mind what is sometimes treated in schools as

aquisition of knowledge to realize how lacking it is in any fruitful connection with the ongoing experience of the students — how largely it seems to be believed that the mere appropriation of subject matter which happens to be in books contains knowledge. No matter how true what is learned to those who found it out and in whose experience it functioned, there is nothing which makes it knowledge to the pupils. It might as well be something about Mars or about some fanciful country unless it fructifies in the individual's own life."[21]

Dewey's rejection of philosophical dualism and his adaptation of experience as the basis of education gives rise to a central idea in his philosophy of education - the idea of the experiential continuum. Dewey argues that the opposite of dualism is continuity. The educational dualisms which Dewey rejects include such things as the separation of mind and body, authority and freedom, experience and knowledge, and dozens of others. Dewey criticizes all of these dualities because they result in a lack of continuity within experience. By his idea of the experiential continuum within educational experience, Dewey hopes to stop duality before it ever gets started.

Dewey illustrates the need for an experiential continuum in education by contrasting the ideas of authority and freedom in education. The old educational methods which Dewey inherited put almost complete stress upon authority in education. This stress upon authority in education stemmed directly from the presuppositions of rationalism. That is, the student was to learn the ideas of the past, which the teacher deemed important. This stress upon authority created a basic schizophrenia in education in a society which claimed to value freedom, democracy, self direction, and personal responsibility. Dewey argues that the result was that the actual experience of the student under the yoke of education was in no way similar to the basic values espoused by the surrounding culture. Therefore, there was no continuity in the experience of the pupil. What was expected in school was docility, passiveness, and submission to authority. What was expected in the "real world" was aggressiveness, self initiative, and a democratic response to authority.[22] Dewey argues that the ultimate goal of education is to make an experiential continuum where the **process** of education, that is **how** a student learns, is given equal footing with the **content** of education.[23]

Dewey wants to take the primary and reflective aspects of all experience and apply them to education. Dewey does not downplay the important role of subject matter, or reflective experience, in education (as superficial critics have claimed). He does want to get away from the obsessive preoccupation of traditional education with secondary experience. Just as Dewey looks to the work of the modern scientist as an example of his basic philosophical method, so too does he look at the education of the scientist as an example for his views on education. Dewey argues that the old methods of education are incompatible with the education of a good experimental scientist. For Dewey sees the good scientist as having cultivated a keen ability at questioning the world around him, rather than simply committing it to memory. I argued in the philosophical method section of this paper that the ultimate goal of knowledge for the scientist was the formulation of the hypothesis as predictive of future experiences. It can be seen here, drawing from the basic method, that education must stress other ideals than the old methods did in order to produce a good scientist. These ideals must include freedom, inquisitiveness, and experiential continuity, as well as the received materials from the past.

SUMMARY AND CONCLUSION

The goal of this paper was to outline Dewey's basic philosophical method, and then to connect it with his philosophy of education. The basic philosophical method was outlined starting with Dewey's rejection of metaphysical and epistemological dualism and his adaptation of experience as the starting point for all philosophy. Two other technical terms in Dewey were introduced — the fallacy of selective emphasis, and the primary and secondary aspects of experience. The paper then connected Dewey's philosophy of education with his basic philosophical method. This was done by showing Dewey's rejection of traditional education's obsession with the secondary aspect of experience and the resulting stress upon docility and passivity in the educational process. Dewey's discussion of freedom versus authority in education was used to illustrate the effects of dualism in education. Finally, the important role of Dewey's idea of continuity in education was illustrated using both the freedom-authority example and the training of the experimental scientist.

In conclusion I want to argue that Dewey offers a coherent and sensible pedagogical theory. I will argue that Dewey's educational philosophy is as relevant today as it was in 1920. Dewey offers a source of inspiration to future and present educators who are confronted by timid and reactionary educators screaming for "back to the basics" and the elevation of a rationalistic principle of education to a supreme status. Dewey also offers a strong warning to those who, in

their zeal for reform would neglect the role of content in the educational process. One only need look at some products of innovative education who are very much "in touch with their feeling" but who cannot write a coherent sentence.

Dewey demands of professional philosophy the highest standards of the application of his theory. For those of use in the field of educational philosophy, Dewey reminds us that philosophy is not an isolated discipline, disconnected from the issues of everyday life. I am here reminded of the modern professor of ethics who is an expert at doing ethical analysis using modal operators, but who is rendered speechless when asked by a pregnant student if it would be ethical for her to seek an abortion. He is also warning us about the other modern ethics professor who spends long hours in the demonstration picket lines in support of a cause, but who is scared to death when confronted by convincing arguments that he may be less than totally right in his convictions.

In short Dewey is demanding that philosophers and educators begin and end their work from the category of experience. As Dewey himself said, "I remarked incidentally that the philosophy in question is, to paraphrase the saying of Lincoln about democracy, one of education of, by, and for experience. Not one of these words, **of**, **by** or **for** names anything which is self evident. Each of them is a challenge to discover and put into operation a principle or order and organization which follows from understanding what educational experience signifies."[24]

Jasper Hunt, M.S. is a former Outward Bound wilderness instructor. He is currently a teaching assistant and Ph.D. aspirant at the University of Colorado, Boulder, in educational philosophy.

FOOTNOTES

[1] John Dewey, *Experience and Nature* (LaSalle, 1925) p. 51. Henceforth referred to as E.N.
[2] Morton White, *Science and Sentiment in America: Philosphical Thought from Jonathan Edwards to John Dewey.* (New York, 1972) pp. 269-273.
[3] Paul K. Conkin, *Puritans and Pragmatists: Eight Eminent American Thinkers.* (Bloomington, 1968) p.350.
[4] John Dewey, E.N. p. 198
[5] John Dewey, E.N. p. 24
[6] John Dewey, E.N. pp. 37-66
[7] John Dewey, E.N. p. 1
[8] John Dewey, E.N. p. 1
[9] John Dewey, E.N. p. 6
[10] John Dewey, E.N. p. 23
[11] John Dewey, E.N. p. 7
[12] John Dewey, E.N. p. 23
[13] John Dewey, E.N. p. 334
[14] John Dewey, E.N. p. 334
[15] Richard Bernstein, *John Dewey,* in *The Encyclopedia of Philosophy* (New York, 1967) pp. 383-384. Vol. 2
[16] John Dewey, *Experience and Education,* (New York, 1938) p. 17. Henceforth

referred to as E.E.
[17] John Dewey, *Democracy and Education.* (New York, 1926) p. 340. Henceforth referred to as D.E.
[18] John Dewey, E.E. p. 17
[19] John Dewey, D.E. p. 377
[20] John Dewey, E.E. pp. 20-21
[21] John Dewey, D.E. p. 389
[22] John Dewey, D.E. pp. 95-116
[23] John Dewey, E.E. p. 20
[24] John Dewey, E.E. p. 29

BIBLIOGRAPHY

1. *Puritans and Pragmatists: Eight Eminent American Thinkers.* Paul K. Conkin. Bloomington: Indiana University Press, 1968.

2. *Art As Experience.* John Dewey. New York: G.P. Putnam's Sons, 1934.

3. *Experience and Education.* John Dewey. New York: Collier Books, 1938.

4. *Experience and Nature.* John Dewey. LaSalle: The Open Court Publishing Company, 1929.

5. *Democracy and Education.* John Dewey. New York: The Macmillan Company, 1926.

6. *Pragmatism and the American Mind.* Morton White. New York: Oxford University Press, 1973.

7. *Science and Sentiment in America: Philosophical Thought from Jonathan Edwards to John Dewey.* Morton White. New York: Oxford University Press, 1972.

8. *The Encyclopedia of Philosophy:* Paul Edwards, Editor. Eight Volumes. New York: Macmillan Publishing Company, 1967.

9. *"Recent Philosophical Work on Dewey". In The Southern Journal of Philosophy.* Gary M. Brodsky. Memphis: Memphis State University Press, 1976.

10. *"Dewey's Enduring Vitality". In Human Studies.* Gary M. Brodsky. 1978.

WHAT MEANS THIS
Experience?

by Alan R. Drengson

There is a sharp contrast between the North Dakota steppes and the mountains of the Pacific Northwest. Some areas of North Dakota are flat for miles. The hills and valleys are gentle contours in a slightly rolled plain. The sky dominates the land, and terminates the reach of the ground in all directions on a low horizon.

In the mountains of the Northwest the horizon is often hidden by a circle of high jagged ridges. The sky is an almost insignificant background to the vertical thrust of rock, ice and snow.

If one's early years have been spent on the plains, viewing mountains for the first time can be a profoundly moving experience, filled with awe, wonder and mystery. Unless told, one would not know what one is seeing. Perceiving details and relationships is something that develops slowly in concert with cognition, but it eventually becomes an assumed background of one's experience.

One must slowly learn to *see* as well as see. After first impressions, the young person can learn to see a mountain, and recognize its various features, such

Alan Drengson *is a member of the philosophy department at the University of Victoria in British Columbia whose particular interest is applying philosophy to solving contemporary problems—and most particularly to solving environmental problems.*

as aretés, faces, buttresses, scree-slopes, glaciers and snow fields, cols, couloirs, etc.

My first experience of the mountains began when I was ten, and I still remember this vividly over thirty years later. As a result, I know I do not see the mountains as I did then. As recalled, that earlier experience

> "We cannot reach a mature understanding of the natural world without the process of experiential learning."

was primarily a matter of receiving impressions. It was simple seeing. It had a lack of clarity because the experience as a whole had very little organization and structure.

In the process of learning, experience itself becomes more coherent and integrated. What we know and believe interacts with and shapes our on-going experience. Future experience is conditioned by the original experience and everything that went on in between, such as the

accumulation of knowledge, the acquisition of new concepts, the grasping of relationships. We learn faster as we develop greater understanding, less time is spent trying to understand what we sense.

We live partly on the shoulders of our past experience, and partly under its control. With respect to seeing mountains, the original excitement can at times still be there, but the accumulated experience, the cognitive processes of conceptual organization, and the understanding of basic patterns of interrelationships, all these forever alter our perceptions. A different quality of experience has been born as a result. (My experience of the mountains today is not that of the first time at ten.)

In what follows I will reflect on what constitutes experience in relation to perceiving, knowing and understanding the mountains. The mountains (and plains) here will stand for environmental processes (the world), and experience will stand for all of the processes of experiential interaction and knowing. My aim is to chart the experiential mountains on the conceptual map, so that the levels of knowing interaction between self and mountains (world) (subject and object) become clear.

The primary purpose is to illuminate what is meant by, or constitutes experience, experiential learning and experiential knowing. What is experiential learning in relation to the environment and the self?

Experience: Conceptual Background

As Hume observed,[1] all knowledge begins with experience, but as Kant[2] was to add, it does not all arise out of, or even end with, experience. "Experience" for Hume meant primarily the reception of sense impressions, although he did recognize that experience in this way produced ideas (copies of impressions) which are ordered by means of principles of association and custom (habit).

The result of this twofold process is that we develop certain beliefs about the world, and we come to have certain expectations.

Now if this is all there is to our experience, we would be confined to knowledge that was based only on inductive processes, but we would never understand why things in our experience have a regularity and coherence that we do not get from sense impressions alone.

In addition, unity of self and the sense of continuity within personal identity implies that there is some transcendental ground for the order of this coherent, whole experience.

To grasp and understand significant interrelationships and their laws is to turn information into knowledge. As Kant saw, impressions might be copied and stored, but it is not an accidental, confused, or disorderly affair.

We proceed as if nature is uniform and as if we can with effort discover her laws. This discovery is part self-discovery and part discovery of settled patterns that make self-awareness itself possible.

To know ourselves we must know that which is not ourselves. We must distinguish ourselves from our background, both from nature, and from other groups. Eventually we must distinguish ourselves from the group to which we belong.

The spirit quest of the Amerinds had partly this function.[3] One found one's self in the natural world away from one's tribal relationships, then one returned to integrate onself with the community. Thereafter one's whole experience contained several ordering elements which were set in hierarchies of value and generality.

In the area of experiencing nature as object, as physics, Kant allowed that the basic forms of this experience (concepts) were themselves ordered systematically by means of general principles, that actually entered into the very constitution of our experience of the world of nature.[4]

Thus causality is not a concept we derive from simple impression: rather, it is one that we apply logically and consistently within and to sensory experience. The actual experience of seeing is in its original act (seeing the mountains for the first time at ten) already ordered and synthesized by some of the conceptual forms of order and organization that suits those impressions to the kind of beings we are. The principles of causal order are found uniformly in all humans.

But this level of experience of nature does not include moral laws, values and social ordering principles. All of these can be seen as organized around central, cultural themes, mythic story-lines, archetypal rituals, etc. As we said above, experience might begin with simple sense impressions, but it does not end there, not does it depend only on impressions. Experience is involved in all learning, but its intensity and clarity can vary considerably, its scope and coherence and one's resulting understanding undergo continuous development.

Even straight classroom reception of information involves experience, and can alter subsequent experience. Thus, we must find some way to mark the difference between experiential learning, when it is to be contrasted with this least experien-

tial form of (classroom) learning.

The classroom lecture then, restricted to conveyal of information, or perhaps just data, will stand as an example of one extreme of learning that is least experiential. The experiences of the mountain and wilderness travel will represent the other extreme.

In a strict sense, information does not become knowledge for us until we have "made it our own . . ." until, that is, we interact with it, relate it to what we already know, integrate it with our insights, and apply it. Then, to the fullest extent possible, this knowledge becomes part of our on-going experience.

In a wilderness journey one is forced to interact directly with the elements of the natural environment. One comes to know a mountain (environment) not from books or second-hand experience, but through direct sensing of the mountain. One's accumulating perceptions of the mountain present it in all different guises, through the day and night, over the years and seasons, in different weather. One could study the mountain (environment) on maps, in books, and through pictures, but one would not know it as mountain, as significant other, until one has been on it, in it, over it, around it, with it.

This accumulated experience and knowledge can pave the way to a return to the original unity of seeing of the mountain for the first time. But it will differ from the original in that the seeing has deepened and broadened, and one can be unified with the mountain, and not just be absorbed in one's impressions of it, as one might have been as a child.

In the child, subject and object have not clearly differentiated; in the young adult, and for most of us, they have separated into subject and object; in full maturity, it becomes clear that these boundaries can be transcended to know the mountain directly in subject-object interrelationships.[5]

At this highest level of seeing there is once again subject-object unity, but it is transpersonal and not merely prepersonal. We will unravel these strands of whole experience by means of ways of knowing and its elements.

"Significant experience is not sense-impression alone. As an on-going contact with reality, it provides a constant source of values and understanding."

Listening passively to a lecture is experience, and something learned from it can alter subsequent experience. After hearing one's philosophy teacher expound and critique natural theology's proofs for the existence of God, one might never again be able to see theology in the same way.

Before, theology might have been seen as a closed system of rational demonstration. Ever after, it might be seen as something other than an exposition of God's geometric rationality. It might now be seen to be about the mystery of worship, and how humans can come to approach most closely the reality (that is God).

What is this ultimate reality, and how do we come to know it?" If this becomes one's question asked seriously, one's life must be different.

On the other hand, wilderness travel alters one's (practical) approach and not just one's seeing. If one learns in the classroom the concepts of ecology, biospheric processes, and the laws

of entropy, one's "seeing" of the world is altered. One's experience changes by experience with the world in application of what has been learned.

In the case of wilderness travel one applies what one has learned (concepts, laws, etc.) to the environment through one's personal experience. These concepts had pure form before, or were vaguely given content, but they become useable tools only when they can be applied to the content they help to organize. The direct visual, auditory, olfactory and other sensory-cognitive elements are engaged cludes a perception that might be called trans-conceptual rather than conceptual or preconceptual. It is not bound by concepts, but it uses them as a means to get in direct contact with the world.

Thus it might be said to be post-conceptual. It is the knowing of the mountain (reality) directly by an intuitive process that contacts the immediate presence of this mountain (world), and perceives both the difference and unity between self and mountain (world). One is immediately aware of this and the boundaries between one's

But in our two pure cases, the ten year old has precognitive sense impressions of the mountains, the young classroom person who has never seen them, but has learned of them conceptually, has first impressions that are cognitively and conceptually conditioned and mediated.

In going on a wilderness journey this young person learns to apply the learned concepts directly to the mountains. They mediate his/her experiences of the mountains, give it structure, extend his/her concepts and mind to the sensory field, and eventually enable grasp of the relationships, patterns and features that characterize the mountains for a human consciousness.

This on-site experience is what we normally think of as experiential learning, for it involves active doing, and it is this that makes one's concepts one's own; it completes one's knowing through them.

This process of experiential learning might eventually lead the way to a direct, whole perception of the mountains that is immediate in both mind and sense as details in unity. All of one's sensing and cognizing capacities are unified with the mountains (world) in this case. Here all former beliefs and conceptual networks are seen as devices for bringing us into touch with the world (the mountains) at a higher level of awareness. This involves the subject-object opposition transcended, rather than a sinking into pre-conceptual oblivion.

It involves a mastery that is able to use or not use various conceptual tools without becoming attached to them.

In sum, these ways of knowing and experiencing the mountains can be described as follows. There is first the original, vague, preconceptual sense-impression of the mountains. There is the learning of concepts and conceptual systems, general principles and the like. Then there is application of these concepts (cognitive forms) to the mountains

---

"Experiential learning is a holistic process, where conceptual, linguistic and perceptual elements are blended with direct impressions of the environment."

---

with the world. Physically applying these learned conceptual and other skills with the whole body-mind to the other, the object, sets feedback processes in motion.

One eventually begins to understand that the neat conceptual-theoretic models by means of which one learned, were too sharp, and one's conception of the actual Being of mountains (world-environment) was too vague.

However, seeing the mountains for the first time at ten is vague as well, even though it is vivid experience. It is vague not because the impressions are dull, but because one's understanding of relationships and features is not formed; one is lost in details, awe-struck in the total scene.

The ultimate seeing of the mountains is not either of these, however. It involves all of these prior experiences, but it also in-

responses, while aware of the patterns of the other. One's concepts, which initially mediated the mountains in experience, now form a transparent foreground that disappears as the experience intensifies.[7] In the wilderness silence, this direct (intuitional) knowing becomes known.

The elements clearly recognizable in the spectrum described above are the following. Initially there are sense impressions of the mountains. This is the situation of the ten year old who sees the mountains for the first time, with no preconceptions, no prior beliefs about them. Then there is seeing them after one has acquired concepts of them, as a young person in the classroom. There is also the intermediate case of one who grows up with mountains who also acquires concepts in concert with sense impressions.

(world) by means of activity in them involving such things as problem solving, etc.

Finally, through all of these processes it is possible to reach direct awareness of the being of the mountains. In this the concepts become transparent. They are seen through, rather than being clouds which partially hide and reveal the mountains. The experiential interaction of sensory and cognitive elements with the mountains matures our learning to completion as experiential knowing. Our concepts are valuable at least to the extent to which they facilitate this knowing. The ways of knowing mentioned so far can now be ordered more carefully.[8] We will do this by means of using Spinoza's "ways of knowing."[9]

The Ways of Knowing

Spinoza noted that there are four basic ways of knowing: 1. by vague experience; 2. by signs (reading and conversation); 3. by means of universal notions (concepts) and common notions (axioms and scientific laws); and, 4. by means of intuitive understanding.

All of these ways of knowing have been described in the examples above. These forms of knowing are part of our total experience (as adults). Experientially learning the mountains as environment involves all of these ways of knowing.

In the case of the fourth way of knowing, there is no vagueness left. What might have been theoretical at first is now a direct practical knowing. We might want to say that as we acquire information and concepts (2 & 3), vague sense experience is becoming less so, and it is taking on cognitive dimensions. As we learn language and acquire concepts from an early age, most of us carry on both processes simultaneously. As a result, our perceptions are early formed by imprecise words, opinions and beliefs.

Spinoza thought that most of us have only vague experience, even with cognitive elements, for most of us give little attention to the discipline necessary to acquire real knowledge (which requires the fourth way of knowing).

If we become reflective, and make learning a discipline, then we begin to apply the mind to clarifying its concepts and more precisely stating these in our

use of words. Further, by means of learning to see the patterns of movement and change in the world (mountains), we begin to understand the principles of movement, and as a consequence experience begins to lose its vagueness in the development of discursive knowledge. This necessarily involves a process of active involvement.

Experiential learning is this holistic process, where conceptual, linguistic and perceptual elements are blended with direct impressions of the mountain (environment), while we are active there in a practical way: solving problems, getting lost and found, listening to the silence, attending to the sky, catching the nuances of colour in the sunrise, smelling the fleeting odor of dying fir, hearing the lush stillness of a rain forest broken by a wren's song. If we are fortunate, our journeys to the mountain wilderness might culminate in the fourth way of knowing.

The fourth way of knowing involves conceptual mastery but non-attachment to concepts and views. In vague experience (at the outset), imagination plays a role and concepts begin to mediate experience. With the fourth way of knowing, knowledge is not mediated, but it is rather a direct and active understanding. One is alert *and* relaxed, receiving impressions, but one is also actively involved in knowing as an immediate, aware, intelligent, perceptive act.

This fourth way of knowing is active insight-awareness, and it is only through it that we can come to know Being directly. To know intuitively in this way is to know the object directly as a subject, as it is in and for itself, its essence, and not merely our concepts of it. One also knows in this direct, non-mediated way, as an essential, vital presence, not as history and belief as through a self-image.

All but the fourth way of knowing Spinoza regarded as knowing "as if through a cloud." They are forms of mediated knowing which are incomplete without the fourth way. Information, sense impressions, propositions, models, theories, etc., can be stored in books and computers. They can be conveyed by means of a medium (language, e.g.); clearly they are not the mountains in reality. They are a way to help us to see the mountains in new ways, which can facilitate learning to understand what we see, while we see it. What we see takes on meaning, as we try to apply these elements to what we see; thus we learn their usefulness and limits. We also learn the extent of our own ignorance.

Through this process we approach that which we seek, knowledge and understanding of the mountains (world, environment) with ourselves as part of what is immediately known or directly understood. Our theories and concepts are meant to put us in touch with the world. They help to develop our capacity for insight.

Insight-awareness is difficult to reach and to maintain. This direct understanding is an intelligent awareness that is aware of its awareness in a unity with that which it knows (self-knower and other-known). By means of the fourth way we are able to transcend these particular conceptual maps; we are able to reconceptualize at will, and also able to cease conceptualizing in

order to appreciate fully the Being of oneself and of the other.

This is an intense unity which Spinoza characterized as involving love and respect, for love and joy perfect our capacities for knowing. This direct knowing is therefore an affection that is love.[10]

Spinoza was a pantheist. For him, ultimately, the only nature is the divine reality of all that there is. However, all particular modes of this divine Being have their way and attempt to main-

vision in our experienced world, but at the fourth level this division between ourselves and the mountains is transcended. Then the mountains are known directly as they are in themselves.

This is a direct, experiential knowing, whereas all of the other ways of knowing are mediated and indirect. Experiential learning (and education) is the process of practical, active engagement with concepts and skills applied in the practical set-

---

"Experiential knowing is not a fixed body of knowledge, but a continuously modifying stream."

---

tain it. This is to be understood and respected as part of the divine.

To know the mountains (environment-world) and its life as divine modes of Being is to know free of fear and aggression, out of love and respect. With respect to the natural wilderness environment, knowing in the fourth way leaves the fears of "big bad wolves" behind, for wolves (as wild nature) can be understood in their way, as expressions of the divine nature, as modes of power and energy formed around the intrinsic values inherent in the wolf-form-of-life. (The actual wolf lives-a-divine-concept for itself.)

Knowing Mountains

If we are to know the mountains (the environment-world) in an objective way, we must know it directly on its own terms, and not as we think it must be, or as an object that threatens or challenges us to subdue it. In this way we come to know the mountains neither limited by fear, nor compelled by avarice.

Cultural beliefs and human chauvinistic attitudes create di-

ting, through physical and practical mental activity. If unapplied, theoretical, speculative, conceptual learning does not lead to experiential knowing.

We cannot understand the wolf (wild life) in the mountain wilderness by remaining aloof and apart from them, whether this be locked in our study, or locked in rigid concepts and faulty beliefs. Thus, the (wilderness) experiential process is as much a process of erosion of beliefs, as it is a deepening of knowledge. By this means we eventually reach the fourth way of knowing. The fourth way points beyond mere survival as our prime activity, to the possibility of living a fully human life based in an understanding that frees us of our bondage.

Life flourishes in love and joy (this is Spinoza's claim); it reaches its greatest authenticity and touches reality most completely, when we know in the fourth way by being in them. At this point, the mountains are no longer the unknowns of the child, nor the concepts of the classroom learner. They stand forth as a reality in which we participate and through which we understand.

Thus the culmination of experiential learning (and education) is that through it we come to know in this experiential way, as a fully alive, direct, on-going activity.

This is the ultimate raison d'être of all learning, for through it we become fully alive as knowing, valuable, valuing persons. In this completing activity persons are perfected as knowers of mountains (and the world as divine Nature).

We could not reach this mature understanding of the natural world without the process of experiential learning. This is its ultimate meaning.

Conclusion

Direct contact with the world (the mountains) is needed, if we are to compensate for the incompleteness of our "maps." This enables correction of errors and short-comings within accumulated, linguistically encoded beliefs.

This accumulated body of beliefs and information is passed to our children through classroom learning, and other means, but if they are to make this their own and correct it to knowing, they must apply it in the experiential process we have attempted to describe herein.

The difference between naive seeing (sensing) and experiential learning is that the latter includes cognitive, personal and cultural elements. At the fourth level these elements can be used appropriately, since there is direct experiential knowing as an unbroken, ongoing unity between knower and known.

"What means this experience?" What it means to us, its significance, is not just as sense-impression alone, but as an on-going contact with reality it provides a constant source of values and understanding. It is also the story of our lives in the rich symbolism of the journey of self into world and its return to its source.[11]

The mountains (environment-world) become more than sense impressions for us as we learn to see their features and inter-relationships. If we learn to know them in the fourth way, through experiential learning, then our vague experience becomes a clear, direct, perception of the mountains in all their on-going Being and mystery.

Experiential education releases energies of experiential learning which can in turn lead to experiential knowing of the world. Experiential knowing is not a fixed body of knowledge, but a continuously modifying stream of aware-knowing in relationships.

We come to understand the environment in no other way, but through this process which takes us from pre-conceptual impressions through conceptualization to trans-conceptual awareness. At this level the mountains (world) are not just the mountains for a western, human person. They are not just impressions, nor only concepts.

They are now only mountains, nothing more, nothing less. The mountains (world) and mountains (world) experienced become one in awareness. In this is the perfection of a life that flowers on the mountains, which rest upon the plain.

Footnotes

1. See David Hume's *Enquiry Concerning Human Understanding*, Selby-Bigge edition, (Oxford: Clarendon Press, 1975).
2. Immanual Kant, *Critique of Pure Reason*, Norman Kemp Smith, Trans., (London: MacMillan, 1963).
3. See Doug Boyd, *Rolling Thunder*, (New York: Delta Books, 1974); and, Richard Erdoes, *Tame Deer: Seeker of Visions*, (New York: Simon and Schuster, 1972).
4. *Ibid.*
5. For a more complete discussion and some slightly different accounts, see the following: Ken Wilber, *The Spectrum of Consciousness*, (Wheaton, Ill: Quest, 1977); and, K. Wilber, *Up From Eden*, (New York: Doubleday, 1981).

6. Here I take "God" to mean the same as "ultimate reality." That this ultimate exists, as Hume said, we cannot doubt. But what this U.R. is, we do not know. It is claimed by mystics that it can be "known" directly. It is said by many to be that which we seek to know (as in the Hindu-Vedic tradition).
7. Consider this in the case of learning a word. Hearing the word for the first time is experience. So too is learning its meaning through and by use. Mastery through practice implies fluency of use that is not consciously mediated by rules. The word becomes transparent in the fluency of masterful use.
8. Or, we could say the elements of whole experience as knowing include the following: Sense impressions, aesthetic and emotional response, cognitive forms, data, historical development, genetic information, principles of systematic analysis, principles of systems interrelationship, values, experiential feedback through application of all of these, direct trans-conceptual contact of self and other in dynamic, aware, knowing. These could each be further broken down. For reasons of simplicity I prefer Spinoza's shorter scheme.
9. Spinoza, *Ethics* (New York: Hafner, 1955). For an excellent, clear discussion of Spinoza's ways of knowing see, Paul Wienpahl, *The Radical Spinoza*, (New York: New York University Press, 1979). I have relied heavily on Wienpahl's book, and his interpretation is much influenced by his knowledge of Zen.
10. On knowing the world through love and respect see Doug Boyd's book on Rolling Thunder, Op. Cit. pp 51 ff. In spirit Rolling Thunder's outlook is very close to Spinoza's.
11. For a discussion of wilderness travel as an example of this story see, Alan R. Drengson, "Wilderness Travel as an Art and as a Paradigm for Outdoor Education," *Quest*, 32 (1), (1980), pp. 110-120.

WILLIAM JAMES, PHILOSOPHICAL FATHER OF EXPERIENCE-BASED EDUCATION
"The Knower is an Actor"

by GEORGE W. DONALDSON and RICHARD VINSON

A book published at the turn of the century provides a significant base for current thinking in experiential education.

William James is being re-discovered by educators. How appropriate that this re-discovery goes on apace especially by those whose instincts and experience tell them that cognition alone constitutes a poor substitute for what James called education, "the organization of acquired habits of conduct and tendencies to behavior". The philosophy of pragmatism is central to experience-based education. William James was the first well-known pragmatist. His thoughts are as relevant today as when he was uttering them over three quarters of a century ago. Experiential educators are well advised to get to know this most unusual man.

James was a member of a family which included a brother, Henry, a distinguished novelist, and a sister named Alice who, while not as well-known as her brothers, was an outstanding woman of her time. (Such was the fate of female scholars even in those days.) Born into a well-known and wealthy New York family, the youngsters were reared in a gad-about fashion by a father whose mind jumped about as much as the family's locale did. William was born in New York in 1842 but spent his infancy in

Europe. He attended school in New York from 1852 through 1855 but was schooled and tutored in England, France, Switzerland and Germany from that time until 1860. His first ambition, to be an artist, was promising but short lived.

He entered the Lawrence Scientific School of Harvard in 1861 and the Harvard Medical School in 1864. 1865-1866 were, notably, occupied with a scientific expedition to Brazil with Louis Agassiz of "Study Nature, not books" fame.

James studied and recovered from a period of ill health in Germany from 1867 to 1872. He became healthy by what he described as "an act of will". Many students of his life and works believe that this period in his life was decisive in his evolution from medicine to physiology and through psychology to philosophy. The disciplines in the late nineteenth and early twentieth centuries had not reached the rarified separatism which is so apparent today. Typically, psychology, philosophy and pedagogy were taught in what would now be characterized as "an interdisciplinary method". In any event, what had appeared to be a brilliant but peripatetic life settled into a life-long career when he began to teach philosophy courses in 1880. However, he was still defining himself as a psychologist when, in 1899, he delivered the series of lectures which became his most specific advice to educators, *Talks to Teachers and Students*. [1]

George W. Donaldson is *Professor of Outdoor Education at Northern Illinois University.* **Richard Vinson** is an outdoor educator from Halifax, Nova Scotia, assigned to work with students in grades 7-8-9. He completed his Master's Degree in Outdoor Education at Northern Illinois University in August, 1979.

[1] James, William. *Talks to Teachers and Students.* New York: Henry Holt, 1900.

Understanding James, the man — his times and place — helps to understand James, the pragmatic philosopher. His sister, Alice, remarked that his summer home in Chocorua, New Hampshire, had fourteen doors, **all opening outward**. What a symbol of this outreaching man! He was described at the height of his career as ". . . short, spare, bearded, blue-eyed, vigorous. Bronzed and ruddy, often clad in rough tweeds, he did not look like a scholar, or speak like a college professor."[2] He was by no means the dull philosophical lecturer; rather he was mercurial, even mischievous. As inconsistent as it may appear on the part of an empirical scholar, he constantly dabbed in the occult. His illness, his discovery of Renouvier's doctrine of free will and his recovery from melancholia probably had a bearing on his own interest in the mystical. The fact that his father was an avowed mystic may have had some influence on him, too.

A spirit of intellectual ferment was abroad in the land then, especially about the Harvard campus and in Cambridge. The era of the Transcendentalists was far from past. In addition to Emerson, Thoreau and Fuller of that group, Oliver Wendell Holmes, Henry Adams, John Fish, Chauncey Wright, Louis Agassiz and Charles Sanders Peirce were all his contemporaries. Their thoughts were reflected in his — and **vice versa**. Harvard throbbed when these great minds, representing several disciplines, wrestled with the "future shock" of post-Civil-War industrialism, with the theories of Charles Darwin and with the "new Science" and its questing, doubting mode.

It was only natural that the **empirical** stance which James assumed in the field of psychology would lead him to what was coming to be called the **pragmatic** approach to philosophy. Although he never claimed to have invented either the terminology or the substance of pragmatism, crediting Charles Sanders Peirce, the logician, with its origin, he must certainly be acknowledged as the person who fleshed it out, elaborated on it and made it understandable. His lectures at Harvard and elsewhere, and his writings, made him by far the best known philosopher, as well as the most easily understood, in America. There was no substantial challenge to his preeminence until John Dewey, almost twenty years his junior, emerged out of the Middle West to become Professor of Philosophy at Columbia University. Both were empiricists, both were pragmatists and, although Dewey more explicitly applied the doctrines to education in the burgeoning industrial society, it was still James who spoke and wrote most clearly. Such was his insight and clarity that few misunderstood him. Dewey was more obscure.

The philosophy of pragmatism made itself felt in all areas of American life — in politics, in law, in religion and, most especially, in education. It fell to Dewey, however, to spell out most of the educational implications of their jointly-held philosophy, probably because he came on the national scene later, as well as because of his association with Teachers College, then by far the best known center for teacher education in the United States.

Indeed, James addressed himself specifically and in depth to the education (then pedagogy) profession only once in his several books. But what he said in the lectures, which later became that one book, made so much sense to educators that he is known to those teachers fortunate enough to know about him at all, almost exclusively as the author of *Talks to Teachers and Students*. Although his remarks in those lectures reflect the historical period in which he spoke, (Teacher-Female), many of the principles he stressed apply to today's teachers and students as if he had spoken yesterday.

Pragmatic philosophy is so central to the theoretical framework of experience-based education and group work, regardless of the widely diverse terminology currently used to designate such education (experiential education; out-of-school education, outdoor education, risk education, community-based education, etc.) that a book published eighty years ago remains "must reading" for anyone who believes in and seeks to practice what folk wisdom has called "the school of hard knocks". If there is substance to the age-old notion that "experience is the best teacher", then William James is a major prophet in the experiential school.

In order to stress the relevance of the William James philosophy to teachers and other group workers interested in experience-related learning, the authors now ask their readers to engage in an imaginative exercise, as follows:

Imagine that the planning committee for a special convention of the Association for Experiential Education has arranged, through the familiar time-warp of science fiction, for William James to meet with members of the organization on the shore of Walden Pond. Professor James, in preparing for his presentation has read much of the literature generated by the recent interest in experiential education. He extracted from it eleven (11) statements or inferences (principles, if the reader wishes) as to the fundamental beliefs of the movement.

For his presentation Dr. James, being in one of his "larky" moods, has chosen a put-on topic: "But I said that in 1899!" Following are James' conceptions of ten "principles" of experiential education, supported by statements from *Talks*:

1. ONE LEARNS BEST BY HIS/HER OWN ACTIVITY

    "He (the learner) must take the first step himself." p. 39[3]

    "Don't preach too much to your pupils or abound in good talk in the abstract." p. 71

    "Instruction must be carried on objectively, experimentally, anecdotally." p. 93

2. INTEREST IS OF SIGNAL IMPORTANCE TO LEARNING

    ". . . in teaching, you must simply work your pupil into such a state of interest in what you are going to teach him that every other object of attention is banished from his mind . . ." p. 10

    "In real life, our memory is always used in the service of some interest; we remember things we care for or which are associated with things we care for." p. 134

[2]Morris, Lloyd. *William James*. New York: Scribner's, 1950.

[3]Each quotation in the remainder of this article is from *Talks to Teachers and Students*.

"If you only care enough for a result, you will almost certainly attain it." p. 137

Feed the growing human being, feed him the sort of experience for which from year to year he shows a natural craving, and he will develop in adult life a sounder sort of mental tissue . . ." p. 148

3. SENSORY EXPERIENCE IS BASIC

"The more different kinds of things a child thus gets to know by treating and handling them, the more confident grows his sense of himself with the world in which he lives." p. 59

"To have grown up on a farm, to have haunted a carpenter's and blacksmith's shop, to have handled horses and cows and boats and guns and to have ideas and abilities connected with such objects are an inestimable part of youthful acquistion." p. 147

"Living in the open air and on the ground, the lop-sided beam of the balance rises to the level line; and the over-sensibilities even themselves out. The good of all the artificial schemes and fevers fades and pales; and that of seeing, smelling, tasting, sleeping, and daring and doing with one's body, grows and grows." p. 258

4. EFFORT AND VIGOR MAKE FOR GOOD EDUCATION

"Sweat and effort, human nature strained to its uttermost and on the rack, yet getting through alive, and then turning its back on its success to pursue another more rare and arduous still — this is the sort of thing the presence of which inspires us . . ." p. 272

"Even if the day ever dawns in which it (muscular vigor) will not be needed for fighting the old heavy battles against Nature, it will always be needed to furnish the background of sanity, serenity, and cheerfulness to life, to give moral elasticity to our disposition, to round off the wiry edge of our fretfulness, and to make us good-humored and easy of approach." p. 207

5. EDUCATION MODIFIES BEHAVIOR

"An impression which simply flows in at the pupil's eyes or ears, and in no way modifies his active life, is an impression gone to waste." p. 33

"Action seems to follow feeling, but really action and feeling go together; and by regulating the action, — we can indirectly regulate the feeling — ." p. 201

"Education, in short, cannot be better described than by calling it *the organization of acquired habits of conduct and tendencies to behavior.*" p. 29

6. GOOD EDUCATION IS HOLISTIC

". . . man is too complex a being for light to be thrown on his real efficiency by measuring any one mental faculty taken apart from its consensus in the working whole." p. 134

"The total mental efficiency of a man is the resultant of the working together of all his faculties." p. 114

7. IMITATING EXEMPLARY BEHAVIOR IS SOUND LEARNING

"We become conscious of what we are ourselves by imitating others . . ." p. 48

"The teacher who meets with most success is the teacher whose own ways are most imitable." p. 49-50

"The child will always attend more to what a teacher does than to what the same teacher says." p. 92

8. LOVE AND UNDERSTANDING ARE IMPORTANT TO LEARNING

"The teacher who succeeds in getting herself loved by the pupils will obtain results which one of a more forbidding temperament finds it impossible to secure." p. 44

". . . to apperceive your pupil as a little sensitive, impulsive, associative, and reactive organism, partly fated and partly free, will lead to a better intelligence of all his ways." p. 196

9. EFFECTIVE LEARNING IS INTERDISCIPLINARY

'When the geography and English and history and arithmetic simultaneously make cross-references to one another, you get an interesting set of processes all along the line." p. 97

10. RESPECT FOR INDIVIDUAL DIFFERENCES IS ESSENTIAL

"The first thing to learn in intercourse with others is non-interference with their own peculiar ways of being happy, provided those ways do not assume to interfere by violence with ours." p. 265

"Every Jack sees in his own particular Jill charms and perfections of which we stolid onlookers are stone-cold." p. 266

11. SOUND EDUCATION IS SPECIFIC

". . . learning poetry by heart will make it easier to learn and remember other poetry, but nothing else; and so of dates; and so of chemistry and geography." p. 130

Conclusion: Teachers and youth leaders who truly believe in teaching the whole person **in** and **about** the whole environment in which life is lived will provide every learner with many direct experiences. These experiences may take place anywhere people are in the modern world — classroom, community, natural areas, schoolyards, parks, farm, inner city — anywhere! Helping the young **to live** in a wider and wider continuum of reality experiences is what experiential education is all about.

Suggested Readings —

1. James, William. *Principles of Psychology.* New York, Henry Holt, 1890.
2. _____. Pragmatism: *A New Name for Some Old Ways of Thinking.* New York, Longman, Green & Co., 1907.
3. Morris, Lloyd. *William James.* New York, Chas. Scribner's Sons, 1950.
4. Perry, Ralph Barton. *The Thought and Character of William James* (2 vols.) Boston, Little, Brown & Co., 1935.

SPIRITUAL FOUNDATIONS

THE
Spiritual Core
OF EXPERIENTIAL EDUCATION

by F. Earle Fox

We take for granted things that are going well. It is when gears grind and axles squeak that we focus our attention upon them. Experiential education is no exception. One might say that the very experience of education has become problematic so that special courses, even whole curricula, are being devised to focus on what in ages past must have been taken quite for granted. Indeed, I would say that even more profoundly the very ability to have experience at all and to make rational sense of it is becoming increasingly marginal for many people.

To have experiences is a given part of life. But to be able to make coherent sense of these experiences, to experience a coherence between oneself, the world, and the source of life does not seem to be a reliable part of the modern package. For several decades our art forms have been signaling danger. Dramas such as *Endgame* or *Waiting for Godot* by Samuel Beckett, or on the music scene, the appearance of punk rock (or rock at all), are clear signs of a culture in deep trouble. We are at once the most individualized and independent and free wheeling culture in history, and at the same time, it seems, the least comfortable with our individuality.

And so, as might be expected, we are appointing committees and writing books and inventing curricula to deal with this strange malady. It is not merely that educational *systems* are out of whack or not doing their job with the 4 R's (add "religion"), though that is certainly true. It is rather that for an increasing number of young people coming through our educational systems, experience of *any* sort is not educational. One might say that it never was. Youth has always been recalcitrant. But the fact is that the educational

systems of the past were on the whole able to discipline and train and shape experiences of their students so that a common culture and common values were possible and shared to a degree we find impossible. It would be facile to assert that that was simply because of the autocratic and authoritarian nature of old educational processes which were able to stamp out mechanically produced specimens made to fit the preconditions ordained by the inherited culture. Clearly any culture has a certain amount of oppression and conformism. But looking back in particular at our own western history, the ages of greatest artistic achievement have come out of a substratum of basic values and a world view shared more or less freely and openly by the populace. A great deal of conformity has been genuine and powerful and immensely productive.

But something has happened to us in the 20th century that will require more than another committee, another curriculum, another Ph.D. thesis to set aright. For despite our intense pride on being modern, the most educated and most informed people at any time in human history, we have a strange panicy sense that it is all coming apart at the seams.

And so we focus on what seems to be the area of deficiency, namely experience. We put together "experiential education", as though education could have ever been anything else. The irony is that we do indeed seem to have invented a non-experiential sort of education, not by design so much as due to the fact that our whole culture has drifted strongly in a schizoid direction. We have retreated over a period of several centuries from feelings and relationships into individualization and abstract thinking. We are living to an extraordinary degree in our heads rather than our emotions. When experience gets too chaotic, we try to control it by force or manipulation, or we retreat from dealing with it into thinking about it. Rock music, self-discovery courses and workshops, gurus and meditation, and experiential education programs are all various ways of trying to deal with that fact through a "new kind"

Dr. F. Earle Fox *received his Ph.D. in Science and Religion from Oxford University. He has served Episcopal pastorates in Connecticut and is currently Chaplain at Becket Academy, East Haddam, Connecticut.*

of experience.

I would like to offer some suggestions about the nature of experiential education and its relation to the spiritual life. My connections with experiential education in the institutional sense of the word are not yet extensive, having only recently become a chaplain at an institution that engages in experiential education. But listening to talk about programs, aims, failures, and successes, and engaging in some of it myself, I am very impressed with the correlation between what is happening at (in my case) Becket Academy and what I gradually and somewhat painfully came to experience my job to be during ten years of parish ministry.

I am also impressed with the fact that without exception all of the successful reform movements in the Church have been non-academic (not anti-academic) but rather experiential in nature — from the early desert fathers, through the Benedictines, the Franciscans, the Jesuits, the Quakers, Methodists, right down to the present day "charismatic renewal". All this was not to the exclusion of serious academic work. But it was the experience that came first which provided the fodder for the rational mind to work upon. The Judeo-Christian tradition is profoundly experiential, not to the exclusion of reason, but as the precondition of it. That is, the material upon which reason exerts itself is precisely those experiences of ours which needs ordering and coherence.

Let us add one further element to this picture. Faith, for the Judeo-Christian community, is not "belief in something no matter how stupid". It is not blind belief. It is not dogmatism or belief despite all the evidence to the contrary. Nowhere in the Bible from Genesis to Revelation is faith presented in such a manner.

On the contrary, nothing in the Biblical story makes sense unless faith is taken to mean "a teachable spirit". Not a gullible spirit, but a spirit that is *open* to experience and to reasoning about that experience. Faith means openness to reality.

The Problem at the Center

So how can experiential education make a difference to the massive needs of our time? Sometimes answers are staring us in the face, laying about the landscape, as it were, though we are blocked by our prejudices from seeing them.

The Judeo-Christian tradition is not available to most moderns. It is too close to us and we are in rebellion against it. And yet it is infinitely far away, out of reach because it seems so contrary to the modern secular mind-set concerning the nature of the world. (Viewers of Carl Sagan's brilliant TV series "Cosmos" would have experienced this in a powerful way.) But even more important, the Judeo-Christian tradition is simply not known. It is a forgotten wisdom. We moderns, despite our pretense to knowledge, are abysmally ignorant of the spiritual and cultural foundation stones long ago laid, and upon which still rests the great weight of contemporary western culture insofar as it still holds together at all. We do not know our own roots.

It can be said that the western spiritual tradition rooted in the Bible has wrestled with two elemental themes — one the problem, the other the solution.

The problem is the child side of ourselves, our contingent, dependent, and somewhat broken nature. We experience our dependency as an unwelcome aspect. We yearn for self-sufficient adulthood, the immortality of the gods. Our vulnerability to the slings and arrows of outrageous fortune is more than we can tolerate, and so we tend to build a closed, defensive circle about ourselves.

One might imagine oneself as three concentric rings, the outer ring representing the body, the middle ring the soul, and the center the spirit:

The soul is composed of our psychological aspects of mind, will, and emotions or feelings. But the soul, not being self-sufficient, cannot be its own center. The spiritual center is inhabited by whatever we choose to put at the center of our lives, that which we depend on for our integrity, identity, and sense of well being. The spiritual center is the throne room. Whatever occupies that throne will shape and form how we think, choose, and feel, our three psychological aspects.

Our problem lies in finding something to put at the center that is itself secure and strong enough to rely on, and at the same time friendly to and supportive of our well being. There are not many such possible friendly, supportive, and secure centers in the world. And so we tend to experience our center as insecure, as in need of protection from outside threat, and also as itself ambiguous toward our well being. The very thing we rely on is not all that trustworthy. We experience the center of our life not as something we can freely share in relationship. There is a part of me that I keep hidden even in my most intimate relations.

The most common way we try to deal with our dependency and vulnerability is to deny it. If we cannot be at the center of ourselves, and if we cannot put something there that is "on our side" in the game of life, we try to create the illusion of invincibility and invulnerability and self-sufficiency by putting something there that we can at least control or manipulate. International power struggles are nothing more than this process writ large. The child within continues to dream of the mythical adulthood, super-hero self-sufficiency, failing which we resort to defensive walling strategies. If you can't beat them, hide from them.

The troubled youth who are the clientele for so much experiential education are no exception. A large part of their maladaptation to life can be explained as faulty dealing with the experiences of being not self-sufficient.

Dealing with our hurts and fears and insecurities through defensive mechanism, power plays, and manipulation works for a while, or we would not be tempted into these ploys. But most of our defenses have the disadvantage of increasingly cutting us off from reality. That part of us that is being defended, the hurting, frightened child within, by that very defense is frequently cut off from the learning experience that could possibly heel and strengthen and mature. Our castles become our prisons, and finally our tombs. The resentment I harbor against being accused prevents me from discovering and working creatively with the truth of the matter, whatever it may be.

The Risk of Faith
The second elemental theme after the problem, naturally, is the solution, namely faith. Now suppose that faith, as taught and lived in the Bible, is not the nonsense that so many Christians and non-Christians alike have tended to treat it as. If that is the case, then this kind of faith becomes the *sine qua non* of experiential education. Openness to experience and to reasoning about it is clearly a prerequisite to any truly educational process. Faith, then, is not the closed attitude that bars one from true knowledge (scientific or otherwise), it is the precondition of living in reality and of having any serious knowledge at all.

The problem is that reality is not always experienced as a friendly place in which to remain open and vulnerable to learning experience. The

school of hard knocks can be just that. And so we can develop habitual responses to life that in fact preclude the fullness of the learning experience. We defend ourselves against any vital and sensitive contact with the very reality we supposedly want to know and understand. We keep reality at a distance, we build walls, we paint and therefore distort our public image so as (we believe) to preserve our acceptability and our viability in a hostile and alien land. A defensive move is always a move of un-faith.

"We become like what we worship."

The life of faith, then, is the choice to risk the hurt and rejection and disappointment, at whatever cost, to experience and know the truth, whatever it may be, and to put that at the center. We are saved and made whole, as Jesus indicated, by our faith. That works, of course, only if in fact ultimate reality turns out to be gracious and friendly despite the hard knocks. If it is not, to expose oneself in such a manner is to be annihilated. That is the risk of faith. That is the leap. But the leap is into the light, not the dark. It is the leap out of my defenses into intimate touch with the truth, the relationship, the person I want to know.

Faith, then, also necessarily means learning with the whole of me. I become, as it were, my own antenna by which I receive messages from reality "out there". If a part of me is cut off by defensive walls, that part of me will at best perceive and relate only in a distorted and partial way.

The Judeo-Christian view wants to say that God, the ultimate reality, has invested Himself in this process as well. The very meaning of Biblical revelation presupposes that investment. The impact of the Christian view of the incarnation of the Son of God is that God makes Himself supremely available and vulnerable — able to be touched, experienced in the deepest kind of mutual sharing, which is holy communion. God does not "defend" Himself — which is the only possible basis upon which we can shed our defenses. To paraphrase Dr. Frank Lake, an English psychiatrist: The only foundation possible for mental health is the gracious nature of God, ... for that alone transforms our brokenness from that which at all costs must be avoided to that which at all costs must be accepted.

Thus, not only because God is my creator, but because God is not hiding behind walls of defense, He alone is able to be the center which can speak to and touch and heal and mature the whole of me.

Experiential Education and Renewal

What then of experiential education? A great deal, though not all, of experiential education is remedial or therapeutic in intent. Many wilderness or "outward bound" type programs are intended to benefit people who have learning or behavioral or emotional difficulties. They are programs which subject students to a great deal of stress along with the experience of personal loyalty which will see them through to success. One is unavoidably confronted with his dependencies — hopefully in a way that he can begin to accept himself and to share that real self in the student-teacher and peer relationships.

What I am saying would certainly apply to such programs, but I believe it would also apply to *any* type of education that aims beyond the surface into the depths of learning and maturation.

If experiential education is to fulfill the goal it has taken for itself — a profound reordering of the educational process which can assist the healing and maturing of the whole person — then it must provide the context within which one can experience the *need* and *desireability* and *possibility* of facing rather than avoiding the brokenness within. That is, experiential education must provide the context within which one can re-experience one's dependency and come to terms with it as a good thing rather than a thing to be denied and defended against. I must experience the ability and the right to be myself and to share that self without denying, hiding, or making excuses for my dependency and lack of self-sufficiency. Until I can find some place (ultimately some person) in which to invest my dependency, my spiritual center, which I can experience as safe and nourishing and supportive, it will never be possible for me to let the defenses down which prevent the growth and maturing I hopefuly seek.

Needless to say, this is never a one shot process. It is a way of life, a pilgrimage. But as experiential education provides the context of unfailing acceptance with uncompromising discipline — what might be called the mothering and fathering sides of life — the hurting child within begins to experience the encouragement to return to full relationship with life. And that means learning and growth. The child begins to experience the freedom to choose the open road of faith rather than the closed circle of defensiveness. That is the context of Tough Love: I will never let you down, I will never let you off. It provides the space where I can fall apart and still be accepted. I can experience success *with* my dependency. And that is exactly what has to happen at the very deepest level of our existence.

That kind of loyalty combined with toughness that characterizes so many experiential education programs is, I believe, one of the foundation stones of success. Both the religious and educational institutions of our culture, church and school, have by and large abandoned any such concept of education. The signs that we may be recovering some of that Tough Love are encouraging.

I would suggest that we find the archetypal model for that kind of love right in the mainstream of the Judeo-Christian spiritual tradition in the person of Yahweh who called Abraham, Moses, and the prophets into a living experience of His presence, and even more concretely in Jesus' relation with His disciples. Tough Love leads us through the holocaust of facing our brokenness, death to self, and into the fullness of personal resurrection on the other side.

Our experiential education programs must introduce students not only to the abstract and theoretical reality of their spiritual center and dependency, but to its concrete reality, real people, real feelings, real decisions. That is the function of Tough Love — absolute love and acceptance married to absolute truth and discipline. Wilderness programs have the virtue of having discipline and hardship built in along with isolation from so many extraneous distractions. But the same crucible of maturation and healing can be created in any community where the leadership is committed to that kind of openness and sharing and self-discipline, and where the leadership will share together a common center of that quality.

That is part of the meaning of being made in the image of God. We become like what we worship. We have not a choice about that. That choice lies in whether sitting on the throne will be something which itself is dependent and defensive and impersonal and therefore inadequate, or whether it will be the person who is in fact the source of my being, gracious, personal, and totally secure, who Himself lives by faith and therefore can afford to allow me to live by faith.

THE NORWEGIAN
Nature Life
APPROACH

An increase in the development of remote natural areas has been matched by a decrease in the skill level of people using these areas.

Photo courtesy of Sarah Pendleton

by Sarah Pendleton

My two year association (as apprentice and mentor) with the Norwegian Seminar for Nature Life has deeply affected my vision of the tasks facing all educators and has enhanced my belief in the value of an experiential approach to educating for ecological awareness. My experiences in Norway as a "mentor of nature life" inspire me to share the perspectives of the Norwegian "nature life approach" with those interested

Sarah Pendleton *lives in Jackson, New Hampshire and is just back from two years of teaching in Norway. She is looking for opportunities to adapt the nature life approach to programs in this country.*

in or already involved in experiential education in this country.

Some of the ideas presented in the following introduction to "nature life" will be familiar to most experiential education programs. Yet others have grown out of the Norwegian Seminar's integrating of an inherently Norwegian ecological paradigm, the traditional ways of upbringing among the Sami (native peoples in northern Scandinavia) and the age old Norwegian tradition of enjoying nature. Some of my word use may be uncommon; the meanings should become clear before I am through. And if they don't, take a walk in your nearest back woods, on a friendly mountain's ridges or along some flowing water's edge, and give these ideas another chance to take root.

Traditional Values

The spirit of the "nature life approach" resides in a seeking out and a nurturing of joy in and with Nature. The Norwegian culture has grown up in a stark setting on farms under the shadow of high mountains, reflected in the deep clear waters of the fjords, washed by ocean waves, and fed by a thousand waterfalls. For more than a thousand years, Norwegians have been confronted by a nature more powerful than their human skills, yet more beautiful than human crafts, and so ever-present that it could not be shut out or forgotten. Living rurally for the most part, by farming, fishing and hunting, theirs was an outdoor life. The values of outdoor life as a free-time pursuit were first articulated by people who lived in more urban areas and who spent more more time in houses than in the 'outdoors'. Yet in both the urban and rural family, the skills and lore of outdoor life were passed on.

Imagine growing up in this "home of the giants". Then imagine learning from one's parents: how to dress to be comfortable with heat and cold; how to eat while staying in nature for a day, a week, or longer; how to read the signs left by wind and snow on mountains and trees; how to recognize the safe paths from those which "trolls" or forces beyond our imagining inhabit; and how to travel with rather than against the rhythms of the living waters, woods, and mountains. Now you may begin to grasp some of the essence of "nature life" — or "friluftsliv' — the traditional Norwegian outdoor lifestyle.

"The assumption underlying the 'nature life approach' is that familiarity with nature fosters friendship with nature..."

The values of the traditional "friluftsliv" have also ben expressed by the likes of John Muir, Aldo Leopold, and Henry David Thoreau — grandfathers of the conservation and ecology movements in this country. Yet here, as in Norway now, the simplicity of traditional ways of outdoor life and the focus on enjoying journeying through woods and mountains and by living waterways in celebration of nature's intrinsic value has been forgotten by many.

Commercialized recreation and sport as competition against man, woman, or nature has claimed more and more devotees. An increase in the development of remote natural areas to accommodate sports and tourism has been matched by a decrease in the skill and awareness level of the people "using" these areas.

This is the trend which Nils Faarlund and a few other Norwegian mountaineers hoped to reverse with the founding of the Norwegian Seminar for Nature Life (NSNL) in 1967, a center for teaching courses in "nature life" (in the ways no longer taught at home). Faarlund believes in "keeping it simple", and the "school" has still not grown out of his home in Hemsedal (a mountain valley in central Norway). Yet the circle of "mentors" and schools reached by NSNL reaches up beyond the arctic circle in Norway and into Sweden and Denmark.

More than just preserving a certain tradition of outdoor live, Faarlund and NSNL are committed to educating for a greater understanding of nature and a deeper awareness of oneself in relationship with Nature. (I write Nature with "N" to mean the physical/spiritual whole encompassing all life forms, even human on and of the earth). Ths is a process of healing, or making whole the now splintered relationship between most humans and the earth-region they inhabit: The founders of NSNL were motivated by seeing eco-crises affecting even the "home of the giants".

At the root of any eco-crisis, whatever its particular form, is the split between human beings and Nature. Whole societies of people now live beyond their means and on human terms that ignore nature's terms. In these societies, we no longer identify the needs of other life forms as our needs, nor do we identify their joys as our joys. Cut off from nature, we have lost a sense of a sacred reality, we reject spiritual value and neglect our own and others' spiritual needs. The focus on one physical reality — on material objects, on the aspects of things, people, and events that can be measured and compared against each other — dominates all areas of our lives.

Even in the field of experiential education, there has been too little effort made to allow the sacred to be reconciled with the physical reality of our experience. It is in this area that NSNL and the "nature life approach" has made a contribution. Part of the inspiration for this comes from our own continent. Native American philosophy teaches that wholeness or heal-ed-ness results from a reuniting of physical and sacred realities. "Nature life" reestablishes a close physical relationship between person and nature that in turn leads to a new spiritual understanding. The assumption underlying the "nature life approach" is that familiarity with nature fosters friendship with nature, and based on this friendship, people develop a commitment to living lightly with simple means, that is, more in harmony with Nature. "Familiarity" refers to the process of getting reacquainted with nature, inherently an experiential process, a matter

Norwegian Nature Lifers take to the mountains.

Photo courtesy of Sarah Pendleton

of learning though living in close contact with nature. NSNL recognizes that in order to transform our attitudes towards nature, we must promote experiences that affect us deeply, experiences that call into question our underlying assumptions and values and inspire us to reevaluate the roots of our world view.

In the "nature life approach", people with many years' experience in traditional "friluftsliv" teach the living skills, nature lore, and nature crafts which enable students of nature to travel as skillfully and with as little trace as a Native American scout, a John Muir, or a Sami reindeer herder. Learning focuses on what is touchable, practical, general, and useful. Self-reliance is stressed from the beginning, along with the norm of journeying and living within one's capacity. During a course, students learn to live on nature's terms. They are urged to cultivate a habit of participation in evaluating and decision making; they are made co-responsible for the

actions of the group and for the outcome of the course and journey and act within their capacity as a group. The "mentor" is both teacher, "grandparent," and member of the group — guiding, evaluating capacities and situations, and choosing moments that are "ripe with learning possibility". The mentor reaffirms the value of experience and of vernacular knowledge (nature lore as opposed to scientific knowledge), or process and path rather than product and goal. The mentor is responsible both to the students and to nature, and thus evaluates situations both in terms of the familiarity the group has, (the extent to whch all members do participate), and asks whether nature will be freed or bound by the encounter. The stated norm is "let nature live free", meaning let nature's rhythms unfold freely. It is the experience of "free nature" that gives us feelings of joy and can teach us spiritual values. Nature life must ultimately be a joyful learning.

A New Perspective in Experiential Education

I would like to elaborate on some of the points just mentioned that express a difference between the "nature life approach" and what I perceive in other programs that use nature for experiential education. My intent is that these differences will point towards a new perspective in experiential education.

The focus of the "nature life approach" is on the fellowship and interaction between human being and nature, rather than on the development of the individual divided from nature. One learns about oneself in relationship *with* Nature. "Nature life" requires that intellect and intuition cooperate, that one's whole self is engaged in a learning process. Yet, "nature life" is not meant to be a way of life in itself. It is a path in upbringing, enabling people to choose a way of life. It is a fusion of experiences that nurtures us spiritually as much as physically and that keeps our joy

Norwegian alpine soup kitchen.

and creativity alive while we learn valuable skills.

NSNL has developed the "nature life approach" on the premise that "how" we teach/learn is integral to "what' we teach/learn, which in turn is integral to "why" we teach/learn. Deep ecological values — the "why" — motivate us to teach awareness of and familiarity with other life forms — the "what" — which can only be gained through a personal and "experiential" encounter — the "how". For example, needing an over-night shelter, students dig a snow pit and seek out the differences in each snow layer. Finding different types of snow leads them to think about how these differences came about. They gain familiarity with how snow changes and builds up and can test in their snow pit for when and where the snow will slide on itself. Having tested the snow in this way, they are themselves responsible for choosing a route that steers clear of avalanches. As well as practical knowledge or "snow lore", they have gained an affinity for snow that they could not have experienced in a lecture on snow and avalanches.

"True satisfaction comes not through passively consuming but only through actively creating."

The immediate focus, then, in "nature life" is on learning practical skills, crafts, and lore. These strengthen the individual's and the group's ability to take care of itself on nature's terms for longer periods of time and under varying conditions. The greater the group's capacity to live on nature's terms, the more each individual has the chance to step outside of the paradigms of the technological age and to feel a sense of belonging in Nature and a respect for nature's intrinsic value.

Through practicing "nature life" skills — sleeping in snow caves, or under sheltering branches or trees, orienteering by sun and stars, and following natural "paths" in the terrain — one feels a physical closeness with nature. One feels steadily more familiar and at home. This familiarity may conflict with the assumptions and values that one hitherto has lived by. A discussion of values, attitudes, and lifestyles flows out of these experiences of physical interaction with nature and the conflicts they pose. It takes time to develop a readiness for such discussions. But in time, they lead to greater awareness of what there is to learn and to a deeper understanding of the value of the practical lore. Thus the "why" leads back to the "what".

There is one other concept that is significant for all three aspects of "nature life" — for "what", "how", and "why". That is creativity. It is present in handcraft as well as in "making do" or solving problems with simple means. It is the key to teaching and mentoring joyfully; and it is the unifying principle of all life. The purpose of "nature life" can also be explained as "to nurture creativity". Handcraft or creative handwork is an important element of the "nature life approach", a complement to nature life skills and lore, where one works with natural materials and hand tools.

In traditional cultures, handcrafts have been important for survival and comfort. Practical and aesthetic considerations were combined in the task of creating the tools one used in daily life. In this way, daily tasks were infused with creativity, and simple tools were also works of art, expressing the traditions of the tribe and the character of the individual creator. In such handcraft, tradition and spontaneity meet and are reconciled. Innovations are still balanced by an understanding of traditional form and function. The use of handcrafted and individually created clothing and tools make visible the interaction between functional and artistic, and between physical and spiritual realities.

People learning handcrafts experience a sense of joy which is part of creating, as well as the satisfaction of having "made something." True satisfaction comes not through passively consuming (be it objects or experiences), but only through actively creating or participating in a creative process. Where there is no

---

"An increase in the development of remote natural areas to accommodate sports and tourism has been matched by a decrease in the skill and awareness level of the people 'using' these areas."

---

opportunity for creativity, nor for the expression of joy, life is experienced as toil and oppression and becomes an endless cycle of wanting and consuming. Yet when one is involved in creating for oneself and others, satisfaction becomes possible. One can experience more using less. While the relationship of the consumer to product or thing being consumed is passive and impersonal, the one who creates learns to care for and respect both what she uses and what she creates. In nature crafts, nature and craftsperson cooperate. Working with clay, the potter moulds but is also moulded.

"Nature life" is meant to be a creative life in nature, where this same exchange between people and between person and nature takes place. It is creative in the sense that each participant helps to create a given course, and must give of herself in order to receive the gift of insight and experience. And for each situation there is a different creative response.

Living on nature's terms is demanding, yet there is constant opportunity to be creative. These concepts are not so easily grasped by people who have long been students in conventional schools or members of a consumer society. Starting with simple handcrafts on a "nature life" course, students become more familiar with creating. The clay bowl or wooden spoon crafted by hand will be a constant reminder of the differences between creating and consuming, and will help one to understand the meaning of "creating one's own experiences". These warm objects can also become a symbol of friendship between self and nature. Learning and sharing songs and writing haikus or other poetry teach one that creating can take many forms.

Creativity is the Key

Part of creating is to be searching, to be in doubt, going forth from the given to the unknown, and living with questions instead of with answers. This is the open and questioning attitude the "nature life" mentor aims to cultivate in students. The creativity nurtured in handcraft is then shown to apply to learning through life in nature, to trying new ways and questioning new values. If "nature life" isn't creative, it is dead. With no creative spirit, it is just technique. As with handcraft, one proceeds forth towards the unknown within one's capacity to create a way of living with what is yet unknown. Exceeding one's capacity is irresponsible and has no purpose, since participating and creating will then be out of the question.

In an experiential approach, there must be room for being creative. The "nature life" journey begins always with the known and unfolds according to the preparedness and capacity of each individual. Each participant is responsible for choosing paths where the group can journey according to capacity and on nature's terms. Consensus is the norm in decision-making. Thus, "nature life" does not aim to simulate a grim struggle for survival, nor to use nature as a challenge ground to stimulate per-

formance and achievement. The aim is rather to nurture ways of creatively adapting to nature's terms in ways that are protective of both human and nature's welfare.

In this respect, the perspective of the mentors at NSNL is quite different from that of many outdoor leaders in this country. Specifically, the Norwegians criticize "risk and high adventure activities" for being very human centered and for causing a greater impact (read "negative") on remote natural areas, while failing to nurture deeper ecological values and the creative attitude. Intense experiences are valuable for personal growth. But in our time, they often serve only by curing the symptoms and not the underlying problems produced by a technological society.

As our lives become more tamed and isolated from "untamed" nature, we seek intensity and risk in our outdoor and recreational experiences. These repair and refuel us for coping with our tame lives again. What we really need is to learn from these experiences how to change paths — how to infuse our daily lives with the harmony as well as the challenges we experience in nature, and with the skill and care we exercise there. We who use the "wilderness" for education have an *obligation* to nurture friendship to nature and a sense of union with a greater Self at the same time as we nurture the in-

dividual's sense of self. It is the experience of being a part of something greater than ourselves, rather than of conquering ever greater challenges, that will ultimately make us more integrated and whole. Our self-concept must accept its membership in a greater Self (unity in Nature), *feel* this friendship, and live accordingly. We must nurture every tiny moment of joy and be careful not to overshadow it by intensifying the challenge and the stress. Our joy is our greatest strength and healing power.

This then is the message of the "nature life approach": that the process of freeing, empowering, and enabling individuals must also "free" nature if it is to be valid. This is the responsibility of every individual, but especially of those who would enjoy nature's beauty and "wildness" at nature's expense. The "nature life" experience will not be conflict- or struggle-free. It is through conflict that we question our established values and assumptions, as well as our life-habits. But we will be supported in this conflict by the joy we discover through living on nature's terms. And as we recognize our emotional and spiritual bond with nature as one not less real than our physical bond, we can begin to live more in tune with the earth, thereby freeing Nature.

"Afjords fembring"
Restored square-rigged wooden boat used now by students at Fosen Folk High School in Rissa, Norway.
Photo courtesy of Sarah Pendelton

EDUCATION AT ITS PEAK

THE ASSOCIATION FOR EXPERIENTIAL EDUCATION

by Jolene Unsoeld

You can't see my knees knock.

You can't feel my stomach churn and flutter.

Why am I afraid?

For the last several weeks--no, months--I've been asking myself, "Why am I going to Colorado?" "What in the world am I going to do?"

Why _am_ I here?

If Willi had been here he would have sauntered up, stroking his chin, looking for all the world like an incompetent prospector and then he would have picked you up and taken you on a wilderness search to encounter your spiritual roots.

That would have been Willi.

I have so many drawbacks to speaking here today.

I don't have any lyrical metaphorical subject and I'm hopelessly non-verbal.

I'm a doer--not a speaker. But I'm here to tell you something about Willi and--more important--to try to tell you why you're here.

First, Who Was Willi?

We were just a couple of college students who climbed mountains together and fell in love. We met at the base of a mountain--an Oregon State College Mountain Club climb.

He used to say he was smitten because I was wearing G.I. mountain pants.

In fact, he lied. There was another student wearing red shorts. He

108

went out with her first.

But I had an unerring eye for quality. He had the best mountain stove and he was the finest story teller.

He had hitch-hiked around the world and climbed in the Himalayas by the age of 23. He was bitten by the "Why?" of the world. Gave up physics and embarked on his quest. We were married and had 4 kids while he was in graduate school.

Teaching at OSU was all theory.

Peace Corps was all doing.

Outward Bound helped identify some ways of changing people.

TESC provided the opportunity to apply it all--the theories and the doing.

Willi did a lot of public speaking. He would come sauntering up here stroking his shaggy beard and tell you that as a species modern folks have lost touch not only with this earth but also with our fellow humans.

He would take you on a walk through wilderness to encounter the holy. He would use the spirit and magic of wilderness to make you see yourself in a cosmic perspective. And then he would bring you back and tell you that the only thing important in this life is how we treat each other.

As Willi saw it, a major part of any curriculum should be aimed at the moral values within a social context. (Alexander Mickeljohn, Education Between Two Worlds.)

Willi felt that we were alienated from our emotions...

We're alienated from each other. (Kitty)...

Alienated from nature...

We're in control and that alienates us.

We don't have to take into account reality.

We're in control and we prefer it that way.

He would suggest that this alienation from nature constitutes the key
to the other alienations. Nature, which includes us, is a seamless robe
which we deny by our process of analysis. We say that we can chop down a
tree, pave a valley, dam a river, and it doesn't affect anything else.
There's no necessary connection between chopping down a tree and all the
rest of us in this room.

Willi's assertion was the exact contrary--that nature is a seamless
robe to a degree far beyond our awareness. We're connected and when you
shake any portion of it, the rest trembles. And then he would go on to say
that the way we treat things affects how we treat people. And that when we
start abusing the physical things of this world, which our culture is based
on, then the abuse of each other follows as automatically as the day follows
the night.

The final product of this whole tendency is not only an alienation from
ourselves and from each other and from nature, but a total loss of meaning,
a total loss of "at homeness" in the universe. A de-sacrilization of the
universe which results from our objectification of our entire experience.

This was what made the wilderness experience religious to him. Defining religious as anything having to do with that in which we hold ultimate concern. Ultimate concern. What keeps us going? What makes it all worthwhile? The answer to the question, "Why bother...at all?" "Why you? Why me? Why anything instead of nothing?"

And that's where he used nature--the beauty and the risk of wilderness--to provide that other dimension.

His approach to the beauty, and hence the meaning, was always keyed to the risk that's present in nature. The riskiness of climbing or kayaking. The willingness to take a risk of being wrong, of having people jeer at you. The risk of riding your first bicycle or going skiing. That little inner quiver that alerts you and mobilizes your whole resources. And for him that was critical. One of his more profound philosophical observations was...life is tough.

And students got madder'n hops at that at Evergreen. Some of them didn't want it to be tough. They wanted it to be beautiful and painless. He saw our youth being conditioned on the other side of the track too much. Being warped over here to the conviction that if it's risky, it's bad. And besides, it's your right, your birthright to have it all laid out for you.

"You aren't going to have to work as hard as I did, kid." Well, we know all about that now--the indulgent parent murdering the soul of the child who is fighting for a suffocating breath of air to try to get out with a chance to do his or her own thing. And it's latched onto a self concept which arises from meeting risk and learning you can cope with it.

"We pay too great a price when we excise risk from our total economy," he used to tell them in Outward Bound when parents came round to ask, 'Can you guarantee the safety of our son Johnny?' (No daughters in early O.B. programs.) He said they finally decided to meet the question head on.

"No, we certainly can't ma'am. We guarantee you the genuine chance of his death. And if we could guarantee his safety, the program would not be worth running."

"Well! If that's all you have to say..."

"No, I have one more thing to say. We do make one guarantee as one parent to another. If you succeed in protecting your boy as you're doing now and as it's your parental duty to do...you know we applaud your watchdog tenacity. But if you succeed, we guarantee you the death of your child's soul."

He felt there was a mystery in nature which is one of its great attractions for us. There's the hiddenness of organic growth, of how a seed decides to be an oak tree. No matter how much reference we have to the genetic coding of RNA and DNA, somehow it doesn't come out totally explained. There is a mystery there in which we are engulfed.

He was, of course, greatly impressed with the mystery of mountaineering. The very mundane question, "Will it go?" "Well, will it?" "I don't know." "What are you doing here if you don't know." But that is the fascination. You have to find out. So you go a little farther and you never know until finally you reach the summit and then you know. Except, "How about getting down."

And his final test of this wilderness experience that we all have known, his final test of its efficacy--because having been there in the mountains, alone, in the midst of solitude, and this feeling, this mystical feeling if you will, of the ultimacy of joy or whatever there is--the question is, "Why not stay out there in the wilderness the rest of your days and just live in the lap of satori or whatever you want to call it?"

And the answer--his answer--to that was, "Because that's not where people are." And the final test for him of the legitimacy of the experience was, "how well it enables you to cope with the problems of mankind when you come back to the city."

And so he saw it as a renewal exercise leading to a process of alternation. You go to the wilderness for your metaphysical fix--your reassurance that the world makes sense. It's a reassurance many of us don't get in the city. But with that excess of confidence, of reassurance, that there's something behind it all and it's good, you come back to where humans are, to where humans are messing things up, 'cause they tend to, and you come back with a new ability to relate to yourself and to your fellow humans and to help them relate to each other. And that's the kind of alternation which he saw crucial for experiential education.

<u>And that's the peak of education for which he was reaching.</u>

That was until one stormy Sunday in March.

Suddenly a test of our own theories of risk and the purpose of our lives and the meaning of mountains to me.

113

I lost a daughter in the mountains. I lost my husband and partner. I nearly lost a son. One could say the mountains have been cruel to me.

And I've known those who have turned away from the mountains after losing loved ones there. I'm lucky. I responded to and understood what mountains are before I met Willi and that understanding and love for the high places was constant throughout our lives together and today remains unchanged.

But there is no easy way to handle death. The days and weeks and months pass, but the pain lingers and sometimes still it leaps out to grab me most unexpectedly.

For a long, long time--3 years in fact--there were things of beauty such as a crimson sunset, a full moon, certain pieces of music, and other things that could bring back an agonizing overwhelming sense of loss. I would find myself driving down the highway in the late afternoon and becoming aware of the glorious sky and clouds as the sun touched the horizon. Suddenly I would be overcome with excruciating pain at the reminder of Devi's death and then Bill's death.

And then one day I became aware that I was looking at this glorious sunset and it was not the sense of loss that was overwhelming me. Rather, I was aware of the beauty that was their lives and I could feel that beauty as very much a part of this universe. I could feel all that Willi was on this earth, all that we were together and it was all very much a precious part of me.

I still know the loss, but I have found strength from what we _were_ together and what we still are.

Now I want to switch gears and pull a "Willi".

He'd use his family in any way imaginable to illustrate what he wanted to talk about. He'd do it with or without permission and with or without accuracy. One of our kids would come innocently hitching into town totally unsuspecting and be accosted by someone they'd never seen before. This stranger would come up to gush over the graphic details of the latest "affair of the heart" and the cosmic overtones with which Willi had invested it. What may have really happened was of no importance. Willi would simply glomb onto whatever flimsy shred of truth could be used to illustrate his latest moral imperative.

And so...I have a son who is surviving his first year of teaching high school. Two of the subjects he's never even been exposed to: consumer economics and law. It is the freshman in his law class that captured my imagination: they say the only reason they don't go out and steal a car or knock off a 7-11 store has nothing to do with right or wrong or moral conscience. Rather, their choice of action is determined by whether it is legal or illegal and their chances of getting caught and their fear of punishment.

A 1981 survey showed only 13% of the Class of 1980 felt that "working to correct social and economic inequalities" is very important. Some 31% rated "having lots of money" as very important.

This is precisely the challenge that all of you practicing "education at its peak" find yourselves up against.

Success is not a destination--it's the quality of everything you do.

It's how you respond to those things that are going on around you--and the example you set for others.

You are educators not only for what you tell your students, and what you get them to experience but, probably more importantly, for the example--the role model--you provide.

Most of us want to shut out the world and what is happening. When approached with a petition to get an initiative on the ballet, a young professional woman said,

"Oh, no, I never sign petitions."

She never asked what the issue was. Never asked how it affected her.

A recent letter to the editor described the scene of an Olympia intersection one Friday afternoon. The writer was a witness to a collision and stopped to help. One man stumbled out of his truck and lay motionless on the road.

The other man was gushing blood from his head and she ran to give him assistance. As she was trying to stop his bleeding, <u>other cars</u> drove by--<u>respectable people</u>--<u>my age.</u> She made eye contact with them and yelled, "Help me!" They looked away and continued driving.

We have a strong desire to have government--and other unpleasantries-- just leave us alone.

But the world can't be shut out--

Tear down the walls and have a look.

You will see examples of inspiration--the two guys spinning through Olympia recently--paralyzed from the waist down wheelchairing from Spokane and back to collect money for Handicapped Unlimited.

The 10-year-old who pulled her grandparents to safety when their car plunged off a highway and was submerged in eight feet of water.

When the family car stopped at a busy intersection and burst into flame, and while her mother and older brother were struggling to get a baby out of a jammed car seat, nine-year-old Karen got her three younger sisters out of the back seat as smoke and flames poured from the hood and underneath the car. "I was very scared," Karen admitted. "Other drivers, who had to stop because of the car fire, were angry and yelling at us and I was trying to comfort my sisters. I got them onto a nearby safety island, then when the light changed to walk, I led them across the street to a gas station."

Sarah Doherty (25), a physical therapist and rehabilitation expert from Seattle, was struck by a car while riding her bicycle to a junior high track meet in 1973. She lost a leg and part of her hip. An artificial leg can't be fitted to her. She must travel on one leg and two crutches, one in each hand. Despite her handicap she climbed Mt. Rainier and then Mt. McKinley this last spring. Now she's looking for a higher mountain.

But in spite of these stellar examples of human behavior, there is some pretty horrible stuff going on in this world, too.

The White House has decided that the United States will formally cease to recognize the authority of the World Court except in non-political cases. We are afraid we'll be found guilty for our actions such as in Nicaragua so we're picking up our marbles and going home.

Never mind that our participation in the World Court is needed. It is a matter of principle to our government that we not be accountable for our actions.

While our economy is still ravaged from the last undeclared war, we now have an administration that says:

"Social expenditures are inflationary, but the same expenditures to rearm an American empire are necessary for this country's welfare and security."

Without the social security trust included in the budget, the U.S. spends 50% for military, 25% for servicing the national debt, and the remaining 25% has to pay for everything else.

In the mid '50s corporations paid 25% of the national taxes. It is now about 6%. Boeing was refunded $267 million and Weyerhauser $139 million.

And some of those same military contractors who don't pay their share of taxes are charging thousands and thousands of dollars for gifts, ship cruises, and entertainment, private club dues and then, in some cases, charging $99 to $340 per-hour labor costs of $750 pliers.

I'm known as an "activist". How did it come about?

Married young, didn't finish college. Four kids during 7 years of grad school. Stayed home until we went to Nepal with Peace Corps and youngest in kindergarten.

When we came back from Nepal in 1967, I had cultural shock.

Compared to the Nepali people we had so much--and yet we had so little.

I didn't know how to translate my own desire to make this world better into action. Things were just too complicated. I did't know how to make a difference so I shut out the world for a year and baked cookies or some darn thing.

We had never had television...starving Biafrans.

TV brought automated warfare and assassinations into our living room and a kid that said to his parents, "Well, what'cha goin' to do about it?"

Wow! You either abdicate parenthood or your start examining your own image as a role model for your kids.

And so now I'm trying to get industry in Washington state to help pay for their share of protecting our environment. I happen to think they ought to share in the cost of keeping our Puget Sound sparkling and vibrant, healthy and productive. I'm working to try to get industry to participate in keeping our groundwater free of pollutants.

90% and 10%. 50% get their drinking water. Organic toxics.

Industry is fighting me. The AWB says there is no proof that there is a problem and they put tens of thousands of dollars against me in my election campaign. I imagine they'll put more in this time.

But those are some of the battles worth fighting. And it's exciting and challenging. When you lose, you go back to your cave and lick your wounds and start plotting how to whip them next time. And, oh golly, when you have a victory, it's the sweetest nectar.

Read the newspapers and what do you find?

The head of OSHA recalled a brochure on occupational safety because he was "offended" by a picture on its cover--of a brown lung victim--not by brown lung disease.

Suspicious burglaries in a Seattle sanctuary-supporting church. The only things taken were membership information and notes of telephone calls to a pastor in San Salvador.

And now the administration wants to have the legal authority to examine your private tax and insurance records.

You'll read about corporations who--as a matter of lofty principle-- insist on their right to pollute, to avoid taxes, and to endanger the health of their workers and their communities.

Who can forget the 2,000 people who were poisoned when gas leaked from the Union Carbide Corporation pesticide plant in Bhopal, India?

Asbestos--and asbestosis--

Agent Orange--

Dumping pesticides--

Love Canal

PCBs, EDBs, nitrates, drinking water contaminated:

16 million kids in the U.S. have no health care.

Canada spends 8% of its GNP--everyone is covered.

The U.S. spends 11%--20% of our people are not covered.

I'm asking you to read the newspapers and weep.

Read the newspapers and vomit.

Once you get over vomiting, do something about it!

These are the battles that have to be fought for social justice. These are the battles that have to be fought to keep our earth a living place--as a participant.

Staying on the sidelines is deceiving yourself into believing it doesn't make any difference, that you don't make any difference.

These are times filled with battles worthy of your skills.

I was really tickled to read last month about a citizen effort to keep a hydro project off the North Branch River and to read that Susan and Richard Herman were in the thick of the battle.

And recently Tom Herbert was selected by USA Today as one of the top 10 teachers.

I would hope no member of AEE would turn away from someone bleeding in the street.

I would hope no AEEer would refuse to enter that gaping maw of bureaucratic battle.

I would hope no AEEer would flinch at speaking out against "official" injustice--even when it's unpopular.

That is the beginning: the example you set for your students.

And that's why you're here. That's the summit of educational experience.

You can change things--you can make a difference. It is your example, the way you approach an injustice, and what you do to make this world a better place that may make that bigger difference in the lives of your students.

Yeah, the earth will continue to spin if you turn away--
    the world will go on.

You can't do everything. But you must do something.

And you were made for challenge.

So bring on the giants!

    Bring on the dragons!

You can handle them!

Hope for the People and the Planet:
Truly Powerful Survivors

by John Breeding

The Concept of Survival

The concept of survival provides a key lineage of experiential education. One thinks immediately of literal physical survival, the teaching of "survival skills," making it in the wilderness, dealing with the elements, fundamental knowledge and skills necessary for living without technological luxuries. Today our wants appear to be our needs, and luxuries are seen as necessities. The teaching of survival skills, experiential education with minimal "things" and maximal reliance on self and environment, challenges this development and takes pride in encouraging self-reliance, confidence and self-esteem.

The concept of survival gained profound attention when the horrors of World War II, and the Nazi concentration camps in particular, shocked our consciousness and forced a stark reexamination of human nature and human potentialities. Study of experiences in these camps led to formulation of the concept of "Survivor." This was truly a basic and literal use of the word; essentially avoidance of death in the face of horror and mass murder. Bettelheim (1952) examined the message that "survival is all, it does not matter how, why, or what for," that a man's true obligation is to "embrace life without reserve." So in order to sur-

John Breeding was a therapist at New Moon Wilderness Program in Austin, Texas. He is now a counselor in the Eating Disorders Program at Hays Memorial Hospital in San Marcos, Texas.

vive a horrendous experience like a death camp, anything is acceptable.

What does this have to do with surviving in the 1980s? It may seem easy, while in comfort, to reject this notion. On the literal plane of physical survival, there are few if any reading these words that feel immediately threatened as individuals. Yet there are horribly many on this planet who are not surviving; in fact, 30 to 40 people die of hunger-related causes each minute as you read this article (OXFAM, 1984). The '80s also present a unique dilemma; that is, we now have the power to extinguish ourselves by our nuclear arsenal. Then there are no survivors. Surviving takes on other macabre twists when one considers the unlikely possibility of limited nuclear war, such as depicted in the recent TV movie "The Day After." It is difficult for the imagination to express such possibilities of a terrible perverted existence. Physical survival is also threatened as never before by impending environmental debacles; contamination of air and water, incredible waste of precious natural resources; greedy, thoughtless, often desperate striving for more, without consideration of our connectedness to planet and universe. The link between experiential and environmental education must grow ever stronger.

To Survive We Must Be Able to Respond

The tragedy of starvation, of nuclear terror, and of environmental degradation is that they are preventable, absolutely unnecessary. So we are responsible. Responsibility means "ability to respond." What is our response? How can we respond? How can we let this happen?

123

Bettelheim points out that the United States' denial of events made us partly responsible for the extermination of the Jews. He says that concentration camp survivors, in order to save themselves the difficult task of integrating traumatic events into their personality, generally resorted to denial, and that it didn't work. We use this same strategy today in referring to arms issues: "Disagreeable consequences" means the death of 15 million fellow citizens; "acceptable loss" means more than 20 million of our men, women and children; "theater war" means the extinction of Europe; "modernization" means more and more deadly weapons...Even we revolted at calling the most destructive weapon of terror in history a "Peacemaker"!

Denial remains a powerful force in the '80s, and it takes a disastrous total. Joanna Macy points out that psychic numbing, or closing off of thought and emotion toward a present danger, critically reduces our capacity for healthy fear and deep caring. This results in avoidance and feelings of being helpless and hopeless. It allows us to dehumanize our adversary. We lose our aliveness, our capacity to care for the fact that so many are starving, in the '80s, while our own tax dollars go to unnecessary weapons of terror or to support regimes which thwart the development of people, many of whom are not allowed to survive.

What has this to do with experiential education? Consider Frank's (1967) comments about surviving. He describes the behavior of our leaders as:

"strangely similar to that shown by mental patients; they, too, try to cope with threats to their personal security by behavior that aggravates them, and for the same reason. That is, they try to deal with adult problems by methods appropriate in childhood, and while they know what they are doing increases their problems, they do not know how to stop...the main source of trouble in human life seems to arise from inability to rise to new challenges because of constraints created by self-reinforcing distortions of perception and maladaptive patterns of behavior..."(pp. 3,9)

The basic premise of experiential education, especially wilderness programming, is that new, unknown challenges stimulate fresh perception, greater self-awareness and new modes of adaptation. This is an appropriate response to the problems described above by Frank and a fantastic way

to break through the defense of Denial, and the feelings of helplessness and hopelessness.

Survival Depends Upon Interconnectedness

So we see that the question of physical survival necessarily spills over into concerns with psychic health. Many have made the point about alienation in modern times, the breakdown of community and support. Like Fox (1983), I view this as a spiritual crisis, a powerful struggle with issues of meaning and purpose (our greatest hunger) in a world seemingly gone haywire, yet so full of opportunity.

Our principal dilemma is that we are seemingly bit by the hand that feeds us. The very progress of Western science which allows our luxury and leisure, and our unparalleled growth opportunities, at the same time imperils our survival. The most powerful mythos which has created this situation relates to notions of dominion and control. With visions of unlimited progress and manifest destiny, the belief of Western science and technological progress has been that we can bring nature even more under our control since it is so clearly separate and external to us. Our strongly entrenched belief in Western progress, our great hope, has turned out to provide the very tools of death, not only failing to preserve life, but making death possible on a so much grander scale. The alternative worldview, shared by most in the fields of outdoor education is, of course, that we are truly connected rather than truly separate. American Indian philosophies most beautifully espouse this view. The overarching concept to deal with this spiritual crisis is that of "Interconnectedness."

"[While it is true that] humankind's misunderstanding and misuse of power has created the current threat,... [it is also true that] abdication of power results in feelings of hopelessness and helplessness."

"The belief of Western science and technological progress has been that we can bring nature ever more under our control since it is so clearly separate and external to us. The alternative world view, shared by most in the fields of outdoor education, is that we are truly connected rather than truly separate."

We have lost our sense of connectedness. Therein lies the heart of the tremendous threats posed by nuclear proliferation and environmental degradation, and the challenges posed by future shock and dehumanization. Roszak (1979) creates a most lucid and meaningful viewpoint from which to examine our dilemma of survival. The prime beauty of his writing for me is his ability to establish a clear link between threats to our planet and threats to our persons, between global crisis and failures of individual development. Roszak states that:

"The needs of the planet are the needs of the person.
The rights of the person are the rights of the planet."

The fact is that at a time when we are creating horrendous planetary debacles, we are also creating an unprecedented personal growth movement in which countless individuals are transforming themselves and adopting a beautiful holistic worldview (Ferguson, 1980). Never before has it been an innate human right not only to survive, but to find your own unique personhood, your true vocation; to seek optimal growth and development, not as an alienated individual carved by the rough edges of competition, but as a person nurtured to experience self-discovery. What a profound difference! What a beautiful, shining ray of hope! Assertion of our personhood is the greatest contribution we can make to our planetary survival and to our own spiritual growth. To meet our physical needs is one thing; to experience our full human potential is an incredibly different way of living. It is this task which I now will address.

Developing a "Survivor Personality"

Siebert (1983) has intensively studied people who have survived a major crisis through personal effort, emerging from the experience with previously unknown strengths and assets. He describes the characteristics these people share as a "Survivor Personality." I will highlight four major qualities. First, survivors transcend polarity. They are paradoxical, transcending any unidimensional explanation. They are both serious **and** playful, hardworking **and** lazy, self-confident **and** self-critical. This may be viewed as evidence of the value of flexibility and adaptation. The relationship between response choices and survival is fundamental. Ken Keyes (1982) dedicated his book on consciousness and the arms race "to the Dinosaurs, who mutely warn us that a species which cannot adapt to changing conditions will become extinct."

Siebert's second observation about survivors is that they share a major motive of synergy; that is, the need to have things work well for themselves and others. This central, organizing principle can also be seen as a special case of the transcendence just cited; survivors overcome the selfish-unselfish dichotomy by achieving a state of selfish altruism. This seems to be a natural offshoot of deep realization of our unity, our interconnectedness.

The third point is that we humans have an inborn drive to have an effect on our environment. This drive functions as a desire to get rid of negativity and enjoy positive actions which result in things working well. This may be seen as an issue of power; note the contrast between a sense of power and the aforementioned feelings of hopelessness and helplessness that stem from denial and withdrawal.

Siebert's final point has to do with the learning process itself. Synergistic survivors learn directly from life's experience. They are intrinsically motivated, alive and fluid. The alternative is to **try** to function as directed by others, motivated by extrinsic concerns. Here we are getting to the heart of experiential education, of "learning what no one can teach." The bottom line is that survival responses are more likely when we are not concerned with having to seek approval or unnecessary help. I strongly believe that experiential education nurtures all four qualities just described.

Developing Values Appropriate for Survival

A question which applies to virtually all aspects of our lives is "HOW MUCH IS ENOUGH?" The concept of "enoughhood" provides a way to confront the threats posed to our growth and survival in the 1980s. This question has a profound connection to self-esteem. Those who grow up in an atmosphere lacking love and care, or manifesting gross inconsistency, achieve no sense of inner security. M. Scott Peck (1978) puts it well:

> "Rather, they have an inner sense of insecurity, a feeling of 'I don't have enough' and a sense that the world is unpredictable and ungiving, as well as a sense of themselves as being questionably lovable and valuable. It is no wonder, then, that they feel the need to scramble for love, care and attention wherever they can find it, and once having found it, cling to it with a desperation that leads them to unloving, manipulative Machiavellian behavior that destroys the very relationships they seek to preserve." (p. 104)

On the personal level, true security can only come from within. The principle applies on a global scale as well. How many of you really feel more secure when we amass more arms, to enhance our "Security"? Roszak points out that there is no such word in our economics as "enough." While poor people need lots of everything, especially food, how much of that is here wasted by our attitudes of self-indulgence? Enoughhood relates to global connectedness as well. Six percent of the world's population consume about forty percent of the world's resources. Our country's projected military budget for the next five years is over one billion dollars **per day** while so many starve every minute. There are over 50,000 nuclear weapons between the two superpowers when 200-300 will devastate a continent. How much is enough?

The value that is appropriate for survival is that "Less is More." More and more people are moving beyond materialistic values to choose outwardly more simple and inwardly more rich lifestyles. Values lying at the heart of Voluntary Simplicity are: Material Simplicity, Human Scale, Self-Determination, Ecological Awareness and Personal Growth (Elgin & Mitchell, 1977). Experiential Education nourishes these values.

Humankind's misunderstanding and misuse of power has created the current threat: blind ambition, misguided attempts to control, thoughtless exploitation, unconscious absolute faith in the myth of progress, a view of self as separate from nature. All of these are manifestations of an inappropriate and often dangerous use of power. Another very dangerous use of power is to not use it. Abdication of power results in the feelings of hopelessness and helplessness discussed earlier. While there is truth to the statement that "Power corrupts and absolute power corrupts absolutely," the inverse is also true: "Powerlessness corrupts and absolute powerlessness corrupts absolutely."

The remedy for denial and feelings of being helpless and hopeless is Empowerment. Empowerment is an important value for experiential education. It is the experience of power, but a benevolent and proper experience. What are the keys to such a wonderful potentiality? The first is that of openness, what Fox described as Faith, "a spirit that is **open** to experience and to reasoning about that experience." The process of being open requires trust and support. The universal law of transcendence, or the paradox of change (Small, 1982), is that I can change (or move to a higher level) only when I have fully accepted where I am now.

Encouragement, or "putting courage in," facilitates this step. Encouragement is any action that conveys to someone that they are respected and trusted, and that you believe in them (Dreikurs, 1964). Experiential exercises provide a beautiful opportunity for this. Properly done, they provide that unique blend of unfailing acceptance and un-

> **"[Those with a 'Survivor Personality'] are paradoxical, transcending any unidimensional explanation. They are both serious and playful, hard-working and lazy, self-confident and self-critical."**

compromising discipline which, as Fox points out, is so conducive to a renewal of faith.

This movement, this involvement, is the next requisite for an experience of positive power. Boyd (1974) wrote, in reference to a powerful Indian medicine man, that "My association with Rolling Thunder was based on his idea that we learn the truth by struggling against ignorance in ourselves and in our surroundings." Experiential educators know that to really learn is to do, that working and learning is the same process. To move is to grow.

Conclusion

Where does this leave us as we move further into the 1980s? For one, it leaves us with the simple, but not easy, awareness that our best chance of survival is through creation of "Survivors," people who are developing their full potential as human beings, who love and care and know the joy of exercising power. The current "manifesto of the person" is, indeed, a response to the planet's needs. Bobby Bridger (1981) puts it beautifully in one of his songs:

"Knowing the wind and knowing the wing,
Knowing the currents and the streams,
I am the hawk and before I die
One time you must hear me scream,
'Oh how will you teach your children to think
What will you teach them to feel
What will they do when the earth needs their wisdom to heal?'"

The earth does need our wisdom to heal. Those in outdoor education know also that we need the earth to heal ourselves and to gain the necessary wisdom. We need to love, know and trust ourselves, so that we can provide proper love and guidance to our children. So this is always the first step: Know Thyself. Make yourself free, loving and full of power. Only then are you truly able to provide the right blend of unconditional love and uncompromising discipline to nourish growth. Our own self-esteem must be so great that we can truly nourish the seeds of our children's natural development, rather than expecting them to meet our needs. The structure and philosophy of experiential education is ideally suited to heal the wounds of our clients, but we must take care of ourselves first. The people of this planet are moving forward; there is no other way. It is up to us to help emerge new human beings who are synergistic and who are survivors, who know how to exercise true and loving power. That is how to do it, how to survive in the '80s.

REFERENCES

● Bettelheim, B. *Surviving and Other Essays*. NY: Vintage, 1980.
● Boyd, D. *Rolling Thunder*. NY: Dell, 1974.
● Bridger, B. "The Hawk". In *Heal in the Wisdom*. Golden Egg, 1981.
● Dreikurs, R., & Soltz, V. *Children: The Challenge*. NY: Hamilton, 1964.
● Elgin, D.S., & Mitchell, A. Voluntary Simplicity: Lifestyle of the Future? In *The Futurist*, August 1977.
● Ferguson, M. *The Aquarian Conspiracy*. LA: J.P. Tarcher, 1980.
● Fox, F.E. The Spiritual Core of Experiential Education. In JEE, 6, 1, 1983.
● Frank, J.D. *Sanity and Survival*. NY: Vintage, 1967.
● Keyes, K. *The Hundredth Monkey*. Coos Bay, Ore.: Vision, 1982.
● OXFAM America, Ed. Pub. #1, 1984. Available through American Friends Service Committee.
● Peck, M.S. *The Road Less Travelled*. NY: Simon & Schuster, 1978.
● Roszak, T. *Person/Planet*. NY: Anchor Press, 1979.
● Siebert, A. The Survivor Personality. Paper presented at WPA Convention, San Francisco, April 1983.
● Small, J. *Transformers: The Therapists of the Future*. Hollywood, Fla.: Health Communications, 1982.

PSYCHOLOGICAL FOUNDATIONS

EXPERIENTIAL LEARNING AND INFORMATION ASSIMILATION: TOWARD AN APPROPRIATE MIX

by JAMES S. COLEMAN

In an address given to the 6th Annual Conference on Experiential Education in St. Louis. Missouri, 1978, a prominent educator separates out some of the major functions of experiential learning.

I must say that I address you this morning with a great deal of diffidence. For in any consideration of experiential learning, it is those who *do* it, and not those who theorize or talk about it, to whom one's admiration must flow. Those of us who attempt to analyze, to dissect, to generalize about experiential learning are as parasites, gaining *our* life blood from the vitality of those who do it. Perhaps the one justification for the kind of analysis I'm attempting here is the same as that which occurs in the discussions that typically follow specific experiences themselves: such analysis can sometimes aid understanding and give greater value to the experience. My aim here will be, then, to attempt to stimulate some insights about the functions of experiential learning in education, and how it can best accomplish these functions. For if experiential learning is to have a strong and secure place in the learning environments of the future, we need a better understanding of just what functions it fulfills.

Having begun with the diffidence, I will nevertheless go on to say that the formation of an Association for Experiential Education in 1977 A.D. is curious indeed. For at first it appears to be a throwback, an anachronism. One might expect the formation of an association for computer-augmented education in 1977, but hardly an association for experiential education. For experiential education has always been with us. The innovation is elsewhere. The innovation is in education through assimilating information, education through being taught via a symbolic medium, learning by being given the distilled experience of others, direct memory-to-memory transfer of informa-

tion. Those innovations are extraordinary, for they have made it possible for persons in one generation to assimilate a vast store of accumulated knowledge, and for persons in one part of the world to know a great deal about what is going on in other distant parts.

It is, however, the very abundance of these innovations in learning through symbolic media that makes necessary now, as never before, a focus on experiential learning. For the very wealth of information with which we are bombarded, the very richness of the accumulated knowledge that is thrust at each neophyte to the society, increases an imbalance which has become extreme, and can have serious consequences for the making of a person. This is the imbalance between information and experience. So long as the techniques by which information is gained *without* experience were scanty and primitive, much of a person's information came through experience, and such an imbalance could not come about. The experience, and information gained through experience, constituted a strong contextual base for assimilating the information obtained by methods that bypassed experience. The latter was made meaningful by the former. For a child who has seen a grandparent grow old and die, the words "old age" and "death," have a rich fabric of meaning unknown to the child without such experience. And when the child grows up, and reads news stories about nursing homes and participates in political decisions about the elderly, the fabric of meaning provided by those experiences provides a context for action that is otherwise missing.

Suddenly, we have a poverty of experience in life. And children, who most need this nourishment, are most deprived of it. The household, which was once a productive unit, overrun with people, activity, strife, demands, love, and work, where the child could gain experience without undue danger, has now become antiseptic, a boarding-house where family members come to sleep, and some-

JAMES S. COLEMAN, *is professor of sociology at the University of Chicago. He was chairman of the President's Science Advisory Council which authored* Youth, Transition to Adulthood. *He is co-author of* Equality in Educational Opportunity, *often called the "Coleman Report".*

times to eat, a place where their paths cross as they go back and forth to their specialized activities.

The child's specialized activity is the school which acts as a protective shield against the mine, the factory, the farm field, the streets, where the child was once exploited by adults and where he learned in the school of hard knocks.

We have intentionally cut off the child's nourishment by experience, for experience always contains difficulties and dangers that parents, looking back on their experiences, want to protect their children from. This deprivation of experience is accomplished largely by the school, aided by the increasingly sterile home which houses the child between school days.

It is at least partly in this context that one can see the various aspects of the youth movement that burst forth in the mid-sixties: that is, as a demand for experience — first in the pilgrimage from the cities of the North to the sit-ins and demonstrations and marches in small towns of the South, and then in the demonstrations and violence on college campuses. The subsequent accounts of these experiences by those who took part in them describe far less the goals of the actions and the larger aims of the movement than they do the texture of the experience itself, the feeling of oneness with one's fellows, the sense of collective euphoria, the emotions upon witnessing a demon-

To say, then, that the school is too rigid, that the school is blind to experiential learning, that the school must change, simply misses the point. For the point is that what goes on inside the school and what goes on outside play important complementary roles. We cannot say what the school should be and do in abstract, without knowing what goes on in the life of the child *outside* the school. For the school has always existed to provide a set of *auxiliary* skills and *supplementary* knowledge, to augment the basic skills and knowledge the child gains through experience.

The task, then, if we are to be serious about designing appropriate environments for children and youth, is to carry out a detailed examination of just what functions experiential education is intended to perform. What do we want experience for?

To carry out such a detailed examination certainly goes beyond what I can do this morning. I can, however, suggest some points that are preliminary to such an examination.

It should be apparent to anyone who reads the program of this conference, or to anyone who talks to two or more people involved in experiential learning activities, that different people are looking for different things. There is not a *single* goal, but different goals. I'll try to identify a few of these.

The very wealth of information with which we are bombarded increases an imbalance which has become extreme, the imbalance between information and experience.

strator being beaten, how it felt to spend a night in jail, the excitement of confronting authorities to whom one once paid deference.

Can we say then that something is wrong with the school, that it is too rigid in its focus on basic academic skills of reading, mathematics and the like? Certainly not without some serious question. David Copperfield went to a school far more rigid than those of today. But this narrow focus upon learning through symbolic media that took place in his classroom was preceded by and accompanied by an overwhelming torrent of experience — on the streets of London, in his friendship with Mrs. Peggity and with Mr. McCawber, his experiences with Uriah Heep, his struggle to get from London to Dover, and the odd assortment of households in which he found himself. For children of his time and experience, the narrow concentration of the school provided supplementary information that enriched, and could be assimilated by the base of existing experience. The school of today is in the same role for some children, but for most children, two changes have occurred: there is a multitude of *other* media outside the school, from books to newspapers to television, to supply information which bypasses experience; and there is, for many of these children, only a weak experiential base on which to build.

I will begin with a function of experience that is most close to the traditional and central aims of the school, and most fully implements these aims. I will consider the two "basic" skills around which most achievement testing and most achievement concerns are focused: reading and mathematics skills. The property of these two skills is that they both involve manipulation of symbols, symbols used to stand for other things. The symbols of language are designed to stand for the whole range of human activity, while the numbers and operations of arithmetic are designed to stand for certain types of operations with quantities.

There are two ways of learning a language, as anyone who has tried to learn a second language in school knows. One is the way all children learn a first language: the "natural" way, by being in the linguistic environment, by trying and failing and finally succeeding, in making oneself understood and understanding others. It is a painful, time-consuming, and emotion-producing experience, but an effective one. The second way is the typical method of school learning of a second language: learning the rules of grammar, learning the meanings of words, not in terms of experience, but in terms of the words of the first language one knows. This process is less painful, less emotion producing, and less effective. Why? Because the first method grounds each word, each phrase, each declarative statement, each question, in a rich bed of experience. One remembers a word, a phrase, *because* of the very emotions it provoked when it was not understood by another, or when it was understood and evoked a response from the other. One cannot forget it, because its usage is an intrinsic part of the fabric of experience that institutes one's life.

Or at a more mundane level, there is the common expression about new words in one's first language: "Use a word three times and it's yours." The statement is not, "Have a word defined three times. . . ," nor even "Hear a word three times. . . ," but "*Use* a word three times. . . ." Usage is action and action generates response, and becomes a part of one's experience, a part of one's personal history.

Language is a reflection of experience, of the daily activities one carries out. Murray Durst reminded me last night that Eskimos have one, or at most a few, words for plants, corresponding to the English "tundra." But they have many words for snow, for their activities revolve around snow. Or as Otto Klineberg, the social psychologist, once pointed out, Arabs have many words for our one word, "camel."

Learning to read is of course different from learning a

anthmetic game devised by Layman Allen, which has been used in some schools, and with which some research has been done, by psychologists at Johns Hopkins. They find an extraordinary effectiveness of the game, and of team play with the game, in raising scores on basic ability tests which involve numerical operations. The rich experience of acting in a setting that involves responses of others, that evolves emotions, that generates mutual aid and support, appears again, as in the other instances, to create a structure of meaning and association that provides a base for further learning.

This then, is one goal, one function, of experiential learning: the creation of a solid experience base, in one's own life, for the very symbolic media that are subsequently used to transmit information bypassing experience. It needs hardly be said that only if these experiential foundations are strong — whether they are built in the home or by an extensive use of school time in play with language, games with printed words, or in still another way — only then can language and reading serve as the vehicle by which information that bypasses experience can be assimilated.

But this has very little to do with Outward Bound, very little to do with alternative schools as we know them, very little to do with urban explorations, not much more to do

---

One goal of experiential learning: the creation of a solid experience base for the very symbolic media that are subsequently used to transmit information.

---

language. But there are ways of learning to read that are experiential learning, and there are ways that are not. Word games, crossword puzzles, games involving letters, stems and parts of words — all these embed the written language in one's own experience in a way that some traditional methods of teaching reading do not. As an aside, I believe that the major different between "advantaged" children and "disadvantaged" children in learning to read is the extensive experience in playing with words and with language that the "advantaged" child has from an early age, long before school begins, and the "disadvantaged" child does not. One of the reasons for the success of Sesame Street, I believe, it that it recognizes this: it *plays* with letters and words, and the child who watches it has, not a true experience, but a vicarious one, with those letters and words.

With numbers and the operations of arithmetic, it is the same. One of the things I have done, of which I am most proud, is to devise a game for playing with numbers, a game in the order of chess, but with numbers as pieces, and one which a six year old can play. I've played it a lot myself, and I've watched children play it, and as a result of playing it myself, I have a different view toward odd and even numbers than I ever had before. I think of a three in a special way, and a four in a different way. Or there is an

with Lance Lee's Apprenticeshop, although perhaps something more to do with Eliot Wigginton's cultural journalism and certainly more to do with Mary Kohler's children tutoring children.

I have begun with this one function that is most close to traditional goals of schools to show the fundamental importance of experiential learning even there. But obviously many kinds of experiential learning are intended for different goals, designed to do different things to a young person. What are these?

Consider first a program like Outward Bound. (Here, as I discuss these programs about which others have so much more experience and understanding than I, my diffidence increases, because I will surely be in error. But perhaps these errors will themselves stimulate the necessary corrections by those who can do so.)

It seems clear that one of the central functions of an experience like Outward Bound has to do with a person's relation to *himself or herself*. A person after Outward Bound is a different person — perhaps more confident, perhaps with more humility, and sometimes with both. An activity like Outward Bound has to do with the *intense* experiences from which many young persons are now protected in the sterile environments we have created for them. It is intense experiences, critical events, that give us knowledge of ourselves, that put us closer to ourselves, make us less fearful of our faults, more able to address them in a straightforward way, without fear or favor. This the school was never designed to do, and in a society that provided a rich set of intense experiences, like David Copperfield's early life in London did for him, the school was properly unconcerned with such things. But it has come to be time to recognize that for many young persons, there is a vacuum outside the school, devoid of such intense experiences that give one self-knowledge. And it has come to be time to design learning environments, whether in school or in another setting, that contain those experiences that move one along the path to self-knowledge.

This discovery of oneself is of course not all that happens in an Outward Bound program, or in other intense experiences engaged in with other persons. But I will content myself here with this one function, that I believe is of central importance, and turn to other kinds of experiential learning.

One kind of experiential activity that is widely engaged in, and takes on a number of different forms, is community studies — whether as urban exploration, as cultural journalism in a rural environment, or in another form. A few of these experiential activities produce a product, such as the Foxfire books, that is of clear value to others beyond the

and went to Chicago one summer to live and work in skid row, West Madison Street. That experience was an important one for me — but not one my parents or school would have designed or even approved of. And such individual search for experience is far more prevalent among the protected young of today than it was among the less protected young when I was growing up. This very increase in search by youth themselves, this very demand, indicates the vacuum, and the need for some way of filling it, or at least some way of facilitating the young person's filling it short of self-destructive activity. It is worth pointing out, in this connection, that not only has the search for diverse experience by the young increased, in recent years; also self-destructive actions such as suicide have sharply increased as well, as Edward Wynne has cogently pointed out in his book *Growing Up Suburban*.

It is not clear just how this vacuum of experience beyond one's orbit can be filled; it is clear, however, that the experience of community studies of various sorts, such as those practiced by some of the persons at this conference, constitute a stride in this direction.

In outlining these three functions of the various activities that are called experiential learning, I have not attempted to be comprehensive. I have tried to show that some forms of experiential learning are essential to acquisition of the

---

The need for such experience lies in the "sanitizing" of a young person's environment which has resulted in part from the conscious attempts by parents to protect their children from bad experiences.

---

participants, although many do not. The importance for the participants themselves of such an externally valued product is great, for it provides an external validation of the value of one's activities. But I want to address another function, shared by all these community studies. This is the function of providing a direct experience with persons, events, settings, neighborhoods, life histories that would be totally outside the realm of experience of these young persons. Again, the need for such experience lies in the "sanitizing" of a young person's environment which has resulted in part from the conscious attempts by parents to protect their children from bad experiences, and in part from the general movement of society toward institutionalization of the young in schools. In the age of the small, heterogeneous community, where children from all social classes rubbed elbows and walked down the same streets, such experience was part of life itself. For some young persons of today, whose parents move a lot, or those whose parents suffer sudden reverses that throw them into a different environment, or those who on their own seek out such experiences, the vacuum is partially filled. (The demand by protected youth for such experience is not a weak one, and leads at times, as I have suggested, to movements like the civil rights marches in the South in the 60's.) When I was in college, I felt such a need,

basic skills that schools attempt to teach, that other forms provide the kind of intense experience that begins to bring self-knowledge, and that still others give a young person some direct experience with other lives and settings far beyond his own. I have not discussed the function, shared by many forms of experiential learning, of broadening and deepening the kinds of relations one has with others — both those his own age and others of different ages. And there are other functions as well that I have ignored.

But the reason I have attempted to *separate* these functions, to identify them as distinct kinds of things that a young person learns, is this: I believe that if we are to provide not merely schools for the young, but environments which aid them toward a satisfying adulthood, it is important to identify the separate components. For then we can work toward providing the mix of various kinds of experiential learning and classroom learning that will address these components. I view this analytic activity toward which I have made a small attempt this morning, as parasitic upon the creative experiential activities which are represented by persons in this room. But as with some parasitic relations, the analytic activity may itself aid the central activity on which it depends, by helping to establish a firmer place in the young person's environment for these activities.

How Experiential is Your Experience-Based Program?

by Maurice Gibbons and David Hopkins

To avoid a vague and destructive definition of experiential education, it may be desirable to construct a "scale of experientiality".

In a west coast elementary school, a fifth grade class is watching Jacques Costeau's documentary on the octopus as part of its study of marine biology. Not far away, near the docks, a seventh grade class is sitting in the cafeteria of a large sugar refinery listening to a company engineer describe the extraction process before he leads them on a tour through the plant. Inland, a group of sixteen-year olds are preparing to overcome their fears and climb a steep face of rock under the watchful eye of their Outward Bound instructor. Nearby, members of a geography class are listening to a lecture about the major land forms that surround them before they separate to search out the rock samples described on their assignment sheets. Spread through the downtown area, students in career education are spending their weekly afternoon working with specialists in various fields of vocational interest. In the suburbs, members of an elementary grade class are negotiating contracts for the Walkabout challenge activities they will design and conduct in the areas of adventure, inquiry, practical application, service, creativity and academic concentration. And on the edge of town, in a barn converted into a sound studio, a rock group is concluding an afternoon practice in preparation for making the tape they will submit for course credit.

All of these activities are examples of experiential education programs that are based on concrete experiences and field studies. The programs are intended to complement or counter-balance the theoretical, abstract studies typically conducted in classrooms. Although each of the activities is experiential, the degree of experientiality among them varies considerably. Subject matter is more directly comprehended through photographs than through words in a book, but pictures, movies or TV programs are less experiential than direct sensory contact with the subject in its natural form and setting. A guided tour is less experiential than a personally conducted investigation. Similarly, a biology lesson held outdoors can be much more experiential than one held in a classroom. That lesson will still be less experiential than a personal challenge in which the student reaches as far as possible beyond his normal performance in an effort to reach such a risky goal as studying the Rocky Mountain goat in its natural habitat. And finally, there is a considerable difference in experientiality between an annual field trip to the farm and a sustained challenge in which a student develops demonstrable skill by a standard effort while in the demanding circumstances of real situations, such as those experienced by a 4-H Club member who plants, cultivates and markets his own crops.

When such a wide range of different programs are referred to as experiential, the term loses meaning and opens the field to misinterpretation and malpractice. A term that does not distinguish between a bus tour and a mountain climbing expedition is too vague. Then critics can select weak forms of experiential education through which to attack the whole concept, the term is too vulnerable. When practitioners can implement a class holiday at the beach and call it a challenge program, a Walkabout or Outward Bound, the term is misleading and permits practices that discredit the field of experience-based education. One solution to these problems is to create a scale of experientiality.

By creating a scale with clearly defined categories, we can not only make the nature of the field and the distinctions between different kinds of programs clearer, but we can solve other problems as well. First, the scale will give consumers a framework for examining programs critically before choosing the one they will buy. Second, it will help the consumer to select an appropriate step on the scale for entry into experience-based programming. Third, the steps will provide a pattern that teachers can follow in developing programs that progress from simple beginnings to full-scale experiential curriculum. Too often experiential education is a one-shot affair, ending after the bloom of newness and the air of excitement pass. Experiences can be

Maurice Gibbons is a Professor of education at Simon Fraser University. David Hopkins is a sessional instructor at Simon Fraser and has written a book, Adventure Education, which will be published in 1980.

used simply as concrete illustrations for abstract classroom lessons, but experiential education is also a major route to competence and excellence. An adequate scale outlines a sustained developmental pattern by which students can master a field of activity through experiential education.

A term that does not distinguish between a bus tour and a mountainclimbing expedition is too vague. When critics can select weak forms of experiential education through which to attack the whole concept, the term is too vulnerable.

All educational programs are composed of experiences, whether they are conducted within a school or outside it. Some experiences, however, are more experiential than others. The question is, what criteria can we use to scale learning events according to the degree of experientiality potential? One criteria is that experience becomes fuller when it is less mediated—by language, for instance—and more directly sensory in nature. We experience objects, forms, features and processes when we are in direct contact with them in their most natural form. A learning event also becomes more experiential when we are involved in the planning and the execution of the activity. The degree of experience increases as the participant becomes more responsible for the experience that occurs, and more responsible for mastering the activity involved to the fullest possible. Experienced-based programs reach their highest level when they contribute directly to the growth of individuals as persons by helping them to establish initiative, industry, competence, and identity; to negotiate the transition from adolescence to adulthood; and to meet the other challenges of the maturing process as they occur. At its upper register, the scale of planned experience-based learning merges indistinguishably with the activities of life. The scale we have devised translates these aspects of experiential learning into five modes, each representing a major increase in the fullness of experience involved. Since the scale is cumulative, each mode can include the kinds of experience in the preceding modes, but adds an important new dimension to the potential quality of the experience involved. The five modes are:

I. **The Receptive Mode:** Experiences, or representations of them, are presented to students who remain a passive audience throughout.
II. **The Analytic Mode:** Students conduct field studies in which they apply theoretical knowledge and skill in order to study some event, analyze some aspect of the environment or solve some practical problem.
III. **The Productive Mode:** Students generate products, activities and services which have been assigned or are of their own devising.
IV. **The Developmental Mode:** Students pursue excellence in a particular field by designing and implementing long term programs of study, activity and practice.
V. **The Personal Growth Mode:** Students learn to understand themselves and their relationships with others. They accomplish the tasks presented by their stage of development toward maturity and make contributions to the lives of others.

These modes can be broken down further into different kinds of activities. For parsimony, the practices common to each mode have been divided into only two subgroups. These subgroups are organized into a

---

The degree of experience increases as the participant becomes more responsible for the experience that occurs, and more responsible for mastering the activity involved to the fullest extent possible.

---

pattern of increasing wholeness or fullness of the experience potential in them. This pattern of kinds of activities is the scale for measuring the degree of experience offered by experience-based programs.

I. Receptive Mode:
    1. **Simulated experience:** The student passively experiences slides, pictures, films and other simulations of reality.
    2. **Spectator experience:** The student experiences the object of study with all senses, but as an observer.
II. Analytical Mode:
    3. **Exploratory experience:** The student is exposed to interesting sites and encouraged to explore the possibilities of the materials at hand.
    4. **Analytical experience:** The student learns by studying field sites systematically often applying theory to solve problems in pratical situations.
III. Productive Mode:
    5. **Generative experience:** The student learns by doing—by building, creating, composing, organizing or otherwise

generating products in appropriate settings.

6. **Challenge experience:** Students are challenged, or challenge themselves, to pursue goals of productivity and accomplishment they must struggle to achieve.

IV. Developmental Mode:

7. **Competence experience:** Students focus on a particular field, practice the skills involved, become absorbed in the activity and achieve recognized competence in it.

8. **Mastery experience:** Students go beyond competence, developing commitment to a set of high personal standards in their pursuit of excellence in a field of activity.

V. Psychosocial Mode:

9. **Personal growth experience:** Students gain understanding of themselves as unique individuals, and learn to direct their own activities effectively and responsibly.

10. **Social growth experience:** Students become more socially competent with people of all ages, and act in more socially responsible ways, using their accomplishments in service to the community.

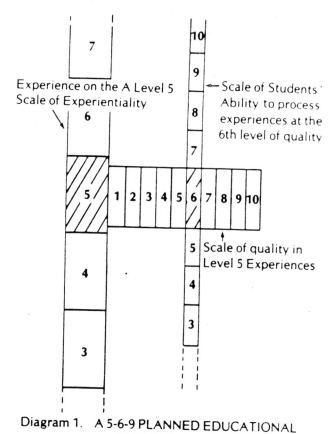

Diagram 1.   A 5-6-9 PLANNED EDUCATIONAL EXPERIENCE

As we examine each stage in the scale of experientiality, two other scales must also be kept in mind—a scale of quality, and a scale of the students' ability to respond. Observing Sir Laurence Olivier's stage performance of **Hamlet** would be a "2" on the scale of experientiality, but a "10" on the scale of quality. One student may not be prepared to respond nor capable of it and so is "1" on the scale of responsiveness or readiness to learn from the experience. Another student—having read the play, discussed it with others and attended other performances—may rate "9" on the responsiveness scale. Part of the process of planning experience-based programs is to consider not only how experiential the program will be, but also the standards of quality for a program at that level and the training students will need in order to benefit from it. While the scale of experientiality is emphasized in the following comments, the demands of quality and the students' capacity to respond are equally important considerations.

The first and most basic level, **simulated experience,** is vicarious experience. It includes all forms of visual aids from picture sets to audio recordings to TV cas-

settes. It may also include objects brought in out of context to illustrate or exemplify some part of a lesson, such as rock samples brought in for a class dealing with

---

Part of the process of planning experience-based programs is to consider not only how experiential the program will be, but also the standards of quality for a program at that level.

---

geology. If the class cannot go out of the classroom, images and simulations of reality can be brought in to it.

At the second level, **spectator experience,** the student has direct sensory contact with the phenomena, but is not actively involved in doing anything with it. This is the field trip to the farm or zoo, the guided tour of the factory or the government buildings, or the nature walk in which the student is a nonparticipating member of an audience. This level also includes visits to the art gallery, museum and theatre. Obviously, the quality of experience can vary greatly at this level, depending on both the excellence of the presentation and the students' ability to process it. It is also clear that students-as-audience may be apparently passive, but actually be very dynamically involved in a play, a painting, or any object of their viewing. Students can increase their ability to process experience and guidance, but the scale, as we have pointed out, cannot account for such personal variables.

The third level, **exploratory experience,** is open-ended, offering the student opportunities to participate, explore the materials, play with them, or attempt to do things with them. This includes discovery learning in its many forms and open-ended creative activities. Activities at this stage may include sensory awareness exercises such as those described in **Awareness: Exploring, Experimenting, Experiencing** by John Stevens; activities for "Messing About in Science," such as those described in the work of David Hawkins; and such imaginative ways of experiencing outdoor environments as "Let's get into the pond and experience it from the eye-level of a frog," described by Steve Van Matre in **Acclimatization.** Being an unorganized or open experience, exploration is often a component of programs rather than a complete program in itself. In its more cunning forms, lessons are built into the experiences for the explorer to find. Examples include learning stations in an open classroom and the specially designed learning materials of the Montessori Method. In its intense form, exploratory experience includes learning to survive and cope in a stressful environment by discovering survival and coping from the situation itself.

Analytical experience is basically field work and clinical experience. As such, it involves the application of theory in real situations, and learning by systematically analyzing the setting or by solving problems in it. A nurse learns to apply a theoretical model of diagnosis during clinical experiences on the wards. An Outward Bound patrol must cope with a simulated disaster far from camp. The geology class must apply the theory of land formations to work out the historical development of a particular river valley. The apprentice in the career-education program must learn by analyzing the behavior of the master craftsman as she throws pots on a potter's wheel.

In **generative experience** students learn by conducting field projects which lead to the creation of products. Students learn by taking part in the process of production. The product that results is both the purpose of learning and the proof of the learning. If the project is to produce a newspaper, for instance, the student discovers what he must learn by examining or attempting the task. When the task is completed, the quality of the newspaper will be the basis for judging how much was learned and how well. A wide range of field projects is possible. Students may raise crops as 4-H participants, launch a small industry as members of a Junior Achievement business group, develop a service as Youth Volunteers of America, conduct a mountain climbing expedition as members of an alpine club, build a glider, launch a project in the fine, applied or performing arts, participate in an education campaign, or become involved in recording local history as a member of a cultural journalism project. The list is limited only by the boundaries of psychological and physical safety, legality and social acceptability.

The shift from **generative** to **challenge experience** in the productive mode changes a single, but significant feature. Being productive in any form is a challenge, but at level six, students are challenged or challenge themselves to reach as far as possible beyond their present behavior to accomplish the most difficult tasks they seem capable of handling. Within the range of possible challenge experiences, those that are assigned to the student are considered to be less experiential than those that students select, plan and implement for themselves. Outward Bound is an example of the first and Walkabout is an example of the second kind of **challenge experience.** In the Outward Bound program, instructors confront students with a fairly fixed set of physical challenge activities through which the students are then guided, such as repelling, kayaking, hiking, the ropes course, a solo and various tests of initiative. In the Walkabout and in challenge education generally, students design their own challenges, conduct the activities involved and demonstrate their accomplishments. The students also plan their own projects in several fairly fixed fields, in consultation with a teacher and another adult. During **challenge experiences,** students may confront their personal limits, but programs at this level are not designed to deal systematically with that confrontation. Such concerns, however, are central in the development mode, the sustained pursuit of competence and mastery.

As stages in the scale, **competence** and **mastery** share a number of distinguishing features. First, they both involve focus on one field of activity. Second, they involve a sustained effort in that field. Third, they involve the achievement of demonstrable skill according to a set of recognized standards. Being two stages of the same mode, they are also different in degree: the apprentice develops competence, the master develops mastery of the field. While competence is usually developed by initiation and practice, mastery requires personal style and originality. And while competence means working to a standard of effectiveness, mastery involves commitment to high personal standards of quality. While still learning through experience, students in these stages settle down to the persistent effort required to master a particular body of knowledge and skills. The more fleeting excitements of peak experiences give way to sustained absorption in the activity. Participation becomes its own reward.

These two stages mark degrees in becoming expert in some performance activity through a sustained pattern of experiences. The task, learning to function as an expert does, has traditionally been accomplished by apprenticeship. In such a system, the beginner faces a clearly defined set of competencies that comprise a craft or trade, and clearly defined stages of progress leading from apprenticeship to journeyman and master-level skill. Apprenticeship still plays an important part in such vocational training programs as Experience-Based Career Education. In lesser work-study programs, the simple act of being on the job, "getting a taste of what it is like to work," is considered adequate experience for high school students. Artists, craftsmen, athletes and members of businesses and trades achieve their education largely through experience, often outside formal educational institutions. Preparation for the professions, whether medicine, law, teaching or engineering, is not considered complete until the student demonstrates competence in such supervised experiences as internships, articles, practicums or field assistanceships. In addition, many achieve their expertise through self-teaching and self-directed study. A pianist, for example, may achieve mastery as an "apprentice" to a great musician or as a student of a great teacher, but he may also teach himself, practice on his own and "pay his dues" for recognition as an expert by playing wherever he can under any prevailing conditions, as many folk, country and jazz musicians have done. Experience provides access to competence and mastery that cannot be gained by abstract studies alone. It opens a much greater range of ways to achieve excellence. Experience provides the means for achieving and demonstrating usefulness, worth the ability to deal with the world that is fundamental to personal growth, the development of personality and character, and a hopeful approach to the future. Yet, there are very few schools, if any, with significant experiential programs designed to lead to competence and mastery. This absence may account for the fact that experiential education has not yet been taken seriously as a dimension or form of public schooling.

Experience in the psychosocial mode is the highest on the scale because it can have the most significant and lasting effect on students. Through **personal growth experiences** the students gain an understanding of themselves, face the tasks of maturation and prepare for the transition to adulthood. The fact that experience-based programs are uniquely appropriate for the cultivation of these attainments in personality and character is one of the greatest arguments of their importance. At this stage, experiences must help

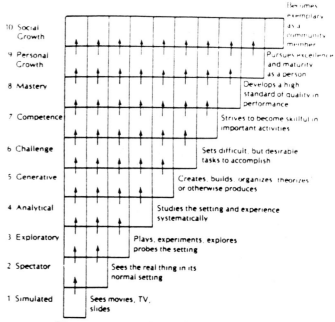

Diagram 2. A SCALE TO MEASURE
THE LEVEL OF EXPERIENCE
IN AN EXPERIENCE-BASED PROGRAM

students to become a powerful force in shaping their own lives. Students who have developed competence already have a solid basis for self-esteem and identity. Further development can be encouraged in many different ways, including:

1. Self-directed education in which students learn to plan, implement and manage their own experiences, and in the process, learn to shape their own development.
2. Creating experiences appropriate for the students' stage of growth so that adolescents, for instance, experience adult responsibilities with adults in real community situations.
3. Intimate conversations with a trusted person, which may later be internalized as intimate conversations with oneself.
4. Humanistic psychologies and philosophies such as Gestalt and Transcendental Meditation, which are designed to teach individuals ways of experiencing their inner lives more vividly.
5. Learning such self-instructional strategies as behavioral self-modification and methods for creating positive self-imagery that are recommended in the whole range of self-help literature.

Helping students to deal with the personal difficulties encountered in self-directed education enables the teacher to deal with inner experience in terms of action rather than as psychological problems. Self-doubt and anxiety may cause students to resist making decisions. Teachers can deal with that doubt and anxiety as decision-making problems and thus assist personal growth without playing psychiatrist. (It is interesting, however, that the psychiatrist is performing the same task as the teacher at this level, teaching his patients to function independently and healthfully in real situations.)

This is the highest goal of experience: a person who relates openly and affectionately to others and becomes an exemplary community member.

If this stage is conducted successfully, students learn to manage their own experience and therefore, gain power over their own development. Learning to cope, to be independent, to be responsible, they not only learn to deal with current situations, they also prepare to cope with an uncertain future.

All of the previous levels on the scale may involve interaction with others, but at level 10, interaction is essential. It is the purpose and medium of experience at that stage. A number of experts, most notably, James S. Coleman in **Youth: Transition to Adulthood,** have criticized schools for locking students into single age-grade groups that deprive them of normal interaction with people older and younger than themselves. These critics recommend that students become involved in a range of social experiences with others of different ages. These experiences can include tutoring those younger than themselves, working with adults at adult activities, and helping those much older than themselves. As a result of such experiences, young people can learn social skills, have the interactions necessary for the development of personality, learn to make their way in the social world, and learn to express caring for others by contributing to the community. This is the highest goal of experience: a person who relates openly and affectionately to others, and becomes an exemplary community member.

How can this be accomplished through experience-based education? The first requirement is contact with a range of people; people of different ages, socio-economic levels, races and beliefs. Second, participants must have an increasing share of the responsibility for what happens during those contacts: initiating, deciding, acting, and so on. Third, students require models of constructive social interaction. And finally, they need a program of activities and tasks which teach them responsible social action, such as those catalogued by The National Commission on Resources for Youth. These experiences can be supplemented by

training programs in communications, interpersonal relations, small group interaction, leadership skills and the like. Human relations training programs and transactional analysis are examples of recognized programs in these areas. Most basic is a close relationship with at least one other person. Unless the student has primary experiences of intimacy, warmth, caring, empathy, openness and trust these characteristics are difficult to teach.

Just as there are stages below this scale's first level, measured out in words and symbols and formulas and theories, there are also stages above the highest level. These stages beyond deal with transcedent, non-ordinary experience. As such they are, at present, matters for individual conscience more closely akin to religion than public education.

Teachers can use the scale to...
* Select appropriate experiences as part of a course such as English, Geography, Art or Science.
* Help them gradually increase the level of experientiality in their courses.
* Implement established experience-based programs (e.g. Walkabout or C.B.E.) with all the features required by programs at that level.
* Create a completely experience-based program.
* Guide individual students, or groups, in designing their own experiences in self-directed programs.

Diagram 3.
USING THE SCALE OF EXPERIENTIALITY

Experience is an essential part of all learning. It is the bridge between classroom theory and out-of-school realities. A good example and metaphor of experience-based learning is pilot-training. Ground school leads to the experience of flight, and supervised flying practice leads to the license to fly one's own missions. Experience complements theory and is the means by which the teacher enables the student to function independently. In addition to being real-practical-applied-technical-clinical-field-apprenticeship learning, experience is also a testing ground for the students' emerging personality and a rehearsal for the activities of adulthood. In a fully realized program, the complete sensory contact, the energy of physical as well as mental involvement, the spice of risk, the richness of social interaction, the potency of designing one's own educational acts and the sense of achievement in striving successfully to do something one couldn't do before, all play their part. When we can harness this power and richness in coherent programs designed to achieve long range educational goals, then experience will take its rightful place as an essential part of all educational activities.

Current Theory and Research in Experiential Learning for Adults

by Ernest M. Shuttenberg, Ed.D. and Brent W. Poppenhagen, Ph.D.

Can college and university students participate in their own learning? The author presents theorectical and research findings that suggests holistic models of learning for postsecondary education.

The value of experiential learning has been one of the main tenets of adult education theory and practice for decades. In the more academic sectors of postsecondary education, however, especially in colleges and universities, experiential learning has been traditionally viewed as necessary, perhaps, for some aspects of "professional" training, but definitely inferior to cognitive study. Participation by the student in the learning transaction was sanctioned, but only under controlled conditions. The model of the teacher as expert and the student as novice held sway even when the students were mature adults.

Today, however, postsecondary educators are rethinking and revising their traditional views of the learner. Where students in colleges and universities were once regarded primarily as passive receivers of knowledge, they are today being recognized as active, integrating learners. New theoretical developments backed by important research suggest a future where many types of learning will be feasible and desirable in all types of postsecondary institutions. Learning will be recognized as both intellectual and experiential, resulting from the integration of cognitive and interpersonal developmental processes. This article introduces exemplary theory and research findings bearing upon adult experiential learning. Three emerging active learning models are described. Implications for the future for individual learners and postsecondary institutions are highlighted.

Emerging Learning Models

Experiential approaches to learning have been gaining understanding and respect in postsecondary educa-

tion over the past decade. In the tradition of John Dewey, Kurt Lewin and Carl Rogers, education is being seen to involve not only subject content, but the growth processes of the learners as well. Weathersby has pointed out that "people's learning interests are embedded in their personal histories, in their visions of who they are in the world and in what they can do and want to do."[1] Mere intellectual knowledge is being increasingly recognized as sterile without the commitment of the learners to give it vitality.

In 1971, Hampden-Turner[2] proposed a model of psychosocial development that pictured all human growth and development as a series of risk-taking initiatives toward the world in general and toward particular individuals. Feedback from each such foray would result in a new integration of a person's identity at a higher level of complexity. Applied to the field of education, this model pictured self-initiated learning episodes resulting in higher and higher levels of educational attainment and personal competence.

Research, theory and practice in adult education, while considered irrelevant to college and university education for many years, have recently become a major part of the foundation for the myriad of "nontraditional" degree and nondegree programs.[3] Several other factors, too, have helped boslter the active and self-directing role of the learner in postsecondary education. For one thing, the realization of the prophecies of the futurists regarding the exponential growth rate of knowledge has finally revealed the passive role

Dr. Ernest Shuttenberg is Associate Professor of Education and Acting Chairperson of the Department of Educational Specialists at Cleveland State University.

Dr. Brent Poppenhagen is Assistant Dean of the College of Education and Coordinator of the Master's Degree Program in Postsecondary Education at Cleveland State University.

1. Rita Weathersby, "Life Stages and Learning Interests," in The Adult Learner (Washington, D.C.: American Association for Higher Education, 1978), p. 19.

2. Charles Hampden-Turner, Radical Man: The Process of Psycho-Social Development (Garden City, N.Y.: Anchor Books, Doubleday and Co., 1971).

3. J.R. Kidd, How Adults Learn (New York: Association Press, 1959); Robert M. Smith, George F. Aker and J.R. Kidd (eds.), Handbook of Adult Education (New York: MacMillan Publishing Co., 1970); Malcolm Knowles, The Adult Learner: A Neglected Species (Houston: Gulf Publishing Co., 1973); Ronald Gross, The Lifelong Learner (New York: Simon & Schuster, 1977).

of the learner as ineffective and obsolete.[4] The proliferation of alternative routes to higher learning under the auspices of institutions such as business and industry, the military and proprietary schools has also caused administrators and faculty members in higher educational institutions to rethink their missions and approaches to learning. The coming shortage of students in the traditional age group for collegiate education has reinforced the other trends mentioned.

At both the undergraduate and graduate level, traditional learning models have persisted by and large, although internships, practicums and field-based courses have been part of professional education for years. There is a growing movement, however, toward more actively involving students in all areas of learning projects and in emphasizing experiential learning strategies.[5] Colleges and universities across the country have begun to offer programs which credit learning activities of an experiential nature.[6,7] Poppenhagen and Byxbee have recently discussed the changing role of faculty members fostered by emerging learning models.[8]

Explorations in Active Learning

In postsecondary settings, three current approaches to the investigation of active learning suggest the richness of efforts to achieve understanding and to improve practice. The first approach, by Lenore Borzak and Barbara Hursh, centers around the study of students' cognitive development and changes in self-perception stemming from experiential learning. Another thrust, by Allen Tough, focuses on the exploration of strategies and processes that adults employ in designing and carrying out active learning programs of their own choosing. David Kolb, in a third perspective, deals with an investigation of individual learning styles and their interrelationships within a theory of experiential learning.

Borzak and Hursh,[9, 10] suggest that experiential learning may, paradoxically, foster many of the qualities of learning traditionally sought in classroom-based programs of liberal education. Focusing their research on undergraduate students in communications and community service, these authors explore the cognitive and emotional consequences of field-based internship experiences.

One outcome sought for in liberal education is that a person become aware of and know how to use multiple perspectives in dealing with personal and societal problems. Another key learning result of liberally educated persons is that they be able to achieve mutually satisfying and productive relationships with others in work and social settings. These two processes—flexibility, on the one hand, and mutual influence, on the other—are respectively termed **decentering** and **reciprocity** by Borzak and Hursh. They find that the combination of decentering and reciprocity "produce a

synergistic effect, with both affective and cognitive outcomes."[11] Some of these outcomes are "an improved attitude toward learning about oneself and others, an increased sense of competence, an increased ability to solve problems, more effectiveness in interpersonal communication, the ability to integrate material from diverse sources."[12] Not only are these outcomes desirable from a liberal arts point of view, but they form the basis for competent professional practice as well.

Experiential learning—that is, educational experiences that include components of both academic and vocational responsibilities—often produce role conflict in students due to differences in expectations that arise at the institution and the work site. In one reported study, students attempted to deal with this conflict in four ways: (1) emphasize the college perspective, (2) emphasize the work-site perspective, (3) reject both perspectives, and (4) blend or integrate the two perspectives.[13] Students who adopted the fourth approach developed "metaperspectives",[14] and they were able to utilize the decentering process to a high degree. The key factor, according to Borzak and Hursh, in being able to integrate multiple perspectives, was the degree of reciprocity present at the work site. They found that "in the absence of reciprocal influence, students will be less likely to achieve a feeling of internship success."[15]

Decentering and reciprocity are interrelated processes, it would appear, that have a direct bearing on the quantity and quality of active learning. Experiencing and learning how to employ these two processes resulted not only in cognitive development, but in a strengthening of self-concept. Students saw themselves as more active than passive, more autonomous than controlled, and more responsible than powerless.

4. Edgar L. Morphet and David L. Jesser (eds.), **Designing Education For The Future, No. 4** (New York: Citation Press, 1968); Alvin Toffler, **Future Shock** (New York: Random House, 1970); Harold G. Shane, **The Educational Significance Of The Future** (Bloomington,; IN: Phi Delta Kappa, Inc., 1973).
5. Brent W. Poppenhagen, "Issues In Alternative Graduate Education", **Alternative Higher Education** 4 (1979): 5-10.
6. Carol P. Sosdian, **External Degrees: Program and Student Characteristics** (Washington, D.C.: Bureau of Social Science Research, 1978), pp. 9-19.
7. Norman Somers, "Graduate Credit for Prematriculation Experiences", **Alternative Higher Education** 4 (1979): 32-33.
8. Brent Poppenhagen and William Byxbee, "Experiential Education At The Graduate Level: A Perspective on Faculty Role And Development", **Alternative Higher Education** (in process).
9. Lenore Borzak and Barbara Hursh, "Integrating the Liberial Arts and Preprofessionalism Through Field Experience: A Process Analysis", **Alternative Higher Education** 2 (1977), pp. 3-4.
10. Barbara Hursh and Lenore Borzak, "Toward Cognitive Development Through Field Experience," **The Journal Of Higher Education** 50 (1979), pp. 76-77.
11. Borzak and Hursh, "Integrating the Liberial Arts," p. 4.
12. Ibid.
13. Ibid, p. 10.
14. Hursh and Borzak, "Toward Cognitive Development," p. 76.
15. Borzak and Hursh, "Integrating the Liberial Arts," p. 10.

Allen Tough, a teacher and researcher from the Institute for Studies in Education in Toronto, Canada, has focused his studies on how adults engage in self-developed learning projects. He has determined that "the typical adult conducts five of them per year, altogether spending 500 hours on major learning efforts." Moreover, while some of these learning projects take place in formal classroom settings, "more than 70 percent are self-planned, and others rely on friends and peer groups." [16]

> Decentering and reciprocity are interrelated processes, it would appear, that have a direct bearing on the quantity and quality of active learning. Experiencing and learning how to employ these two processes resulted not only in cognitive development, but in a strengthening of self-concept.

In explaining why so many people elect to learn on their own rather than making use of coursework developed by colleges and other institutions, Tough cites the recent study by P.R. Penland. [17] Penland surveyed adults from all over the United States, and he found that the most frequently encountered responses regarding the popularity of self-initiated learning had to do not with lack of money or transportation problems, but with the desire of learners to set their own pace, to employ their own language style, and to structure the experience according to their own learning needs.

Even though learners may initiate their own projects, the approaches to planning the details of content, sequence, and duration of learning episodes within the projects may differ. Tough identifies four planning methods, or "planners": (1) the learner himself or herself; (2) a nonhuman resource, such as programmed instruction or audiotape; (3) another person, such as a peer or tutor; and (4) a group of persons with whom the learner is joined. [18]

In order to maximize the potential of adult learning projects, learners must engage in a number of steps and develop several skills related to self-directed learning. Some of these are planning skills, such as "deciding the specific activities, methods, resources, or equipment for learning," or "deciding where to learn". Other skills involve the implementation of the learning plan. Examples are "deciding the pace at which to proceed", "finding time for the learning", "setting specific deadlines or intermediate targets," and "obtaining the desired resources." In addition to planning and implementation skills, the self-directed learner needs evaluation competencies such as "estimating the current level of his knowledge or skill," and "detecting any factor that has been blocking or hindering his learning." [19]

Why do adults spend so much time and effort in pursuing self-directed learning projects? Tough has stated that "the benefits anticipated by the learner are not only intellectual, cognitive, and material; many are emotional or psychological, including pleasure, satisfaction, self-esteem, impressing others, and receiving praise." [20] Tough's research seems to validate the assertions of Maslow and McGregor that persons naturally seek self-actualization and they will put forth great effort in the pursuit of goals that they find meaningful. [21]

A third researcher and theorist, David Kolb, from Case Western Reserve University, has devoted many years to the study of adult learning styles. Taking as a point of departure the experiential learning model developed by Kurt Lewin and his associates, Kolb and Ronald Fry define two primary dimensions of the learning process: **quality of experiencing** and **level of activity**. They maintain that "learning requires abilities that are polar opposites and the learner, as a result, must continually choose which set of learning abilities he will bring to bear in any specific learning situation." [22]

On one end of the quality-of-experiencing continuum is Concrete Experience (CE) and at the other end is Abstract Conceptualization (AC). Persons whose mode of learning tends toward CE rely heavily on feeling-based judgements and prefer to become involved with other people in specific learning episodes. Learners tending toward AC, on the other hand, are more rational and conceptual in their approach and prefer symbolic more than personal learning interactions.

The level-of-activity dimension has at its one extremity Active Experimentation (AE) and at the other, Reflective Observation (RO). Active experimenters have a "doing" orientation to learning that involves trying things out and modifying behavior in the light of success or failure. Reflective observers prefer careful observation rather than involvement, and they learn best by thinking about and comparing ideas.

16. Allen Tough, "Major Learning Efforts: Recent Research and Future Directions", The Adult Learner (Washington, D.C.: American Association For Higher Education, 1978) p.9.
17. Allen Tough, The Adult's Learning Projects: A Fresh Approach To Theory And Practice In Adult Learning, 2nd Edition (Austin, Texas: Learning Concepts, 1979), p. 174-175.
18. Ibid., pp. 78-79.
19. Ibid., pp. 95-96.
20. Ibid., pp. 45-56.
21. Abraham H. Maslow, Eupsychian Management (Homewood, Illinois: Richard D. Irwin, Inc. and The Dorsey Press, 1965); Douglas McGregor, The Human Side Of Enterprise (New York: Wiley, 1975).
22. David Kolb and Ronald Fry, "Toward An Applied Theory At Experiential Learning" in C. Cooper, Editor Theories Of Group Processes (New York: Wiley, 1975), p. 36.

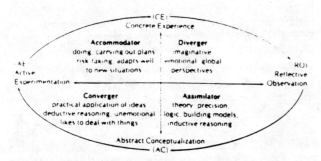

Source
David Kolb, BUILDING A LEARNING COMMUNITY:
A START-UP PROGRAM FOR ADULT LEARNERS
(Washington, D.C.: National Training and Develop-
ment Service, 1976). Summary of learning style types
inserted by authors.

Figure 1:
The Experiential Learning Model and Learning Styles

If these two learning dimensions are seen as the axes of a grid, four learning styles can be defined based on the emphasis one places on CE or AC, on the one dimension, and on AE or RO, on the other. Thus, a high reliance on CE and AE is characteristic of the Accommodator—one whose learning style stresses risk-taking and intuitive problem solving. Emphasis on AC and RO defines the Assimilator learning style, where theory building, inductive reasoning and conceptualizing are key learning activities. The Converger's learning style, defined by high AC and AE, stresses the practical application of ideas, while the Diverger's style, high CE and RO, tends to utilize imagination, creativity and generalization to a great degree. [23]

Kolb has developed a self-assessment instrument, the Learning Style Inventory (LSI), which enables a person to identify his/her patterns of learning in terms of the two major dimensions and four learning styles. A good deal of research with the LSI has been conducted by Kolb and others regarding the learning styles of adults in a variety of settings. [24,25,26]

Theoretically, according to Kolb, although persons early in life tend to adopt one of the four learning styles above the others, the maturation process over years should enable them to develop a more complex approach to learning. In other words, "growth proceeds from a state of embeddedness, defensiveness, dependency and reaction, to a state of self-actualization, independence, proaction and self-direction." [27]

In the light of this developmental concept, the design of learning experiences for adults becomes an opportunity and a challenge to enlarge the learning repertoires of the participants. As Kolb points out, "continuous life long learning requires learning how to learn and this involves appreciation of and competence in diverse approaches to creating, manipulating and communicating knowledge." [28]

Implications for the Future

Educational rhetoric has traditionally viewed students as active participants in learning and, therefore, central to the learning process. Only in recent years, however, has research of the type discussed in this article emerged to support the conversion of rhetoric to practice. As postsecondary institutions move further in the direction of learner-centered education, a variety of implications will surely confront individual adult learners as well as the organizations which serve them.

Within college and university classrooms, experiential learning has the potential to change the very nature of instruction, while at the same time to enhance the role of field learning. This is possible because any

---

> Educational rhetoric has traditionally viewed students as active participants in learning and, therefore, central to the learning process. Only in recent years, however, has research of the type discussed in this article emerged to support the conversion of rhetoric to practice.

---

discipline, no matter how specialized, can adopt active learning strategies and, in so doing, address the learner's affective as well as cognitive learning needs. Kolb has suggested that collegiate institutions might come to, "...provide the integrative structures and programs that counterbalance the tendencies toward specialization in student development and academic research." [29] Integrative development, as Hursh and Borzak [30] and Weathersby [31] point out, cannot occur unless personal growth is recognized in the learning environment. It is time, then, for institutions to emphasize integration; to, in Kolb's words, "counterbalance" the effects of specialization in cognitive disciplines. Implications for institutional change growing from experiential learning confront at least one other traditional goal of postsecondary education. That colleges and universities

23. David Kolb, *Learning Style Inventory: Self-Scoring Test And Inter-pretation Booklet.* (Boston: McBer and Company, 1976), p. 7.
24. Kolb and Fry, "Toward An Applied Theory," pp. 37-40.
25. Richard D. Freedman and Stephen A. Stumpf, "What Can One Learn From the Learning Style Inventory?" *Academy Of Management Journal,* 21 (1078), pp. 275-282.
26. David Kolb, "Student Learning Styles and Disciplinary Learning Environments: Diverse Pathways for Growth" In A. Chickering, Editor. *The Future American College* (San Francisco: Jossey Bass, in process).
27. Kolb and Fry, "Toward An Applied Theory," p. 41.
27. Kolb, "Student Learning Styles," p. 44.
29. Ibid.
30. Hursh and Borzak, "Toward Cognitive Development," pp. 76-77.
31. Weathersby, "Life Stages", p. 19.

help adults learn how to learn has been true only in part. Postsecondary education will better serve this important goal in the future by encouraging the integration of learning through experience.

For individual adults, the most dramatic implications related to experiential education stem from the opportunity to grow both emotionally and intellectually during learning experiences. Hursh and Borzak's term "integrative humanism" [32] may best exemplify this idea as it calls upon learners to experience academic perspectives and to integrate these perspectives with the world of human interaction. Through integration, experiential learning activities provide adults with participation in nearly all aspects of the learning process while encouraging the use of a variety of learning strategies. The result seems to be the movement of adults toward a genuine merger of emotional and intellectual development.

Beyond the rhetorical claims reproduced in countless college catalogues over many years, there now exists a promise for the fulfillment of intellectual and interpersonal developmental needs through the utilization of already existing and viable learning models. That these models might be the basis for new strides in holistic learning may prove to be the most exciting development in postsecondary education in the coming decades.

BIBLIOGRAPHY

Borzak, Lenore and Hursh, Barbara. "Integrating the Liberial Arts and Professionalism." **Alternative Higher Education** 2:3-16.

Freedman, Richard D. and Stumpf, Stephen A. "What Can One Learn From the Learning Style Inventory?" **Academy of Management Journal** 21:275-282.

Gross, Ronald. **The Lifelong Learner.** New York. Simon and Schuster, 1977.

Hampden-Turner, Charles. **Radical Man: The Process of Psycho-Social Development.** Garden City, New York: Anchor Books, Doubleday & Co., 1971.

Hursh, Barbara and Borzak, Lenore. "Toward Cognitive Development Through Field Experience." **The Journal of Higher Education.** 50: 63-78.

Kidd, J.R. **How Adults Learn.** New York: Associated Press, 1959.

Kolb, David. **Learning Style Inventory: Self-Scoring Test and Interpretation Booklet.** Boston: McBer and Company, 1976.

Kolb, David. "Student Learning Styles and Disciplinary Learning Environments: Diverse Pathways for Growth." **The Future American College.** Edited by A. Chickering. San Francisco: Jossey Bass, in process.

Kolb, David and Fry, Ronald. "Toward An Applied Theory of Experiential Learning." in C. Cooper, (ed.) **Theories of Group Process.** New York: Wiley, 1975.

Knowles, Malcolm. **The Adult Learner: A Neglected Species.** Houston: Gulf Publishing Co., 1973.

Maslow, Abraham H. **Eupsychian Management.** Homewood Illinois: Richard D. Irwin, Inc. and the Dorsey Press, 1965.

McGregor, Douglas. **The Human Side of Enterprise.** New York: McGraw Hill Book Company, 1960.

Morphet, Edgar L. and Jesser, David L., eds. **Designing Education For The Future.** New York: Citation Press, 1968.

Poppenhagen, Brent W. "Issues in Alternative Graduate Education." **Alternative Higher Education,** 4: 5-10.

Poppenhagen, Brent W. and Byxbee, William. "Experiential Education at the Graduate Level: A Perspective on Faculty Role and Development." Cleveland State University, 1979.

Shane, Harold G. **The Educational Significance of the Future.** Bloomington, Indiana: Phi Delta Kappa, Inc., 1973.

Somers, Norman. "Graduate Credit to Prematriculation Experiences." **Alternative Higher Education,** 4: 32-33.

Sosdian, Carol P. **External Degrees: Program and Student Characteristics.** Washington, D.C. Bureau of Social Science Research, 1978.

Smith, Robert M., Aker, George F. and Kidd, J.R. eds. **Handbook of Adult Education.** New York: MacMillan Publishing Co., 1970.

Toffler, Alvin. **Future Shock.** New York: Random House, 1970.

Tough Allen. "Major Learning Efforts: Recent Research and Future Directions." **The Adult Leaner.** Washington, D.C.: American Association for Higher Education, 1978.

Tough, Allen. **The Adult's Learning Projects: A Fresh Approach to Theory and Practice in Adult Learning,** 2nd Edition. Austin, Texas: Learning Concepts, 1979.

Weathersby, Rita. "Life Stages and Learning Interests." **The Adult Learner.** Washington, D.C. American Association for Higher Education, 1978.

---

32. Borzak and Hursh, "Integrating the Liberial Arts," p. 15.

TEACHING FOR ADULT EFFECTIVENESS
Article by DR. DOUGLAS HEATH

Building on his studies of adult maturity and effectiveness, Dr. Heath distinguishes between the dimensions of maturity and educational techniques, challenging that concentration on technique at the expense of a clear conception of purpose may lead to ineffectiveness.

I involve my students in experiential learning in every course that I teach: fieldwork in nursery schools, alternative schools, old age homes; cooperative modes of teaching and learning; action research on significant social issues; experiential involvement in the classroom with theoretical concepts; student participation in the teaching process itself. What have been the effects?

Upon students? Apprehension about what will happen next; avoidance of my courses by the overly intellectualized as well as the academically weak student; arousal of emotional ambivalences in a few toward me; increased "aliveness," motivation, and curiosity in many but not all students; great spurts by some in fulfilling academic potentials not previously sensed; a feeling of emotional-intellectual exhaustion by the end of the course; an understanding of the power of learning by *praxis.*

Upon colleagues? Distrust and wariness of what Heath is up to now; dismissal by some of such experiences as frivolous, time-consuming, and not "basic;" desire by others to block such courses out of the curriculum, or at least consciousness, but inability to do so completely because enhanced student interest and growth, even mastery of basic content, are known; mystification; the feeling that "Heath can do it; he can get away with it; I can't."

Upon me? More emotional hassles with students as they struggle with formerly suppressed ambivalences toward teachers; greater demands of me for energy, time, and, most of all, sensitivity; increased awareness of the maturing effects in students when they assume responsibility for their own growth; fleeting desires to return to the infinitely easier authoritative didactic role in which it is clear that a teacher is a teacher and a student a student; strengthening my belief that if what we learn is to endure it must affect the character of a student — his passions, values, concept of himself, personal relationships as well as his mind; recognition that such expe-

DR. DOUGLAS HEATH, *is Professor of Psychology at Haverford College.*

rientially based courses will not survive in the long-run if they are not also academically demanding.

I have learned other important lessons. The academician needs the insights of the experiential educator about how to create more powerful transforming educational settings. The experiential educator needs the academician's knowledge of intellectual skill development as well as his rigorous demands that can assist a person to use his problem-solving talents in a diverse range of settings, including the academic. Perhaps the two most important lessons that I have learned are that both need to be much clearer about their priority goals and that both need a persuasive, coherent, theoretical understanding of what healthy growth means and what the educational conditions are that promote such growth.

Regardless of our different perspectives, all of us face an extraordinary challenge: how to prepare today's young people to be effective adults for the uncertain, perilous world of the 21st century. It is the rare faculty that has self-consciously sought to identify the qualities that will be required to live in those unpredictable years. Proctor Academy, one of our country's leaders in experiential education, identified the three most important qualities to be compassion, self-confidence, and adaptability. It is an even rarer faculty that deliberately seeks to educate for such qualities and then has the courage to assess whether it is successful or not. I think of the faculty of Alverno College that has dared to do just that. Common to such efforts and to the thinking of those at the forefront of education in many parts of the country is the growing conviction that a priority goal should be to empower a youth to become a more adaptable, self-educating, autonomous learner. Unfortunately, such a goal remains more a slogan than a specific program for action. Although some academicians and experiential educators claim they achieve such a goal, I remain skeptical that most of us are as successful as we may believe.

How can we go beyond slogans and rhetoric to discover what are the actual qualities that make an adaptable adult? Presumably such a person is one who has learned to fulfill various adult roles reasonably well. I suggest that we examine in depth just what such adults are like in our society. What qualities predict their effectiveness? Can we begin to draw out of such studies and our own collective experience as academicians and experiential educators insights about the principles that further such adaptability that can be implemented in our work with young people?

Effective adults: What are they like?

I have just completed a study of men in their early thirties who typically fulfill our American stereotypes of successful, effective persons. They are highly educated and productive contributors to society. They are physicians, lawyers, scholars, engineers, business managers, poets, accountants, writers. Most are married; they have at least two children. They are financially comfortable. More importantly, they are living very full lives: they rate themselves to be between moderately and very happy persons. I have more than a hundred different measures of what they were like as adolescents and more than 400 measures of their competence as adults. Extensive material about the men has also been secured from their wives, closest friends, and colleagues.

What have I learned about effective adults, persons who have learned how to cope with the demands of diverse adult roles? First, as an indicator of their adaptabil-

had higher quantitative aptitude scores when in high school, for example, were, 15 years later, less well integrated persons, had less accurate views of themselves, were rated by their colleagues to be more distant and aloof in their relationships, were less mature. As other studies of gifted young people have shown, high intellectual aptitude and achievement in and of themselves do not guarantee subsequent happiness or effectiveness. More likely than not, too accentuated cultivation of just such potential strengths during adolescence to the exclusion of other kinds of growth may imbalance the personality in the long-run and rob a youth of the socio-emotional growth that contributes, apparently, to adult effectiveness. When I studied the qualities that contributed to the men's vocational effectiveness, I found an impressively large variety of traits that most of our academic measures just do not assess: ability to anticipate, imaginativeness, empathy, tolerance, interpersonal sensitivity, persistence, ability to schedule and plan, and so on.

But the most important finding from the study was the clear demonstration that it was the psychological maturity of a youth and, later on, of an adult, that was the most powerful predictor of his subsequent effectiveness.

"The men who had higher quantitative aptitude scores when in high school, for example, were, 15 years later, less well integrated persons, had less accurate views of themselves, were rated by their colleagues to be more distant and aloof in their relationships, were less mature. As other studies of gifted young people have shown, high intellectual aptitude and achievement in and of themselves do not guarantee subsequent happiness or effectiveness."

ity and ability to continue to grow, the men had continued to become more mature and psychologically healthy since their graduation from college. Growth does not have to stop once one has reached 17 or 21 or even 30. Second, the men who were well adapted vocationally were also much better husbands and more competent fathers. This singularly important finding tells us that there is a set of qualities that apparently mediate effective adaptation in a wide variety of different adult roles. If we knew what such qualities were, we might be able to nurture their development more directly in school. Third, the men's happiness was not related to their academic grades when in school, their income when adults, or to most other measures of material achievement in our society. Instead, the happier person was the one who had continued to grow and become more mature since he had graduated from college. It was the person who had not changed much, whose attitudes and values had not been challenged, whose relationships remained in the same old ruts, who was less happy. Also, the happier person was more mature, particularly interpersonally. Fourth, measures of the men's adolescent scholastic aptitude and college achievement just did not predict much later in life. What the aptitude tests did predict, however, was unsettling. The men who

Of the hundreds of qualities that I measured, it was his psychological maturity that contributed most to his vocational adaptation, happiness, marital sexual compatibility, and his competence as a father. My findings confirm the results of other studies of highly competent, creative, and productive persons. A highly effective adult must be an adaptable person, capable of creating some optimal satisfying relation between the demands of his own needs and the demands of the various roles that he plays. The more mature is the person the more likely he will have the qualities necessary to continue maturing and adapting. Maturity is its own condition, in other words, for continued healthy growth.

The adaptable, self-educating person

I have mentioned that the emerging consensus among educators is that we must more self-consciously educate a youth to be a more adaptable, self-educating person. Four qualities are essential to be such a person; each is enhanced by a person's maturity. We know that a self-educating person has a self-concept that he is growing and can continue to learn and grow. Since what we think we can do can affect our motivation to risk trying, our ideas about ourselves can become self-fulfilling prophecies. A solo experience in the Hurricane Island

Outward Bound program can reassure a youth that he can survive on his own and powerfully alter his estimate of his competence to achieve in other ways as well. A student who believes that he cannot learn algebra frequently will not try to learn. Self-confidence in one's capacity to learn and adapt, therefore, becomes an indispensable quality that enables a youth to risk extending himself. Much evidence now indicates that the more, in contrast to the less, mature person has greater confidence in himself.

A second attribute of a self-educating person is that he has a desire to learn, a curiosity about his world that spurs him to explore and to learn. Yet, we teach in our traditional schools, even our best ones, in ways that tend to snuff out that curiosity. A study of one of New England's best public schools has shown that only 43% of the fourth graders and 13% of the 12th graders evidenced any genuine intellectual curiosity or eagerness to learn in the classroom. The relation between healthy growth and curiosity becomes very clear even by third grade. Studies show that it is the healthy, mature third grader who is the more curious student.

A third attribute of a self-educating, healthy growing person is openness to learning from his peers and teachers. A defensive youth, whether manifested in

> "Mastery of self-educating skills is too often only a fortuitous consequence of either approach. Why? Primarily because we have not clearly identified the priority skills we want our students to learn and then planned, organized, and educated in ways that deliberately further such skill development.

hyper-sensitivity to criticism or in passive negativism, is not educable. Again, we know that the more self-disclosing, interpersonally open person is a more mature, well integrated person.

The final attribute of a self-educating person is that he has learned that knowledge and those skills that can assist him to educate himself. He has learned how to get control, so to speak, of the processes of his own growth. For example, a self-educating person knows how to establish realistic goals, organize his available resources to achieve such goals, and evaluate whether he has achieved his expectations. Yet, we seldom teach for such skills in our traditional classrooms; and I am not certain that we teach for such goals as systematically as we could in our experientially based programs. Too frequently, we reverse the logic of the educational process. We select a course or program to offer primarily in terms of its content or appeal and ignore the more functional adaptive skills a youth needs. The traditionalist plans to "cover" the content of the course, even if it means racing through to the final chapter, progressively leaving more and more students behind, ignoring the effects of such pacing on their self-concepts, and intensifying student passivity as lectures dominate more of the class-

room. The experiential educator becomes enamored by a novel experience, a simulation, or some other "turn on" experience which, sometimes, becomes the goal in and of itself. Mastery of self-educating skills is too often only a fortuitous consequence of either approach. Why? Primarily because we have not clearly identified the priority skills we want our students to learn and then planned, organized, and educated in ways that deliberately further such skill development. I have identified for each course that I teach the principal skills it lends itself to teaching most effectively. Then I focus very systematically on the process of teaching to create the learning conditions in and outside of the classroom to further such skill development. For example, a self-educating skill that students will need in the years ahead is induction, one that experiential education ideally is capable of nurturing. One of the potentially more powerful ways to learn such a skill is to become immersed in the complexities of a real-life problem, like trying to understand and work with nursery school children. Simply working with such children several hours a week does not necessarily lead to improved inductive skill. I have learned that much more active teacher-reflective involvement is required, however, if the skill is to be "fixed." I deliberately confront students by having them discuss together questions like, "What did you learn? What generalizations or principles were evident in the behavior of the children? What is the relation of what you have been observing to the material you have been reading?" But I find that this constant prodding in many diverse ways is not very productive. My hunch is that a more effective way to teach induction is to be with the student while working with the children and illustrating the process by modeling it at the actual time such inductions are appropriate.

What prevents the contributions of the traditional and the experiential teacher from synergistically assisting the other is the lack of a common philosophy of education, or, as I have already suggested, the lack of a shared conception of healthy growth and of the outcomes of the educational process. If both can accept that a primary goal of education should be to enhance a youth's adaptability and capacity to educate himself, then I think we can create a more rational theoretical underpinning for our joint efforts. The demonstration that psychological maturity not only contributes to a student's ability to educate himself but also is the best predictor of how effectively a person adapts to a variety of adult roles provides the opening to the creation of such a common developmental understanding of our goals.

The process of healthy growth

What do we know about the process of maturing and what are we learning about the educational principles that we can implement to further the maturational process? Any growing person, regardless of his or her sex, ethnic, social class or cultural background, grows as an organismic system, not just in the head. All persons grow in certain common ways as I have described elsewhere.[1] If we stretch that growing person out of shape by emphasizing too exclusive development in only one sector of his personality, like the academic, we eventually create stresses in his personality that may interfere with continued growth in the over-emphasized sector. I think this is one reason why many very talented persons have turned away from formal academic work to immerse themselves in experiential learning. But too exclusive involvement primarily in the affective modes of learning may also satiate a person, particularly those who sense that they also need the rigorous demands of a disciplined intellectual education if they are to fulfill their nascent talents. We are systems that need to integrate both the affective and the cognitive if we are to release the full adaptive potential of each. We hobble a gifted youth if his talent is not yoked to passion; we drown the passionate youth if his emotionality is not disciplined by intellectual skills.

So how does a person grow healthily? He matures in five interdependent ways: he becomes more able to *symbolize* his experience, more capable of taking a *multiplicity of perspectives*, more *integrated*, *stable*, and *autonomous* in his concept of himself, his motives and values, interpersonal relationships and intellectual skills. I describe each dimension and then illustrate one of several educational principles we are now discovering that contribute to healthy development on that dimension.

Toward increased symbolization: When confronted with a difficulty, one of the most powerful potentially adaptive responses that we can make is to represent the elements of the problem symbolically. We notice its details, different meanings, and seek to articulate the essence of the problem that is troubling us. Such awareness enhances our power to retrospectively learn from our past experience to similar problems, imagine the possible outcomes, and anticipate their consequences. Our increasing ability to label and articulate more carefully leads to increased reflectiveness, self-insight, and understanding of our motives and those of others.

How can we more systematically prod healthy growth on this dimension? At this point, I must distinguish between an educational principle and a technique. I am dismayed by teachers who ask me how I teach, believing that my specific teaching methods will necessarily help them. We do not empower others by offering them our techniques; we empower them by helping them internalize principles of broad generality that provide guidelines to them for creating their own techniques. For example, one educational principle of which all of us are aware but few self-consciously implement in furthering healthy growth is to *contrast, confront, and challenge*. This principle is close to the heart of the success of many experiential programs. While good teachers use such a principle to provoke thought about course content, few of us use it to disrupt a student's typically passive and dependent mode of learning to help him learn how to become more aware about his own idiosyncratic way of growing. One *technique* that I use the first day in a class of 35 students is to immediately break the class into small groups of five each. I present each student with a list of goals, one of which is to begin to learn the skills of cooperatively helping each other learn. I then list a detailed series of steps by which they can begin to learn such a skill. After 45 minutes, the class is brought back

together for the first time as a class. I challenge them to tell me why I began the course that way. Some are usually perceptive enough to know that I am disrupting their typically passive mode of learning as well as their assumption that I am there to "teach," if not "entertain" them. They know that I am forcing them to confront the fact that most are not very autonomous learners. Such disruption of years of passive learning creates frustration in most, anger in some, and great anxiety in all. But they are involved, many for the first time, in the first step leading to reflection about their own learning processes. Now such a technique may not be useful or appropriate for other teachers or students; the underlying educational principle, however, remains valid. If you wish to provoke a person to become more aware, learn how to reflect, think freshly, then disrupt his usual patterns by forcing him into situations that create contrasts, confrontations, and challenges.

Toward increased allocentricism: The second interdependent dimension that describes the adaptive process or maturing is technically known as allocentricism, the growth away from self-centeredness and narcissism to self-objectification and the capacity emphatically to take other divergent points of view toward issues

---

"I am dismayed by teachers who ask me how I teach, believing that my specific teaching methods will necessarily help them. We do not empower others by offering them our techniques; we empower them by helping them internalize principles of broad generality that provide guidelines to them for creating their own techniques.

---

and towards one's self. Such a growth underlies the capacity, when confronted by a difficulty, to analyze the problem from different viewpoints, to think more logically, to communicate more clearly. It enables a person to predict more accurately what others think of him; he becomes a more tolerant, accepting person as he more deeply understands how others feel about the issue that may be the source of the difficulty.

Of the several educational principles I am learning that further such growth, there is one that again many experiential educators intuitively know; namely, *provide opportunities for students to assume alternative roles*. One of the powerful contributions to healthy growth that drama, for example, offers a youth is that it sanctions playing a role, dramatizing a range of feelings or interactions, that he otherwise might not be able to allow himself to experience. As one learns on the stage how to be affectionate or cry, even be dependent or assertive, one learns that such feelings are not necessarily evil, that one can control their expression, and that there are ways they can be integrated into one's experience. Within an academic classroom, I use the technique of encouraging students to assume the role of teacher, first in dyads, then in small groups, and then in the larger class itself.

Scarcely a novel technique; one that may fail with some students, with some faculty. But the underlying *principle* is one we could more deliberately use in more imaginative ways to further allocentric maturing.

Toward increased integration: A maturing person gets himself together; his thinking becomes more differentiated and relational; he is more natural and spontaneous in that he can be himself in his relations with others; his values and actions become more consistent; and he becomes more able to work cooperatively in mutually respectful ways with others. When adapting to a difficulty, a mature person not only is more aware of its various aspects and seeks out alternative solutions, but also tries to formulate some line of solution that brings together, synthesizes, integrates the various elements of the problem.

Much of the maturing power of experiential education is due to its integrative potential. Unfortunately, in most traditional classrooms a student passively sits and inefficiently absorbs information that is not integrated with his experience. As wise educators have always known, a critical educational principle that furthers healthy growth is to provide *reflection upon experiential types of learning.* Experience forces action; when we must act, our in-

Toward increased stability: A maturing person becomes more stable, though not rigid. Recall that too extended development on one dimension, relative to growth on the others, can distort a person's integrity and result in maladaptation. A person's intellectual skills become more stable, though still resilient; when confronted with personally meaningful or anxiety-arousing challenges, a more mature person is able to maintain his judgment, his analytic efficiency, his ability to recall the relevant facts of a problem. And if his judgment does become colored by his biases or he temporarily blocks on an exam, he can recover more quickly than the immature person can. As Erikson has told us, a mature person also has a more stable sense of who he is; his values are more stable and he has the capacity to create more enduring relationships with others.

Of the educational principles necessary for mature stabilization to occur, the requirement for *constant externalization of what we think we know and its correction by action* is very familiar to experiential educators. By virtue of their emphasis on action, experiential educators are several steps ahead of traditional educators in creating more powerful conditions for stabilizing what is learned. The value of constant practice

"*Much of the maturing power of experiential education is due to its integrative potential. Unfortunately, in most traditional classrooms a student passively sits and inefficiently absorbs information that is not integrated with his experience. As wise educators have always known, a critical educational principle that furthers healthy growth is to provide reflection upon experiential types of learning.*"

tellects, concepts of ourselves, values, feelings, and interpersonal skills are involved. What we learn becomes integrated with many different action systems and so becomes stabilized more readily. But as the early Greeks knew well, experiencing is not enough; there must be self-conscious reflection about it if it is to have integrative maturing effects. For example, for years I taught students about psychoanalytic theory by talking about repression, resistance, and free association. But even those who recited back the correct definitions of such terms never seemed to really understand what such concepts referred to. So now as an optional experience, pairs of students, each alternatively assuming the role of patient and the other that of a psychoanalyst, actually free associate for twenty minutes and in the process discover that at times their minds become blank, that nothing comes to mind, and that such blocking is what Freud meant by repression. They then reflect about what they discovered that interfered with their associating. Finally, the larger group comes together to reflect similarly about the variety of ways that "resistance" to associating had occurred. A student now knows by way of his body, not just by way of his head, what the abstract concept of repression means.

in action is scarcely a revolutionary insight; it has been known since parents first began raising their children. But most of us do not *self-consciously* capitalize on the value of the principle. For example, few high schools and colleges require students to write frequently; if they do, they seldom ask students to re-write and then re-write again until they have made perfect what they have written. They are externalizing their students' thoughts and language skills but not correcting them by remedial action! No wonder students do not know how to write. One technique that I use to "fix" what the students learn is to use students as guides, resource persons and teachers whenever possible. For when they explain, demonstrate, assist, they externalize what they think they know. They soon discover in the process how well they communicate to and teach others. Too often, even in experiential programs, the teacher or leader fails to "let go" his teaching or leadership at the appropriate time when students verge on the edge of being able to accept the responsibility of becoming teachers or leaders themselves.

Toward increased autonomy: A maturing person becomes a more independent person; he can take what he has learned in one situation and apply it to increasingly different problems. He can stand up for what he believes, and resist the lures of peer pressure or the imperious demands of his own impulses. He gradually comes into command of his own talents and energies.

Experiential educators have told us much about the educational principles that further mature autonomy that could be applied to the traditional classroom. Again, the principles are obvious, but again most of us fail to implement them systematically in the way that we teach in the classroom. Few of us deeply understand, for example, the psychology of learning that is involved in *consistently encouraging a youth to assume responsibility for his own growth early in life.* Experiential programs that test a youth's capacity to assume responsibility for himself and for others can profoundly alter a youth's concept of himself. An Outward Bound program taught my son that he could alter his own life if he but chose to do so. He has a self-confidence now that has freed him from the fear that he can not make it on his own wherever he goes. But I know few academic programs that similarly challenge their students to become autonomous self-educating persons and that progressively wean them of the need for directed guidance and structure within the classroom. I try to teach so that students as-

we could what we have been learning about how to create more effective learning conditions in the traditional classroom. Given tighter future budgets, the retrogressive implications of the "back to basics" movement, the increasingly conservative educational temper in the country, the experiential education movement as a movement risks suicide if it does not articulate more convincingly what it is learning about how to help a youth become more mature and so more adaptable. The model of maturing I have proposed may provide the theoretical map by which to identify the potential strengths of experiential education; it may also provide the bridge to synthesize the strengths of both the traditional and the experiential approach to education. It maps the core qualities that facilitate effectiveness in a wide range of adult roles. Society expects schools to prepare youngsters to be more effective adults. Experiential education offers numerous educational principles which if consistently implemented within the classroom and school experience could greatly enhance the power of education to contribute to a youth's future adaptability.

A future task for all of us is to identify those educational principles that contribute to growth in the symbolization, allocentrism, integration, stability and au-

"Given tighter future budgets, the retrogressive implications of the "back to basics" movement, the increasingly conservative educational temper in the country, the experiential education movement as a movement risks suicide if it does not articulate more convincingly what it is learning about how to help a youth become more mature and so more adaptable."

sume more and more responsibility for their own education as they progress through each course. I share with them as much of the educational process as they are willing responsibly to assume. And as I have already mentioned, I alert them the first time they come to class that I expect that they will become in time more self-educating, autonomous persons.

Maturing and experiential education
We experiential educators, sometimes because of anti-academic attitudes, sometimes because of our failure to bring a disciplined reflectiveness to what we are doing, sometimes due to a reluctance to analyze and examine what the enduring effects of our programs are upon the participants, sometimes because of our lack of understanding about the adaptive potentials of our own programs, have not communicated as persuasively as

tonomy of a youth's self-concept, values, interpersonal relationships, and intellectual skills. Contrasting, confronting, and challenging, providing opportunities for assuming different roles, encouraging *reflection* upon experiential learning, requiring constant externalization and correction by action, and consistently encouraging the assumption of responsibility for one's own growth are only the more obvious principles that experiential educators know well. I believe that there are numerous others,[2] known to educators for centuries, but ones that need to be re-affirmed and given new meaning through the vehicle of experiential education to the wider educational community. If we accept that challenge, our contribution to the broader educational scene will justify society's continued support of our innovative searching efforts to create more humane and transforming learning experiences for our students.

Heath, D.H. *Maturity and Competence: A Transcultural View.* New York, Gardner Press (Halsted Division of Wiley), 1977.
Heath, D.H. *Humanizing Schools: New Directions, New Decisions.* Rochelle Park, N.J. Hayden Book Co., 1971.

THEORY MISAPPLIED:
TEACHING BY OBJECTIVES
AND COGNITIVE LEARNING

By taking a basically sound educational theory and applying it uncritically, educators run the risk of alienating their students. This can be seen in an unfortunate application of Bloom's educational taxonomy, which can result in student alienation.

by Stanley J. Spector

Many times it is difficult to make the transition from what has been theoretically formulated to its practical application, since the constraints demanded by concrete situations restrict theory's applicability. In fact, these constraints often cause theory to be misapplied. In educational theory and practice this happens too frequently, and unfortunately, it is the student who is most affected. As an example of this misapplication of theory and the resultant harm to the student, we shall consider the currently widespread practice of teaching by objectives which emerged as a teaching style as a result of the theoretical base provided by Bloom, et. al., in *Taxonomy of Educational Objectives: The Classification of Educational Goals. Handbook I: Cognitive Domain. Handbook II: Affective Domain.*[1] Prior to the publication of these handbooks, teachers had also been teaching by objectives, although in a haphazard way. With the appearance of the systematic structure of the kinds and levels of learning, though, teachers could plan more specifically the types of activities appropriate to the kinds of skills necessary for a particular kind of learning. This new emphasis on teaching by objectives was soon affected by more recent concerns of teacher accountability; and since accountability is measured in terms of student success, teachers have been forced to prove their student's success. To do so they have had to write objectives that measure student success by some objective criteria. That this emphasis on objective measurement is a misapplication of Bloom's theory will be made clear by a review of the projects of the cognitive and affective handbooks. That this misapplication is harmful to the student in that it alienates him from the contents of instruction will also be made clear by an analysis of the consequences of the emphasis on these objectives.

Since it was generally agreed that a recognition of the kinds and levels of learning would enable teachers to teach more effectively, Bloom and the Committee of College and University Examiners began classifying educational goals and objectives to facilitate curriculum planning and student learning. Learning was defined as a change of behavior; and so, in order to classify kinds of learning, the committee first observed and classified types of student behavior. They then classified different areas of learning correlating with different kinds of behavioral change, and they found that people learn, that is, they exhibit changes of behavior, in three domains: psychomotor, cognitive and affective. Each of these domains is representative of a different kind of learning; the learning of gymnastic skills, for example, is a function of the psychomotor domain. Cognitive domain learning happens as a student develops skills in the intellectual manipulation of specific content, and affective domain learning happens as that student's attitudes and interests towards that content change.

The first domain for which the Committee developed the classification of goals was the cognitive domain since it is the domain

> ... in which most of the work in curriculum development has taken place and where the clearest definitions of objectives are to be found phrased as descriptions of human behavior.[2]

This was a natural starting point for the Committee since the clearest examples of the correlations of changes of behavior and educational goals are most easily observed in the cognitive domain.[3] In this domain, a student recalls a content, comprehends it and applies it. He then analyzes it into its parts, synthesizes it with new comprehended content, and finally evaluates it by comparing the content with a pre-established objective criteria. Each level of learning in this domain correlates with distinguishable behavioral changes since a student can demonstrate if he can perform a skill or not.

In the affective domain however, correlations between a student's interests and his changes of behavior are not as easy to observe and measure; therefore, the classification of goals in this domain was a more difficult project which took an additional eight years to complete. As a result of their investigation into affective goals, the Committee discovered that a student often "internalizes" what he is cognitively learning. That is, in addition to manipulating pieces of content on a cognitive level, a student brings to that process feelings and meanings of his own. In this domain, a student perceives the content and becomes aware of it; and as he is willing to attend to it, he responds to it with a positive feeling.

> At some point in the process he conceptualizes his behavior and feelings and **organizes** these conceptualizations into a structure. This structure grows in complexity as **it becomes his life outlook.**[4]

What the committee means here is that when a student learns, he does not first exercise and master cognitive goals and then exercise for affective ones; it is rather that as he learns cognitively, he simultaneously learns affectively. Whenever a student encounters a content, he brings to it a structure of meaning that he has been developing since he began thinking, and as he works with this content to improve an intellectual skill, he also changes his structure of meaning.

The Committee accounts for the simultaneity of these two behavioral changes with their notion of the unity of the organism. It is a single student that is being observed, and the Committee correctly realizes that although it is useful for analytical and classificatory purposes to separate the cognitive and affective domains, they cannot be separated in fact since behavior results from the simultaneous interaction of all domains and not simply from one domain or another. As a student encounters instructional content, he comes to it neither as a cognitive being nor as an affective one, but as a human being. As such, he is an organism that has an essential unity. Therefore, when there is a change in his behavior in one domain, there is accompanying change in the other domains.

To apply this theory accurately, teachers would have to write objectives for both the cognitive and affective domains since a student, as a unitary organism, learns both cognitively and affectively with each new learning experience. Unfortunately, the theory is misapplied today since teachers write objectives almost exclusively for the goals of the cognitive domain. They emphasize cognitive learning because a student's improvement and success can objectively be measured by the objectives of this domain; and since the criteria

of evaluation is an objective standard, a student can be tested to determine if he has learned something or not. Teachers need to prove their students' success now because of accountability demands; for if a student learns, then it is the teacher who has taught. Teachers can prove that they are teaching well if they can prove that their students are learning; and since it is possible to prove a student's achievement with cognitive skills, teachers emphasize cognitive learning.

On the other hand, the success of affective domain goals is subjectively determined by the teacher since there is not any objective criteria for how and to what degree a student internalizes as he learns. Teachers neglect, therefore, except idiosyncratically, the affective domain. That is, teachers in a vague and general way really want their students to like what they are learning; however, they do not plan objectives for these goals with the rigour that they plan cognitive goals since it is cognitive learning that is being emphasized. As a result of the emphasis on objective measurement, teachers teach students as if it were possible in fact to separate the cognitive and affective domains; and with their neglect of affective domain goals, they have misapplied the theoretical foundation of the *Taxonomy of Educational Objectives.* They have moved away from the notion of the unity of the organism and with it their emphasizing of cognitive learning they have established learning conditions whereby a student does not internalize into his own structure of meaning as he learns. He, instead, objectifies content and performs cognitive operations with it. He externalizes as he learns and does not incorporate the content of instruction into his own structure of meaning. Therefore, even though teaching cognitively satisfies accountability demands, it does a disservice to students since as a student learns cognitively and externalizes, he becomes alienated from the content of instruction, the world and himself.

He is alienated in that as he cognitively deals with content and encounters the world objectively, he is not responding as an organism that has an intrinsic unity, but as an organism that has clearly defined parts. As his sense of unity disintegrates, so does his structure of meaning; and since it is through his structure of meaning that he understands himself and the world, when his structure of meaning disintegrates, so does his understanding. He is alienated in that his own existence loses its meaning for him as he encounters the world objectively. He does not internalize a structure of meaning, but becomes indifferent to what he is learning and to himself.

In conclusion, by emphasizing the cognitive relationship with the content of instruction, teachers cause students to become indifferent to their learning. If Bloom, *et. al.*, are correct, and a student really has an essential unity, then the emphasis on cognitive learning reflected in the current teaching by objectives style is certainly a misapplication of a theoretical formualtion. It also follows that this misapplication harms the student because of his resultant alienation. To teach in accordance with the *Taxonomy of Education Objectives* requires that teachers perceive their students as single organisms and plan their objectives to account for the whole of the student and each of his domains of learning.

Stanley J. Specter, M.Ed., is a former English and alternatives instructor for the Baltimore City Public Schools. He is currently a graduate student in philosophy at the University of Colorado, Boulder.

FOOTNOTES

[1] We note that anti-behavioralists can argue against the validity of Bloom's theory; that, though, is not the purpose of this paper. However, since the situation in the country today is such that most states require their teachers to teach by objectives, this paper will inquire into the philosphic foundation of this style of teaching to point out how its misapplication has a detrimental affect on students.

[2] Bloom, Benjamin S. (Ed.), *Taxonomy of Educational Objectives: The Classification of Educational Goals. Handbook I: Cognitive Domain,* David McKay, N.Y., 1956, p.7.

[3] We note that since Bloom and the Committee felt that there is a limited applicability of psychomotor skills to the classroom goals of K-12, they did not develop a taxonomy for this domain; consequently, when discussing Bloom's work, we shall limit ourselves to the cognitive and affective domains.

[4] Krathwohl, David R., Benjamin S. Bloom, and Bertram B. Masia. *Taxonomy of Educational Objectives: The Classification of Educational Goals. Handbook II: Affective Domain.* David McKay, N.Y., 1964, p.27.

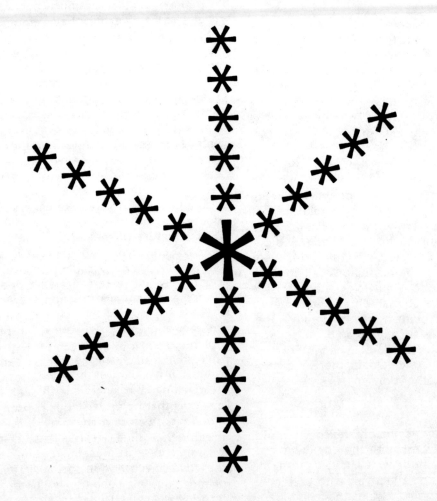

ON DEFINING
EXPERIENTIAL EDUCATION

It is helpful to move from a vague notion of experiential education to a more structured one. Here, a five stage model with nine defining characteristics is presented to further clarify what is meant by experiential education

by Laura Joplin

The premise of this paper is that all learning is experiential. This means that anytime a person learns, he must "experience" the subject — significantly identify with, seriously interact with, form a personal relationship with, etc. Many educational settings only partially promote learning. Those aspects which yield learning can be defined by an experiential model, whether intended or not. Much that is done under the guise of education does not involve learning. Likewise though all learning is experiential, not all of it is deliberately planned or takes place through an educational institution or setting. This paper is designed to define or identify those aspects of education that are experiential, i.e. those portions of experiential learning which are deliberately planned. This paper includes two approaches to defining experiential education:

1) A five-stage model generalized from reviewing the processes and components of those programs calling themselves experiential

2) A review of nine characteristics developed by comparing experiential and non-experiential programs and describing the implicit and explicit assumptions in the experiential programs

THE FIVE STAGE MODEL

Beyond particular agency and client related tasks, experiential programs begin with two responsibilities for their program design: providing an experience for the learner and facilitating the reflection on that experience. Experience alone is insufficient to be called experiential education, and it is the reflection process which turns experience into experiential education. The process is often called an "action-reflection" cycle. The process is generally referred to as cycle, on-going and ever-building with the later stages being dependent on the earlier stages. Most program descriptions and experiential educators hold these statements as "givens" in defining experiential education.

The five-stage model was developed to communicate an experiential action strategy to teachers as they planned their courses. The intent was to enable teachers to more deliberately design their courses and thus increase the experiential nature of those designs.

Briefly stated, the five-stage model is organized around a central hurricane-like cycle, which is illustrated, as challenging action. It is preceeded by a focus and followed by a debrief. Encompassing all is the environment of support and feedback. The five stages are one complete cycle, where completion of the fifth stage is concurrent with commencing the first stage of the following cycle.

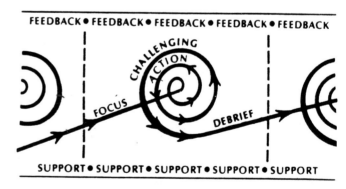

The model is both "maxi" and "mini" in scope. A one semester course could be viewed through the five stages of the model, and also have the limitless repetitions within the whole course. Following the initial

premise that all learning is experiential, everytime a person "learns," these five stages are involved in one way or another. Thus the interpretation of each of the stages for any one situation is very dependent upon the degree of "maxi" or "mini" that is under study. A flash of insight would be describable in these terms. However the initial purpose of the model is to enable teachers to design courses and course components. Thus the model is intentionally simple. For purposes of defining learning, the model is far from appropriate and should not be scrutinized for its relation to learning theory. Rather the model should be viewed so that regardless of what mental processes and brain functions may be involved, these five stages remain the responsibility of the facilitator of learning.

FOCUS is the first stage of the cycle. Focus includes presenting the task and isolating the attention of the learner for concentration. It defines the subject of study and prepares the student for encountering the challenging action that is to follow. A good focusing stage is specific enough to orient the student but not too specific so as to rule out unplanned learning. Most experiential programs expect and intend students to learn things that their fellow learners did not learn; it is the nature of individualized education. Focus facilitates that by helping the learner prepare for what he or she views as important. Focus also works to tell the student what the course and/or teacher holds as important and thus explains the expectations placed on him.

The actions in the focus stage are dependent upon the activity to follow as well as the activity rating on the "maxi-mini" scale. Focus actions may include meeting as a group and having each member discuss his expectations, desires, or needs. It may also include having students use learning contracts. Reading an article relevant to the ensuing action is focusing as well as the teacher's explanation for the next class activity. Focus can also be indirect such as when a rockclimbing instructor opens a packsack and begins laying out an array of climbing paraphenalia.

ACTION is the hurricane stage of the model. This stage places the learner in a stressful or jeopardy-like situation where he is unable to avoid the problem presented, often in an unfamiliar environment requiring new skills or the use of new knowledge. Action may be physical, mental, emotional, spiritual, or of any other dimension. Action involves the student with the subject, occupying much of his attention and energy in sorting, ordering, analyzing, moving, struggling, emoting, embracing, etc. The action phase gives the learner great responsibility.

Different actions — such as wilderness experiences, environmental education and internship programs — have often become confused or synonymous with experiential education. The design of the action com-

ponent should not be confused with the educational approach being used. All of these, and many more, can be characterized by the same model or philosophy. Recent work in brain research promises the most complete description of action as it relates to the brain's operations. Leslie A. Hart in "How the Brain Works" has explained that the brain is innately active. The brain is 'on' when it is actively choosing, ordering, making decision, etc. The brain is not 'on' when someone is attempting to pour information into it. Therefore to design an action component for experiential programs, it is mandatory that the student and his brain be given responsibility in the learning process. Reading a book is a challenging action for an experiential program, IF it gets the student responsible for processing the information within it. The student can be given such responsibilities as choosing the book to read on a teacher assigned topic; defining the reason for reading the book; searching for an answer to a problem in a book; using the book as a reference; or defending a personally held value position.

Another cross-reference for defining action, is the use of "original sources." Watching a film of someone rockclimbing is far different from climbing the rock oneself. Similarly reading about business administration is much different than interning in a business office. A history class studying the United Nations might take the dramatic field trip and visit that august facility in New York. However original sources for studying the United Nations could also be interviewing people about its current activities or reading newspaper clippings during a time of great debate on it. Textbooks are a supposedly efficient means of giving information to students. However textbooks innately deny much responsibility from the student. The textbook author decides which source he will cite, what the correct references are, and the important points of the topic. All of this denies the student and his brain the opportunity and necessity of deciding, sorting, or actively pursuing information.

The overarching strategy which helps implement these ideas of original sources and a brain that is "on," is student responsibility. A student climbing a rock is allowed to succeed and fail on his own, indeed he must do it on his own. In a classroom a student must be given the freedom to fail. A teacher who leads the student through an assignment has not given the student the responsibility for that action phase. Increasing student responsibility does not mean leaving a student to struggle with a problem that is beyond his capacity or background preparation. The problem must be appropriate to the learner and it is the teacher's responsibility to design it accordingly.

Using a student responsibility schema requires great faith in the learner. Students often express great anger and resentment when first introduced into a responsibility oriented experiential situation. Tricks to get teachers to assume their overly helpful habits will be tried by many students; students will often exclaim that they are unable to solve the problem. The teacher's only assurance in this situation is his own experience and faith that the student can master the task. The teacher needs to gain faith in the students as more capable than many educational situations accept. The stages of support and feedback in the model mediate the student's anxiety and the teacher's responses.

SUPPORT and FEEDBACK exist throughout the learning experience, maxi and mini, Adequate support enables the student to continue to try. Adequate feedback will ensure that the student has the necessary information to be able to move ahead.

Support provides security and caring in a manner that stimulates the learner to challenge himself and to experiment. Support demonstrates that the learner is not working alone but has human responsiveness that accepts personal risk taking. Support is implemented in many subtle and obvious ways. Support is demonstrating interest in the learner's situation and letting him know that help is available if needed. Having the group share individual frustrations will help each member see that his feelings are not unique. Support can be physical, verbal or written.

Feedback provides information to the student about what he has been doing. It can include comments about how the student works, his manner of interactions, or the substance of his work. Feedback works best with an equalization of power between learner and facilitator. The teacher should distinguish between those ideas that the teacher holds as true, and those ideas that the teacher believes most professionals in the field hold as true. The areas given to student discretion should be made clear. Feedback is also more easily understood the more specific it is. Specific examples help clarify the meaning, especially those coming from mutually experienced activities.

The fifth stage in the model is **DEBRIEF**. Here the learning is recognized, articulated and evaluated. The teacher is responsible for seeing that the actions previously taken do not drift along unquestioned, unrealized, unintegrated, or unorganized. Debrief helps the student learn from experience. Debrief is a sorting and ordering of information, often involving personal perceptions and beliefs. In experiential learning — as opposed to experiential education — debrief may occur within the individual. However in experiential education debrief needs to be made public. It can be made public through group discussion, writing of themes or summary papers, sharing of personal journals, doing a class project, or a class presentation. It is the publicly verifiable articulation which makes experience and experiential learning capable of inclusion and acceptance by the educational institutions. The public nature of debrief also ensures that the learners conclusions are verified and mirrored against a greater body of perception than his alone. The process of reflecting on the past often includes decisions about what needs to be done next or how it should have been done initially. The public nature of debrief helps turn these comment into focusing agents for the next five-stage cycle.

This five-stage model presents the general actions and responsibilities that a teacher maintains through experiential education. The nature of the actions chosen by a teacher at each stage of the model can be further clarified by looking at the overarching characteristics on experiential programs. The descriptors to be presented have one unifying parameter; they are based on an 'involved' paradigm.

Experiential education is based on the assumption that all knowing must begin with the individual's relationship to the topic. The involved paradigm explains that everything is connected to everything else. Therefore to learn, we must investigate those relations. Among other things, this necessitates including personal perceptions and values. The process of learning may involve being as objective as possible in any given situation. However the innate subjectivity that characterizes all knowing must be recognized and accounted for in our learning systems. Following are nine characteristics which further clairfy how this involved paradigm is characterized in educational settings.

NINE CHARACTERISTICS

Student based rather than teacher based. Learning starts with the student's perceptions and current awareness. Much of typical course design attempts to start with an orderly format based on the teacher's ideas of the ideas of the textbook author or the schoolboard. These starting points and the context organization may or may not be relevant to the learner. Experiential education starts with the student and goes at his pace of learning. It does necessitate some latitude given for including unplanned topics and not including all that might otherwise be covered. Though less teacher decided material may be covered, more material may be learned because of the student oriented process.

Personal not impersonal nature. The learner as a feeling, valuing, perceiving being is stressed. Experiential education starts with the individual's relationship to the subject of study. How a student feels about a subject is valued along with the student's prowess or factual recall. The relationship of educational experiences to personal growth is allowed to be incorporated into the classroom. There are degrees of psychological change that are not appropriate to the classroom. However the ordinary maturing process of a person often accompanies and effects increasing knowledge. Thus the person who is learning is as important as the subject which is being studied.

Process and product orientation. Experiential education stresses how a student arrives at an answer as well as how 'right' that answer may be. The product of the study is valued within the context of the thought and work processes behind it. This is especially important in the evaluation process. Student evaluation is commonly a 'products only' evaluation. Experiential educators also need to assess a student's ideas developing processes and work strategies. These are readily monitored by student journals. The process of idea investigation can be viewed by looking at the reasons a student chose a book, why it was finished instead of being put aside, and how the ideas within it relate to his problem of study.

Evaluation for internal and external reasons. Much of educational evaluation is done for agents external to the student's learning experience, such as parents, schoolboards, entrance to other educational programs, etc. Evaluation in experiential education also includes evaluation as a learning experience. Evaluation is not something that is only 'done to' the student. Students can be encouraged to develop self-evaluation skills and take part in the monitoring of their learning. Competence in evaluation skills can help a student become more of an independent self-directed learner. Students participating in their own evaluation increases their responsibility.

Holistic understanding and component analysis. Experiential education includes both the explanantion of phenomena through statistical equations and describing the variety and depth of the qualities of the subject. Narrative descriptions, interviews, personal reports, inventories, questionnaires, or group discussions can provide information. Representing the complexity of situations is stressed over the simple summation.

Organized around experience. Direct experience provides the substance from which learners develop personal meaning. Since the learning starts with the learner's experience, the subject organization must start there also. A problem or thematic approach can provide a strong organization for experiential education. Rather than building from the simple to the complex, experiential situations start with a complex experience and analyze it as the follow-up study. Enlisting student

participation in choosing among a set of topics to be covered as well as the order of study, helps the teacher organize the course around the student's experience.

Perception based rather than theory based. Experiential learning emphasizes a student's ability to justify or explain a subject rather than to recite an expert's testimony. His ability to articulate and argue his position in the light of conflicting theories, facts, and first hand encounters will be the test and learning medium. Expert testimony is one source for investigating an idea. Experiential education stresses knowing the subject from the ground up, starting with the student's perception and moving to the expert testimony as verifier of views.

Individual based rather than group based. Experiential education stressed the individual's development in a self-referenced fashion. Group comparisons or norm ratings are useful as supplemental information. Norm-referenced grading can be a part of experiential education, especially for target audiences such as school systems and college entrance boards. However the emphasis and goal within experiential education is toward monitoring the individual's growth and the development of self-awareness. Group identity and socialization skills are often involved in experiential programs. The emphasis is however on the individual's relationship and role within the group and that person's awareness of group functioning and his part in it.

These nine characteristics and the five-stage model taken together can provide the stimulus and home base for a teacher's course design endeavors. They are intrinsically individually based, for teachers as well as learners. How a teacher implements the ideas will depend on that person's characteristics, perceptions, and goals. The model necessitates that the teacher be a learner along with the student. The model demands continual responsiveness that can only work when the teacher is an active perceiver and learner in the situation. Deliberate exploration of these ideas can help a teacher know himself, his goals for his students, and his ability to implement the type of experiential program that he desires.

Laura Joplin, Ph.D., is the director of Learning Designs, in Denver, Colorado.

Piaget—A Psychological Rationale for Experiential Education

by Mitchell Sakofs

Broadly defined, experiential education is a philosophical orientation toward teaching and learning which values and encourages linkages between concrete educative activities and abstract lessons to maximize learning. Through these experiences it is hoped and believed that learners attain a qualitatively superior level of knowing than can be achieved through abstract lessons alone; this goal is accomplished by confronting the learner with elements of reality which augment their understanding of the materials under investigation because reality demands that the learner more fully engage themselves in the learning process (i.e. experience the learning process) in ways that abstract teaching tools such as books cannot accomplish. It is important to note that experiential education refers to a philosophical orientation and method of presentation rather than a content area. In fact, experiential programming can be applied to all academic fields.

Although much has been written on the philosophical aspects of experiential education, when front line educators seek to implement experiential programs within their schools they often find that the administration is resistant to promoting such projects. This resistance is often rooted in the failure of the experiential education movement to overcome its association with the now tainted progressive education movement led by John Dewey, and legitimize itself with currently accepted psychological learning theories.

To aid teachers generate more support for the development and implementation of experiential programs within their school based curricula the following brief discussion of some recent research in the field of psychology is offered.

Dr. Sakofs is the Director of the AEE and teaches courses for the University of Colorado School of Education.

STAGE THEORY

How children learn is a direct function of how they think and grow intellectually. To an understanding of these processes the Swiss psychologist Jean Piaget devoted much of his life and developed a theory of learning which all involved in education should be familiar. Through his more than 30 years of research related to learning Piaget identified various stages of cognitive development in children. The stages of development which Piaget identified were: 1) sensory motor (ages 0-2), 2) preoperational (ages 2-7), 3) concrete operational (ages 7-11), and 4) formal operational (ages 11-14). Although the age parameters have been identified for each stage, Piaget acknowledged that they may vary from culture to culture and/or as a function of experience.

Although children operating within Piaget's sensory motor, preoperational, and concrete operational stages are dramatically different, a fundamental thread which ties them together is that in each of these stages the child is dependent upon concrete interactions with the world in order to promote intellectual growth and true learning. Thus it is not until the last stage, the stage of formal operations, that children are capable of cognitively manipulating abstract concepts in an effective manner.

Since, according to Piaget, most people attain the level of formal operations between the ages of 11 and 14 years, it seemed reasonable for schools to develop lessons which required such capabilities, for conducting lessons on an abstract plane is more efficient in terms of time, money and energy, than structuring experiential lessons. Evidence to the acceptance of this position can be found most everywhere in our nation's schools. For example, at a very early stage in a child's schooling the vast majority of lessons are taught through abstract means, i.e., various media such as books, movies, filmstrips, and the like. Since these tools of education

159

are essentially one dimensional, and thus devoid of stimulation beyond the abstract manipulations of the mind, they require the student to possess the cognitive capabilities to effectively process this information; that is they must have the cognitive constructs which Piaget defined as Formal Operations.

Unfortunately, however, although the lion's share of information presented in our nation's schools is done so at the abstract level, recent research has shown that the vast majority of students attending these schools operate below this level of functioning. More specifically, work by Epstein and Maynard indicate that nearly 85% of all middle school and 69% of all high school students in the United States are functioning within Piaget's stage of concrete operations. Thus, the research indicates that our educational system is emphasizing methods of knowledge acquisition which require the students to use cognitive skills which they do not possess. Furthermore, the research also suggests that the byproduct of such demands on the students is that they "turn off" to school and learning, and become frustrated and dissatisfied with education.

EXPERIENTIAL EDUCATION

In contrast with traditional school programs which emphasize learning formats requiring formal operations, i.e., the use of books and other media to facilitate learning, experiential programs, by their very nature, focus on concrete experiences to facilitate learning. As a result of this focus on the concrete, experiential programs are more in tune with the cognitive capabilities of the majority of students in attendance in our nation's schools on up through high school.

These facts are critical for all educators to understand if they are to teach effectively, minimize the frustrations experienced by their students, and promote true learning. In addition, such information provides teachers with a psychological foundation upon which to base a proposal to develop and implement experiential programs into their curricula.

BIBLIOGRAPHY

Dewey, J. *Experience and Education.* New York: Collier Books, 1963.

Maynard, G. "A Middle School Identity." *Transescene: The Journal of Emerging Adolescent Education,* Vol. 3, 1975.

Piaget, J. *The Construction of Reality in the Child.* New York: Basic Books, Inc. 1954.

Sund, R. *Piaget for Educators.* Columbus, Ohio: Merril Publishing Co., 1976.

Experiential Education — One Reality

by Martha Cray-Andrews

"A good teacher doesn't just say 'Here are the materials. You figure it out for yourself.'"

This confident, competent student was so sure of her definition of the good teacher. In her view the "good" teacher is time efficient and task specific. The "good" teacher does not waste students' time by holding back information such as: how long the report should be, what is the expected result of the experiment or where is **the best** source for the information. The "good" teacher offers clearly stated directions, defines his or her expectations by outcomes, and structures an orderly progression through a hierarchy of skill or concept acquisition. As a student in this teacher's classroom, you know where you are, where you're going and you expect your efforts to get you there.

Experiential educators can't compete with this view of "good." The teacher who creates a laboratory environment does not fit the above criteria. Laboratories are not clock-hour efficient. The writing process, scientific inquiry, and creative problem solving do not fit neatly into fifty-seven minute periods. They do not squeeze nicely into controlled learning packets. One cannot always predict when the student will finish, when the idea will strike or when the best solution will present itself. What kind of teacher attempts to create a place for learning which operates on waves of understanding, not steps of competency? What does the experiential

Dr. Martha Cray-Andrews is an educational consultant based in Francestown, New Hampshire who specializes in Learning Styles and Gifted and Talented Education.

learning environment offer? At what cost to teacher, student, and school do we create such an environment? Who really benefits?

Some students learn best through an orderly progression of information and skills.

The Reality

For experiential educators the real world of learning is steeped in active, involved processes. For this Mind view the focus of learning is on "how to" rather than on "what."

This Mind view of reality uses the present as a window to the future. Looking ahead while standing on the threshold of the present means that there is a disregard for the tried-and-true solutions of the past. We should be gathering experiences which may be used at a later time to solve other, related problems. Our task is to go beyond what has been and move into what might be with as few constraints as possible. This is a Mind set comfortable with letting go. It is a reality ready to jump ahead, comfortable with challenge and ready to rise to meet the competition.

What links the people who are drawn to this reality? How can we describe those who find comfort, efficiency and value in "how to" and in choosing options? This view of the world is one of the four Mind channels or Learning styles (Gregorc, 1982) open to each of us but preferred by the experimenters among us. These experimenters are also known as dabblers, option-finders, go-for-it folks or the ones who would be the survivors in a "marooned on a desert island" simulation. Included in this group are the fixers who, in idle moments, tighten bolts, change recipes or try a different route just because "we need a change."

In a tour of the building, there will be evidence of their presence. Piles of stuff (they call it resources) fill brown cardboard boxes and are stacked precariously along walls. Gadgets, equipment, media, technological apparata collect in their work space. They are expensive people to have around. Their kitchens, workshops, classrooms are filled with the best, top-of-the-line products which allow them to do things they could not do before.

You hear these classrooms before you see them. Conversation, movement and diversity of activity are standard. Groups of students engage in activities and the casual visitor is hard pressed to identify the common link among the groups. It is evident the students are busy at tasks but the diversity of the tasks makes defining the single purpose of the activities difficult. In these classrooms, students and teachers are equals, working along side each other in quest of solutions.

These teachers ask questions rather than answer them. They are the ones who claim "'I never answer a student's question. I ask the appropriate question to help the student find the answer." Teachers with this view cruise around their classrooms, operating by an intangible ability which enables them to sense when a group of students is at the end of its rope and arrive in time to ask the appropriate question or make the appropriate observation which serves to help the group get back in gear.

These teachers are rarely the custodian's delight as the debris from these laboratory-like environments defies description. The hands-on, resource-rich, gadget-gathering program fills whatever space is alloted and then spills over to the space given up by friendly neighbors. Marvelous scroungers, these teachers have an ability to gain access to every nook and cranny in their buildings

> "...these channels of Mind or learning styles are available to each of us. We share the basic human capacity to function in each but we do not share the ability to function equally well in each."

and can pull from the community at large when necessary. They never throw stuff out because one never knows just when one might need it.

These teachers are the ones who expect an administrator to go away and administrate. A good administrator from their perspective works to gain resources, space and options for the staff. The administrator then trusts the staff to use those resources well. A competent administrator is one who has done the job rather than read about it or "studied" it. The important credentials are the scars and experiences of having been through it, having done the task, having risked the journey.

These teachers expect students to be willing to experiment, take risks, create new products and generate novel ideas. They expect students to be filled with energy and ready to take off on a moment's notice, physically or intellectually, to explore the territory. They expect students to rise up to a challenge and they assume each student is comfortable with and able to negotiate their own guidelines for projects or products. They expect students to be able to work in groups with cooperative action in pursuit of a common goal as well as be comfortable working and spending time alone in pursuit of a solution to a problem.

The students who share this Mind view are natural experimenters. They explore places, materials, environs looking for options. They are natural negotiators. These are the students who, upon hearing that the assignment is to be five pages long, have the automatic response "How about four pages and a diagram?" These are the students you do not leave unattended in a science wing for an extended time for fear of reading in tomorrow's headline--SCHOOL LOSES WEST WING TO STUDENT EXPERIMENT. These students alter the assignment to create the challenge: moving from trying to light the bulb to trying to make the bulb burn extra brightly or from showing the standard proof for the math problem to trying to find **another** way to prove the theorum.

These students are packers. They lay in supplies of string, gizmos, gadgets, and snacks, bringing in enough to fill desks, lockers, backpacks, pockets and purses. At irregular intervals they check on their paraphernalia by fiddling, reorganizing or engaging in checking-on-my-stuff activity that amazes and annoys those who do not understand this Mind view.

The above characterizations of teachers and students reflect a learning style we all have the basic capacity to use. We do not, however, have uniform abilities to use this point of view well. For some people the demands of this view are necessary in order for them to feel competent and fulfilled.

Traditionally, schools and the teachers in those schools have inadequately answered these demands. Individuals who teach best through investigations, process-orientation, experimentation and stimulation have not had resources, space or training to enrich or deepen their abilities. Students who learn best through these vehicles and strategies have had precious little opportunity to develop their abilities fully. At present, our schools are out of balance in resources, time and space. Experiential educators may be able to aid in shifting that imbalance.

The Danger

There is danger in viewing the world through one reality. We are more complex than one uniform picture tells. While experiential educators as a group can be collectively described as the process-oriented experimenters Gregorc refers to as having Concrete Random preferences, individuals in that group can be expected to show wide range and great variety. It is through the variety and range that each individual will make his or her contribution to the group. Each member will strike a balance among the four Mind preferences or learning styles which enables him or her to feel competent, efficient and fulfilled.

Students are actively involved in learning about the environment through a service project to combat beach erosion.

(National Youth Leadership Council)

Some students thrive on intellectual activity such as research and analysis.

While this article focuses on the Concrete Random Mind view, each of the realities offers a potential contribution. Consider the other learning styles available to each of us.

Concrete Sequential Reality:

This is the practical, precise world of the refiner. It is a neat and orderly world where everyone has a task and the goal is to complete the task well. In this world view, task commitment and clock hour efficiency are the principal measures of value. How well and how quickly one does the assigned task is the foremost criterion for advancement. Advancement proceeds along steps which are defined and arranged in hierarchical order. People who live this reality believe the world to be a patterned, organized place. They believe our job is to recognize those patterns and work hard to fulfill our defined task of maintaining and perfecting the patterns.

Abstract Random Reality:

The people-centered, colorful, motion-filled world of the aesthetic offers a different focus. In this reality, the concept of global village lives. They believe we are all connected by our humanity. Our role in this world is to connect one to another to understand, sympathize with, and empathize with one another. Task rarely takes precedence over person. These people will be late for appointments, forgetful of meetings and unmindful of clock time in their efforts to spend time with friends. Their sense of humanity and connection to others guide their actions from group to group, person to person, friend to friend.

Abstract Sequential Reality:

This fourth reality favors intellectual understanding of our place in history. These people value tradition, credentialed experts and logical analysis of issues or problems. In this reality it is important to know and understand what has gone before. In that way we will know our mistakes and avoid repeating them. In this reality there is logical decision making which is based on the best data available. These people want to know how one idea correlates with another in a continuous effort to link ideas together to form systems. Wanting to know "the big picture," they will research indefinitely in order to reach expert status in their fields. Comfortable in solitude, these people search for the grand "overview," the time when all the connections will be defined. Our task in the interim is to proceed to connect, recognize — through logical connections — the relationships which comprise our system called earth.

According to Gregorc, these channels of Mind or learning styles are available to each of us. We share the basic human capacity to function in each but we do not share the ability to function equally well in each. Our preferences and strengths cause us to seek out certain channels. We create in the image of those preferred channels. We value people and environments that reflect our preferences well. We may choose to surround ourselves with like-Minded people and deny views different from our own. We can then rule other-Minded people to be inferior, inadequate or deviant. "Our group" can then work hard to make others just like us in their Mind set.

It is a short step from denying alternative views from others to denying those views from ourselves. We begin by "keeping a lid on" our own unacceptable ideas and behaviors. We work hard being good at the "normal" behaviors of our group. We fake it. We compete on false grounds, making claims we have no business making. Like-Mindedness can be a comfort; it can also be a prison.

The Opportunity

The opportunity created by understanding these realities of Mind is immense. Understanding the variety in these realities will aid in teacher-to-teacher communication and teacher-to-student communication. Knowing the reality or learning style through which we teach will enable us to understand the demands we make on learners. We make those demands, not because they are THE appropriate demands but because they reflect the reality we, as teachers, create in that classroom. Each reality enables us to create a classroom with demands and each will have students who respond negatively to those demands.

Recognizing the demands we make on students and the expectations we have for fellow-teachers will enable us to become better classroom designers. We will be able to differentiate between the real demands of teaching and the style-specific demands we make. We will be better able to exercise our creative abilities to design an enriched curriculum which reflects the full array of realities rather than the impoverished narrow band of Mind preferences owned by the individual in charge.

Developing an enriched curriculum requires teachers who have a natural understanding of the Mind's realities and who can effectively offer those realities to others. These teachers will be able to openly share the demands and explain the demands rather than expect students to recognize unspoken rules. They will be able to offer access to students by cracking the codes of each learning style and by recognizing that students have preferences too. The students will have alternate pathways to learning rather than the single pathway so often presented today. These new educators will be able to differentiate between access to content and understanding of content. They will recognize the viable variety of ways people learn. Most importantly, they will be able to understand and accept their own weaknesses as educators without dismissing those abilities as unimportant in educational programming.

New educators will be able to work with fellow staff members who do not share their strengths in order to create a richer environment for learners. The education this collaborative effort will create

Students are involved in cooperative learning groups.

has the capacity to surpass past efforts of reform which were based on the perspective of educators with one Mind view. We need groups of educators secure in their purpose, understanding of their strengths, and cognizant of their weaknesses. Through such groups the imbalance in education can be righted. Cooperative efforts may yield new educators able to understand the place and time of the Concrete Sequential's world, the people and color of the Abstract Random's world as well as the experiment and variety of the Concrete Random's world.

REFERENCES

- Cray-Andrews, Martha. Mind's View (a film). Gabriel Systems, Inc. Maynard, MA, 1984.
- Gregorc, A.F. *An Adult's Guide To Style*. Gabriel Systems, Inc., Maynard, MA, 1982.
- Gregorc, A.F. *Inside Styles: Beyond The Basics*. Gabriel Systems, Inc., Maynard, MA, 1985.

Programming the Transfer of Learning in Adventure Education

By Michael A. Gass

When evaluating the effectiveness of any learning experience, educators have often focused on how learning will serve the student in the future. This concern has become particularly true in the field of adventure education. Whether it has been a young adolescent developing more appropriate social behaviors, a freshman student obtaining a more beneficial educational experience at a university, or another program where adventure is used as a valid educational medium, the credibility of programs using a challenging environment has been based upon the positive effects they have on their students' or clients' futures.

This effect that a particular experience has on future learning experiences is called the transfer of learning or the transfer of training. In our attempts to simplify the essential, most adventure educators call this phenomenon 'transfer'. Transfer is valuable to many programs in the sense that their success, continuation and/or livelihood is based on the effect their program has on the future of their students or clients. For example, when describing the value of adventure programming as a milieu used to prevent delinquency, the U.S. Department of Justice states that despite having some plausible theoretical or correlational basis, wilderness programs without follow-up (transfer) into clients' home communities "should be rejected on the basis of their repeated failure to demonstrate effectiveness in reducing deliquency after having been tried and evaluated."

While transfer is critical to the field of adventure education, probably no other concept is so

Michael Gass is Coordinator of Outdoor Education at the University of New Hampshire and a doctoral candidate at the University of Colorado.

often misunderstood. Much of the confusion plaguing the transfer of learning has resulted from two main factors. First is the concern that the initial learning usually takes place in an environment (e.g. mountains) quite different from the environment where the student's future learning will occur. Second is the lack of knowledge concerning the variety of methods available to promote transfer. Neither of these problems are limited to adventure education, but there are certain theories, models and techniques that pertain directly to the field and can assist in eliminating much of the confusion surrounding the topic and enable individuals to strengthen the transfer of their program's goals.

THEORIES CONCERNING TRANSFER

Concerning the application to adventure education, three central learning theories pertaining to transfer exist that explain how the linking of elements from one learning environment to another occur (see Figure 1). Bruner describes the first two, specific and non-specific transfer, in attempting to show how current learning serves the learner in the future.

"There are two ways in which learning serves the future. One is through its specific applicability to tasks that are highly similar to those we originally learned to perform. Psychologists refer to this specific phenomenon as specific transfer of training; perhaps it should be called the extension of habits or associations. Its utility appears to be limited in the main to what we speak of as skills. A second way in which earlier learning renders later performance more efficient is through what is conveniently called non-specific transfer, or, more accurately, the transfer of principles and attitudes. In essence, it consists of learning, initially, not a skill but a general idea which can then be used as a basis of recognizing subsequent

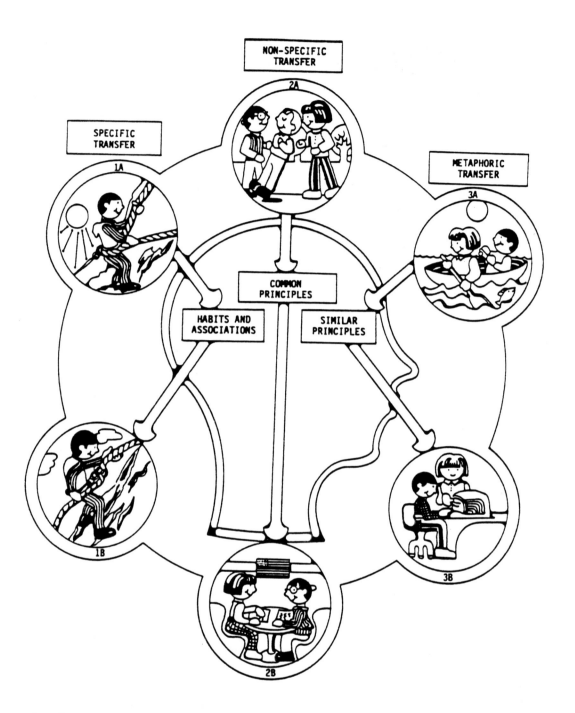

Figure 1. THREE THEORIES OF TRANSFER IN ADVENTURE EDUCATION. The above diagram illustrates how learning in adventure education is linked to future learning experiences. In the first theory, specific transfer, the learner takes the habits and associations acquired during a previous experience (Diagram 1A - the hand skills of belaying) and applies them to a new experience to assist him in developing a new skill (Diagram 1B - the hand skills of rappelling). In the second theory, non-specific transfer, the learner generalizes the common underlying principles received from a previous experience (Diagram 2-A developing trust from an initiative game) and employs them in a new learning situation (Diagram 2B - developing trust with peers at school). The third theory, metaphoric transfer, shows the learner transferring the similar underlying principles from canoeing (Diagram 3A) to working with other individuals in a business corporation (Diagram 3B).

problems as special cases of the idea originally mastered." (1960:17)

The following example from a student's notebook serves to illustrate the use of specific transfer in adventure education:

"Today during the class we learned how to rappell. Initially I was quite frightened, but I ended up catching on to the proper techniques and enjoying it quite a bit! One thing that helped me in learning how to rappell was the belaying we did yesterday. With belaying, our left hand is the 'feel' hand while the right hand is the 'brake' hand. With rappelling, it is the same; our left hand is the 'feel' hand and our right hand is used to 'brake' our rappell and control our descent."

In this example, the student's previous experiences of specific hand skills learned while belaying positively affected her ability to learn the necessary and correct hand skills of rappelling. Figure 1 illustrates these events occurring — the initial stage of learning how to belay, the development of the proper and safe habits while belaying, and finally, the use of these skills while rappelling.

The next example from another student's notebook highlights what Bruner describes as non-specific transfer, or the use of common underlying principles in one learning situation to assist the student in a future learning experience:

"...(as a result of the wilderness course) I've seen myself developing more trust in my friends at school. The no-discount policy¹ helps me quite a bit, but I think what helped the most was learning how I receive as well as give support to others. I felt that this was the most important thing I learned (while on the wilderness course)."

In this second example, the student had taken the common underlying principles that she learned about developing trust (i.e. receiving and giving support from/to others) from the wilderness course and generalized those principles and attitudes to a new learning situation (i.e. school). This ability to generalize by the learner is crucial for non-specific transfer to occur. Figure 1 shows the connection of two learning situations by common underlying principles or non-specific transfer. In this example, the student, through an initiative such as the willow wand exercise² supplemented with a no-discount policy, learns valuable principles and attitudes about developing trust in peer relationships. She takes these principles, generalizes them, and transfers them to a new learning situation, such as developing meaningful relationships at school based on trust.

The third transfer theory associated with adventure learning also requires the student to generalize certain principles from one learning situation to another. But the principles being transferred in this theory are not common or the same in structure, but are similar, analogous, or metaphorical.

The following passage illustrates a student making the connection between the similar underlying principles of canoeing and his group working together:

"There has been a certain jerkiness in the group. It's like the progress of a canoe. When the people on each side paddle in unison, with each person pulling his weight, the canoe goes forward smoothly. If certain people slack, or if there is a lack of co-ordination, progress becomes jerky. The canoe veers (from) side to side. Time and energy are wasted." (Godfrey, 1980:229)

In this particular situation, the student is not using the principles of efficient canoeing for future aquatic learning experiences. He is instead transferring the concepts or principles of canoeing as metaphors for another learning experience that is similar, yet not the same.

This third type of transfer, metaphoric transfer, is also illustrated in Figure 1. Here the student takes the similar underlying principles mentioned in the example above, generalizes them and applies them to a future learning experience with similar elements. The future learning experience represented in Figure 1 for metaphoric transfer is a group situation where the necessity of everyone working together efficiently is vital (in this case, working for a business corporation).

Probably the individual who has done the most investigation into the use of metaphoric transfer with adventure learning is Stephen Bacon. In the following passage, he further explains how using experiences that are metaphoric provide a vehicle for the transfer of learning:

"The key factor in determining whether experiences are metaphoric is the degree of isomorphism between the metaphoric situation and the real-life situation. Isomorphic means having the same structure. When all the major elements in one experience are represented by corresponding elements in another experience, and when the overall structure of the two experiences are highly similar, then the two experiences are metaphors for each other. This does not imply that the corresponding elements are literally identical; rather, they must be symbolically identical." (Bacon, 1983:4)

¹ The no-discount policy is a technique from Gestalt psychology used by some adventure programs. It asks that all participants (voluntarily) enter into a 'contract' with the other group members, agreeing not to discount their feelings as well as the feelings of the other members in the group. Members of the group are asked to confront any discounting behavior and this will often lead to a group discussion.

² The "Willow Wand" exercise is an initiative used to introduce the concept of trust to a group in an adventure experience. It often serves as a lead-up activity to a trust circle or trust fall.

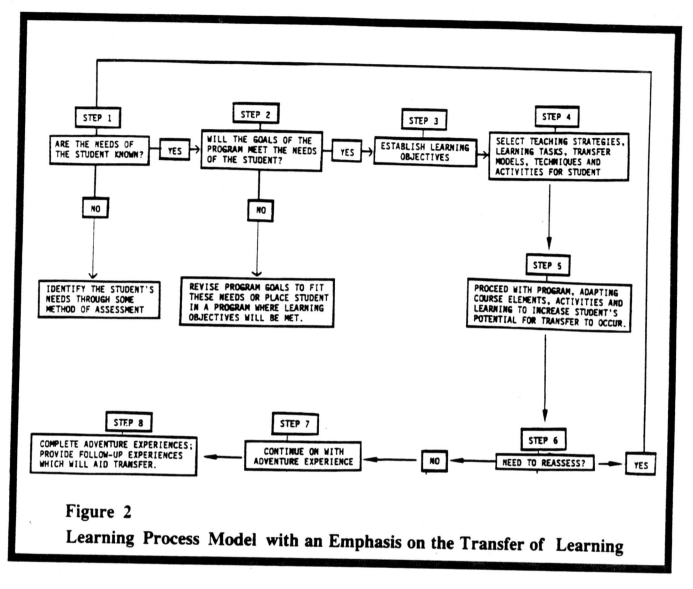

Figure 2

Learning Process Model with an Emphasis on the Transfer of Learning

A PROGRAM MODEL
FOR TRANSFER

When reviewing the three transfer of learning theories discussed previously, it can be seen that the key to increasing transfer often lies either in the selection or design of appropriate learning activities or in the teaching methodology. One of the major faults of adventure education has been the lack of planning for the transfer in these areas. Transfer must be planned, much in the same manner as an educational objective, or a properly planned learning skill.

Figure 2 portrays the learning process of an adventure program interested in procuring positive transfer for a student.

As seen in the model, once the needs of the student and the goals of the program are properly identified and matched, the learning skills, activities, teaching strategies and transfer models and techniques are planned. A strong emphasis is placed here on providing the connection between the present and future learning environments to increase the amount of transfer which will occur. Note that throughout the program, if the needs of the student change, the model directs the instructor to assess these changes and adapt new learning activities and transfer elements to the student's new behavior. At the completion of the adventure experience, follow-up activities are also used to enhance positive transfer.

169

FACTOR/TECHNIQUES THAT ENHANCE THE TRANSFER OF LEARNING THROUGH ADVENTURE ACTIVITIES

Given the information in Figure 2 for programming transfer, what are some of the factors or techniques adventure educators can use to assist them in increasing the transfer of their students' learning? (Shown by Step 4 in Figure 2). Many researchers have presented exhaustive lists of elements which can lead to positive transfer, but some of these are unalterable (e.g. genetic factors concerning intelligence) while others have little application to the 'non-traditional' atmosphere where most adventure learning takes place.

As stated in the program model, it is necessary for the adventure educator to select not only the proper transfer of learning theories but also the techniques and activities involved with the increase of transfer applicable to their program. Ten techniques adaptable to the transfer of learning occurring with adventure activities are presented here as examples. However, many other techniques exist and should be selected for their ability to transfer the goals of the specific program and what theory of transfer one is using. (A bibliography is included with this article and sources that address this topic to a greater degree are noted by ***.)

1. Design conditions for transfer before the course/program/learning activities actually begin. Several steps can be done prior to a learning experience that can aid in the transfer of learning from an adventure activity.
Examples of these steps include:
a) Identify, develop or establish a commitment to change in the student.
b) Have a student set goals for the experience.
c) Write and set tight learning objectives for the student in the program.
d) Place the plans and goals made by the student in writing to create a stronger commitment for transferring the learning.

2. Create elements in the student's learning environment similar to those elements likely to be found in future learning environments. Learning environments with strong applicability to future experiences have greater potential for a more positive transfer of learning. The following example of a disaffected youth in a wilderness program shows how elements of the program were created to assist him in transferring a behavior, in this case, a greater self concept, into a subsequent learning environment.

"Throughout the course, Kurt was presented with a variety of challenging tasks. He overcame strong personal fears and doubts and succeeded at many of the tasks that required a great deal of initiative. The staff noticed that after he had developed a stronger belief in himself, he was especially zealous on tasks that required a great deal of trust and responsibility (e.g. belaying). Throughout the course, the staff continued to place Kurt in progressively more difficult situations that demanded a strong, realistic belief in himself as well as other members in the group. Many of the discussions at night were about the relationships between the elements they faced as individuals and as a group in the wilderness and those they would find when they returned to their communities."

Other learning behaviors are often presented in a similar manner to increase their relevance and application to future learning environments for students. Certain programs have found that by approaching problem solving and decision making skills in a general manner, their students succeed in creating elements valuable for future use. (Gass, 1985:5)

3. Provide students with the opportunities to practice the transfer of learning while still in the program. There was probably no better time for Kurt to practice the skill to be transferred (i.e. an increased self-concept) than during the course. The variety of contexts in which to practice transfer, the number of times Kurt could practice transferring the skill and the strong support group that developed during this outdoor adventure program all helped Kurt to focus on the generalizing and conceptualizing skills he needed to strengthen the bond that his transfer needed for different learning situations.

4. Have the consequences of learning be natural - not artificial. One can think of the consequences of learning as either being natural or artificial. "Natural consequences are those that follow or would follow a given act **unless** some human or human system intervenes. Artificial consequences follow or would follow a given act, if, and only if, some human or human system **anticipates** or responds to the initial act and causes the artificial consequence or modifies a natural consequence." (Darnell, 1983:4)

Superficially viewing the field of outdoor education, one would think that all learning takes place in the outdoors would have natural consequences. Unfortunately, far too often this is not the case. Whether it has been from an 'overly' caring instructor or an overpowering one, too often the student becomes dependent on, is shielded by, or anticipates the instructor as a reinforcer of learning. Once the course is over and the reinforcer (i.e. the instructor) is removed from the student, learning behavior is severly hampered or terminated. In this way, with artificial consequences the result of learning transfer is extremely limited.

However, if outdoor programs could make their students' learning more experiential, natural consequences would be more likely to occur. This would result in the stronger formation of learning behaviors likely to be available in future learning situations, hence, the increase in the amount of transfer. Some experiential learning techniques that could foster the development of natural consequences include relying upon the students' intrinsic rather than some external source of motivation; placing more responsibility for learning on the student (see 8); and not shielding the learner from the consequences of their learning, whether they be positive or negative.

5. Provide the means for students to internalize their own learning. The ability for a student to internalize his/her own learning creates the concepts and generalizations central to the transfer process. Adventure educators have differed to a great extent on how this is best accomplished. Many believe that by getting their students to verbalize, or place their own learning into words, the internalization of the concepts to be transferred is increased through self-awareness and reflective thinking. (Kalisch, 1979:62) Others feel that conscious efforts such as verbalizing are secondary to other methods of internalization, such as the subconscious development of metaphors for transfer. (Bacon, 1983:2)

All methods which ask students to internalize learning behaviors from adventure programs strongly support the use of **reflection** to aid internalization. It seems that any process an instructor can use that enables the student to identify personal learning would lead to a greater applicability of learning for future situations.

An example of a process often used by adventure education programs that increases transfer through reflection is the "solo" experience. Certain programs feel that such an experience reinforces the learning that occurs in the adventure program and helps students/clients to identify how they are going to use the experience in the future. (Gass, 1985:6)

6. Include past successful alumni in the adventure program. Sometimes the incorporation of successful alumni in courses or programs assists

in the transfer of learning for students/clients. The following examples demonstrates how one program uses this technique:

"By listening to how these alumni used the skills they had learned from the program in their lives, students began to envision how they might use elements of the program in future situations. While not always advisable or possible for some programs, many individuals felt this 'vicarious' method of planning future transfer strategies aided in the transfer of learning for students." (Gass, 1985:5)

7. Include significant others in the learning process. The inclusion of other individuals closely associated with the student's/client's learning process has often been found to heighten the transfer of learning (Gass, 1985:2). Some of the persons used to fill this vital role have been peers, parents, counselors, social workers and/or teachers. The following example illustrates how one program includes significant others in the learning process to provide positive transfer for a student:

"Before Cristina participated on the adventure portion of the family therapy program, several objectives were established for her family, counselor and school teacher — as well as herself. Cristina and her family met with the staff, other participants and their families prior to the adventure experience in order to familiarize both the students and the parents of the reasons for their participation on the course. Another reason for this meeting was to inform them of possible changes in the student that could occur. The program continued to stay in close contact with Cristina's family in order for them to adjust to and support possible changes in Cristina's personality and behavior.

Cristina also created several "goal contracts" in a pre-trip meeting with the assistance of a staff member in the areas of personal, family, school and peer development. The contracts were discussed on the course and monitored monthly, with proper adaptations, for the next six months. Cristina's teacher also participated on several portions of the wilderness course, enabling him to support, reinforce and try and use the observable changes during the adventure program with Cristina in the classroom."

8. When possible, place more responsibility for learning in the program with the student/ clients. Many programs, especially those invested in teaching adventure education experientially, believe that placing more responsibility with the student in the program not only increases their motivation to learn but also their incentive to apply their learning in future experiences. Examples of this range from some programs involving students in the planning of food menus to other programs that have students organize and conduct an entire adventure experience on their own. Certain programs have implemented strong service components that have a definite focus on future experiences outside of the adventure experience (MacArthur, 1982:37-38) and enhance the self-responsibility within the student which could lead to a greater transfer of learning.

No matter what techniques programs use to involve their students/clients in the planning and operations of an adventure learning experience, their involvement should depend on their ability to accept responsibility for learning and their willingness and desire to do so. A person that willingly accepts responsibility for learning will transfer information much more readily than an individual who approaches such a task with a sense of indifference or resentment.

9. Develop focused processing techniques that facilitiate the transfer of learning. In many adventure education programs, processing/debriefing/facilitating is often used to enrich a student's learning experience. The length and intensity of these debriefings can differ from a quick and informal sharing of the day's occurances to a lengthy and formalized discussion of a particular incident with a specific set of rules and guidelines. Despite this vast difference in the application of techniques, there are certain general characterics that, if included in the processing of an experience, will assist in the transfer of learning. Some of these characteristics are:

a) Present processing sessions based on the student's/client's ability to contribute personally meaningful responses.
b) Focus on linking the experiences from the present and future learning environments together during the processing session.
c) When possible, debrief throughout the learning experience and not just the end of it, allowing the students to continually focus on the future applicability of present learning.

10. Provide follow-up experiences which aid in the application of transfer. Once a student begins transferring learning, the presence of follow-up activities (e.g. continued communications, feedback on learning decisions, processes and choices) serve to heighten transfer abilities. Again, one reason for this might be the positive effects of reflection between learning situations. Reflection gives the student the opportunity to see and evaluate the results of past learning behaviors, garner learner motivation and plan future learning strategies and directions.

CONCLUSION

As educators who use the outdoors and challenging situations to help students to learn more efficiently, we all aspire to teach our students something useable; and therein lies the value of our program. But, unless we assist our students in providing their own linkages, bridges and connections to their learning, the utility of much of the education we care and work so hard to bring about is put away in the equipment room along with the ropes and backpacks. As we strive to become better educators and proponents of the value of adventure education, let us look upon transfer as a device to excite students by showing them the future value of their current learning experiences. This motivation, provided by the opportunity to use their learning again, can furnish one of the strongest incentives for our students' continued learning and the field's success.

REFERENCES

*** Bacon, Stephen. *The Conscious Use of Metaphor in Outward Bound*. Denver, Colorado: Colorado Outward Bound School, 1983.
● Bruner, Jerome. *The Process of Education*. New York: Vintage Books, 1960.
● Darnell, Donald K. "On Consequences, Learning, Survival and 'The Good Life'." An unpublished report. Department of Communications, University of Colorado, 1983.
*** Gass, Michael A. *Strengthening Adventure Education by Increasing the Transfer of Learning*. Durham, New Hampshire, University of New Hampshire, 1985. ED.
● Johnson, Grant, Tom Bird, Judith Warren Little, and Sylvia L. Beville. (Center For Action Research, Inc.) *Delinquency Prevention: Theories and Strategies*. U.S. Department of Justice: Office of Juvenile and Delinquency Prevention, June 1981.
*** Kalisch, Ken. *The Role of the Instructor in the Outward Bound Process*. Three Lakes, Wisconsin: Honey Lakes Camp, 1979.
● MacArthur, Robert S. "The Changing Role of Service in Outward Bound". *Journal of Experiential Education*. Volume 5, No. 2, Summer, 1982.
● Mitzel, Harold, editor. *Encyclopedia of Educational Research*. (American Educational Research Association). 5th Edition. New York: Free Press, Volume IV, pp. 1947-1955, 1982.
● Rhoades, John S. "The Problem of Individual Change in Outward Bound: An Application and Transfer Theory" Doctoral Dissertation: University of Massachusetts, August 1972.
*** Richardson, Brian L. "The Transfer of Learning from High-Risk Activities in Adventure-Based Outdoor Education Programs". An unpublished report, Northern Illinois University, July 1978, p. 22.

INTERNALIZING LEARNING: BEYOND EXPERIENTIAL EDUCATION

by

Larry Prochazka

Learning without doing may not be learning at all. Yet, experientially designed learning activities do not insure learning occurs either. What is learning? How does learning take place? How does an individual learn to internalize information, integrate it into his or her personal life, and assimilate it to determine what fits and what does not? These interesting issues pose a challenge to those in education and learning related fields.

What is Learning?

Surprisingly few teachers have a clear working notion of learning. Most know what teaching is. It is generally the delivery of information, the one-way process of telling learners about information. In this traditional view of teaching, learning is measured by test scores and written assignments. But does this system really measure learning or simply assess an individual's test taking and memorization ability?

Educators favoring experiential methods of teaching would have a broader view of learning than teachers ascribing to more traditional views of education. To them, learning somehow involves "doing." Learning activities are centered around getting students involved in experiencing situations illustrating relevant information. By absorption in the activity, students are learning the material. But, is there something beyond experiencing a process? Is a deeper level of learning possible?

An Experiential Dilema

The question of going beyond experiential learning was raised for me several years ago. I was teaching a class in communication skills. This was one of my first major tests at designing and applying the experiential process. I believed learners would really learn communication skills if they "did" communication skills. Off to the library I charged! After I reviewed a variety of textbooks and journals, I collected numerous experiential exercises which support the basic "content" I had identified as essential to enhancing communication. The class learned about active listening and then performed active listening exercises. They learned about barriers to effective communications and then experienced situations where these barriers were present. After three weeks of this exciting adventure, the class took a "thinking" oriented test. Questions were designed around real-life situations. Learners were to analyze the situation, identify one communication skill recently learned, apply it to the situation to enhance the described communication pattern, and imply how the outcome could be modified by using the skill they selected. They did marvelously well on the test. However, over the next few days, learners showed little or no change in their communication pattern! What happened? If experiential activities enhance learning, why were communication patterns left unchanged once the obstacle (the test) was hurdled. What does it take to go beyond the experiential exercise; for an individual to draw the information inside themselves and somehow integrate it into his or her life? This was my next challenge, to go beyond experiential learning to the process of internalizing learning.

Internalizing Learning

A large part of education centers on information and facts. Information may enter the brain and be recorded for a short period of time before evaporating into the universe. For example, how much do you remember from your high school civics class? Probably very little. Data is stored by memorization until its usefulness is terminated. Then, poof! It's gone. This is what I will call the first level of "learning." At this level, memorization is the primary process involved and the focus is on content.

The next level involves a little more than memorization but is still primarily intellectual or cognitive activity. At this level, the learner may have an attitude of interest, an attitude of "I think I know what this means." They are primarily working with data and may or may not be involved in experiential activities. There is perhaps a feeling of familiarity with information but the ability to apply it is lacking. Master of "content" is again the focus of the learning process.

The third learning level is experiential. Here the data has been organized in such a way to allow learners the opportunity to experience it. In the communication example, learners listened to and discussed information concerning communication skills. Then they participated in activities structured to accommodate experience and use the skill. The experiential level is deeper and more personal than the first two levels of learning. It involves not only a focus on "content" but on the "process" of learning as well. However, it may not connect with the individual in such a way that they take new skills away from the experience. A glowing example of this is the statement, "do as I say, not as I do." It genuinely indicates there is information stored somewhere in the gray matter that has not been registered in the organism, the person. Consequently, intellectual awareness of facts is not an indicator that learning occurred "internally."

Now we arrive at the level of "internalized" learning. At this level of learning, learners ask themselves such questions as, "What can I create with this new information? How can I make it a part of my life and use it? What can I choose to do differently now?" It is at this level that the individual learner becomes intimately involved in the "process" of bringing the data into reality. Content is still involved but the process of bringing the content into a personal reality is of greater significance.

"Internalization" can be thought of as an inside-out process. The learner takes the information inside themselves to a deep, personal, feeling level, a level deeper than that of cognitive recall. Here the learner has responsibility for creating something with the new information. A responsibility to take the information and integrate it into their life, and act upon it. The learner acts on it by looking outside themselves into the real world around him or her, and identifying a goal for applying this new

174

learning. The learner might ask, "How do I get there from here? What is it going to take? How can I use this information to get there?" It is in this process of "getting there" that learning becomes internalized and a part of the individual. As an example, if I had encouraged learners involved in the communication session to keep a diary, and the purpose of the diary would have been to "live" one communication skill and record the experience, learning would have taken place at a deeper level. Had the learners taken the information on active listening, designed a plan to live it and used it for one day, and recorded their feelings about the experience, learning would have occurred at a deeper level. They would have been personally responsible for literally trying on new information and seeing how it fit into their life. Learning at this level has significant impact on the individual! They are touched and involved at a deep personal level.

So what happens inside? Information is no longer sterile. Learners are invited to become intimately involved with growing, changing, and learning. They become their own teachers and guides. They are, in essence, learning how to learn. The "process" used during internalization can be transferred to any aspect of their life, any class, any new information they wish to learn.

The Role of the Teacher

I remember reading once that learners learn more from "who" you are as a teacher or person than from "what" you say. Therefore, the first responsibility of the teacher is to role model what he wants learners to learn. Strict "black or white" thinking will not model creativity, open-mindedness, or curiosity. "Right answer thinking" models conformity. "I have all the answers" thinking models "you are only a student" behavior. Whatever the subject, the teacher must be aware of his behavior and what it is saying. To believe in internalized learning is to demonstrate it. Some native Americans had a concept called the "give away." During certain rites of passage and celebration, a family would give away everything they owned. The only reason to own anything was to give it away. You cannot give away anything you do not have! The same is true for the teacher. A teacher can only share what they have developed as a person.

A role important for teachers to play is "asker" instead of "teller," of questioner instead of possessor of all the answers. People learn more from talking than listening, yet perhaps 80% or more of the time spent by learners is spent listening. The mind disengages while the hand furiously takes notes. This is a nice exercise to improve motor skills but not for developing higher order "thinking." An example of this was shared with me by a man who was trying to help children understand why it is wrong to tell a lie. The child was told it was wrong to lie and did not understand. He could not connect the action of lying with the command not to lie. But when the child was asked if he told Johnny the truth, he replied "no!" When asked how he felt inside, he felt nervous and uncomfortable. He felt like he was unfair and dishonest with Johnny. Now he understands why it is improper to lie. The feelings of anxiety and dishonesty were the real teacher, the teacher became a questioner directing the child to discover his own answers. Teachers must be proficient at asking questions that guide learners to new awareness rather than meeting them head on and "telling" them all they need to know.

Positive manipulation can be a powerful tool. The martial arts teach learners how to use the momentum of an opponent for their defense. Go with the flow and use the momentum, never go against it head on. Teachers can use the same principle to create more stimulating learning environments. For example, there is a strong survival mode among learners. They will do nearly anything that is required of them for points or credit. This momentum can be used to involve students in stimulating learning activities. I have begun requiring cognitive maps at the beginning of class when new topics are to be presented. Learners have to read the material to complete the map. The map is designed to be done on one page and includes the major concept covered in the reading, sub-topics related to the major concept, and supportive information for each sub-topic. The mapping process integrates the hemispheres of the brain and facilitates greater understanding. Never before have I had an entire class read what they were asked to read. Now, not only have they read what they were asked to read but they are prepared to discuss key concepts from the material. Rather than resort to lecturing on the topic, we can now share in discussion. I bring my questions, learners bring theirs, and off we go into a world of curiosity, discovery, discussion, and personal involvement. Higher levels of thinking and communicating are involved as well as intimate, internal views of the learners. Significant internal levels of learning are achieved when emphasis on memorization of information is reduced and greater emphasis is placed on understanding and discussing. Learners are encouraged to use the information, to try it on and "live" it! Furthermore, interpersonal skills are being developed which is seldom a priority in traditional classrooms.

Conclusion

There are as many different definitions of learning as there are teachers. Most have not explicitly defined it so they subconsciously stab at accomplishing it. It may be looked at on terms of the level of learning a teacher hopes learners can reach. Memorization is a rather shallow and short-term intellectual skill. Deeper levels of learning are possible which encourage the personal committment to grow and improve as a person. It is only by experiencing this growth that teachers can share it with others. Perhaps a guiding question would be of use to teachers interested in the internalization process, "What do you want learners to know or be able to know when they finish your class?" Do you want them to be masters of information and the memorization process or do you want them to grow as people?

*****

About the author: Larry Prochazka is an Assistant Professor with the Department of Recreation and Leisure Studies at California State University, Northridge. He has been studying learning for several years in an attempt to empower learners in the classroom and help them "learn how to learn."

BOOK REVIEW

by MARY ANNE C. JOHNSTON

Jean Piaget, Science of Education and the Psychology of the Child, *London, Longman Group Ltd., 1971.*

"Psychological research on the development of rational operations and on the acquisition or construction of fundamental ideas provides data which seem decisively in favor of the active methods, and which require a much more radical reform of intellectual learning than many supporters themselves of the active school imagine." (Piaget, 1973, 94). The most compelling justification for encountering Jean Piaget is his comprehensive theoretical support for "active" education. Experiential educators have always felt that their ideas on learning were powerful and accurate. Now these intuitive feelings have validation from an abundance of psychological research.

As Director of the School of Psychology and Educational Sciences at the University of Geneva, Switzerland, Piaget has proposed a developmental theory of learning based upon years of direct observations of children within their natural environment. Piaget describes the child as an interactive, cognitive organism who constructs his knowledge of the external world as he acts upon that world. He is neither purely passive nor reactive within his environment. He is a selective organism who invariably organizes and adapts his actions, thoughts and feelings to the surrounding milieu. A child will progress through successive developmental stages, sensory motor, preoperational, concrete operational, and formal operational, but he will move through these stages at varying rates, dependent upon his interaction with the environment.

At the sensory-motor level from birth to 2 years, the child knows his world through his actions. He learns to coordinate his behaviors to adapt successfully within his environment. With the development of symbolic thought at age 2 to 4, the child enters the preoperational stage (2 to 7 years). Symbols are private signifiers which allow the child to represent those objects and events which are not present. At this stage, deferred imitation, symbolic play and language development increase the child's ability to understand himself and his external world. In the concrete operational stage (7 to 11 years) the child develops structural changes which allow him to perform logical operations on the environment. He can now attend to several perceptual dimensions while problem-solving or operating in the external world. The child must still work with concrete objects or representations of such objects. It is only in the formal operational stage (11-12 to 15 years) that the child may deal with hypothetical situations and propositional thinking. At each stage the child's knowledge of the world is qualitatively different from other stages. If Piaget's cogent analysis of child development and learning is con-

sidered seriously, then pedagogical goals and methodologies should become more responsive to the developing child.

Piaget has published volumes of essays, articles and books expounding his psychological research and its implications for education. *Science of Education and the Psychology of the Child* (1971) and *To Understand is to Invent* (1973) are among the most accessible and readable for educators concerned with constructive pedagogical change. Both books demonstrate the depth and scope of his brilliant thinking. Piaget has focused primarily on the development of logical, rational thinking. The current movement to explore the intuitive, metaphoric mode of thinking should not necessitate a denial of the significance of the rational, linear mode of thinking. "It is the polarity and the integration of these two modes of consciousness, the complementary workings of the intellect and the intuitive, which underlie our highest achievements." (Ornstein, 1972, 80)

For Piaget, the significant goal of education is the cognitive and moral development of the individual child within his own society. "Affirming the right of all human beings to education is to take on a far greater responsibility than simply to assure to each one reading, writing, and arithmetic capabilities; it is to guarantee fairly to each child the entire development of his mental faculties and the acquisition of knowledge and of ethical values corresponding to the exercise of these faculties until adaptation to actual social life." (1973, 53-54) This adaptation of the child to his cultural milieu is in no sense conformist or restrictive. The child emerges as a powerful agent for social and political change. Piaget advocates values "such as those of justice based on equality and those of 'organic' interdependence" in the moral realm and "coherence and objectivity on the intellectual plane." (1971, 180, 160) These values are interdependent and significant in the ultimate growth of the individual and the society. They reflect a strong need for the child's development in both affective and cognitive areas. "If the child's thought is qualitatively different from our own, the principal aim of education is to form its intellectual and moral reasoning power." (1971, 160) This power is conducive to the child's discovery and exploration in both cognitive and affective domains.

Educational methodologies manifest profound philosophical and psychological assumptions about the nature of learning. An "active" methodology assumes the child is the active constructor and creator of his own knowledge. Each adaptive child is uniquely different from every other child. He brings to every learning experience a

Mary Anne C. Johnston, *is a graduate student in Education at the University of Colorado.*

history of other experiences which have enabled him to develop his own intellectual and moral understanding of the world around him. He can not be expected to soak up information as a sponge but must be invested physically, emotionally and mentally with his world. The teacher is no longer the prime speaker, manipulator or authority in the classroom. The child must have the freedom to interact with his peers as well as his teacher — questioning, testing, evaluating the ideas shared in the classroom. "What is desired is that the teacher cease being a lecturer, satisfied with transmitting ready-made solutions; his role should rather be that of a mentor stimulating initiative and research." (1973, 16) The teacher may no longer assume that every child is able to understand concepts at a specific age level. He must be a sensitive listener, evaluating the developmental stage at which a student is functioning, in order to plan judicious learning experiences.

Every excellent pre-school teacher has always sensed the significance of play in the development of young. Piaget supports this intuitive judgment. "And just as the games of animals constitute a method of exercising particular instincts, such as fighting and hunting instincts, so the child when it plays is developing its perceptions, its intelligence, its impulses toward experiment, its social instincts, etc. This is why play is such a powerful lever in the learning process of very young children, to such an extent that whenever anyone can succeed in transforming their first steps in reading, or arithmetic, or spelling into a game, you will see children become passionately absorbed in those occupations, which are ordinarily presented as dreary chores." (1975, 155)

The methods and environment which facilitate the developing child to construct his own knowledge will necessarily invite experimentation, interaction and adaptation on the part of the child.* Piaget challenges us as educators to continue the difficult task of designing those creative experiences which will enhance the growth of human wisdom. Society, as well as the individual, will benefit from this growth of wisdom. "To the degree in which childhood is thought of as endowed with its own genuine form of activity, and the development of mind as being included with that activity's dynamic, the relation between the subjects to be educated and society becomes reciprocal: the child no longer tends to approach the state of adulthood by receiving reason and the rules of right action ready-made, but by achieving them with his own effort and personal experience; in return, society expects more of its new generations than mere imitation: it expects enrichment." (1971, 138)

*There is increasing evidence that adults need similar experiential interaction for their continued intellectual growth.

Bibliography

Omstein, Robert E. *The Psychology of Consciousness.* New York: Penguin Books, 1975.

Piaget, Jean. *Science of Education and the Psychology of the Child.* London: Longman Group Ltd., 1971.

Piaget, Jean. *To Understand is to Invent.* New York: Grossman Publishers, 1973.

IN REVIEW

Reviewed by Herb Stockley

The Practice of Multi-Modal Therapy, Arnold A. Lazarus, McGraw-Hill Book Company, New York, 1981. $18.95.

As experiential outdoor "treatment" programs mature, there will be an increased focus on the quality of the therapeutic aspects of the program. Experiences offered by outdoor programs are great, but they fall short of being a panacea for the client's problems now being referred to them. In the past these programs have been innovative. In order to maintain their reputations and quality with other professionals, they are going to need to put aside the magic of "going to the woods to get well", and include persons trained in the field of behavior and behavior change.

Kurt Hahn was an innovator, and the challenge of the 1980's will be to take the knowledge presently available, and translate it into the experiential outdoor treatment programs in an innovative way. The information that is contained in Lazarus's book will undoubtedly be familiar in these settings. This information will be as basic to outdoor programs as lining a canoe through swift water, or sidestepping down a steep, tree filled hill in powder snow with a heavy pack. Programs will be unable to offer quality experiences without it.

Lazarus's Multimodal therapy acronym is BASIC I.D. (B is Behavior, A is Affect, S is Sensation, I is Imagery, C is Cognition, I is Interpersonal Relationships, D is Drugs/Biological Functioning). We all behave, have emotional feelings, sense our environment, imagine, think, have interpersonal relationships, and biologically function. The BASIC I.D. model provides a procedure to access systematically personal problems, and their interactions within the human system.

The book includes a questionnaire and many practical suggestions for compiling a BASIC I.D. "profile." There will be phenomena which need to be increased and phenomena which need to be decreased in each modality. For example, an individual may wish to decrease the frequency of yelling at friends, increase the number of pleasant feelings, decrease the number of traumatic childhood images, and increase the frequency of social interactions in their lives. After the profile is completed, strategies can be selected which match with the particular problems identified. If you can't identify an appropriate strategy to address a particular problem area, Lazarus lists over 35 strategies with brief explanations. If the strategy summary is still inadequate, references will direct further reading.

A second use of the BASIC I.D. assessment is to overcome impasses in treatment. An example may make this clearer. If you drink (behavior) a glass of water, you might "sense" the water in your throat, "imagine" the last time you drank out of a cold stream, and "think" about watering your houseplants. If you are somewhat dehydrated (biological), someone hands you the water (interpersonal), and you feel pleased (affective), then you have covered all the modalities.

If you understand this point, imagine the impasse of a sixteen year old throwing repeated tantrums causing potential harm to self and others. By applying the BASIC I.D. concept to the impasse, one might find images of childhood abuse, thoughts of hurting someone, and feelings of anger. You as a professional might be frustrated in dealing with the behavior only. Lazarus's assumption then is: the more modes of human functioning addressed and changed in treatment, the more durable the change will be, and the less likely a relapse will occur. So to modify the child's tantrum (B), the frequency of negative images (I), anger feelings (A), and thoughts of hurting others (C) must be reduced. A reduction in tantrums will follow.

The Practice of Multi-Modal Therapy is organized around 11 chapters and three appendices. The appendices include Multimodal Life History Questionnaire, Glossary of Principal Techniques, and Marital Satisfaction Questionnaire. It is followed by a list of references and an index.

Lazarus has done an excellent job of organizing the information. The information he presents in the book should be required reading for anyone interested in working in programs which specialize in the "treatment" of people. Programs are utilizing the latest technology in hiking and camping equipment. It is now time that we begin to utilize the excellent behavior change technology available to provide constructive, long lasting interventions for our clients. This book is the place to start.

THEORY AND PRACTICE

THE DESIGN OF INTELLECTUAL EXPERIENCE

by DONALD L. FINKEL and G. STEPHEN MONK

Sharing experiences with students is essential to learning, but difficult to accomplish. The authors suggest a workshop approach, give a detailed example, and discuss basic principles for worksheet design.

Why Teach?

Beneath the conscious goals and motivations that drive a teacher's daily activities lies a basic human impulse: the desire to share intellectual experiences. Most teachers have felt for themselves the striking pleasure that results from the work of intelligence, whether experienced as insight, beauty, connectedness, or resolution. Ideally, they would like to lead their students to such pleasures; yet, the accomplishment of this ideal is rare.

Few teachers adopt the explicit goal of sharing experience, and those who do must be struck by the difficulty of actively pursuing such an aim. This is not the sort of pedagogic goal about which one's colleagues talk. Moreover, what kind of methods could be formulated for achieving such a personal and insubstantial goal? Too easily, the dimension of experience is ignored altogether, leaving teachers with only the products of their disciplines to present. Yet, it is the processes that lead to these products which yield the intellectual excitement they wish to share. For students to experience such excitement, the formal systems of knowledge must be undone, so that students can feel what it is like to put those systems together for themselves. Thus, *teachers must learn how to convert academic subject matter into activities for students.* Because it is just these intellectual activities that lead to understanding, the students' gains and the teachers' gratification stem from the same process.

This article will describe a framework for converting formal knowledge into structured activities for students. We shall examine an example and draw from it six principles for designing such activities. This discussion should make concrete the goal of sharing intellectual experience and indicate its benefits to both students and teachers. We must begin, however, by confronting the dilemma which faces any teacher who takes this goal seriously.

The Dilemma of Sharing

Suppose you return home from a trip to Nepal. You are brimming with the excitement of the experience and wish to share it with your friends. Your first inclination is to describe to them in detail all you can about the people, the landscape, and the customs, illustrating your adventures with as many slides as possible. Your first impulse is the *Impulse to Tell.* After several hours of slides and talk, you cannot avoid a conclusion: Since your friends have never experienced anything like Nepalese culture, they cannot possibly get from your description what you feel you are putting into it, or anything like what you got from the trip.

Perhaps it is impossible to tell about important experiences, to give them directly to others. Maybe you should wait until your friends' lives naturally take them to Nepal. Then, when they return, you will finally be able to share the experience. The Impulse to Tell has given way to the *Impulse to Let It Happen.* Following this impulse is not satisfying either, since you may have to wait forever, and you want to share your trip now. Compromises are possible, and you may urge your friends to travel. Yet even if amenable, they will probably experience Nepal quite differently. More likely, however, your urgings will awaken a long buried desire in them for travel up the Nile, and then you will be faced with the inevitable evening of Egyptian slides and monologues.

These two opposing impulses, The Impulse to Tell and the Impulse to Let It Happen, are inherent in the attempt to share experiences, and each has the unfortunate tendency to drive you to an extreme. If you sense you are telling unsuccessfully, you are likely to tell more and more, and to tell it in greater and greater detail. If you withdraw to let something happen, careful to avoid imposing your own experience on others, and nothing happens, then you will withdraw even further to leave a wider arena free for the others' experience. The dilemma of sharing is this: What do you do when you have discovered that neither telling nor refraining from telling is a successful mode of sharing?

Teachers also find themselves caught in this dilemma. In the classroom, the Impulse to Tell leads to lecturing or expository methods of presenting subject matter. The Impulse to Let It Happen is found in various non-directive teaching modes that have arisen in reaction to exposition. We do not oppose these forms in themselves but rather the

Don Finkel *is a faculty member at The Evergreen State College, Olympia, Washington and* **Steve Monk** *is an Associate Professor of Mathematics at the University of Washington, Seattle, Washington.*

results that flow from them. Teachers who seek change by following one of these impulses find themselves either expounding in ever more exquisite detail or refining even further the role of non-leader. Since telling does not provide a genuine experience and letting things happen does not produce the particular experience you had in mind, neither of these impulses leads to the genuine satisfaction that comes from sharing an intellectual experience.

This claim immediately raises two questions. What are *intellectual* experiences and what does it mean to *share* them? Does going to a Beethoven concert with your friend constitute sharing an intellectual experience? What about watching a football game together? Returning to the previous example concerning the trip to Nepal, you cannot be sure that even bringing your friends with you to Nepal would have satisfied your desire to share the experience. To address these questions, we must distinguish between the external events or objects (the musicians, the musical sounds, the football game, the people of Nepal) from what we make of them (our perceptions, ideas, interpretations). These mental constructs are what we *use* to interact with the external events; without them we can have no experience. Thus, events in themselves are neither intellectual nor non-

that even bringing your friends with you to Nepal would have satisfied your desire to share the experience. To address these questions, we must distinguish between the external events or objects (the musicians, the musical sounds, the football game, the people of Nepal) from what we make of them (our perceptions, ideas, interpretations). These mental constructs are what we *use* to interact with the external events; without them we can have no experience. Thus, events in themselves are neither intellectual nor non-intellectual. These terms refer only to the nature of our interactions with events. Interactions may be characterized as more intellectual to the degree that they engage and promote the development of more elaborate and comprehensive systems of ideas. Listening to Beethoven can be non-intellectual depending upon *how* one is listening, while watching a football game might be a most intellectual activity if it were part of a comparative analysis of games.

Now, what does it mean to *share* an intellectual experience? Suppose you are listening to a record of a Beethoven quartet with which you are not familiar, and you suddenly become aware of a structural similarity among all of Beethoven's late quartets. Full of excitement, you invite a friend over to hear your new record. You have had an

Few teachers adopt the explicit goal of sharing experience, and those who do must be struck by the difficulty of actively pursuing such an aim.

intellectual. These terms refer only to the nature of our interactions with events. Interactions may be characterized as more intellectual to the degree that they engage and promote the development of more elaborate and comprehensive systems of ideas. Listening to Beethoven can be non-intellectual depending upon *how* one is listening, while watching a football game might be a most intellectual activity if it were part of a comparative analysis of games.

Sharing Intellectual Experiences.

The solution to the dilemma lies in the intriguing possibility that a teacher can design an experience which has intellectual consequences for students, the very consequences the teacher wished to share in the first place. Our central thesis is that such pedagogic activity is possible and that teachers can best share intellectual experiences by designing them.

This claim immediately raises two questions. What intellectual experiences and what does it mean to share them? Does going to a Beethoven concert with your friend constitute sharing an intellectual experience? What about watching a football game together? Returning to the previous example concerning the trip to Nepal, you cannot be sure

intellectual experience and wish to share it. As you listen to the record together, are you sharing an intellectual experience? It is most unlikely that your friend will make the same discovery you made by just listening to the record. When the record ends you look at your friend expectantly to see if "it happened," and then you recall that for a teacher to merely expose students to archetypal examples is precisely to yeild to the Impulse to Let It Happen. It is tempting to think that something fruitful must result from such exposure. After all, how could one read Shakespeare and not be improved by the experience? However, teachers who simply trust in such invisible and delayed effects forgo a sense of direct contribution to their students' understanding. Implicit in the idea of sharing is that we teachers have something valuable to give, not Beethoven or Shakespeare, but ways of thinking about them, ways of understanding and ultimately of interacting with music and words. We would like to give our students the systems of ideas, the perspectives, the concepts that make possible these interactions with music and words. Yet, to adopt such an approach sounds as though we are back to Telling. If only we could collar our students, reach into their heads with a mental hand, and alter their patterns of thought! Once again, we face the dilemma of sharing.

To resolve this dilemma, we must focus on two crucial propositions about these patterns of thought we would like to alter. First, there is no way to interact intellectually with anything in the environment except through such mental patterns. Every student brings some form of conceptual system to new material; the student initially understands the material in the best way he or she can, interpreting it according to his or her present patterns of thought. This proposition is encouraging because it means the teacher is not attempting to get students to elaborate complex theories from nothing. It can also be discouraging, because it means that the teacher must work with students' systems no matter how primitive, fuzzy or ill-conceived those systems may seem when compared to the system the teacher would like the students to develop. The second proposition is that the structure of the system of ideas which engages with an external event will never match perfectly with the structure of the event. One's own mental system will inevitably influence the way one "sees" the event. At the same time, interaction with the event can influence the system of ideas.

It is possible to influence someone else's patterns of thought by means less direct than a mental hand. *The teacher can design an environment, and activities for stu-*

Moreover, it is the act of restructuring such systems which provides the pleasures of intellectual work we assume teachers wish to share with their students.

An Example

The most prominent feature of teacher-designed intellectual experiences, or "workshops" as we call them, is that students work on their own in groups ranging in size from two to seven. The teacher roves from group to group, observing, guiding, questioning, and "teaching," in response to the needs of specific groups or individuals. The students' work is directed by a set of written instructions and questions which we call a "worksheet." Thus, the teacher is present in the students' environment only through the written worksheet and occasional interactions.

The following worksheet is for a college-level workshop in developmental psychology, sociology, or the philosophy of education. The intellectual experience it attempts to share is the understanding that the way one thinks about child development is inextricably linked to one's conception of society. The authors hoped to induce their students to make this connection and to crystallize it by formulating alternative versions of the possible relations between society and the developing child.

What do you do when you have discovered that neither telling nor refraining from telling is a successful mode of sharing?

---

dents within that environment, which will engage their current conceptual systems in such a way that these systems will be induced to develop. These activities must aim to create a kind of mismatch between internal structure and external event that leads the student to refine, differentiate, and restructure the conceptual system. This approach to teaching is neither Telling nor Letting It Happen. In designing such experiences for students, the teacher must draw upon personal intellectual experiences, but the students will have their own experiences in working through the activities. No one can directly engineer an experience or guarantee the outcome for another person. However, designing focused activities within a concrete environment makes the chances of converging experiences likely, and such a convergence is as close as we can come to sharing.

We thus propose designing intellectual experiences for students as a means for sharing the pleasures of the mind with them. To design, in this sense, is to structure a specific environment for student interaction in order to promote the restructuring of the students' systems of ideas. We take the goal of conceptual restructuring to be of paramount importance because it is the students' systems of ideas that stay with them and shape their vision of the world

There are four parts to the worksheet. As you read them, try to picture a classroom full of students engaged in these activities. Further, try to determine how each part of the worksheet requires a different style of work from the students. Finally, ask yourself these questions: Is the worksheet likely to engage the students' current patterns of thought about development and society? Is it likely to result in a restructuring of the students' ideas on this topic?

ELOISE AND THE PHILOSOPHERS

There are four parts to this workshop. Part I is to be performed in pairs. Parts II and III are to be done in groups of six, formed by combining three of the previous partnerships from Part I. Part IV will be completed with the class together as a whole.

Part I *Eloise is an 11-year-old girl who has decided to keep a diary during her sixth-grade year, which she has just begun. You will find attached the first entry in her new diary, written during the lunch hour of the first day of school. After reading the entry (which appears below, after Part IV), agree on and write down the answers to the following five questions.*

1. List the five different activities in which Eloise participated during her morning.
2. For each activity, describe what you think were the teacher's underlying goals (or strategies) in having the children participate in such an activity.
3. Now consider that the school and its teachers are primarily agents of society, and that one of society's tasks is to employ the school to affect children's emotional and intellectual development in such a way that they are prepared to enter society and be useful members. Then each of Eloise's activities can be viewed as meeting society's goals well or badly, but *on two levels*: on the level of *content* (fractions, writing skill, ecology, etc.) and on the level of *form* (the way the activity is organized.) Ignoring the content of Eloise's morning, describe how society is affecting her through the form of each of the activities. Why is each activity structured the way it is?
4. Note the basic similarities and differences among the five activities, based upon your responses to question 3. Overall, do the forms of the different activities tend to be consistent with each other, or inconsistent?
5. What are some different ways to view the possible relationship between the developing child and society? List at least three different relationships.

Part II *Form groups of six by combining three partnerships. Each group should choose a scribe to keep a written record of its results. The group will be given a set of 14 index cards, each with a quotation on it. [See below for example]. These quotes are from philosophers and educators, old and new.*

1. Each quote implies a certain relationship between the developing child and society. Sort the quotes into a small number of categories (between 3 and 5) that reflect the differing relationships. Try to agree on the groupings.
2. Formulate and agree upon descriptive labels for each of your categories.
You will probably have to go back and forth between questions 1 and 2, sorting some cards, deciding upon a tentative label, and re-sorting some of the original cards. If you cannot reach agreement, record minority opinions.

Part III *Remain in the same group of six.*
1. Together with your original partner from Part I, share your answers to Part I, question 5, with the group. Compare these answers to the categories your group devised in Part II. Did categorizing the quotes alter your original views significantly? If so, in what ways? Compare the effects of Part II on your views with its impact on other partnerships in your group, and have the scribe record general trends.
2. Using your current set of categories from Part II, your group should place each of the following systems into the appropriate category:

(a) Summerhill (as seen in the film last week),
(b) the school you are now attending, (c) the way your parents treated you (in general),
(d) the way you intend to treat your children,
(e) today's workshop.

Part IV *The class will reassemble as a whole. We will hear the results of each group's work from the scribes, and then discuss the entire exercise.*

ELOISE'S DIARY

Dear Diary: It was great to get back to school and see my friends again, especially Susan. Before the bell rang, I told her all about our summer trip to Mexico, and about Manuel, and our trip to the beach together. This year I got Mrs. Morgan. She's okay, but I wanted Mr. Brown. Susan's so lucky she got him! After attendance the first thing we had to do was write a paper about what we did over summer vacation. Why do teachers always give that dumb assignment? Well, I wrote about Mexico City, and the market place, about all the things you can buy there. Some people read their papers out loud, but I didn't. Then we had math. Mrs. Morgan explained about multiplying and dividing fractions. We had all that stuff last year, but no one seems to remember it. Even Mrs. Morgan made a mistake at one point! Of course, everybody loved that. We learned a little poem, so we know when to flip the fraction upside down, and when not to. (I forgot the poem already! I never was good in math!!) Then we saw a movie about a lake in Africa —like the ones on TV. Mrs. Morgan said for science we are going to learn a new thing called *ecology*. The first thing we had to do was list all the animals we saw using the lake and tell how they used it. Then Mrs. Morgan asked us what would happen to all the plants and animals if the hippos got killed and could never bathe in the lake. Richard said there would be a lot of dead hippos around and the whole class laughed. Richard's so dumb! But Mrs. Morgan wouldn't tell us the answer, even after we tried. Then we had gym. I love gym, but Mr. Brown's class creamed us in volleyball. If only I could get those creeps in our class to set up the ball, I'm sure we could win. When we got back, there was a policeman waiting in our room. Everyone was excited for a minute, but it turned out to be a lecture on drugs. He showed us all these pills and needles and stuff and said it was all bad. Borrring! Now it's lunch time. Oh, here comes Susan — see you tonight, Diary.

• • •

SAMPLE QUOTES

[We include the following three quotations to give the reader of this article a flavor of the quotations used. We have chosen three rather extreme cases, but the full group of 14 index cards presents a formidable task of differentiation and categorization.]

"Give your scholar no verbal lessons; he should be taught by experience alone; never punish him, for he does not know what it is to do wrong; . . . May I venture at this point to state the greatest, the most important, the most useful

rule of education? It is: Do not save time, but lose it."

"Having thus very early set up your Authority, and by the gentler Applications of it, shamed him out of what leads towards any immoral Habit . . . (for I would by no means have chiding used, much less Blows, till Obstinacy and Incorrigibleness make it absolutely necessary) . . ."

"What is the least that we can say about an organism's development? Everybody admits that two things must be said: First, it develops by getting habits formed; and second, it develops by getting new adaptations which involve the breaking up or modification of habits."

• • •

To appreciate the experiential flavor of the workshop, you should now switch gears and actually *do* the problems which make up Part I. Readers usually tend to resist becoming more active in this way, but you will sense the power of this approach only if you overcome this resistance.

Principles of Design

The most striking quality of this worksheet on first marized in a list at the end of this section.

Environment. The student's environment in a workshop has two chief components: an external shared event and the other students in the group. The external event can take many forms; in the above example it was Eloise's diary and then the quotes on index cards. Whatever the form, *the event must be specific, concrete, and present.* These features are required to engage effectively the students' conceptual systems. Any material (texts, data, graphs, journals) with which the students are going to work must be ready at hand in manageable quantities. The material must be sufficiently challenging to engage the students at diverse levels of sophistication, but not so complicated as to overwhelm them.

The group of students working together on a worksheet provides a second aspect of the environment. Students can help one another in a number of ways: They can provide mutual support and a sense of common purpose; their exchanges can promote the externalization and articulation of ideas; finally, the diversity of points of view provides a continuing source of puzzlement and constructive friction. This last feature of group work propels the card sorting task in *Eloise,* while externalization and clarification of ideas lies behind the use of

If only we could collar our students, reach into their heads with a mental hand, and alter their patterns of thought!

reading is its variety. The students work in pairs, groups, and as a whole class. They read the imaginary diary of a sixth grader and later classify quotes from philosophers. In addition to reading and sorting cards, they must express themselves to classmates, argue for their views, and reflect upon their own experiences. In order to reveal the orderly design within this apparent kaleidoscope of educational activities, we must break down the overriding goal of workshops into a set of interlocking principles. Recall that the teacher's goal is to convert an intellectual product into a sequence of activities for students. The six principles that follow will suggest how such a conversion may be facilitated and will illustrate why the authors of the previous worksheet designed it as they did.

A worksheet must always set forth an environment, and activities for students in that environment, which engage their current conceptual systems in such a way that these systems will be induced to develop. We will first examine the nature of that *environment,* then describe the structure of the *activities,* and finally discuss the resulting role of the *teacher.* Our six principles emerge from the discussion of these three elements of workshops. They are italicized in the text and sum- partnerships in Part I, the analysis of the diary. The teacher designing a workshop must think through these issues in advance in order to *exploit consciously the collective potential of the group.* Such devices as requiring agreement, fostering debate, inviting exchange of work, and assigning specialized roles use the group productively. With whatever techniques you use, your instructions must implicitly communicate your trust in your students' capacity as a group and your genuine expectation that together they have the resources to complete the task.

However, simply to place your students on their own in groups to explore a stimulating event is insufficient. Beyond the group and the event, a third aspect of the environment is required. *Specific questions and instructions must be written in advance and given to each student.* These questions and instructions constitute the worksheet itself. Sometimes the activities required will not be clear unless they are written. Even when the instructions could be communicated orally or on the board, it is important to distribute them to each student. With the worksheet at hand, the students can interact directly with the event and each other without the need for the teacher's constant personal mediation. These written questions and instructions embody the teacher's wisdom on the subject, yet in this form, they permit the students to take the initiative.

Activities. A great deal of activity can be generated by placing students in an environment that contains concrete events, other students, and specific written questions about these events. However, student activity in itself is not our goal. We wish to induce intellectual change in order to allow the sharing of intellectual experience. To effect intellectual change, activity must have a particular structure. This structure may be summarized by saying that *every worksheet requires the students to solve a problem.*

The best way to alter someone else's thought is to provide a problem which cannot be solved with his or her present conceptions. This requires a three-phase process. First the student must be made to see the problem as a genuine problem that is disturbing and requires resolution. Such a problem must be formulated from the student's own view of the phenomenon. Thus, the first phase requires *activities which elicit the student's current mental structures.* People always have common-sense concepts, intuitions, or general rules-of-thumb for

structure their ideas will guide most teachers to this balance.

In *Eloise,* the single problem which organizes the activities is this: How can we describe the system of mutual implications between views of child rearing and conceptions of social organization? As a question this is very abstract and is unlikely to lead to a productive discussion. With this problem serving as a focus, the teacher must ask: What activities or tasks would be most likely to lead students to understand these implications? In this case, the authors decided to use a categorizing task. By articulating different ways in which a view of child development contains a conception of society (or vice versa), students will be forced to make distinctions and ask questions that are new to them. The workshop now has a central activity, one that will constitute the second phase (disequilibrium) of the three-phase structure. Sorting quotes almost inevitably reveals the inadequacy of students' intuitive views about children and society and may well produce intellectual conflict as the students argue over which cards belong in which piles and why. Indeed, the card sorting is the center of this workshop, and will perplex students and challenge their current thinking.

Your presence at the workshop itself will still be necessary, both to facilitate the students' interaction with the worksheet and to give you the necessary information upon which to base future worksheets.

exploring anything new. These are what must be elicited by the first phase of the worksheet, because it is only from these mental constructs, that intellectual change can proceed. The problem itself only comes into consciousness as a result of *questions that force upon the student the inadequacy of his or her present conceptions.* This is the worksheet's second phase. It must throw the student into a state of intellectual disequilibrium. Conflict between the students' differing conceptions or between obdurate phenomena and unsophisticated theories must make the student feel the problem in all of its perplexing force, and lead him or her to want to solve it.

It is not enough to perplex students and leave them hanging. Relevant information, guides, questions, and examples must be provided so that the students have a reasonable chance of making new distinctions and tying ideas together in a different way. *Activities which lead to intellectual restructuring* mark the third phase, which should result in the creation of a new mental equilibrium. The teacher must strike a balance between withholding too much information, on the one hand, and giving out a pre-packaged solution, on the other. Repeated experience in workshops watching students re-

However, to present the student with fourteen wordy quotes with no preparation might well throw them too far off balance. First, they need to have their own ideas about children and society elicited in a more familiar and concrete context. The questions about Eloise's diary fulfill this function. By the end of Part I, the students' own ideas whould have been articulated, clarified, and written, so they can face the test of the card sorting.

If the workshop were to end after Part II, the students would have only their own shaky products, the set of categories, which might well seem *ad hoc* and of little significance. The students now need to use the categories, applying them to phenomena to see if they shed new light. In addition, they need to bring their ideas into the public arena of the class to present them to their peers and teacher. Parts III and IV of *Eloise* address these needs; they supply the resolution and closure to the experience. Certainly a total restructuring of ideas will not occur as a result of *Eloise,* but a first step will be made in the process. After the groups have compared their categories in Part IV, they will try to resolve their differences through synthesis in the ensuing discussion. Their original ideas (e.g., about free children and harsh societies) will have been shaken, and they will be on their way toward a more refined and complex system of ideas.

In all this it is important to remember that, intellectual or otherwise, *a genuine experience has a style and a texture* as well as an organization. Matters of rhythm and timing must not be neglected. Moreover, it is essential that the worksheet not speak to the students in a voice that is didactic or pedantic; it should speak in the author's natural voice. The finished worksheet should bear the teacher's personal stamp, reflecting a sense of play and purpose. *Eloise* requires students to shift activities repeatedly. It does not try to exhaust the meaning contained in any one source; it progresses, allowing for student work in new modes and in new combinations. The authors attempt to write in the style of a sixth grade girl and provide physical props, the cards with quotes, so that some of the action can be physical. The important point to remember when you are composing a worksheet is that students will actually be doing the things you ask of them, and you must try to envision what it would be like to experience the activities you are designing.

Teacher. In writing a worksheet you have provided a blueprint for an experience. By working backwards from the products of your discipline to activities for students, you have drawn on some of your most creative and pedagogic impulses. Yet your presence at the workshop itself will still be necessary, both to facilitate the students' interaction with the worksheet and to give you the necessary information upon which to base future worksheets. However, your role will be quite different from that of the conventional teacher. Most teachers are held captive by the need to continually direct and organize the activities of the class. The students' attention is almost always focused on the teacher. He or she is bound in place by the students' conviction that the teacher is the vital link between themselves and the subject matter. This traditional role puts the teacher at the hub of the wheel, the common source of support and cohesion. In contrast, the teacher's role in the workshop may be summarized by the phrase: *The teacher is there, but out of the middle.*

In a workshop, it is the worksheet, and not you, which provides the "carrying energy" for the students' work. They are in direct contact with the material and one another, so that you remain outside of their immediate experience. This is just what you need in order to be free to move around and respond to groups of students in a flexible fashion, tailoring your contribution to the needs of the moment. No matter how exquisitely you have designed your worksheet, some students will become stranded in irrelevant details, while others will skim over all that is interesting. Still other students will approach the problem from a point of view you never imagined. All of these students, and many others as well, will benefit from direct interaction with you. As you engage them, getting them started again, deepening their approach or leading them to a new angle of attack, you will feel the most immediate gratification of the sharing of intellectual experiences.

To Summarize, the six principles of design are the following:

Environment:
1. The shared event must be specific, concrete, and present.
2. Specific questions and instructions must be written in advance and given to each student.
3. The teacher should exploit the potential of the group.

Activities:
4. The worksheet must have within it an underlying problem to be solved. To make the problem genuine and solvable requires activities which:
    (a) elicit current mental structures;
    (b) point to the inadequacy of present structures;
    (c) lead to intellectual restructuring.
5. The workshop must have the texture of a genuine experience.

Teacher:
6. The teacher is there, but out of the middle.

Diverse Applications

We cannot convey in this brief article the variety of forms that workshops and worksheets may take. The interested reader should refer to our more complete treatment of the subject[1] where numerous examples are given, as well as more detailed guidelines for designing workshops. To suggest this variety, we present here several examples of workshops written by us and our colleagues. Many of these have been composed in collaboration, because we have found that the most effective method of converting intellectual products into activities is for an expert in the subject to join forces with an intellectually inquisitive but naive partner.

1. *Hot Tips:* An exercise that starts with graphs of the prices of four stocks and moves toward an understanding of rate of change at a point — used in a calculus course for social science majors.
2. *The Ideal Gas Law:* A reconstruction of the Ideal Gas Law in chemistry, which starts with questions about balloons and pistons, and progressively builds toward an understanding of the regularities stated mathematically in the law — used in an introductory chemistry course.
3. *Examination of Assumptions:* An exercise in philosophical analysis, based on the extraction of assumptions in a fellow student's written argument, and using several written exchanges between the two partners — used in an introductory philosophy course.
4. *How Children Form Mathematical Concepts:* A set of questions used to help students digest a *Scientific American* article read prior to the workshop and brought with them to class — used in an advanced developmental psychology course.
5. *The Problem of Identity in "A View From the*

Finkel, Donald L. and Monk, G. Stephen. *Contexts for Learning: A Teacher's Guide to the Design of Intellectual Experience.* Olympia, WA: The Evergreen State College, 1978.

Bridge". An exercise in applying to the characters in a play a psychological concept previously studied, based on the students' re-creation of each character's point of view in a closing monologue — used in an interdisciplinary social science and humanities course.

Workshops can fulfill quite a variety of functions within a course. The following is a partial list.[*]

1. Have students parallel the work of an author before reading about that work.
2. Help students gather and organize a wealth of detailed and confusing information.
3. Articulate an intellectual structure by providing a shift of context.
4. Give practice translating between languages within a discipline to show the power of a new language.
5. Help students crystallize their knowledge in preparation for a test.
6. Let students experience physically something they have studied or will study more abstractly.

Conclusion

We began by addressing a question all teachers

them see their students' progressive understanding. We have proposed one way of creating such exchanges, one that we believe is a significant educational innovation, and one that *does* result in development — for students and for teachers, too.

We have listed elsewhere[*] the detailed benefits to students and teachers of this workshop approach. Here we can only summarize by saying that virtually all college students with whom we have worked have thrived in workshops. Because their teachers have removed themselves from "the middle," they have been able to apply their own intellectual powers to concrete problems, thus gaining an awareness of and a confidence in their own intelligence. Moreover, because their teacher's expertise has not been withheld, the students have felt neither abandoned nor manipulated. Able to interact with an environment constructed by their teacher and to work together in a collaborative atmosphere with their peers, they have made conceptual advances that have altered their mental landscape.

One of the dramatic consequences for teachers who write worksheets first and run workshops based on them is their strikingly sharper view of the effects of their

In a workshop, it is the worksheet, and not you, which provides the "carrying energy" for the students' work.

must eventually face: Why teach? We have ended with a proposal for improving instruction, a response to the question: How can I improve the learning that takes place in my class? We believe that these two questions are inextricably linked. Many teachers are quick to make superficial changes in their courses, employing new curricular packages, new kinds of tests, and new texts, in the hope of improving their students' education. We are proposing an alteration in the very structure of the teacher's experience with students. To suggest such a step would be futile without addressing a teacher's most basic needs and hopes. We focused on the goal of sharing intellectual experiences because we have found in our own collaboration with numerous teachers that it is precisely this consequence of designing and running workshops that is so gratifying and sustaining. Calling for such broad and unspecified goals as "significant educational change" or "faculty development" strikes us as unproductive because such sweeping appeals do not address teachers' immediate desires. Teachers don't want to "develop"; they want to have intellectual exchanges with their students in a way that lets

pedagogical thinking on students. Having completed the intellectual work before the workshop, teachers can then see more clearly the quality of their students' thinking. Such a vantage leads to a ready understanding of how better to design the next workshop. Moreover, in having to work backwards from the intellectual products of their discipline to the activities that lead to them, teachers find they have to rethink many fundamental questions in their field. Their own intellectual excitement in this process parallels the students' enthusiasm in accomplishing the workshops. And within this interactive cycle occurs the genuine sharing of intellectual experience.

References
Finkel, Donald L. and Monk, G. Stephen. *Contexts for Learning: A Teacher's Guide to the Design of Intellectual Experience*. Olympia, WA: The Evergreen State College, 1978.

Suggested reading list:
Dewey, John. *Democracy and Education*. Free Press, 1966
Kohlberg, Lawrence and Mayer, Rochelle. "Development as the Aim of Education." *Harvard Education Review* 42 (1972). 449-496.
Furth, Hans. *Piaget for Teachers*. Prentice Hall, 1970.

[*]Finkel and Monk. *Contexts for Learning*, pp. 38-43 for amplification

[*]Finkel and Monk, *Contexts for Learning*, pp. 99-108

EXPERIENTIAL LEARNING: DON'T OVERLOOK HALF YOUR LABORATORY

by JANE WATKINS

In a very personal address to the 6th Annual Conference on Experiential Education, an ACTION coordinator told of her adventure with experience.

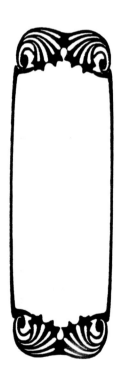

I am delighted to be here for this Conference. Being a journeyer myself, I am always glad to find a group of kindred souls who look on life as an adventure rather than as a burden.

Of course, the absurdity of making a *speech* to a group deeply involved in experiential education has not escaped me. I contemplated suggesting that we all go out and scale a building then return to compare our experiences. But I have, instead, capitulated to that part of me that loves to have a captive audience. However, I do not think of myself as a speechmaker. I like to consider myself a storyteller.

Each of us who is making this journey through life has a story to tell. Unfortunately, there are too many people in the world who, either through actual physical deprivation or, in the developed world, through mental and emotional deprivation, never make the journey. For them, life is a series of crises — endless and unsolvable — or a boring existence full of things like "security" and "conformity" and "properness." But for those lucky few of us — and we are few in the world's numbers — who, through luck or fate or some unknowable force are able to approach life as an adventure, to continue growing not just physically, but spiritually and emotionally as well, we few have a story to tell.

And that is what I want to do tonight. I want to share some of my experiences with you and talk about ways that we can share our good fortune with others . . . ways that

JANE WATKINS *has been the assistant director of AC-TION since 1977. Prior to that, she was administrative assistant to the director of the Democratic Study Group in the U.S. House of Representatives and has served on the board of HEAD START and on the Council of Human Relations.*

we can approach "education" to create an environment in which people may become non-defensive, open to lifelong learning, anxious to examine their own experiences and learn from them — in short, education that enables people to grow in all dimensions and to become whole.

I have called this speech "Experiential Learning: Don't Overlook Half Your Laboratory." I might also have called it, for this group, "Put a Book in your Backpack!" What I want to get across by that, and by this story tonight, is my firm belief that real learning leading to a whole, mature person is not a trick accomplished by taking a backpack into the wilderness, or by sitting in a classroom for 16 or more years, or by attending sensitivity training groups, or by seeing a psychiatrist. Learning to become a whole person requires an openness to *all* those experiences, and a willingness to reflect honestly and critically on your own response to those experiences.

Each of us can, no doubt, point to one or several events in our lives when we make the discovery that something we had been taught, that we knew to be true, wasn't. That is the beginning of the opportunity for real learning. And that is the turning point for people. Those who become defensive . . . who retreat, saying: "Of course that is true and I will ignore my experience because it is too scary to

later when my then 15 year old daughter wanted to pierce her ears, I said, "no." She said "Why?" I said, "Because your grandmother told me that nice girls don't pierce their ears." She told me, "But, Mom, grandmother got her ears pierced last year!" End of discussion. Laurin has her ears pierced. So does my mother. Not me. I'm either scared of needles, or convinced that nice girls don't pierce their ears.) And so the stereotype went. I was a majorette, a debutant, and would become, no doubt, a wife and mother. It was a little embarrassing that I kept doing things like being editor of the high school newspaper and winning a place in the hall of fame or the outstanding Senior award when what I really wanted was to be queen of the homecoming court.

But the forces in my world were about to undergo an upheaval that would change that world and my life. In 1954 the U.S. Supreme Court decided a case called Brown vs Board of Education. Suddenly the deep South had to face its history. Indianola, county seat of Sunflower county, home of Senator Jim Eastland, situated in the rich Delta farmland of Northwest Mississippi, reacted. The Citizen's Council, a modern, milder version of the Klan, was founded in my hometown. During my Senior year, 1955, a pamphlet was distributed in our school explaining that black people were inferior for genetic reasons. We were

---

Real learning leading to a whole, mature person is not a trick accomplished by taking a backpack into the wilderness.

---

face a world without solid truths," those people opt for security, for the comfortable or not so comfortable status quo. But for those who take the challenge — and I like to think of myself as one of those — the world opens up. We begin to see that life is an adventure, not an absolute; that being, becoming, striving to become an open, learning, whole person is hard work — sometimes frightening, sometimes confusing, but always an adventure.

Many of you, I suspect, faced that moment on a mountain trail, or rappelling down a rock face. You faced the challenge and discovered that you could control your own life rather than be controlled by forces outside yourself. And you probably also discovered the joy in sharing that moment with other human beings.

I didn't face that moment on a mountain or a rock face. I got my first glimpse during my Senior year in Indianola high school in a small Mississippi town in the mid-1950's, a town lazily locked into the past. My world was a world of absolutes. Good family, and lots of it; Sunday school on Sunday mornings, or no movie that afternoon; doing well in school to please my teachers and parents; coming home from dates in time to meet my curfew; knowing that nice girls wore lots of underwear and didn't "make out" with boys; knowing that not-so-nice girls pierced their ears and peroxided their hair and "made out" with boys. (Years

told to read the pamphlet, produced by the Citizen's Council, and write a paper about it.

While I had always been aware of the Negroes in our town, I had never, as far as I can now recall, considered the fact that they were not happy with the status quo. That pamphlet, designed to prove to me in writing that the status quo was justifiable, made me mad. I, for some reason, didn't believe it. I had known and loved several black people in my life and I was unprepared to buy that they were genetically inferior. Now that might seem like a logical and rational reaction to you. But consider the context. I had been taught to believe that teachers were always right; that adults were to be obeyed and agreed with; that the world was based on truths about what was right and wrong, good and bad. Questioning the power structure of that school and town was a fairly revolutionary event in my life and one that shook me soundly.

I went to my Mom, a fair and just lady without an evil bone in her body. Well, she announced, "I'll take care of that."

Some years later I learned that she had gone to the Superintendent of schools and told him that she would never stand for her children getting such trash to read from the school. At the time I knew only that I did not have to write that paper. But the seed of doubt had been planted. I had asked the first question about the social order of my life. And I didn't like the answer.

I went on to college — my mother's alma mater — and married at the age of 20 — a man I am still married to I might add, and my best friend as well. College and those first married years spent with Wes in the Navy in Hawaii, were predictable and ordinary ones for a Mississippi Southern Belle living out her destiny. We returned to Mississippi in 1959 for Wes to enter law school at the University. A year later, our daughter was born. But the questions about my world that I had asked so tentatively, lurked around the corners of my mind.

It was during this time that another significant event in my life occurred, irrevocably changing my course. Nothing so cosmic as the civil rights movement this time, but the arrival of a seven year old boy named Gordon, Wes's younger brother, to become part of our family. Wes' parents died while Gordon was still a small boy and it fell to us to rear him. I was in graduate school and learning to cope with a baby of my own . . . I hardly saw Gordon's arrival on the scene as an earth-shaking event. But in many ways it was the real beginning of my experiential learning.

It is safe to assume that I had been learning from my experiences all my life, but I had not, before this time, been forced to pay attention. Those of you who have reared

making him the entire subject of my story, but there is one event that I have related often during the years that was again a moment of revelation for me . . . and the story is about Gordon. It goes like this: When Gordon was about 10 years old, he decided two things. He loved tropical fish and he hated math. Indeed, he had math tutors, summer schools, repeated grades . . . but he absolutely refused to learn the multiplication tables, all the while scoring exceptionally high on math aptitude tests. On the other hand, he was learning everything he could possibly learn about tropical fish. His room was full of bubbling tanks that he had earned money to buy and tended with great care and expertise. One day, I walked by his desk where he was working on complicated mathematical formulas, several sheets of figures strewn over his desk. "Math homework?" I asked. "No!" he emphatically replied. "Looks like math to me." "It's not math," he insisted. "I'm just figuring out how much 'ick' medicine to give my fish."

"There is a message for me here," I thought. Could it be that children learn what they need to know when they understand the reason to learn it? I began to watch Gordon in a different way. Sure enough. When he approached a subject that interested him with a teacher who showed him respect, he could learn anything. When either the interest or the respect was missing, he would refuse to interact.

I, who had learned primarily to please others, was not nearly so well educated as my son, who learned in order to please himself.

---

children know what I mean when I say that some children require that you learn from them. Gordon was such a child. In spite of the fact that he had survived the death of both parents and his beloved grandmother — all of which left him in a shakey emotional state — and despite the fact that he was now having to cope with 23 year old, new parents who had no idea what to do with him, he retained a solid sense of himself, of who he was and what he was willing to put up with.

One thing was clear. He was not willing to put up with the foolish absolutes of my authoritarian approach to life. Neither would he tolerate a teacher's abuse. He was never defiant — just firmly silent and uncooperative.

He finally got my attention, but not before we had chosen a "good" private boys' school for him where elementary children wore suits and ties and played football whether they wanted to or not. We had, upon moving to Washington, D.C. in 1962, looked at a coed, co-op school that had classes in old barns and nature walks on the curriculum. But we decided against that for Gordon because the children called the teachers by their first names and we thought Gordon needed firm discipline and solid subject matter if he was going to be a success. In those days, we never seemed to define success.

I promised Gordon that I would not embarrass him by

While that was a profound lesson for me about my son, it was still some years later, as I taught students of my own, that I gained respect for Gordon's approach. I, who had learned primarily to please others, was not nearly so well educated as my son who learned in order to please himself.

The Washington years brought other lessons. The civil rights movement challenged my racial beliefs. And once I begin to examine such a basic part of my belief system, other questions came.

By 1967, Wes and I knew that we had to return to Mississippi and raise those questions publicly. Again, Gordon chose a tougher path. While we were working through the trauma of being civil rights activists among people who saw us as traitors to our families and our region, Gordon — who never seemed to suffer any form of racial prejudice — was joining forces with the anti-war movement. Now if you think Southerners were upset about race, you cannot imagine their violent reaction to anyone who opposed that war. And if that was not enough, it was becoming increasingly apparent to me that a Woman's role in our society was limited and stultifying.

So there I was: thirty years old, back in my homeland, trying to have some impact on racial injustice, trying to understand a son who didn't want to fight for his country, surrounded by the easy answers of my childhood that no longer worked for me.

And then I discovered "THE ANSWER": Leadership training, as we called it in those days. Group process, sensitivity training, communications conferences, and the human potential movement had come to Mississippi to a small band of us who became true believers. In the same way that I had embraced the easy authoritarian answers of my childhood, I now went around announcing that this was, indeed, the answer.

The training *was* good for me. Through it, I learned the missing piece: To truly learn from one's experiences, one must reflect on them and be willing to change what does not feel right. It was that *reflection* that I had not really understood in my floundering attempts to become "self-actualized" (a word I didn't even know then) or whole.

Of course, I was obnoxious. There is no one more obnoxious than someone who has found "THE ANSWER."

It took me several more years to realize that all my experiences were valuable and useful; that answers do not come easily and only in one way; that people learn what they need to know to survive in whatever way they can figure out at the time. I had been lucky.

The authoritarian upbringing of my youth had been

by intellectual skills."

This is not a plea for the eternally balanced, forever compromisingly-even human being. This is a sharing of something that is true for me and, I believe, may be true for all of us . . . . that we must be open to all of our experiences and develop all of our faculties, intellectual, mental and emotional, to most fully live our lives.

I have tried to take this reality into my work today. At ACTION, we deal always with the human dimension be-cause that is what our programs are about. The VISTA volunteer, the Retired Senior Volunteer, the Peace Corps volunteer are people who choose to confront themselves with experiences that are guaranteed to change the realities of their lives. To choose to become involved with other people, particularly with those in a different culture of social environment, is to choose to confront yourself with a different reality. I have profound respect for our volunteers. Most of them will describe their experience in terms that you and I recognize as learning experiences in the most personal and holistic way. As an agency, we are constantly faced with the problem of how best to choose, prepare and educate these volunteers to face the stress and turmoil that often happens to them both in their physical environment and in their personal growth. It is not an easy task. But the most successful volunteers are surely

---

To choose to become involved with other people is to choose to confront yourself with a different reality.

---

tempered enough by a wise mother to allow me to question and, through that questioning, to grow.

The civil rights movement had taken me into politics, and politics had sensitized me to the inferior status of women in many aspects of our society. In learning to understand the problems that we women face, I came to understand that men, too, face a terrible burden. In fact, the principle applies and the healthiest feminist is one who is able to identify and sympathize with men who are locked into role models that do not fit. In one way or another, the dilemma is the same. The problem is not male or female; the problem comes when any preconceived and defined role is assigned to any human being.

The message is clear to me today (but I do not rule out the very real possibility that it can be clearer tomorrow.) The message is that *no force outside ourselves is the answer.* There is no easy way. Whether we start with too rigid or too permissive an environment, we must seek to examine and experience the opposite if we are to become whole persons. Dr. Douglas Heath who wrote "Teaching for Adult Effectiveness" in the Association's *Journal of Experiential Education* (and with whom I wholeheartedly agree on almost all points) put it this way: "We hobble a gifted youth if his talent is not yoked to passion; we drown the passionate youth if his emotionality is not disciplined

those who know how to learn and adapt from their own experiences.

For a VISTA, a walk down a south Bronx street can be, and often is, as challenging, as terrifying and as growth producing as rappelling down any rock face. I cannot even imagine what it would be like to live, as my sister did, in a small Indian village in the jungle of Peru teaching villagers to raise chickens so that the children would have adequate protein in their diet. It seems to me that these are adventures that take great courage.

And what ever happened to Gordon? Oh, he lives on a mountain in Arkansas in a house he built himself with a wife that we all love, who shares his dreams. And he works sometimes as an instructor in an Outward Bound school. While he questions from time to time the wisdom of my living in polluted air in the middle of Washington, D.C., he understands that my drummer is different than his and that my life is mine to live and no better or worse, only different from his. We have a lot of love and respect for each other and for the experiences that separate us, as well as those that bring us together.

So if I have a message for you tonight, it is the one Gordon helped me learn: Enjoy the adventure. Be open to all your experiences and use all your laboratory. And remember to put a book in your backpack!

194

ACROSS THE RIVER . . . (AND INTO THE BLACK): TOWARD SELF SUFFICIENCY THROUGH CRAFTSMANSHIP AND FOLK WISDOM

Article by LANCE LEE

An exploration of the potential of Apprenticing for developing personal integrity and independence in the modern world.

Moses and the Israelites, ensconced in Egypt, had job security. Pharaoh saw to that. It appears not to have been enough. *Exodus* is an eloquent hymn to the ancient truth that man does not live by bread alone. Observing that the needs of the spirit were absorbing the otherwise productive hours of his guests, Mr. Pharaoh closed up the temporal mouseholes by inviting the Israelites to gather the straw as well as manufacture the bricks. All of this, of course, with no diminution in quantity. Moses and his crowd were soon out of the red, to the still sorrowful and not a little bitter consternation of the other firm.

Pharaoh, as a tactician, deserved to be reduced to a lance corporal. By increasing the demands or load upon his slaves, he increased their capabilities, will, and tenacity. With this newly-found strength they burst out of bondage, crossed the river and began operating solidly in the black.

We are a people in bondage. Our dream is of instant, effortless brick-making, more spiritual time *and* operating in the black. A "service economy" today means having someone else do it and bill you. Increasingly the army of service personnel, garage mechanics, repairmen, carpenters, are *replacers*, not *mechanics*. A replacer orders a part from Mercedes, Sony or General Electric, and then installs it. All but gone is the welder, blacksmith, machinist, rope maker, and wood turner who put raw material — metal, fiber, leather, wood — on a turret lathe, last or shipsaw and came away in a few hours with a totally re-built axle, shoe or windlass.

To the sorry decline in the degree of self-sufficiency of a community must be added the aggravation of waiting for any part not in stock (Taiwan or Germany mean long waits). Add spiralling expenses compounded by fossil fuel-carried freight. Add the sheer aggravation of being helpless when a breakdown occurs. We are in bondage to a dream of purchasing rather than creating, to a dream of not having to do it ourselves but hiring a middle man, and to a dream of charging the service or writing the breakdown off to taxes and thus feeling smug about living in frequent frustration!

We must look again at the dream of an educational structure, the ideal of which is to find a niche in which one can avoid *doing*. For generations parents have said, "My kids are not going to have to labor; we'll get them into college and then into management and office employment, where they'll make more money, do less physically and escape the manual masses for the cerebral elite." We remain in serious bondage to this drastic over-simplification which is leading to an enormous sector of population becoming dependent upon a decreasing percentage of *doers*.

In the language of the radical, there is a parasitical relationship developing. In the language of the future planner, there is a serious danger of food, clothing, shelter and energy shortages which increase exponentially as our dream of doing less and making more with clean hands and primarily academic educations advances. In the language of the Gestalt people, the peril courted by the non-doer whose hands reach only for the pen or the salad fork rather than the drill press handle or the pitchfork is one of waking up distorted, unfulfilled and out of touch with the profound satisfactions of productive as well as creative accomplishment. There is a vital self-assurance factor in having done something which contributes to the physical well-being of the self, family, or community, whether that is growing a cabbage, docking a tugboat, or mending a harness.

Yes, we are a people in bondage. Any reader can make up his/her own list of illustrations. What seems far more critical is acting upon the recognized dilemma, not getting all up tight about it, and laughing a bit on the way to the fields of new straw.

The experiential education movement is virtually a

Lance Lee, is the Director of the Apprenticeshop, at the Bath Marine Museum, Bath, Maine.

195

lifering thrown to a civilization drowning in a sea of lukewarm idealism. The ideal of the instant bricks, or of reaching the far side of the Red Sea by putting the family on a Revolving Charge Account, or the vice presidents aboard a 40-knot plastic Speedykraft with a 200 horsepower outboard guzzling fossil fuels with the same gay abandon as beer at the Oktoberfest, is an ideal unlikely to last. The experiential movement has viscerally shown many thousands that there are no short cuts out of Egypt. Gathering the straw, drawing the water, making the bricks and reveling in the blazing sun rather than howling about adversity, can be a moving way of life and of freeing oneself from bondage. "The planetary conditions are thus," said William James, speaking of the perennial adversity which confronts us all, "and we can stand it."

Where is experiential education headed now? Willi Unsoeld, in the Asilomar Conference just past, pegs the central issue as "How are we going to treat each other in the future?" That is certainly not the wrong question, but is not one closer to the bone in saying, "How are we going to behave with respect to subsistence, well-being and fulfillment, as well as to each other?"

How indeed? We will have to respond actively, with the muscles, and not with the mind alone, and by gathering straw, as well as adventuring in the wildlands and total sex. A two-year-old son is fast teaching me the old bit about "the child being father to the man." He peels out across the living room, riding to hounds on his wooden horse, with a pagan warcry of "Fun, Mama!" The physical world has him enthralled, and that includes passing me logs for the stove, losing *himself* in saying "Bjorn help Dada!" He's still headed towards being a pagan, a primitive, a *doer*.

Institutionally and individually, we need to move toward helping ourselves toward self-sufficiency. A major concern is how institutionally dependent we are becoming. Dependent upon money. It is often said that academic institutions are threatened by experiential ones. The reasons run more to foundation grant competition, than the menace of having to deodorize hair shirts. The reverse is equally true. Experiential schools are threatened by traditional schools.

The clear indication is that any educational ideology or system in our times is nervous, even paranoid about competition from other institutions and the future. This stems from an unhealthy preoccupation with money as the means of continuity. Overt competition for state and local, federal, corporate, foundation, private philanthropic and tuitional funds dominated utterly the educational scene in 1977.

That is more than unfortunate. And it suggests what most of us already know. Sooner or later we will compromise tenets or principles once believed to be sacred, for the patronage or grant with which to ensure that the doors, hatches or tent flaps of our program stay open.

Of much greater concern is a more subtle risk. Dredging hard in the marketplace of money recently, I learned that a major "source," up to which we are all increasingly snuggling, has ruled that earned or generated income in an educational institution makes it suspect and disqualifies it as a recipient. This is a very considerable "source" of potential funding and so the immediate, logical temptation is to relinquish deliberately developed operating practices through which a degree of self-sufficiency has been won. As an alternative, the director/administrator is invited to enter a phase of glorious freedom from fiscal responsibility. In this newfound freedom one must publicly declare that no income to help sustain the institution is being earned. The institution is not helping itself, and is thus totally dependent upon outside sources of funding. Then it qualifies. Then it receives money and is succored. Recall the above comments on being in bondage, and the new ideal of having neither to make bricks nor gather straw while none the less operating in the black. There is very trenchant evidence before us that, if we do not help ourselves, someone else will, and that institutionally, if we make ourselves dependent, we will then be landed free on the far shore of the Red Sea.

Yea. We'll be landed there so weakened in capability, willpower and tenacity that the first wave of adversity (whether the wolf showing up at the north door, the winter blizzard, or the military confrontation) will wash such free spirits into the gutter. The attraction of gathering the straw and thereby attaining pride, independence, and capability begins to compete handsomely with the ideal of financial dependence.

The alternative? Institutions can be run on money or on process. Pharaoh ran a dynamite program, the graduates of which were both liberated from institutionalism and acquainted with how to balance the budget. The tuition was high — paid in the coin of blood, sweat and tears. The result — the graduate Degree of Self-Sufficiency — compares favorably with any degree granted in educational history.

At the risk of being repetitious: The way out of Egypt was almost laughably simple. The Israelites had first to build up their strength, tenacity, and will by developing their physical abilities. This meant embracing adversity, rather than rejecting it. When they had done so, they easily crossed — and does it matter whether they went over, under or through, in double paddle kayaks, Sears and Roebuck waders or Swiss submarines? They emerged from decades of bondage, they crossed over, and they began operating in the black.

In five years, many of our educational institutions (both traditional and experiential) will go under. Many others will be kept afloat and in bondage by "adjusting" their operating philosophy to qualify for specific — and increasingly governmental — aid. But an old/new alternative is rising up, divergent from precedent and made possible by a new interpretation of life, learning, and "how to cross the river." This gambit is one of actively seeking self-sufficiency. It's exciting, satisfying and emboldening. An increasing number of young people — late teens to mid-thirties — are moving in a spreading, swelling current to raise their own barns, goats, competence, *bas relief* frescoes, aspirations, summer squash, self-image, roof beams, and quality of life. They are doing this by lowering their dependence on money and government aid, the size and temperature of their pads,

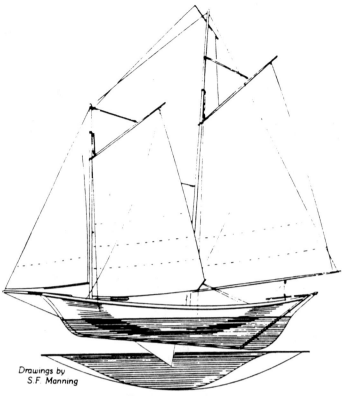

Drawings by
S.F. Manning

Tancook Whaler

and their expectations of a life of ease and affluence as being synonymous with the good life. They are seeking out the last generation — the grandparents and the consummate doers whose lives were bounded by what Eliot Wigginton has marvelously called, "the intricate tricks of self-sufficiency learned through generations of trial and error." It is a scramble, a tight race between seeing those tricks slip back into oblivion, and re-learning them in time to make them the basis of a life, *or an institution's life*, which is not dependent upon money but upon process. What an exciting movement!

I see absolutely nothing of greater hope or significance. Accordingly, our institution, the Apprenticeshop, will concentrate on two "high octane" 1978 projects:

First, the Tancook Whaler: At the turn of the century, on an island in Mahone Bay, Nova Scotia, a community with roots going back to the Empire Loyalists attained a remarkable level of self-sufficiency through a combination of fishing, farming and boat-building. The schooners they built, "whalers", are perhaps the most beautiful and swiftest of all the 19th century workboats. The "intricate tricks" of island life were, in some cases, remarkable. Boats were constructed from a half-model, not from designers' blueprints, and set up "in frame" by an old — apparently German — method which appears to have been extremely swift as well as sure, and may have cut many hours from the construction time of workboats. These small schooners were hauled out on the beach by a trick so simple, low cost and "natural" as to be laughable in the Age of Automation. Sails were "cut", that is, laid out full-size and pieced together, on an ice pond because no loft or floor was large enough. We are ransacking Nova Scotia and this country for photographs, models, written and personal ac-

counts and anecdotes, not of this *story* but this *way of life*. Already we have many hours of discussion with old practitioners from the '80's and '90's on tape (one of the many advantages to be gained from a synthesis of old tricks and modern technology). We are building a (34-foot) whaler, of course, using the tricks. She'll be used to combine sail-training and sail-freight, thus illustrating with the "eloquence" of her extreme beauty the concept of harnessing wind energy again, and training through the natural imperatives of work as well as Nature — here, the sea. We will publish an extensive description of this project, to inspire others and to promote the tricks of a small self-sufficient community. (Yes, we have a special government grant which covers 50% of cost from the National Endowment for the Arts, Folklore Division.

Second, a "BOSUN" Project: Recently, it has become apparent that one critical element in experiential education — as also in communities — lies in active, skilled, and inspiring leadership. Not the "authorizing official" and not the lumper "more fit to carry the hod than the epaulette". Historically, in the Age of Sail, the "translator," who took the orders of the officers and turned them into action with the men, was the bosun, the petty officer or gunnery sergeant, whose physical skill exceeded that of his men. A natural ability to inspire, lead and elicit great endeavor from others marked the finest, rather than an ability to drive. Bosuns operated between the thought and the deed; between the afterdeck and the forecastle; between the bondage of the ideal of idleness and instant bricks and the liberation of a swift passage, a happy ship, an enterprise running in the black. There were good and bad bosuns.

Today, institutionally and individually, we must begin fashioning our own solutions, building our own shops or buildings, machines or communities with muscle and blood, ingenuity and re-cycled materials. To skill, time, timber and spikes absolutely must be added buoyant leadership. We must nurture leaders, project catalysts, "bosuns".

In Bath, this spring and summer we will again construct a sizeable building (2½ stories and 70 x 32 feet) from the reclaimed and waiting timbers of four old buildings. A fifth, a magnificent early 19th century barn — mortise-and-tenon pegged — remains to be studied in its structure, dismantled and set to a new life. A superb leader, John Connolly, and a crew of special volunteers will raise the building. John was an invaluable colleague in the building of the North Carolina Outward Bound School and the Apprenticeshop. Our scheme involves using this building project as an opportunity to train "bosuns" through the subtle process of blood-sweat-and-tears, room, beer and board — rather than classroom lectures and the Seven Cardinal Rules of Leadership. Individuals who aspire to become bosuns — skillful in carpentry and organization, in "pizzaz" and humor, who crave the satisfactions of the tangible and know the stakes are growing higher for a culture which does not lead itself out of the bondage of the idle dream — such will be selected as the volunteer construction crew, trading "learning for labor."

197

A crew of volunteers dismantling one of the recycled buildings of the Apprenticeshop preparatory to mantling a new facility in which to train doers and through the construction of which to train "bosuns."

Institutionally, such enterprises may become critical. There is not enough treasure in Bath to have a construction company erect this building, and there should not be. It will be used to train more hands-on students, in blacksmithing and drafting as well as woodworking. (Bath) high school kids, as well as apprentices from all over the country. The building will serve other display purposes, but most importantly, the project will be on the subject of a small publication illustrating how its construction will serve to train bosuns — for other states, institutions or individual commercial ventures. We'll publish information about this project as well as do it, for we believe that such solutions — using process instead of money exactly as did the "Tancookers" of 1900 off the Nova Scotian coast — ought to be suggested, made available for us all in the next decades. Old new actions, and thinking, will need to characterize our culture soon. (No, we have no grant. We have pegged the entire cost at $16,200.)

On the northeast and southwest of Tancook Island are two shallow coves. No harbors. No shelter. Each Island family had a "stand" — fish tubs, line, gear, cleaning table, perhaps a shack — on established strips of the shoreline. In a sudden gale, there seem to have been three alternatives: you hauled the boats, fast; you sailed or rowed 'round to the sheltered side of the island; you trusted the strength of simple but ingenious moorings. The southwest cove was the harsh one, open to the sea, to the severe conditions, the greatest adversity.

There were easier places to live — to fish, farm or raise families — than Tancook Island. Why did a community choose to make a stand there? More strength, more tenacity, more heartbreak were inevitably involved. It is increasingly tempting to me to ask if the strongest fishermen vied for a stand, not on the north or more sheltered side of Tankcook Island, but in Southwest Cove. How else do you stay in the black?

The Quest for 'Freeorder'

An Interview with the Man Who Discovered the Open Network

Education is where you find it, not always in schools, nor exclusively in programs touting self-discovery and sundry learning. Education in the best sense often flows from one human being who has discovered a convival way of bringing other human beings together, someone with an eye for wondrous experience and a knack for playing any system to that end. Leif Smith is one such person. Several years ago, Leif started an information clearinghouse to help people connect with whatever they needed to grow and explore. He called it an open *network because its structure was dependent on the questions people asked and its content reflected the information they put into the system while pursuing their individual quests. Using a computer, a monthly publication called* Network News, *get-togethers and frequent telephoning, the open network has built up an impressive history of connections between people on the look-out for new ideas and skills. Working on a small scale, it has woven lives together in immensely educative patterns. This interview took place on May 7, 1980, at the offices of Network Research in Denver.*

--Thomas James

T.J. *What is a Network?*

Leif A network is an array of points connected by lines. If the points are people and the lines are things they are saying to each other or devices for carrying the things they are saying, then you have a network. Networks are nothing new. The newness is in running an office for a process we call "open network." I don't know of anyone ever having done that before.

T.J. *What makes a network open instead of closed?*

Leif Let me read you something. It sounds serious, but I mean every word of it: "The open network is a freeorder arising from all aspects of the world in which an explorer of sovereign spirit may rejoice. It is a process and an image. It is not an organization. It cannot be owned and it cannot be controlled. You may connect with the open network through the facilities of Network Research in Denver. We find, invent and distribute tools for explorers of all kinds--from scientists to artists to craftsmen to theologians." This office we operate here in Denver is not the open network. The open network is the process I defined as being comprised of all those aspects of the world in which an explorer of sovereign spirit may rejoice. This is such an open-ended definition that nobody could ever determine what it does and doesn't include--which is the reason I formulated it that way. If what is happening here is anything, it is an attempt to prove the value of tolerance, to create a way people can find each other and talk to each other without straining one another's capacity for patience. It is open to everybody, no matter how much they differ. The value hidden in people's differences, the potential arising from the fact that people don't see eye to eye about things, can be turned to advantage, especially by an organization that doesn't define in advance what it's for.

T.J. *What do you mean by "freeorder." It seems as though you have constructed a paradox with those words.*

Leif It may seem that the words indicate a paradox, but to me they express the highest of all harmonies. Proudhon, a French anarchist writer, said that order is the daughter of freedom, not the parent. The idea is that if you know when to abstain from controlling things you have the power to control, the result is a spontaneous order far richer than anything you could have contrived by foresight. This is especially true when you move beyond the domain of a single individual and look at what happens when people begin to interact. In constructing an open network, we have placed severe limits on ourselves so that we don't prevent that spontaneous order from taking place. One limit is that we do not allow ourselves to classify the data coming into the computer system of the open network. We have no preselected key words or categories; the entries are organized through a key word system, but the users of the network decide what words they want to connect to the things they put into the computer.

T.J. *Do you censor any of the entries?*

Leif Never have. If I became convinced that I was in the presence of outright malice or intent to harm, then things would stop. But I've never run into that here, and I don't expect to.

T.J. *You mentioned a computer system. You also said earlier that the open network is not an organization. Another paradox?*

Leif   The office where we work *is* an organization. But all the office does is to serve people who are involved in the *process* of the open network. The open network is a freeorder not controlled by the office, but supported by it in ways that make freedom possible. If I were to call the office anything, I would call it a network generator. The business of a good network generator is to understand when to stop, to know what to leave alone. We think about what to leave alone as well as what to do. There are many times we don't make connections even though we could. People don't always want more information. We're in the business of facilitating exploration, which often means thinking until you come up with a few pieces of information that could be important to individuals--then you call them or hope they call you.

T.J.   *How does the office function? How do the computer system and staff work to make connections?*

Leif   We initiate people by insisting that no one use the word "members" when referring to the open network. We talk about "users" who "open accounts" with Network Research. This is deliberately impersonal and remote. We don't want anyone to think the use of the network depends on what *we* want. We tell people that when *you* want to build something, think of us as a tool with an adaptable working surface that can become a chisel or a saw. You program us; we don't program you. Network Research is supposed to be programmable by the user. We always want people to take the initiative. Don't expect us to get in touch with you. When you open an account with us, we don't give you this phone number for nothing. Use it. Call up and give us a scenario about what you are thinking about doing with your backyard or your thoughts on keeping your house energy efficient. Or call us up and put something into the computer. At the last open house we ran for users of the open network, a woman walked up to the computer and typed in the word "communities." She was looking for a community to live in. Up on the screen came an entry from another woman who was standing beside her, whose entry was a listing of houses that offered cooperative living arrangements in Denver. You never know what a person might need, which is why we have no preselected set of key words such as energy, education, books, etc.

T.J.   *But aren't you controlling the media through which people are communicating?*

Leif   We control it more than we want to because of poverty. We don't have the resources to get a ter-

minal unit out to the public. The terminal in the network office is on loan from the company we work with. I would like terminals in public places in Denver where people could walk up to them and type in favorite words and see what happens. People who have never used a computer before would be able to find the things they are interested in. Very simple. I would like to have less control over access to the computer.

T.J.   *Obviously, you have a social philosophy that is fundamentally different from that of information systems in education, banking and government. Where does that philosophy come from?*

Leif   Imagine you are in a typhoon in a small boat and somebody says, "We're sinking, why bother to bail?" I reply, "If we don't bail, we'll surely sink; but if we do, maybe we'll make it to land." I'm optimistic insofar as I can see the outlines of a distant shore. So, I'm bailing like crazy because I still think we have a chance to make it.

We are not here to tell people our philosophy. If people walk in and ask, we'll tell them. The telling shapes so much that you begin to see only a reflection of what you said. One of the reasons I started this office was that I wanted a place for my own education. I wanted a place where people with ideas would come to me and where I could learn from them. For myself-for my own education-I have a few compressions of ideas that express what I am trying to do. One is the notion of freeorder that we've been talking about. By freeorder I mean a balance between designed and spontaneous orders which is conducive to exploration. In that definition I make no speculations as to the nature of the balance. I'm proposing that it is worth attending to the balance between designed and spontaneous orders, within individuals, within societies, within organizations- any structure of experience in which one might find oneself. Somewhere in the balance of designed and spontaneous orders there is a social order that is optimum for the explorer, one that does not constrain either by an excess of tradition, binding new conjecture and preventing its test, or by excess of structure impeding access to tools.

Another of my ideas is that if resonance is the end, then freeorder is the means. By resonance I mean an expectation of magic. By magic I mean fusion of four things in real doing: intensity, sensitivity, wonder and a passion for integrity. When I find all four of these things fused in real doing, not in prospect or retrospect, I call it magic. It is simply the magic of exploration and real doing. If there are people who have decided to bet on the explorer within themselves, then we have a tool store for their use-and it is less likely that they will be beaten by circumstances.

In running the office for the open network, I have kept this exposition on freeorder mostly to myself. It is not what we are selling. If a situation comes up and it seems like some of the ideas I have accumulated can be of value, I bring them up piecemeal, one at a time, handling them with great care. Like tools in a tool box. There are two hundred people in the network that have interesting tool boxes, really complex ones like mine. So I am one person people come to, and I usually give them something out of my tool box, then point them to other people. Lots of tool exchange goes on. If I can be paid for doing that, it's perfect.

T.J. *Are there any other networks like this in the United States?*

Leif Everyone has personal networks. Hundreds of millions of networks for all of us. Then there are networks more specifically established as networks-a society for professional engineers, for example. Thousands of those. Every journal creates a network of its own. A business, its clients and its salesmen that offer products constitute a network. Most networks that we know about are what I call focused networks: there is a world view that governs them, such as the network of professional engineers in Denver, the network of people interested in west coast Indian art-it goes on and on, all the definably different ways a network can be focused. The open network is perhaps a first. I've never seen anything like it, where a deliberate attempt was made to avoid all focus. Not because we think focus is bad, but because we think there is something else that needs to be done. People are like artists in their explorations, but instead of a palette with colors of paint they have a palette of focused networks. Give them an open network and the palette increases manyfold. Successful connections through the open network number in the thousands. They are the sort that happen in a matter of thirty seconds and are gone. We never hear any more about them. We did our job and that's that.

Some people get wrapped up in a new network of their own. I tell them: If you ever have any ideas that seem strange and interesting, you have our number. For example, they get this idea to use a computer to keep track of who has what western art in what galleries in Denver. They think, ''Who knows about art in Denver? Who can I talk to?'' They ask one of their companions. No one can

help. If that's what happens, they call the network and we will find someone that they can talk to. The network is also for the person who calls up and says, ''I'm a user of the network and wondered if there was a person in the network who knows a lot about western art. I have a computer and I want to do such and such.'' There is a minimal context created-minimal because we don't lead people to suppose that just because someone is a user of the network, they are people you will want to talk to and be friends with. In fact, there are people in this open network who do not like each other at all.

T.J. *Could you give me an example?*

Leif There are environmentalists in Colorado who put things into the computer as users of the open network. They discover that another user is someone they regard as being close in moral stature to Atilla the Hun. He is one of the world's leading advocates of nuclear energy. This horrifies them. The come in thinking, ''What a fantastic idea, an open network-anybody can use it.'' I show them the book this man has written. They look stunned. ''He's in the network?'' But it's an *open* network, right? The same thing happens on the other side-in the camp of the nuclear advocates. They get interested in the network. Then I tell them that one of the principal organizers of antinuclear demonstrations is a user of the network. We are here as a general purpose tool for explorers. A great many people on both sides are honest people trying to do their very best to see the planet as a good place to live. I'm convinced that both sides of that dispute have a lot to teach each other, and there are very few meeting grounds. If the open network can be one of them and if through that encounter some people's appreciation for differences can increase a little, we may gain a lot.

T.J. *Would you say a little more about how the open networks operates? Besides telephone conversations, open houses and people walking into the office, how do you communicate systematcially with the users?*

Leif We used to run a newspaper with two kinds of spaces, called network research space and user space. It was modeled on the idea of public and private spaces. The main content was in the private or user spaces. Our circulation was not large enough to support that idea, so we have designed a simpler monthly publication. We also will do an annual report for the year, where the main content will be spaces that the users of the network buy and put into it. For example, I have a philosophical venture and I'm a user of the network. I'm a weaver having something called

Mountain Forge, which is a philosophical venture, a focused network. My entry says I'm buying a page in the network annual report and I'm inviting people whose ideas I especially like to sublet or take a grant of space from me where they can talk about what they are doing. The business of Mountain Forge will be to create the context that defines that entire space.

T.J.   *What do you mean by the term "weaver?"*

Leif   Part of the architecture of this network we are propagating is that the main networkers will not be the staff of Network Research. When you think of a question, you call the open network as just one of the many things you do. A more intense form of network, or "quest-facilitation," is not happening in this network but is being done by people I call weavers. For example, one might be a person who works for an underwriting firm bringing new companies to the public. Somebody else might be a career consultant. These are focused networks that use the open network as a place to find people and ideas.

T.J.   *Does the Association of Experiential Education fit in as another network of that kind?*

Leif   Yes, it does. What we are trying to do is to design and implement a good working relationship between office of open network and a tremendous variety of focused networks like AEE, all inhabited by at least one weaver. Maria Snyder has been a weaver for AEE. Weavers are the people who make connections in a network. We are trying to design tools principally for weavers. Five years from now, most of the users of the office for open network will probably be weavers who are using it as a device for enriching what people can find when they come in contact with their particular focused networks. Also, weavers pass people back and forth. Maria Snyder finds somebody who needs some other focused network, possibly through this office, so she pases on the information.

We want to make sure that any explorer can quickly change the array of focused networks they use, so that they don't get stuck. I hope people always remember there is a phone number to call when they are seeking a change of network. Nobody is trapped. We live in a complex web of possibilities where there are no tightropes to fall off of. It's possible to think you are on a tightrope, but you learn to act differently than when you know you are in a sustaining web.

T.J.   *A minute ago you used the term "architecture" when speaking of the open network.*

Leif   Network architecture pertains to the discussion on weavers. It is the relationship that exists between the powerless office for open network and the thousands of well focused, very well organized weavers that surround us. That relationship is central to the architecture of the system that serves open network. There is no end either to existing networks or to the new focused networks that can be created. In fact, the creation of new networks is another purpose of the open network. Frequently people will get ideas for patterns of interrelationships between themselves and others for which there is no supporting network.

For example, someone wants to build an integral urban house-a living unit designed to supply all of its own energy and food from within. As far as I know there is no network in Denver to serve this quest. There is beginning to be one, and much of the reason for it is that the people who are working on ideas having to do with integral urban houses are constantly in touch with the open network. So when we find somebody that might fit in, we pass the information on, and communications begins to occur. Gradually there is a merging of this focused network, with the intent of building an integral urban house in Denver as a demonstration and research project. That requires a good weaver.

T.J.   *How many users are there now in the open network?*

Leif   In the history of the network we have had seven hundred and seventy-one accounts. Of those, approximately six hundred are still active. The density of users is highest in Denver, but I think the right scale for an office for open network is regional. It should be metropolitan and spread for a few hundred miles. I do not see this office generating a nationwide or worldwide business, although we presently have users in thirty states and seven countries.

T.J.   *In what way do you see the open network as a business?*

Leif   I think of this office as a business with the highest aesthetic aspirations. I do not find those notions opposed to one another. All business means is that you tell people, "We have something that might be of value to you. If you can somehow support it to the extent that we can continue, we will provide it to you." The idea of business is that everybody gains. I'd love to make a profit here. The economics of this place will begin to make sense when we have two thousand to twenty-five hundred accounts. Right now it makes no sense at all. An economist would say I was subsidizing the place. I am willing to do that because, in my opinion, what I get from it now outweighs all the money I could presumably find a way to earn by doing something else. I'd rather be doing this, and I think the economics will work out as more people catch on to the value of the open network as a tool for exploration.

T.J. *How can people who read this journal get in touch with the network and find out more about it, or offer their services?*

Leif First, they can give us a call. The number is (303) 832-9764. Second, if they would like information until the end of 1980 we will send out an information package for one dollar. After that it will be two dollars. You can write to us at Network Research, P.O. Box 18666, Denver, CO 80218. We have not kept anyone from using the network because of lack of money, and we don't intend to start. Our access fee is going up like everything else, but we make it plain that we do not want to discriminate against people because they are poor. Right now the access fee is thirty dollars per year.

T.J. *What do you think the future holds for the open network?*

Leif I see the staff of open network as apprentice weavers, because this is not the place, in the long run, where you need a highpowered weaver. It is a lot simpler than that. As more and more people learn to use this system we are creating, it will be less and less necessary for the magic combinations to happen out of this office. I expect this will be a training ground for weavers who are developing focused networks in their own businesses, non-profit organizations, social service agencies, and the like.

The office of open network is one project of Network Research. We are going to have many other projects. Network Research is all about inventing, finding and distributing tools that explorers need to make proper habitats for themselves. What I am concentrating on now is the computer terminal as a tool, mostly to facilitate the work of weavers, but also to be useful to anyone who wanders in from the street, anyone yearning to be an explorer.

"The gods send thread for the web begun," goes the old adage. What would you encounter if you pursued a quest through the open network? The brief history of the process is full of surprise and spontaneous connection. The city of Northglenn devised a plan for a self-sufficient waste recycling system through contacts made in the open network. According to a newspaper account, the recycling system shredded grass clippings and leaves into useable methane and a sludge that was fed to earthworms, which were then processed to make a protein supplement. Other connections included a local restaurant looking for people to design its interiors, a conference called "Windmills Are Tougher Than They Look," the convictions of a man running for political office, information on roofing construction, a solar bookstore, a typewriter repair business for sale, a pantomime duo looking for engagements, and many more: a barter network, a conciliation service to avoid litigation, a holistic health network, a neighborhood organization that monitors government action and disseminates information to citizens.

"The card shark says 'read 'em and weep,' the farmer says 'weed 'em and reap,' " said one of the entries in Network News. Leif, who worked for a time as "philosophical consultant" to the Denver Free University, sees the interrelatedness he has created as a means for his own education as well as that of others: "My principle is never to do anything if you can find someone else to do it better, except for the things you want to do most of all." But he has added a twist of exploration to that statement, making it a call for learning and self-reliance. So the weaving of lives proceeds effortlessly without prescription: neighborhood gardens and community parks, the design of a left-handed pen molded to the natural contours of the hand, venture capitalists looking for interesting investments, someone hoping to find a music teacher, another wishing companionship to explore the visual presentation of mathematical forms in nature, a notice by a kite store on legal restrictions to kite flying, a guide to vegetarian food stores and restaurants, places open in a theater company, classes on how to get published, a quarterly magazine reviewing new books in the field of law, someone looking for allies to save the historic Elkhorn Lodge in Estes Park-and on and on, this thing that exists for no other purpose than to facilitate anybody's quest.

T.J.

Experience, Reality, and Computer-Controlled Technology

by Dennis M. Adams

In 1984 we saw the first signs of a serious backlash against educational computing. We had finally reached a point where people began to rebel against the euphoric hype surrounding microcomputers that had been going on unabated for three or four years. The major serious criticism seemed to revolve around the notion that the computer-based technology might replace real experience — or even real people — in the classroom. In some cases this had happened; instead of using more expensive science equipment, some schools were saving money by limiting students to manipulating objects and chemicals on the screen. Still, in spite of some misuse of technology, the criticism that electronic experiences were replacing "real" ex-

periences on a massive scale were unfounded. Do children **have** to touch something before it becomes real?

After a period of computer bashing, the time may now be ripe for a swing back towards moderation. Those of us who are writing critical and cautionary articles about how microcomputers and television trap children in artificial worlds have more than made our point. Microcomputers, videodiscs and VCRs are a fact of life and are having an impact on how we formulate our perceptions of what's real. Reality itself is changing as rapidly as the technology defining it. Certainly some skepticism and concern is healthy, but exaggeration can kill a new instructional tool before it has a chance to reach its potential. This is particularly true now that a technological synthesis is on the immediate horizon — with a kind of electronic synergism about to take place.

Dennis M. Adams is Associate Professor of Educational Studies of Northern Colorado.

Actual Experience Is Not the Only Connection to Reality

Just as science frequently confuses fact with truth, educators frequently confuse what's found in the physical (non-electronic) environment with what's most real for the child. If it's machine-assisted, it must be mechanized and less valuable than actual (real) experience. The truth is that sometimes it is, and sometimes it isn't. There are limits to actual experience. Intellectual enrichment can come from any direction that stimulates the brain with novelty and challenge. Certainly we want children painting with real brushes — but that doesn't negate the learning experience that can come from doing art on the computer because that too can become part of the "real world."

The form and style of reality is changing. When children use a computer hooked up to a videodisc — or other television media — they can tour an art museum in any way they want, viewing the art from any angle, even calling up printed text information if they like. The force and clarity of this visually based learning should not be underestimated.

The reality of human learning is that there is vast range of different styles in thinking and learning. And adding a computer-based technology to the mix has the potential of opening up avenues for a wider range of intelligences than traditional methods. Of course the manner in which children come across ideas will affect their use. But intelligently programmed electronic devices would seem to only add to the possibilities — discovery **can** take place in both new and old ways. Even the primitive, non-interactive television technology that we have with us now can be intelligently and critically viewed and used educationally. In spite of all its present limitations, it does give us the very first information about what's going on in the real world. Some of what it presents is simply not something that we can experience in our daily lives. Better programming and merger with other media could really change our conception of the medium.

While it's true that learning is powerfully affected by experience, some actual life experiences are not experiential. The abstract "unreal" is, at least occasionally, the most "real." Actual experience is only one way to approach understanding reality. We can, for example, have experience in our heads — or with computer controlled simulations. Like a book, or any other curriculum material, these can be used as jumping off points for the exploration of the limitations of our "real world" models. And, as the technology develops, these electronic excursions will themselves become more and more real.

Real world lessons do not automatically hold true any more than internal (what goes on in our minds) or external (electronic) lessons. The field and the streets are not necessarily more accurate in teaching perceptual truths than our minds or our video screens. You can be tricked by the real world as easily as the electronic one. There are multiple

> **"There are limits to actual experience... Certainly we want children painting with real brushes — but that doesn't negate the learning experience that can come from doing art on the computer because that too can become part of the 'real world'"**

ways of arriving at the "truth." In fact, internal critical thinking skills and external computer controlled video technology can help us balance out some of the illusions thrown at us from our physical environment. There is **some** truth to the expression "seeing is believing." And technology can help us to "see" things that would otherwise not be part of our reality. We can see reality with electronics that we could not see in the real world; building graphic models to represent DNA molecules is one example.

Technology can also stimulate an enriched learning environment by helping us bring distant or uncommon events into our consciousness and change our view of reality. Interacting with historical events and atomic reactors would be impossible in real life. Yet these and other events can enter our personal realities with computer-based technology. But be careful, magazines and newspapers frequently use computers to alter almost anything they want in a picture. The camera simply puts the picture onto the TV screen and a computer allows the editor to rearrange any of the elements. The pyramids, for example, were digitized and rearranged to "fit" on the cover of *National Geographic*. Although prohibitively expensive today it is possible to do the same thing with film; transplanting a moving character from an old to a new movie or television segment. These electronic experiences — along with the internal mental sorting and evaluating may be distant from concrete material ... but they will be just as real.

When real world experience with actual material is a possibility it should take place. Technology should be viewed as a supplement or amplification, not as a replacement. But when actual experience is impossible, the mechanical devices and internal thinking processes can help us build — and take part — representations of real world models. Computer controlled technology can help students understand the relationship between elements and the limitations of the models we use to represent them. Television, particularly when linked to a computer, changes the limits of real time and space in ways that allow us to view both differently. Even in reality scientific models are more like simulations than perfect representations of real world experience — and the better we understand that, the better we understand the underlying process. Technology can help us explore the complexity of such models in a more graphic, concrete and visual manner than is possible by mathematical formula or the printed word.

Educational Computing: Self-Satisfaction or Criticism?

When educational computing was just beginning to get moving (only 3 or 4 years ago) it generated too much self satisfaction — followed by too much criticism. Exaggeration in either direction can prevent the integration of a new learning process. Progress requires a little skepticism and a little faith. But the critic who says that computers in education will fare no better than some previous technologies (like programmed learning and educational television) should remember that we only have an average of one computer for every fifty children in school. (In poorer districts it's one for every seventy.) Dismissing such devices now is a little like dismissing books in 1780. After all, they didn't help much -- and with an average of

"Progress requires a little skepticism and a little faith."

one per class, what came our of primitive printing presses didn't seem as lively (or as real) as those done by hand.

Programmed learning and educational television failed to treat the child as a thinking and contributing individual. The computer is assuming a new role, encouraging children to accept a greater amount of responsibility for their own learning process. Seeing the future of educational computing is a little like trying to envision a 747 while watching the Wright Brothers. Those who are very self-satisfied about the present state of computers in the schools and have accepted the computer as the answer for most of our educational ills are making the same mistake as the critics. Fanaticism or extreme claims can cloud the picture and make everything more difficult for a rapidly changing educational technology. The overly enthusiastic and the overcritical might best be served by a middle course of moderation. If expectations in either direction are too grand, then disillusionment is bound to set in and a powerful learning tool will either fall short of its potential or be lost altogether.

Connecting Everything to Everything

While we are arguing the specifics of early 80s computing, the world is turning and many of these factors might prove to be simply prehistoric distractions from learning in the future. Computer chip technology has now reached a stage where it is possible to process information in almost any frequency — from the human voice to computers, to television and beyond. When these new microchips are put into civilian action, it will be possible to use computer technology to control television sets, personal computers, radios, and other electronic devices connecting everything to the human voice or anything else found in the frequencies of nature.

IBM and AT&T are just two of the larger companies (to say nothing of the Defense Department) that have recognized the possibilities in these breakthrough technologies. (Witness IBM's recent

"Real world lessons do not automatically hold true any more than internal (what goes on in our minds) or external (electronic) lessons. The field and the streets are not necessarily more accurate in teaching perceptual truths than our minds or our video screens. You can be tricked by the real world as easily as the electronic one."

alliance with MCI communications and CBS.) New high speed integrated circuits (VHSIC chips) support the evolution of computer-based electronic systems — with great increases in speed, accuracy, picture clarity, and instant connection to just about any sound or picture that is desired. TV pictures can be stored in computer memories, pictures from several sources can be pulled onto a screen with freeze frames and close ups and even a printed text explanation. The learning possibilities are endless.

At the same time as we are coming up with more powerful learning microworlds, we are getting closer to being an electronic village on a worldwide scale. The time is rapidly approaching when computer controlled technology will make it possible for just about anybody with the proper (inexpensive) computer controlled devices to communicate with anything anyplace else in a multitude of ways. A form of computer-based video may be the key technology for providing alternative paths for learning. The real concern is with the quality spectrum the medium will be programmed to carry in the future — rather than last year's criticism about trapping children in artificial worlds.

Mass communication devices (mainly television at the moment) have enormous intrusive, reality-forming power. Witness the recent hijacking of an airline by terrorists who literally shot themselves into every living room. One jarring moment was when the ABC anchorman (on "Good Morning America") turned to the Shiite Moslem leader Nabih Berri and said, "Any final words to President Reagan this morning?" (The American president reportedly had the TV in his bedroom on.) Even in today's limited format, TV messages can be conveyed to massive publics of billions around the globe. The Live Aid (for Africa) concert is the largest example. It went out to more than fifty countries. There were musicians from England, the USA, Australia, Ireland, the Soviet Union and other countries. And although some of the best

moments were missed by the TV networks going to laxative and pimple cream commercials in the middle of songs, the potential of television for doing positive things should not be missed. The message was essentially healthy, in spite of the greed on the part of the commercial networks — and coverage by announcers who might most charitably be described as mindless adolescents. Of course it was aimed more at the emotional eye than the analytic mind — and its electronically induced reality became an "experience" for billions. People can communicate with machines **and** with other people.

No matter how real or how healthy, conventional television usually shows a few of the facts, but misses the truth. And as it can make complex distant events immediate and concrete, it can also be dangerous. It can put terrorists in our living room or positively mix commercial greed, music and food for starving people. Reality, illusion, or a mix of both can be conveyed to the viewer. When it opens its lenses for a mass audience, TV can even change the essential nature of the event it conveys. The images that television transmits may carry more power than the reality of what's in that image. This is even evident in what's censored out of our reality. The BBC, for example, was recently accused by a Labor Member of Parliament, as acting as "thought police" for not broadcasting a program on the IRA. Prime Minister Margaret Thatcher, on the other hand, was very pleased that they didn't "further the objectives of IRA terrorists." Censorship or a high level of social responsibility? Take your pick.

Regardless of the politics involved, a powerful synergism is emerging from speeding up the interaction of ideas, learning and technology. People do need help in learning how to sift the popular image of what's real from the underlying reality.

Because technology is so much a part of what we define as real, critics miss the point when they say that it prevents students from getting at the

"Technology can help us to 'see' things that would otherwise not be part of our reality."

real world. **Reality is changing as rapidly as video images and computing.** And there is to be no turning back of the clock. We might as well make the best of it by improving the programming and teaching our students how to think critically about these electronics devices and the messages they carry. It **is** possible to use computer controlled technology to explore the complexity of reality; rather than the educational equivalent of the simplified headlines seen on the network news. Teaching critical viewing skills and using interactive computers can help us to deal with the disguises, exaggerations and artificial universe implicit in the technology. The whole process will require new styles of critical thinking, viewing and being on the viewer's part — making visual fluency even more important.

As diverse mediums (including personal computers and television) are giving common connecting points on a world-wide basis, the potential for good or evil, real or unreal, experiential or artificial, are all present. If our educational system is to play its part in the process, then it must not only provide alternative means of thinking about and exploring curriculum topics, but reconceptualize its view of reality and experience. Certainly the best way to learn is through experience. But in light of our evolving electronic miracles we not only must reconceptualize teaching and learning, but what "experience" means.

As antiquated equipment is replaced, some elements of educational computing philosophy may become stronger than ever. The notion of discovery by choice — and user control — behind some of the elements of today's educational computing will almost certainly carry over into a new age; an age where activities in the mind and experience with electronic devices will be considered as legitimate an experience and as "real" as what's picked up in the physical environment.

Computer-controlled electronic elements will be one of the primary means of creating the world of experiences and ideas in the future — in fact, they will be central to thinking, learning and communicating. As technologies merge and integrate, so do traditional divided human skills. We are in the process of major transformations in how knowledge is acquired and communicated. Our range of choices are being dramatically increased. As new technological combinations collect, analyze, and deliver information it is creating new tasks. It is now time to stop attacking the old (early 80's) computer technology and assume responsibility for how the reality of our future is being created through ideas — experiential, internal and electronic.

REFERENCES

This article was done in cooperation with Mary Fuchs.
- Adams, Dennis M. *Computers and Teacher Training*. New York: Haworth Press, 1985.
- Adams, Dennis M.; Fuchs, Mary. "Amplifying Our Thinking: A Synthesis Of Television, Artificial Intelligence, Computers, Science and the Visual Arts", *AEDS Journal*, July/August, 1985.
- Adams, Dennis M. "Expanding Critical Awareness of Visual Media: Gaining Access to the Exploding Electronic Universe", *Electronic Education*, forthcoming.
- Daiute, Colette. *Writing and Computers*. Reading, MA: Addison Wesley Publishing, 1985.
- Geoffrion, Leo D.; Geoffrion, Olga P. *Computers and Reading Instruction*. Reading, MA: Addison Wesley, 1983.
- Michie, Donald; Johnson, Rory. *The Knowledge Machine*. New York: William Morrow and Co. Inc., 1985.

The Stranger Without and the Stranger Within...

Transplanting the Liberal Heart

by Robert S. MacArthur

Editor's Note: This is the text of a speech given at AEE's Northeast Regional Conference on March 30, 1985.

Recognizing that we learn in different ways, I have tried to provide two access points for you. Thus, for those of you who learn best in a linear, left-brained way, I have organized this talk into six propositions. For those of you who learn best in a symbolic, right-brained way, I have attached these propositions to two images.

My first proposition is this:

There is a growing gap between our private and our public lives, a gap that is becoming critical.

Public vs. Private Life

A few years ago, a word merchant coined the phrase, "the me decade" to characterize the 1970s. One wonders what the phrase will be for the 80s. Whatever emerges, it will take into account the heightened materialism of our day. Perhaps the 80s will be called "the mine decade". One of its young media-maids, Madonna, celebrates its philosophy in the daily barrage of the top 40. She sings of the boys who don't measure up:

"They can beg and they can plead but they can't see the light, because the boy with the cold hard cash is always Mr. Right...
we are living in a material world,
and I am a material girl."

Robert S. MacArthur is President of the American Youth Foundation based in St. Louis, Missouri.

The Yuppie phenomenon is even more disturbing. According to Newsweek's special in December, Laurie Gilbert, a 28-year-old lawyer at the Disney Channel says she would be comfortable with $200,000 a year (and more, if she has children)! The Yuppies are known not so much by their willingness to work hard for the corporation, but by their devotion to accumulating power and getting rich. I must read this one:

"When Carrie Cook was a kid growing up on Boston's Beacon Hill, election time meant blanketing the neighborhood with Kevin White leaflets and singing the praises of anyone who ran as a Democrat. Today, however, things are different... (In November election) Cook liked Reagan 'for financial reasons', but because of the Republican stance on abortion and other social issues she eventually voted for Mondale. Not that she actually wanted the Democrat to get elected.

'I knew Reagan would win easily anyway,' she says. 'If I thought it was a close election, I might not have voted for Mondale. I had the best of both worlds. I could vote my conscience and still come out ahead financially.' "

The Yuppies are an extreme example of people who are occupied with a consumptive self interest, those who function within a highly selective and isolated circle of peers.

There are other reasons, however, why people turn increasingly inward and away from the public realm. One reason is just the complexity of the issues facing us today. We need a certain amount of technical information in order to participate in decisions about policy. Because issues seem so convoluted, many of us give up trying to deal with them and concentrate instead on the smaller realm over which we exercise the greatest control — our families and our friends. This is not altogether bad, since each of us needs a private life to nourish and support us. However, when we end up avoiding involvement in public life, we shortchange ourselves, and we contribute to the poverty of everyone's experience of the public.

In an excellent book, *The Company of Strangers*, Parker Palmer writes:

"My thesis is simple. In a society which lacks a healthy public life, both private and political life will suffer. In the absence of a public which knows and cares about itself, private life tends to become obsessive and fearful, while political institutions become centralized, overweening, and even totalitarian. If we want authentic privacy and authentic politics, we must cultivate the public life on which both depend." (1978:71)

Having mentioned the political sphere, let's remind ourselves why fewer people aspire to hold public office. Certainly the lack of financial incentive is one. However, I think the lack of role models worth emulating is another, and this is coupled with the prevailing perception of the compromises necessary or inevitable in public service. For example, within a 3 week period beginning in late February we learned that:

- Director of the Division of Enforcement of the Securities and Exchange Commission, John Fedder, resigned in the wake of public knowledge of his wife beating.
- a federal grand jury indicted Louisiana Governor Edwin Edwards on 50 counts of racketeering and mail fraud.
- Labor Secretary Raymond Donovan resigned, facing trial on 137 counts of grand larceny and fraud.
- and finally, Edwin Meese was confirmed as attorney general.

As Archibald Cox said in a Washington Post article, "In the past, receiving personal financial benefits, as Meese did, and then exercising governmental power in favor of the benefactor has been condemned as grossly unethical — even when there was not proof of a casual connection.

The president of a large university asked me last spring: 'How can you and I continue to try to teach young men and women to recognize moral standards if the Senate votes that what Ed Meese did does not bar his confirmation as attorney general of the United States?'" (1/28/85)

Parker Palmer provides another example of the gap between private and public life, when he talks about our preoccupation with intimacy in relation-

"Because issues seem so convoluted, many of us give up trying to deal with them and concentrate instead on the smaller realm over which we exercise the greatest control - our families and our friends."

ships. This is particularly pertinent to us in experiential education, in that we often impose a false sense of the intimate on our groups, largely because some groups do emerge as intimate communities. Palmer says:

"When intimacy becomes the sole criterion for authentic human relationships, we falsify relations in public... we must learn to accept and appreciate the fact that public life is fundamentally impersonal...
The public life involves those qualities of distance and disinterest which allow us to receive from another without assuming a personal obligation, to give to another without having to make a total commitment. In fact, the public life allows us to view and listen to each other, to be edified and entertained, without forming a personal relationship of any sort... impersonal relations have a validity of their own." (1983:50)

I will assume that this group needs little convincing of the validity of my second proposition: **As citizens of a free society, we have an obligation to participate in the public life, whether it be with our voice in the formulation of public policy, or our presence in service to others; because the consequences of our neglect are so extreme, we cannot afford to abdicate that responsibility.**

With each passing day, the nuclear arsenals grow, increasing our capacity to destroy not only ourselves but most forms of life on the planet. With each passing day, we foul our global nest and deplete its resources.

According to environmentalist Dana Meadows, each day on this planet $2 billion are spent on armaments, 57 million tons of topsoil are lost to erosion; 70 square miles of desert are added;

80 square miles of tropical forest is lost; and one species of life becomes extinct. Each **minute** 60 million barrels of nonrenewable oil are burned at great expense, releasing carbon dioxide into the atmosphere at such a rate as to threaten a global climate change.

I don't think I need to go on. As dwellers on this globe, not to mention educators, we cannot turn our backs on these issues, if life is to survive. We must renew a commitment to the commonweal, and we must find new ways to engage ourselves and our students in the responsibilites of citizenship.

The Stranger

It is time to pause for a moment and attach an image to these first two propositions... Everyone close your eyes for a moment... empty your mind... I want you to picture two or three **strangers** you have encountered recently in two or three different settings... now, I want you to focus on the feelings you experienced in response to those strangers...

Our feelings range from **curiosity** at the people we pass on the crowded sidewalk we share; **indifference,** in the case of an exchange with a sales clerk; **caution** or defensiveness when someone rings our doorbell; maybe outright **fear** when we enter the subway. I think one of the fundamental dynamics at work to exacerbate the move toward private life is simply fear.

The most dramatic recent example of this phenomenon, of course, is provided by Bernhard Goetz. The response of the public to the subway shootings is as significant as the event itself. For many people Goetz' action represented a justifiable response to the frustrations felt at the fear of public places, even with the new evidence that Goetz may not have been the blameless victim first portrayed.

Earlier this year, a report from the Eisenhower Foundation noted that crime rates have in fact declined over the previous year. However, the fear of crime remains as high today as it was in the 1960s. "Because they influence how we live and act, fear and perception are important measures of crime." (Valley News, 3/4/85,p.8)

Because most of our fears are associated with the unfamiliar or the unknown, **the Stranger** becomes a potent symbol of our estrangement from the public sphere. At the same time, **the Stranger** outside really serves as a mirror for the stranger inside us. The immediate public support for Goetz reflects empathy for his being the victim. His fear is our fear. Because he was perceived to have righteously stood up to the intimidation, people projected the response they would have liked to have seen in themselves in a similar situation.

But the Stranger without also has a positive image for us. You may recall the story in Luke's gospel of the two disciples who were walking on the road to Emmaus after Jesus' crucifixion. They are joined by a stranger who walks with them a while. They invite him to eat with them, at which point in the breaking of bread he becomes known to them as the risen Lord. The stranger brings an unexpected blessing. The story is not only a powerful account of the meaning of resurrection, but it is a reminder of the basic law of hospitality through which the stranger is welcomed because he is a stranger and sojourner. Many of us have lost that quality today. Instead, we hide behind bureaucratic rationalizations; we live in homogeneous communities; and we center our work and leisure in a private sphere of achievement and entertainment.

Once again Parker Palmer is helpful:
"...the only limitation on self-interest is other-interest, the sense that we are members of one another for better and for worse...

My argument for public possibilities is based on an assumption which can be stated negatively or positively. Negatively: so long as the primary opportunities of our lives are private, our tendency to deny public relatedness will be amplified. Positively: if people are given opportunities for public experience and expression, the experience itself will evoke their willingness, interest, desire, and ability to be part of the public." (1983:37)

Palmer goes on to say that we need agencies to build bridges between private and public life, and the church is his primary focus. I see education and in particular experiential education as providing another such bridge. It is to this theme that we now turn.

Civic Consciousness

My third and fourth propositions are that 3) **Educators, especially those involved in experiential programs, are in a good position to build bridges between private and public life, and 4) That one vehicle for doing this is by developing a new curriculum for civic consciousness.**

The reawakening to civic consciousness is evident from many sectors. In an article that appeared

"When we are asked by researchers, evaluators, and academics about the persistence of learning from our one shot experiences, how often do we paraphrase Kurt Hahn: 'It is only our task to ignite; it is up to others to keep the flame burning.' I think we have been passing the buck. There are too many stimuli out there igniting flames in people. We don't need more fire *per se.*"

in the Boston Globe not long after the Goetz shooting, columnist David Wilson commented:

"The country has lost civitas, a pride in belonging to a community with legitimate authority to enforce acceptable standards of conduct.

In the absence of civitas, which implies widely shared willingness to place the interest of society before one's immediate personal advantage, the entire US Marine Corps could not maintain public safety in New York." (January 13, 1985)

The 1981 Carnegie Foundation report, "Higher Learning in the Nation's Service" claimed that "the advancement of civic learning must become one of higher education's most essential goals." (p.43), and it called for a restoration of that tired old academic workhorse, "civics."

As a nation, we are becoming civically illiterate. Unless we find better ways to educate ourselves as citizens, we run the risk of drifting unwittingly into a new kind of Dark Age — a time when small cadres of specialists will control knowledge and thus control the decision-making process... In a world where human survival is at stake, ignorance is not an acceptable alternative. The replacement of democratic government by a technocracy or the control of policy by special-interest groups is not tolerable. (p.47)

The winter 1982 issue of *Liberal Education*, the quarterly publication of the Association of American Colleges was devoted exclusively to "The Civic Purposes of Liberal Learning." The heads of major foundations such as Kettering, Carnegie, Exxon, Dana, and Lilly are actively seeking ways to define a new curriculum in the civic arts for liberal education.

At the high school level, various proposals include the civic arts as part of the foundation of reform, including Mortimer Adler's *Paideia Pro-*

posal, Ted Sizer's *Horace's Compromise,* and The Carnegie Commission's report, *High School,* which is best summarized by Dick Kraft, AEE's Executive Director, in the spring '84 issue of the AEE Journal.

"For experiential educators, the Carnegie report is like a breath of fresh air in its call for community involvement, oral and written literacy programs, the importance of a transition to the world of work, the formation of a service ethic in our youth, an experiential base for teacher training, the active participation of the student in his/her learning, and the need for flexibility in schedules, class sizes and programs." (p.11)

Transplants

It's time to pause again for another exercise in imaging. Close your eyes... take a deep breath, and clear your mind... Now let the images flow through when I ask you, what do you see and feel when I say the word **TRANSPLANT?** Experimentation? Plastic parts? New thresholds? Arrogance?

How many of you thought of Gary Trudeau? Did you see the marvelously absurd Doonesbury series earlier this year about transplanting the heart of a liberal into the body of a conservative?

The image is appealing for purposes of my talk, not only for its humor but for the absurd boldness of its assertion: it is an effort to translate civic responsibility to generations that have grown up with the predominant reinforcers nudging them toward the private and self-centered life. Similarly, it is one of the most difficult tasks for experiential educators to transplant or transfer the liberating peak experience into the conforming body of routine back home. Finally, the image of the transplant portrays the difficulties we have translating our alternative programs into mainstream institutions. It is my feeling that a curriculum of civic consciousness provides us with a new opportunity for transplanting today. And, because of the distinctive attributes of our experiential programs, we are in a strategic position within education to serve as the surgeons of this transformation.

The Role of Experiential Programs

When I speak about a "curriculum" of civic arts, I am using the term in its broadest sense. I mean not only academic courses but experiential programs and activities in the larger community. **My fifth proposition is that Experiential Programs have distinctive contributions to make in collaborating with schools and community agencies to develop civic consciousness.**

1. One of the first contributions Experiential programs would bring to the development of such a curriculum would be the **ability to motivate learners by actively engaging them.**

2. A second contribution of Experiential programs to the formation of a curriculum in the civic arts stems from our **ability to enhance in individuals the sense of self-esteem.** Of all the outcomes we claim for our programs, the one which is most consistent, at least as an immediate, short-term consequence, is increased self confidence. A close second may be our graduates' willingness to take more control over their lives.

We need to highlight one of the characteristic elements for achieving these outcomes — the process of risk-taking — standing at the edge of our first rappel or sitting at the dismount of the tarzan swing on the ropes course; performing in front of others; being held accountable as leader for the day. Experiential programs help us manage our fear; we learn to realize that growth in life involves risks — the combination of danger and opportunity, which the Chinese bring together in their word for "crisis."

And living with new people is part of the risk-taking, **the stranger without teaching the stranger within us.** The extent to which the stranger threatens us and we are uncomfortable with ourselves, to that extent are we ripe for growth. Speaking in terms of faith, Parker Palmer puts it this way.

"The religious quest, the spiritual pilgrimage, is always taking us into new lands where we are strange to others and they are strange to us. Faith is a venture into the unknown, into the realms of mystery, away from the safe and comfortable and secure." (p.56)

3. The third way in which experiential programs would contribute to the development of a curriculum of civic arts is through a partnership with academic programs. **Experiential programs provide laboratory settings for applying academic concepts.** The most successful programs at the Dartmouth Outward Bound Center were those in which we sought to complement existing, mainstream "curricula"; the Labs were weekend experiential components within existing academic courses; the Living/Learning Term was a 12 week program constructed around the academic calendar and commitments, and the residential life of the College; the programs in mental health were designed to provide episodes through which patients could see dysfunctional behavior and begin to change, or which therapists could use as a catalyst for more conventional treatments.

Experiential programs need to be integrated with more traditional learning approaches - pedagogically and politically.

4. A fourth contribution of experiential programs to the development of a curriculum aimed at raising civic consciousness is **the ability to provide direct involvement in the basic institutions of society through internships, and interaction with diverse people through service.** Internships and apprenticeships provide an opportunity for students to learn how organizations devoted to government, business, or human services operate. In some cases, this experience is related to exploration of career paths.

5. Probably the most important contribution of experiential programs to the development of a curriculum of the civic arts lies in **the ability to train students in those process skills which underlie democratic functions — skills related to the individual's participation in groups; and skills such as problem-solving, forms of decision-making, and conflict resolution.**

How many of you know about the *National Assessment of Educational Progress?* Well, this is an education research project mandated by Congress to collect and report data, over time, on the performance of young Americans in various learning areas. In 1981-2 the NAEP published its third set of educational objectives for Citizenship and Social Studies. This was the basis for a national survey of 9, 13, and 17 year olds, and it was prepared over a year-long period by several hundred educators and lay persons affiliated with professional and civic organizations.

"Probably the most important contribution of experiential programs is the ability to train students in those process skills which underlie democratic functions — skills related to the individual's participation in groups; and skills such as problem-solving, forms of decision-making, and conflict resolution."

There are 5 major categories and it's interesting to see that experiential programs can play an important role in four of those objectives. Each objective has many subsets. Let me just list a few to give you some examples, and you think of your own programs and the extent to which they address these objectives.

Objective #4: Demonstrates an Understanding of and interest in the ways human beings organize, adapt to and change their environments.

- understands the relationships between individuals and groups.
- understands the relationships among groups, including interdependence, cooperation, competition, conflict resolution.
- understands the relationship between people and the natural environment.
- has a commitment to human rights, for example, by showing concern for the well-being and dignity of others.

Objective #3: Demonstrates an Understanding of individual development and the skills necessary to communicate with others.

- interacts in groups in various capacities among which are
    recognizing divergent roles within a group,
    recognizing emotions operating within a group and allowing for their expression,
    recognizing and permitting the expression of different values, beliefs, and ideas in a group.
- Has effective relations with people having different cultural perspectives.

The list continues, but I think the point is made: experiential programs already deal with a significant number of the objectives of the National Assessment of Educational Progress. And, in many cases, experiential programs can be more effective in achieving these outcomes than conventional classroom techniques.

Civic Arts as A Major Goal for Experiential Educators

In the discussion this far, I have been trying to make a case that there is a gap between private and public life; that educators have an opportunity to work with business and civic leaders to develop a curriculum to help bridge the gap; and that experiential educators can make distinctive contributions in developing civic consciousness. I would like to conclude with my sixth proposition: **It is in our own self interest that experiential programs and the AEE as a network adopt the development of the civic arts as a major thrust for the coming years.**

First of all, an invigorated curriculum in the civic arts is responding to a real and challenging need, one that relates to our survival as a species and perhaps as a planet. We defer major policy decisions to the specialist or the technocrat only at greatest peril. Instead, we must find ways to involve ourselves and our young people in the decisions that affect us. It will not be easy which is why many have withdrawn into their private worlds, but it is no less necessary.

A focus on civic consciousness would enable us to lead from our most effective program outcomes by helping to educate citizens who
- have a confidence in themselves and thus an optimism about the future
- are willing to take sensible risks
- understand their personal values and have an appreciation for the diversity of values around them
- have a sense of responsibility to the larger community
- have the ability to solve problems

Third, the civic arts provides an important ingredient missing from many of our experiential programs — namely, a mechanism for transferring the peak experience back to the activities of routine. How do we reinforce the lessons of the wilderness or the lessons of the intense and isolated, small group experience? When we are asked by researchers, evaluators, and academics about the persistence of learning from our one-shot experiences, how often do we paraphrase Outward Bound's founder, Kurt Hahn: "It is only our task to ignite; it is up to others to keep the flame burning." I think we have been passing the buck. There are too many stimuli out there igniting flames in people. We don't need more fire **per se**. Those stimuli, unconnected, just reinforce the private worlds I have been describing earlier in this talk. Rather we need to invent or recapture ways of feeding more steady increments to fuel to the fires we have ignited. One way to do this is by entering into a more conscious partnership with schools and civic organizations to integrate and reinforce experiential and academic components of learning.

If my last point was a commentary on our pedagogy, my final point is directed toward our politics. I think the civic arts provides not only a philosophical but a political base from which our programs could gain wider recognition and funding.

Conclusion

For most of our history as a network, we in AEE have been looking for a theme or set of themes to unify the diversity of activities represented by our programs. I think civic consciousness or a related set of words, would provide this thrust for the coming years. We would not be alone. I have mentioned the Kettering, Lilly, Carnegie, Dana, and Exxon foundations that are already promoting this theme — we could help them spend their money. The National Assessment of Educational Progress already has us in its objectives for citizenship and social studies. We could help the NAEP report improvements in achieving these outcomes between survey periods. Civic groups have long

been committed to these objectives. We could help them be more effective in their outreach to youth by encouraging them to provide internships and scholarships for our participants. Finally, the AEE would have a broader base for making common cause with other experiential, service, and learning networks to achieve a greater impact in our schools and communities.

The image of the stranger reminds us that we are encountering the novel. It is a time to be wary, for there are inherent dangers, as there are risks to growing or changing. On the other hand, there is the possibility that through the stranger, a greater mystery of knowledge or faith is revealed. The stranger without speaks to the stranger within. Our task is to recapture a sense of hospitality for both.

This process will involve us in some fundamental transplanting - transpiring new life into an old curriculum; transporting the fires of the peak experience to the embers of routine; translating an essentially private world into a new public awareness; and transforming our despair at the complexity of effecting change, into hope, not only for ourselves, but for the generations of the future, for whom we are responsible.

REFERENCES

● Palmer, Parker J. *The Company of Strangers: Christians and the Renewal of America's Public Life* (Crossroad, New York, 1983)
● "Citizenship and Social Studies Objectives, 1981-82 Assessment" (No. 13-CS-10) published by the National Assessment of Eductional Progress, Educational Commission of the States, Suite 700, 1860 Lincoln Street, Denver, CO 80295.
● Boyer, Ernest L. and Hechinger, Fred M. "Higher Learning in the Nation's Service" published by The Carnegie Foundation for the Advancement of Teaching, 1785 Massachusetts Avenue, N.W., Washington, D.C. 20036-1981.
● Kraft, Richard. "A Summary of The Major Reports" in *The Journal of Experiential Education*, Spring 1984.

WHEN WE WANT TO EMPOWER AS WELL AS TEACH

by

Lorraine Wilson

Getting their group over the "nitro crossing" (group initiative) hadn't been too hard for them. Kristen had trouble lifting her feet when she swung across. And no one could carry the bucket of water over without falling off the rope. But after several attempts, they figured out the problem we'd given them.

Then my co-leader and I shifted things around. "Okay, let's use the same equipment: the ropes, the buckets of water, and the tree. But this time, let's make up our own problem to solve."

"Huh?"

An hour later, the seven junior high students had conceived and solved a truly unique initiative problem. It didn't just happen...we had trouble getting started. Then Tara remembered something her teacher once explained about "brainstorming." They liked the idea of concensus, so we designed a final problem which incorporated everyone's original ideas. And when it proved to be easier than we wanted, we made it harder. After all, it was our problem.

Before we broke up, I asked the group if they were usually asked to come up with their own problems.

They all agreed. "No."

#########

I've gotten excited all over again about teaching experientially. I always knew it was an effective way to involve the learner; I knew it was fun. But I've also discovered that within experiential education, there is a tremendous potential for empowering the learner.

This is important for me because learner empowerment is an essential component of the work I do--teaching early adolescents the skills and attitudes of peacemaking and nonviolence.*

My working definition for "empowerment," in relation to peacemaking, is "acting on belief or hope." There are two components to that definition, and both relate to experiential teaching.

The first part is the ACTING. To feel empowered, knowing HOW to act is perhaps not as important as knowing IT IS POSSIBLE TO ACT--though knowing how surely helps us feel we can.

When I began teaching nonviolence, I designed these theory courses to cover the skills I thought were important: conflict resolution, problem solving, communication, etc. I was on the right track, those are the important skills. But my students weren't hooked. It seems that middle school students (fifth, sixth, seventh, and eighth graders) prefer to actually do something rather than talk about what we might do if something were to happen. And there wasn't much happening in these classes.

Rather than keep fighting that energy, I started working with it. Now I offer opportunities for the students to act. In the doing, they discover what skills are needed; we recognize the ones they already have and make plans to learn the ones we need.

The second part of the definition implies that our actions are derived from our hopes and beliefs. It recognizes that the caring, feeling, responsive part of ourselves has hopes, dreams, and visions. It is this part of our being that impells us to be active.

Stephanie Judson, author of A Manual on Nonviolence and Children, believes that children have an innate sense of justice, but since children are so often made to feel powerless, they may not feel capable of acting on that sense.

My objective is to help children develop a sense of their own power to be involved in peacemaking. That means I want them to feel they can respond to their issues and concerns related to their sense of justice or injustice. Just as in other experiential programs where the emphasis may be on leadership or risk taking or problem solving, I am looking for more than the students being able to tell me what these skills are. I want them to actually see themselves as peacemakers (as leaders, risk takers, etc.).

An experienced-based approach affirmed the children's desire to "do something," but was it necessarily empowering them to see themselves as peacemakers--to make that transference from the curriculum to their own lives?

Ron Gager, of the Colorado Outward Bound School, wrote an informative paper entitled "Experiential Education: Strengthening the Learning Process". He advocates that the inductive nature of experiential learning (observation following activity) is the "basis for a level of intrinsical motivation and learner-centered responsibility difficult to achieve through traditional methods." But he goes on to caution that "to simply include an experiential component is not enough and to believe that it is simply sets in motion program flaws which will ultimately cause it (exp. ed.) to disappear. His point is that we must fully understand how and why experiential education works, in order for it to live up to its ability to be a powerful educational vehicle.

I am asking a similar question. I knew from my own experience that experiential education had the potential to be a very empowering process. But some programs lived up to that and some didn't. I wanted to identify what the keys were--what elements made the difference.

For the past two years, I concentrated on that question in my work with early adolescents. They taught me a great deal that I will try to compress into this paper.

"Make it Real"

One of the important things to remember for making an experience empowering is to make it as real as possible. Effecting the transfer of skills from the (curricular) experience to the student's life is one of the hardest parts of experiential teaching. It requires our best expertise at processing. In my case, I needed to effect a transfer of attitudes as well. Why not make that transfer easier by already letting the group act on their own issues?

It was the students who told us about this desire for realness. We often used group initiatives/challenge events on a ropes course when the sixth grade went to camp. Instead of just saying "get your group across these swinging tires" we would enhance it with a dramatic story..."These tires are hanging over a raging river and you have to get some medicine across to a dying heart patient on the other side."

Some groups totally immersed themselves into the fantasy crisis. They told us how much more compelling it was to feel there was meaning in the game. Some groups did not buy into the fantasy but said that if it was real, they would have focused more on the problem and less on who went first. At other times, they told how they wish there was more meaning to the things they did in school. It should be noted that "meaning" was explicitly related to the idea of being needed.

There are two ways to make things more real for the participants. The first is to use real problems or situations. Here are some examples:

The traditional model for Friends Day (a middle school student conference at Friends Select School, Philadelphia) was to enlist a host of resource people to come in and give workshops for the students. It was a good plan, but last year we committed ourselves to making it more real. Six students planned the event, with our guidance.

Tim Foley, a seventh grader, proposed a title, "Stop, Look, and Listen to What's Really Going On" Then they surveyed the four grades to determine what their peers wanted to know about. The choices ranged from birth control to prisons, but the majority were in the realm of social problems (the homeless, drug abuse, nuclear war). Those interest groups met once to set their goals. Then on Friends Day they actually went out to visit places and meet people. The experiences they had that day were with real people with names and stories. They shared from these experiences in a concluding meeting for worship. For some of them it was a risk they took, for some an adventure, for others an inspiration.

Those who work in wilderness programs know the value of using real events as the learning medium. Two of my colleagues ran a summer program, "Select Your Own Adventure," which combined adventure and environmental studies. They sloshed through bogs together, crawled through caves, and orienteered their way out of the New Jersey Pine Barrens. The program was a complete joy for all of them, due greatly to the real experiences they shared.

When the event is real, it's easy for participants to recognize what they have accomplished...."We helped these people at the shelter" or "I was afraid to talk to them but I did it."

"What if it can't be real?"

It's not always possible to use a real event. Sometimes we use simulations or role plays. In those cases it helps to create a larger context in which to view the event. By this I mean that we relate the particular skills and behaviors needed to accomplish this simulated task with ones that are needed in outside real situations. Sometimes you have to point out the realities within the simulation.

We designed a simulation of the Underground Railroad for sixth graders (and now used for families!). It consists of a series of small group challenges: physical obstacles, moral dilemmas, unusual problems, encounters with strangers...done at night in the woods. Though a dramatic simulation of an historical event, the challenges facing the group are in themselves real. For instance they must come up with a way to convince the ferryman to take them across the river or they will never reach the end. They have to ask the doctor for help or one of their members will not be able to continue with them.

Over and over again, the students exclaimed that the Underground Railroad "seemed so real." What did they mean? Granted, our volunteer actors did an excellent job of portraying historical characters, but what they were talking about was the fact that they were challenged to respond to these situations. In a later processing session, they told us that it was so exciting because there was no adult to tell them how to do it. They had to figure it out for themselves. That reminded them of times when they had been caught in an emergency and there was no adult around to tell them what to do. They discovered one "larger context"--and apparently a very empowering one for them.

In this case, there was an even larger context to look at. I didn't create the Underground Railroad so much to teach about the historical event as I did to teach about the skills that are needed to deal with situations of justice and injustice. The Underground Railroad is a recurring event in our history. There are always people who must take extraordinary risks to pursue their dreams for a more just life. But these are rarely extraordinray people; they are people like ourselves. I wanted the students to recognize the strengths and the fears they would have, that these were very much like the strengths and fears real people would have in that situation (though our lives were never really in danger).

I have met several high school students who have actually fled from such countries as Cambodia, Laos, El Salvador, and Guatamala. They were children impelled by a dream.

I wanted my sixth graders to recognize what they were capable of if they were motivated to reach for it.

In both the real experience and the simulation, the facilitator's role is to help the group identify the skills they used, to give them the names, to make sure to affirm their accomplishments. In the paper's opening scenario, somewhere a teacher must have said, "This is a problem-solving technique known as brainstorming" so Tara could own it and use it again.

We need to say something like "That was a peacemaking skill" or "That was very good use of a leadership skill known as..." Sometimes these acts slip by us unaffirmed. For years, I had trouble seeing myself as being the kind of person who takes charge and makes decisions. Then one week I was setting up my first vacation in the Northwest; it was centered around visiting some friends. At the last minute, the friends pulled out of the plan. But I really wanted to make that trip. So I quickly set up some alternatives. And then it dawned on me that I had acted like someone who makes decisions and handles problems. Maybe I was that kind of person.

Ashley Montague once said that the way you become a loving person is to start acting like one!

The opportunity to see ourselves acting in real situations, and to recognize those behaviors and skills when we're using them can develop our sense of our own empowerment.

Give Them a Choice

I remember when I thought I'd reached a plateau in teaching when I could set a goal for the group, design a structured activity to "teach" that lesson, and finally process it all to make sure they got the point. There wasn't anything reprehensible about that, because I chose important skills: cooperation, communication, leadership. But it wasn't very empowering for the group because I was deciding what they needed to learn.

Students caught on and gave me the answers that they thought I wanted to hear. We talked ad infinitum about the need for cooperation, but their voices lacked conviction. They weren't interested in this.

I examined my own learning responses and came up with some observations: 1) I really only (willingly) learn what I want to. As an adult, I have autonomy over most of my learning, but as a child that was rarely true. 2) There's a lot I want to learn, and I'll work very hard to do so. 3) When it comes to my own behaviors, I know better than anyone else what I need to learn, or at least I know

220

what I'm ready to learn. So maybe the kids were the same as me.
Maybe they didn't know how to articulate what they wanted to learn--I
think that's a skill-but they'll be purusing their own goals just the
same.

The second issue to remember when working towards empowerment is
to provide choices for the participants.

What Are Their Goals?

One of the most significant ways we can offer choice is in the
area of goal setting.

At the beginning of the week long training on Adventure-Based
Counseling with Project Adventure in Hamilton, Massachussetts, we
were asked to identify our personal goal for the week, leaders
included. That process let us see that not only were we all there
for a different professional purpose, but for a different internal
purpose as well. The workshop belonged to each of us and we were
responsible for our experience. My journal entry from that week
read:

> "I think this individual goal setting is a
> giant step toward making sense out of these
> activities...a leap toward ownership...a
> tool for the group to help each other. I
> can't wait to try it out."

Providing that space for individuals or groups to set their own
goals is one of the most important keys to making the event
empowering. It sets into motion that vehichle for "intrinsic
motivation" that really lets the experience belong to the learner.

I signed up for this climbing course last spring. Climbing had
always been a painful metaphor for me--it represented all my needs to
perform well. I often left the rocks in tears, but I kept going
back. Not because I wanted to become a class 10 climber, I just
wanted to be at ease with myself on the rocks--to bring a more
playful spirit to this activity.

For this class, I wanted to relearn the set-up skills and have
fun with my friends. After making the first two climbs, the 90%,
nine-hour day wore me down and I mentioned that I wasn't going to
make the last climb.

The instructor didn't know anything about me. But he was sure
that I needed a lecture about pushing myself farther and living up to
my potential. He played on the spectre of self-doubt that remained.
Was I really afraid?

I made the third climb and he probably felt like he'd
accomplished something. But I certainly didn't make it with any

221

spirit of empowerment. Instead, I felt like my own goals had been devalued.

I didn't return for the second class. But I do climbing with my friends.

Interpreting the Group's Themes

There's another way to let a group set its own goals, and it's a bit more complex. Sometimes, particularly with children, it isn't so easy a thing to say, "Oh, peacemaking, well here's what's holding us back from doing that; we're stuck, so could you design some activities for us that will let us work through that issue?"

But as we become very skilled observers, we begin to see that that is what they're saying. Whatever issues are important for a group, either as stumbling blocks, concerns, or strengths, will emerge in their experience. That's how we were able to discover how important it was for our students to feel they were needed--by watching and listening to what they were responding to on the ropes course I mentioned earlier.

I encourage you to listen more to your students. When I was taught about developmental stage characteristics for adolescents, they didn't say anything about their strengths, their concerns, their issues, their dreams. Whenever a group engages in an experience, they will reveal clues about these things. And those themes should be given a place in the program. Where? First in the processing. In Larry Quinsland's article for the AEE Journal, "How to Process Experience," he tells us to prepare ourselves for leading the processing by asking the following questions:

1. What are the most important questions to which I want to respond?

2. At what level are these questions (referring to the hierarchy of thinking skills)?

3. What questions should I use to lay the foundation for the important questions to be answered more easily?

This is a good plan to follow but I would encourage us to think about the first step differently and ask, "What are the most important questions to which my participants seem to want to respond?"

The other way to respond is to design future experiences based on the information you've received (if you have access to that group over time). We intuitively know that we can better plan for a group once we know them. Once we knew that our students wanted to find meaning and purpose in their curriculum, all our future plans were altered to reflect that need.

Other Types of Choices

Another way to provide choice for participants is to offer a choice of activities.

My committee put this type of choice into practice at an intergenerational conference one spring. We wanted the participants to come away feeling more empowered as peacemakers. Each participant chose to be in a workshop which reflected some particular aspect of peacemaking: problem solving, risk taking, envisioning, playfulness, or creative expression.

Initially the facilitators led the activities, to build up the sense of community in the group and to deepen the group's perspective toward the skill. But then the learning focus was shifted back to the group. They were invited to "Choose a risk for yourselves that you will take together" or "Choose a problem you want to work on now"...and so on in each group.

I could never have foreseen what kind of risk was important to my group; it was so different from my own choice.

Sometimes we can choose how we will respond to the task:

I once led a children's program that was part of an adult conference. The kids ranged in age from 6-13. After we talked about why their parents were there (and most of them didn't know), I invited them to make a video about something that seemed important to them. They first chose a format that allowed them a great deal of freedom--a "60 Minutes" type thing. Some of them wanted to interview their peers about their feelings about Quakerism. Some made news flashes about nuclear weapons. There were mystery stories and sports. We showed this tape to their families.

With some trust, some structure, and some choice, those 30 kids put together a complete video production in one day!

Sometimes we can choose when we will undertake an experience. You could offer both climbing and hiking (and the option to do neither) on several days so the student can match their moods with the activity. We're used to doing this in our lives, for children it is not so much an option. Classes run on schedules.

I think choice is inherently affirming and empowering for several reasons. Being given a choice implies that I am capable of thinking seriously about the subject, and making a sound decision. It says that what I care about is important. It says that there is more than one way to do something and that maybe I know just the best way for me. Choice says the leader is not holding all the power or all the answers.

Becoming a Co-Learner

The final key I have so far observed is for the leader to become a co-learner with the group. This involves sharing the power, in ways we have looked at so far. It means revealing some of your own hopes and dreams, some of your own questions, and perhaps some of your own vulnerabilities.

I have pondered some of my deepest spiritual questions with twelve-year-olds who were more than pleased to share their insights. My students have advised me on my problems with my housemates; they have escorted me out of caves when I was disoriented. They have watched me tremble with fear on the high ropes and shiver with joy at the sight of a wild bird.

At first I wasn't sure about it all, if it meant giving up control. If I was going to let the group set its own goals, I could no longer predict how things would turn out--I could no longer take all the credit for what they learned! But in exchange for whatever loss of power or prestige I thought I would incur, I have been more than compensated by the excitement of watching a group discover something for themselves, and feeling their own sense of purpose and importance. And I don't think my "leadership" has ever been forfeited, though I now define my task as that of observing, interpreting, enabling, and connecting.

One of my favorite passages to quote is from Elliot Wigginton's introduction to the second Foxfire where he talks about pushing back the chairs, sitting down on the floor, and finding out what teachers and students can come up with--together.

Summary

When we used an experiential approach to empower groups, there are several important guidelines to keep in front of us: the realness or significance of the experience; individual choice; and leader "vulnerability" (or shared power). I have found these themes to be very valuable in the area of peacemaking. And as many of the skills which are woven into the fabric of peacemaking are also woven into the other types of experiential programs where empowerment is a goal, I hope they are useful to others.

PERSONAL PERSPECTIVES

Adventure
AND
Education

by Erik Leroy

Several years ago I instructed my first Outward Bound course in the Three Sisters Wilderness of Oregon. During that course, a very simple but enlightening experience became the catalyst that since then has sent me puzzling along the paths of adventurers, comparing their experiences in pursuit of their peaks, their poles, their trans-oceanic crossings, with the more humble (but not less significant) adventures of students at Outward Bound and programs like it.

My experience went something like this: In the mist and clouds of a typical Oregon day surrounded by quite wet and very cold Outward Bound students, I was joyfully lost in the preparation of prusiks, butterfly knots, and other essentials that a beginning group makes before a siege of the formidable bergschrund on the Prouty Glacier, much too lost in the minutia of the impending climb to sense the growing consternation of my group.

My ignorance, however, ended quite abruptly when Priscilla, in the vernacular of her Bronx origins, and in a voice full of anger, anticipation, and fear, blurted out that she did not then, or at any moment for the duration of the course, want to "take any more risks." Initially I was flabbergasted, then hurt — and then angered. After all, this woman before me on the Prouty Glacier was from New York City. Now I knew about New York City. I had ridden the subways there and knew quite well how slight the risks were for her on the Prouty compared to her daily menu back home! Or did I? Or could I? Or *should* I?

In spite of her very forcefully articulated con-

Erik Leroy *is former chief instructor for Northwest Outward Bound, interim director of the outdoor program at Evergreen State College, and recently a graduate of law school. He and his wife live in Anchorage, Alaska, where they are pursuing the practice of law.*

cern that she not be subjected to any more risks, Priscilla did walk out onto the glacier that day, and after two whizzing falls, each caught by an equally terrified compatriot, she climbed the bergschrund. Every day thereafter until and including the marathon, she analyzed each boulder, stream, hill, and cloud for its danger-dealing potential. She never flinched for long, though, and in retrospect, she loved every minute of it.

> "**P**riscilla . . . blurted out that she did not then, or at any moment for the duration of the course, want to 'take any more risks.'"

Priscilla begat my interest in the nature of adventure by teaching me a valuable lesson. Back on the glacier, what I perceived as a simple exercise, a Saturday stroll, Priscilla perceived as high adventure, full of danger, difficulty, and the unknown. Priscilla taught me that when we try to understand "adventure," the physical magnitude of the peak, pole, lake, or trail is no more important than the emotional response the task elicits.

In our programs at Outward Bound the magnitude of the thing is much less important. Certainly Priscilla's psychological adventure was monumental, just as deserving of acclaim as anything Amundsen did at the South Pole or Hillary did on Everest. And, in turn, what those elicited emotions of Priscilla the conqueror (of herself) might in turn create are monumental in possibility. In fact, the creation of those emotions and all the potential for self-knowledge and growth that accompany them is the reason for any adventure program's existence; the accompanying possibilities and sense of one's own capacity and self-confidence is a major step to promoting the ideal of an individual with a sense of responsibility towards humanity, which was a very explicit goal of Outward Bound's founder, Kurt Hahn.

Because we should be primarily concerned with the subjective adventure experience, we should look with great interest and familiarity to the experiences of some of the Arctic explorers and their mountaineering counterparts. The adventure experiences of these explorers are different from Priscilla's only in magnitude, and magnitude is an unimportant criterion. In character and psychological ramifications the similarity is striking.

There is one characteristic that sets apart Fridtjof Nansen's account of his struggle with fear and the unknown as he set out to winter over on drift ice near the North Pole from that of a novice in the wilds on a first adventure course, and that is the revealing eloquence with which the former writes. As Vilhjalmur Stefansson, pre-eminent Arctic explorer, noted: "The explorer is the poet of action and exploring is the poetry of deeds." What Stefansson urges us to do if we are committed to action and deeds is to pay heed to adventures and adventurers; they not only will speak of adventure, they will, in their poetry, illuminate adventure. By introducing some of the literature and personalities of our adventuring tradition, I hope to approach more precisely what it is we do with adventure in an Outward Bound setting, as well as perhaps cast the seeds of literary friendships that might prove as fruitful to others as they have to me.

Defining "adventure" is not an easy task. Wilfred Noyce, in prefacing *The Springs of Adventure*, felt it best to eliminate the element of risk, and called adventure, ". . . a novel enterprise undertaken for its own sake." A more traditional definition found in the dictionary as well as in literature includes the risk element as well as "an undertaking of uncertain outcome; a hazardous enterprise; an exciting or very unusual experience." Stefansson being a bit obdurate, offered a more pejorative definition: "Adventure is the result of past mistakes." When Peter Freuchen, reknowned Danish explorer who lived as an Eskimo for many seasons, was asked to define "adventure" he answered, a bit equivocally, "Adventure is not an act in the line of duty. It is not something done for science either. Adventure is a strange experience for its own sake."

Peter Freuchen was a wise man. He knew there was no ultimate definition to be had. We who are the conjurers of adventure for hundreds of seekers each year, are we anymore prepared to define the phenomen than Peter Freuchen was? I contend we are not, nor should we be. An adventuresome experience has a mystery about it that cannot be violated. The twinkle in our own eyes should tell us this when we describe a forthcoming trip as an adventure. Certainly adventure would fascinate us less if it did not contain such a substantial element of the unknown.

Adventure's elusiveness should not, however, preclude us from talking about it. There are things we do, characteristics of the experiences we orchestrate, that are but attempts at replication of the experiences more noted explorers than ourselves and our students have had. Specifically, I can identify four characteristics common to all adventure, and particularly present within our courses that should be expanded upon: difficulty, danger, commitment, and stress — or the need to choose wisely under pressure.

"The immense act is useless in a materialistic sense."

The Degree of Difficulty

What we do in a program or on a course should be difficult for our students. Men and women who have sailed, climbed, and skied have always understood the challenge and difficulty of their enterprise as an aspect of the adventure they sought. Fridtjof Nansen, writing of his impending sledge trip from his ice-shrouded ship "Fram" in search of Franz Josef land to the north, wrote:

> H'm! as if dissatisfaction, longing and suffering were not the very basis of life. Without privation there would be no struggle, and without struggle no life — that is as certain as that two and two makes four. And now the struggle is to begin, it is looming in the north.

Knud Rasmussen, on his sledge journey across Arctic America, found, to his surprise, an Eskimo witch doctor who thought much as Nansen did about these matters:

> All true wisdom is only to be learned far from the dwellings of men, out in the great solitudes; and is only to be attained through suffering. Privation and suffering are the only things that can open the mind of man to those things which are hidden from others.

"We succeed when what we do is reasonably safe for us but seems horribly dangerous to students."

Though the thoughts are similar, the difference between the two is obvious: Nansen chose the ice, the Eskimo was born upon it. Nevertheless, the lesson here is a valuable one. What Nansen would tell us is that if our path is free of privation, we cannot know the meaning of life; whether one is born to it or must seek it out, privation is an explicating element in the experience of life. George Mallory, possibly the first to climb Everest, wrote upon his return from his first traverse of Mount Blanc, "to struggle and to understand. Never the last without the first. That is the law."

The Element of Danger

Another characteristic which we hold in common with more reknowned expeditions is physical risk; what outdoor challenge programs offer is dangerous. "Just by going into the mountains we invite disaster," we are told somewhat quizzically by those "outsiders" who do not understand our purposes. Yet they are correct I think. Mountains move and snow slides. We subject ourselves to these perils and there is, to some significant degree, no escaping them. When we enter these realms, the possibility of injury or death is present for the instructors to a bearably small degree. However, the apparent possibility of the same catastrophes is present for many students to an excruciatingly large degree.

Of course, instructors have a refined understanding of the objective dangers, and the consternation of students is more than three-quarters ignorance. That distinction means nothing and it means everything. It means nothing because even though the danger is really quite slight, the feeling of being *subjected* to danger is overwhelming, and it is the feeling that is important. It means everything because the feeling of danger that the experience elicits is, in a sense, a spiritual preparation for self-growth. We could not in good conscience run our program if the dangers were as great as our students sometimes insist they are. Yet those feelings that lead to students' insistences are filled with growth potential and are actually what we seek. We succeed when what we do is reasonably safe for us but seems horribly dangerous to students. Priscilla's decision to venture out onto the Prouty Glacier was just as significant as Hermann Buhl's decision to attempt the summit of 26,000-foot Nanga Parbet by himself. Both thought they were chancing a great deal.

I can be a bit more specific about the value risk bears. Herman Rohrs, who wrote a biography of Kurt Hahn, said, "the sharp felt impact of an event or a deeply felt personal experience can rouse a man from complacency, and the taking of a risk can have a similar result." Nansen, writing in his journal after months locked in the ice, was just as much to the point:

> Oh! at times this inactivity crushes one's very soul; one's life seems as dark as the winter night outside; there is sunlight upon no part of it except the past and the far distant future. I feel as if I *must* break through this deadness, this inertia and find some outlet for my energies. Can't something happen? Could not a hurricane come and tear up this ice and set it rolling in higher waves like the sea? Welcome danger, if it only brings us the chance of fighting for our lives — only let us move onward!

Months later, Nansen again wrote, "What I would not give for a single day of struggle — for even a moment of danger."

Commitment to Persist

Commitment is another characteristic all adventure holds in common. The demand that an extended course of risk and difficulty makes requires a mental commitment to persist; likewise with the commitment to the unknown that forces a shaky rocky climber out onto the very first nubbin that will turn the trick and unravel the climb. Though there is a subtle difference between these two shades of commitment, there is also a commonality that ties these and all other acts of commitment in adventure together: The eventual outcome is unknown. When a group finally stops talking and starts walking, there is an omnipresent question: "Did we choose right?" Of course they will only find out by seeing their choice through, and that act demands commitment. One of the remarkable characteristics of the Willi Unsoeld Tam Hornbein first account of the West Ridge of Mt. Everest in 1963 was the commitment it demanded. Once through the rock band, there was no turning back; it was up and over the top or perish.

Similarly, Nansen, embarking upon his sledge journey wrote:

> I cannot deny that it is a long journey and scarcely has anyone more effectively burned his boats behind him. If we wished to turn back we have absolutely nothing to return to, not even a bare coast. It will be impossible to find the ship, and before us lies the great unknown. But there is only one road, and that lies straight ahead, right through...

"By endurance, we conquer," was the Shackleton family motto, and there is scarcely a better example of perserverance than Ernest Shackleton's 1913 sledge journey to the South Pole.

Understandable Stress

Commitment, difficulty, and risk in combination are the components of an experience as familiar to our students as to a leader of a polar expedition. Presence of mind under fire or under stress is not a trait we necessarily cultivate in our everyday lives as I suspect our forebears did. It may not even be a trait to which many of us aspire. However, subjection to stress, "understandable stress," can be a highly educative experience and not one to avoid.

The difference between stress and "understandable stress" is the knowledge with the latter that certain correct responses will resolve the crisis. I think Justice Oliver Wendall Holmes spoke as clearly as anyone about the value of the stressful experience when he wrote, "To make up your mind at your peril upon a living question, for purposes of action, calls upon your whole nature." To be able to choose at peril is a sign of a "person complete in all her or his powers." Really quite seldom is our "whole nature" called upon. Yet in our various programs we ask (or at least we should ask) for complete efforts. When all of the elements already discussed combine in a moment of crisis, a complete effort is demanded.

In the famous accidents of mountaineering we find examples of the most complete efforts. While

we do not lay in wait for such moments so we may prove our worth, reading of the events on the 1953 accident on K-2 or of Maurice Herzog's descent from the summit of Annapurna in 1951 or of the incredible self-rescue by Doug Scott who crawled from 24,000 to 18,000 feet down The Ogre in 1977 buoys our faith in our own and generally in our species' ability to survive. Upon a smaller scale, the demand for decisiveness "upon a living question" evokes what capacities our students have and may help create, in Holmes' words, "persons complete in all their powers."

Final Questions

All of these characteristics — difficulty, danger, stress, and commitment to the unknown — define the adventure we orchestrate in an adumbrated fashion. Much more can be said about adventure; however, I don't think we can hope for more clarity. Adventure, afterall, bears a fascination and a mystery that make it in definition somewhat inviolable. Furthermore, we've no need to probe deeper. But there are some questions we should ask: for what purpose does this adventure experience exist? What does the experience mean for our species or civilization? And, finally, and perhaps most importantly for the purposes of this paper, why do we foster adventure experiences in our programs? For the latter, I believe a clear answer exists, but for the previous two, all I can do is suggest possible answers.

To assume in the first place that adventuring such as is found in mountaineering is purposeful could be a step in the wrong direction. Many have said that it is not purposeful. For example, Lionel Terray, a well known French climber, titled one of his books, *Conquistadors of the Useless.* H.W. Tillman, member of several pioneering attempts on Everest, may have had a similar outlook to Terray's when he prefaced his account of the 1938 Everest attempt with G.K. Chesterton's now famous piece of puzzlement:

> ...I think the immense act has something about it human and excusable; and when I endeavor to analyze the reason for this feeling I find it to lie, not in the fact that the thing was big or bold or successful; but in the fact that the thing was perfectly useless to everybody, including the person who did it.

But some answer does lie within this paradox. The immense act is useless in one sense; useless in terms of most characteristics that our culture places value upon; useless in a materialistic sense. Adventure is not a materialistic experience, rather it is a spiritual or perhaps a humanistic experience. Is there any use in our civilization for materially useless, spiritually rich experiences? The question, I am sure, need only be asked rhetorically, particularly when the audience is a crowd of mountaineers.

Ours is a society ruled by scientific process. Explanation, logical and derivable, is expected and usually obtained. The adventure experience doesn't fit this mold. As we have seen, there is a considerable array of questions about adventure that have not been answered, nor are they going to be. Most, if not all, of the things adventures do are useless in the materialistic sense. Yet, there are many who very definitely see it as purposeful endeavor. Sir George Trevelyn commented during the christening of the Aberdovey Outward Bound School's first schooner that, "If youth ever loses the thirst for adventure, any civilization, however enlightened, and any state, however well ordered, must wither and dry up." J.R.L. Anderson, in a book entitled *The Ulysses Factor*, postulated "Some factor in man, some form of special adaptation which promotes a few individuals to exploits which, however purposeless they may seem, are of value to the survival of the race."

Now, how can such spacious generalizations as these be defended? In part, defense is best left to each of our own perspectives on the world, each of our own opinions regarding the efficacy of our civilization. There are some characteristics that adventurous experiences infuse that are, in my opinion, essential for our species' survival. Several, if not all, are held in common with those possible values we all hope to instill: perserverance, strength in individuality, compassion in the multiplicity of group experience, the ability to use one's mind, and to think — or perhaps the reason to think. If we value these attributes and if we believe that they are not handed out at birth or in school or in work within our society, then I think we must agree that the vehicle through which they are offered — adventure — is a very purposeful endeavor, particularly if the spirit of mankind is

to persevere.

Kurt Hahn had the negative tendencies of civilization in mind when he first toyed with the idea that would become the underlying principle of his educational philosophy. From Rohrs' biography.

In its fully developed form, Hahn's answer to the problem is, as we have seen, "experience therapy" — a form of fresh youthful experience which makes it possible for young people once again to feel wonder and astonishment, and so, contemplating, to look outward and upward to new horizons. The experience itself has no more than an ancillary function — namely, to uncover the deeper layers of human personality, which in everyday life have all too often been overlaid by conventions of civilization.

Kurt Hahn recognized the alienating character of a materialistic civilization. His purpose, very specifically and concretely, was to reunite us, one with another, through the instillation of self-knowledge that would allow, finally, "a sense of responsibility towards humanity." That final sense was for Hahn, as I believe it should be for us, the harbinger of unalienated existence.

It is particularly important for us now to remember Hahn's purpose. If we forget it, we also lose track of any purpose we as professionals of his tutelage now have. We are engaged in a purposeful enterprise with clear goals, not a miasma of uncollected and unarticulated reasons for being. And we are not, or should not, be merely a collection of climbers and kayakists who have found in the program for which we work a means of supporting our habits.

Adventure is a purposeful enterprise. It instills characteristics found in few other places of our civilization. Some of those characteristics will, hopefully, break through the alienation accompanying technological life. When one is no longer stranger to another, then "a sense of responsibility to humanity" is not only possible, but nearly assured.

Southwestern
SOJOURN

by Bert Horwood

The institution of sabbatical leave gives a person an unparalleled opportunity for observation and reflection. I had decided to devote my 1982-83 leave to constructing an overview of the theory and practice of experiential education. The bulk of the field work was to be done by observing a number of programs in Colorado and New Mexico. It seemed potentially useful to readers of the Journal of Experiential Education to describe in a somewhat informal and occasionally light-hearted way an admittedly limited and selected view of experiential education in those regions.

It would have run me entirely into the ground to have attempted even a cursory visit to every institution and agency in the area with an experiential educational component. So it made sense to be selective and focus on settings and people that would contribute to a broad view of the field while adding to my insights as an experiential teacher of experiential teachers. Thus I confined myself, and this unvarnished account, to aspects of the field related to experiential education in public and private schools and to issues related to the training and education of instructors, leaders, and teachers. As a consequence of this limitation, no claims of completeness for the picture are being made. Indeed, this is but a peek into one corner of the vineyard.

Home Base at Boulder

Every sojourner should have a place to treat like home. I was lucky to have found a kindred spirit in the person of Dick Kraft at the Toronto Conference of AEE, and he kindly made me welcome as a visitor to the School of Education, University of Colorado, Boulder. There, besides the convenience of an office under the eaves of the education building, I found other amenities in both the physical plant and personnel that were of great comfort.

Chief among these was Dick Kraft himself, a genial and energetic person whose normal work would quickly bury two ordinary mortals. Dick made it easy for me to observe and be part of

Bert Horwood *is a member of the Faculty of Education, Queen's University, Kingston, Ontario.*

his teaching, especially in the graduate courses in experiential education. A hallmark of these courses seemed to be their responsiveness to individual variations among students, combined with substantial expectation of self-directed learning. It was also of great professional interest to witness planning and developmental work as members of the School of Education laboured to bring into being an experience-rich problem-solving mode of secondary teacher education.

Lessons From Schools

An entirely captivating school came to my notice quite early in the leave. It was the Mountain Open High School of Jefferson County, located in Evergreen, Colorado, where the Walkabout Program, envisioned by Maurice Gibbons, was in full flower. It was refreshing to find a school in which the administrative rhetoric seemed to be perfectly congruent with day to day practice. There I spent a number of happy days, interviewing students and teachers and generally getting a feel for both the trials and the triumphs of such a program. Mountain Open High School has sufficient features to justify a much fuller account as an exemplar of experience-based education at the secondary level.

But not all school visits involved such intensive study. A delightful and delicious counterpoint came in the visit to a grade two classroom in Lafayette, Colorado, where the children were preparing and serving sit down lunches for grade one children and sundry adults, mostly parents, who stopped by. It was a trifle hair-raising to watch my diminutive waitress, complete with apron, order pad, and pencil, gaze about her as my plate of spaghetti tilted more and more away from the horizontal. There was a guardian angel that kept her from disaster. The plate arrived before me with its contents a little sloshed, but nevertheless in place. Now, that is experience-based education in the classroom!

A similar interlude that punctuated the autumn routine of participating in Dick's classes and observing at Evergreen was the appearance of grade five/six pupils at the School of Education to instruct the graduate students in the gentle art of constructing, binding, and ornamenting one's very own journal. The subsequent study and practice of journal making was much enhanced by the entries in books that we had made ourselves.

During the winter I was able to visit two cultural journalism projects in schools. One of these was "Worldwinds" at Boulder High School. The students there are all immigrants taking English as a Second Language and combining recovery of their original culture with magazine production in English. (This program was outlined in the Winter 1983 issue of the Journal of Experiential Education.) The second program I saw was embedded in Steamboat Springs High School. Its magazine is "Three Wire Winter", and there, as before, I was able to interview students and teachers. At Steamboat good luck and great willingness of students and staff made it possible for me to join an interviewing team that was learning from the proprietors about the operation of Antler's Bar and Grill in Yampa. There I saw some of the sweat, care, and diplomatic patience that must go into cultural journalism projects.

As a kind of topping to my compote of school visits, I spent a short time with staff and students at the Life Center Alternative School, part of West Mesa High school in Albuquerque. One of the teachers took me along as outrider while he visited some of his kids in community service placements. And while in New Mexico, I was also shown the field center of the Albuquerque Academy and later talked at length with colleagues who were looking for ways to increase subject integration and student involvement through experiential learning.

"It was refreshing to find a school in which administrative rhetoric seemed to be perfectly congruent with day to day practice."

Common Themes and Impressions

Some general impressions emerge from thinking about all of these encounters, whether profound or superficial. First, experiential education in schools is a tough proposition. The principles and practice of teaching through, with, and for experience are inimical to many systems and personnel. There seemed to me to be a general sense that experience-based programs existed more or less on sufferance and continually needed to be careful and to be ready to justify their existence in the world of school. Perhaps that is a healthy, if precarious, state of affairs.

A second common theme was the difficulty students had in learning to cope with the combination of freedom and responsibility which all of the programs demanded. This difficulty was a dominant feature of my observations in all settings and was a prominent component of students' accounts of the difficult aspects of their work. It has occurred to me that most students enter high school quite unprepared to take responsibility for themselves and that one of the great contributions made by experiential programs like the one's outlined, is to require students to become self-directing, independent persons.

This ability, however, is not learned without pain, travail, and trouble, because if it is to be learned at all, it must be practiced by the students. And the first steps are hard to take because the kids are accustomed to being almost fully directed, at least in the school context, if not elsewhere. My general view of this matter is supported by the statements of both students and teachers in most of the settings, that one of the hardest things simply is to get started. "All beginnings are difficult."

Four other general conditions were seen that relate to the freedom-with-responsibility issue: Experiential programs in schools are demanding but appear soft to the casual observer. The demand lies in the insistence that the student take charge of the work. The soft appearance comes from the fact that the teachers, having set up the demand and providing the means for its accomplishments, must leave the students to their own time and decision as to how to proceed. Students told me that the lengthy "messing about" or "goofing off" time (their words) was both essential and distressing. But without it, they never would have been impelled by the conviction that no one else was going to do it.

The second condition is the existence of some kind of group support system for the students who are having trouble in getting active in the program. Support is marshalled both from peers and from instructors. The precise arrangements vary widely among programs. But in all cases, the freedom-with-responsibility demand, which is fundamentally isolating, is enhanced by some kind of group interaction which does not remove the demand but does remove the isolation, and thus provides a framework for individual and autonomous growth.

The third common condition is the presence of an essential characteristic of the teachers. They all seemed to be aware of the demand they were making and were able to discipline their own behavior so as not to usurp the act of commitment required from the students. Many of them told me how hard it was to do that successfully every time. Several told me about the difficulty of finding, for each student, the ideal degree of support and interest that still left the student with the burden of grasping their own learning. I was struck with the realization that this is a very uncomfortable razor's edge which seems to persist despite years of practice. It was apparent, too, that it is very tiring and, not surprisingly, the schools with long-lived programs had ways and means of teachers giving and getting mutual support and rest.

In this connection the students I interviewed displayed substantial understanding of the teachers' dilemma. Almost universally they characterized their teachers as caring, patient, knowledgeable. A well developed and active sense of humor was identified by some teachers and students as critical for survival in the kettle drum.

The final general condition that seemed to be tied to the thrust of all the school programs to make students responsible for their own progress was the presence of an element of risk. Experiential educators usually think of risk in the context of adventure activities. But other forms of experiential education seem to be risk-laden in their own particular ways.

A cultural journalism teacher told me about the astonishment she always feels whenever the magazine actually appears in print, especially in light of the cliff-hanging moments when it appeared likely that the student staff would make a disastrously bad financial decision. Another teacher explained how non-experiential colleagues felt that it was too risky to trust any part of their important work to the kids. They might mess it up. Interestingly, some students seemed to be unaware of risks involved in their experiential program. They felt quite safe, as if whatever risks there were, were safe ones. A few perceptive and articulate students spoke to me about their perceptions of risk in almost the same terms as did their teachers.

The schools mentioned, at least in their experiential components, had some common administrative features. All made provision for students to work in the community or the outside world, but with a secure base and home within the school. The programs had a physical place to call their own, even though it might be empty much of the time. Similarly, all the programs were able to free distinct blocks of the students' time from other timetable demands. Thus there was a controllable and sacrosanct chunk of space-time available. (Protecting, preserving, or increasing that space-time seemed to be a continual problem or potential problem for program administrators.) Finally, all the schools I approached were remarkably cordial in their willingness to accommodate a nosy and embarrassingly direct stranger. Openness was their common attribute.

"Schools with long-lived programs had ways of teachers giving and getting mutual support and rest."

Lessons From Outdoor Agencies

Driving hither and thither on Colorado's main and minor roads brought me close to a variety of agencies which use the outdoors and adventure programming for a wide range of educational, recreational, and therapeutic goals. At these equally receptive places I asked different questions than I had in the schools. Here, the search was for the collected views of those who operate the programs, as to what constituted an effective outdoor leader or instructor and how those attributes were acquired. The nature of my inquisitiveness had shifted from experiential programs in schools to the question of instructor development for adventure-oriented programs.

Over the eight months, I was able to consult with Program Directors of the Colorado Outward Bound School and the Wilderness Experience Program in Denver. In addition to consultation, the Colorado Outdoor Education Center for the Handicapped at Breckenridge made it possible for me to spend some time with handicapped sledders on Peak Nine. You must understand that no one can observe the sledding program in action without getting up on the slopes with the sledders and instructors. Oh, the hardships of research into experiential education when it must be done on skis on the flanks of whacking great mountains in scorching sunlight after an overnight snow fall!

It was impressive and profoundly moving to ski down a run behind a paraplegic in a pulk sled and to share the exhilaration of motion and flying powder. The lift rides not only conveyed us aloft but also gave time for me to pick the brains of both staff and sledders. It also let me catch needed breath.

The roads also led, as mentioned before, into northern New Mexico where, after some wandering, I found the Santa Fe Mountain Center. Again I was made welcome on what must have seemed the worst of all possible days. (But is there ever a good day to have a visiting fireman come to call?) The staff were preparing food, equipment, and itineraries for three patrols due to leave within a few days. The level of activity, while far from feverish was intense in a relaxed and disciplined way.

It was good to be able to watch, talk to staffers as opportunity afforded, and fire my questions about instructor development. The visit to that agency was also physically demanding, for Program Director Deb Harris gave me her undivided attention while we enjoyed a noon hour run. Only it was a six mile loop. . . and every step up-hill. Such is the magic and enchantment of New Mexico. Luckily, I needed my breath for running and so was able to listen to Deb's articulate and emphatic views. Later, my running ability, or rather disability, was kindly attributed to the unaccustomed altitude.

In a way similar to the school situation, there were marked similarities in the message that these agencies had for those who would be or would train instructors for the field. There is simply no substitute for the possession of hard (i.e. technical) skills appropriate to the terrain, time of year, and nature of program. While the extremes of expertise are not required, solid personal competence in some areas and the willingness to acquire it in others seems to be the norm.

The agencies also had an equally great common requirement for "people skills", as one person put it. These are the skills of group process, awareness and sensitivity, and in some cases counseling. All of the people I spoke to seemed to be in accord that most instructors came with greater strength in one or other of the two skill areas but, assuming strong motivation and given the particular staff training of the institution, a satisfactory balance was usually achieved. Balance also could be obtained in the field by matching the varied strengths of instructors in complementing ways.

The agencies were imaginative and resourceful in the way they acquired and deployed staff. Always there was rigorous screening, thorough staff training and development, and some systematic way of getting feed-back to everyone. Learning is definitely not confined to the clients of these programs. Some of the places I saw find a system of internships and assistant instructor positions to be valuable in finding and producing the high degree of competence required. Not surprisingly, this matches the tendency of various educational and training efforts to require future leaders to serve in internship settings.

In a similar way, some agencies have found ways to mobilize the good offices and assistance of skilled workers who are primarily volunteers. Of these, the Wilderness Experience Program in Denver is a striking example, although it is not the only one.

Looking Ahead

It seemed to me that experience-based education is alive and well in a large array of forms, modes, and variations. But the field is scarcely fat. The struggle for funds and appreciative recognition is endemic. There is no end in sight for the struggle to survive, and that is probably the best augur that one can have for the future.

There were two areas of endeavour that struck me as being particularly promising for future development. One was stimulated by visits to almost totally undeveloped archeological sites. Here is a field for learning by direct experience in which only a small number of pioneers are currently engaged. Consider the potential for on-site work by small groups of students under skilled direction. There would be all the problems of outdoor living, plus the labour (and tedium) of the dig, but also all the rewards — the treasured artifacts and the challenge to construct an account of life from them.

The second direction for growth is not unrelated. The increasing coherence of environmental action under the general rubric of the deep ecology movement seems to have real promise for yielding a healthy planet. The integrative tendencies of experiential learning match the integrative, life-centered values and practices of the deep ecologists. Perhaps one of the ways forward is to further develop those connections.

All sojourns end. And my oddessy has provided much to ponder. Unlike the original oddessy, this one perhaps has no heroic qualities, but neither must the traveller find at the end of the need to "rust unburnished". Instead, in my own place once again, where, like Gary Snyder, I would like to "stay for three thousand years and get it right", it seems better to forsake Ulysses and turn to Cheng Man-ching: "I sincerely hope that kindred spirits will forge ahead together."

The Risk of Freedom

By Steve Simpson

I'll tell you straight off that this story has a sad ending. There is joy in it, satisfaction in it, and a few exciting ideas in it, but the end of this story is a sad one. Perhaps the next story I tell will be different.

This story is about my first try at using experiential education in the public school system. The story takes place in a high school in Olympia, Washington. Before I tell you what happened, I should explain what my idea of experiential education is. Unlike most of the experientially based programs with which I am familiar, my methods did not involve wilderness, mountaineering, whitewater, or any other physical action beyond moving chairs around and talking. The most dangerous things we did were saying and writing what we thought. Despite the lack of scenery, I believe our experience was as profound and powerful as anything we could have accomplished on a glacier or an alpine meadow.

I understand experiential education to be education gained from something personally encountered, undergone, or lived through. It can be more simply stated as being what you learn from what you do. What we did was an attempt to learn as much of the standard curriculum as possible while letting the students do most of what teachers normally do in the public school system. What we learned may surprise you.

One of my fundamental beliefs is that no one really understands how the human animal learns things. I believe that people are too complex and subtle to be boxed or labeled or fed some learning system recently thought up by one educator or another. The human animal can grasp an idea intuitively or after painfully rational analysis or by osmosis after reading the back of a cereal box. Learning is in the same ballpark as artistry. If someone were able to define the ingredients that produce artistic ability, then they could gather them up and mix us an artist. The same is true of learning. If we really knew how people learn, we could gather all of those ingredients and whamo, everyone could learn everything. But we can't, and they can't, and this is why I decided to try experiential methods in my classes.

Whatever it is that we humans have inside us which enables us to learn, it is there when we are born and from day one we kick it into gear in order to survive. A mother may teach her child love by keeping it warm or feeding it or petting it or any of the thousand other things mothers consciously do for their children. But that mystical bond that exists between a mother and child cannot be solely attributed to those actions. There is more to it. Somewhere in the womb listening to her heartbeat, or somewhere in her smell or in her voice or in the look in her eye at two in the morning, the child learns things about mother that mother does not consciously teach. The child learns by experience. I believe that students learn by a process based on the whole of an experience and which none of us really understands.

Because there is a dimension of learning gained from doing which simply cannot be gained any other way, I decided to start by letting the students do as much as possible in my classes. I would let the students decide what learning methods they preferred, and we would use those methods. They would decide how they wanted their work to be evaluated and what they felt was appropriate behavior in the classroom. My function as the teacher was to be their guide. Like a guide, I knew the dangers because I had climbed the peak many times. I knew the subject matter. I knew the restrictions enforced by the administration and legislators and parents. I had the ultimate authority in the classroom because I had the ultimate responsibility. My job was to use my skill as a guide and allow the students enough freedom to take risks and yet not allow so much freedom that they climbed a foolish route and got badly hurt. It is a fine line, but I used the simple rule of letting the students do everything I possibly could. If my experiment resulted in failure of the students to learn enough of the standard curriculum, then I would lose my job. On the other hand, if we could pull it off, the students would not only learn the standard curriculum, but they would learn a thousand more subtle, more important, more useful things that can only be gained experientially.

The classes with whom I tried this method were studying sociology. Sociology is supposed to be the study of human groups, and of human institutions so I decided to let the students create a clasroom society, do something with it, and learn from the experience what they could.

Steve Simpson lives in Olympia, Washington, and is a prospective teacher and prospective father.

The first discussions we had were on the purpose of being in school. They talked about the reasons they needed an education, what an education is, and how difficult it is to learn about life when we are literally boxed off from life by the four walls of the classroom and the laws which force us to stay there.

After we had talked about why we were in school and, in a general way, what we planned to accomplish, we began to discuss some of the details of learning. We began with a discussion of what behavior would be acceptable during the class. This was an area which made me particularly nervous. One of the classes consisted of roughly 75% behavior problem students including six or seven drug abusers who came to class loaded and often nodded off during class, two or three loud, disruptive types, and one who had a history of beating up teachers. I was told before the quarter began that most of the students were slow learners and/or behavior problems. Most had failed the class before and were only taking it again because they had to pass the class in order to graduate. I was to be considered successful if only 10 or 15 percent failed the class and no one got hurt. You can understand why I was hesitant to experiment with new techniques.

I gave you more details about this particular class than was necessary because I want to emphasize their success. I believe that no one can simply move from childhood to adulthood and by some magic of modern body chemistry wake up one morning as a responsible citizen. I don't believe that you become familiar with self-control, group behavior or the restrictions of our society by passing a lot of tests. I believe that students learn these social skills through practice. I decided to give the students the freedom to decide what kind of behavior would result in the learning environment they needed. They would create the laws under which their classroom society would agree to live.

I found that when given the freedom to decide what kind of behavior they wanted in the class, virtually every student voted for a system which would be most teachers' dream. Our rules were simple and everyone understood them. The students had to bring their books, paper, and writing materials to class every day. Every student had to attempt every assignment. They had to be in class and on time every day. No student had to talk during class unless he wanted to, but each student had to listen when someone else was talking. No student was allowed to come to class loaded, sleep during class, or disrupt class in any way. Our class rules were based on the principle that every student has the right to learn and if another student (or teacher) disrupts class in any way they are stealing from the others their right to learn.

Like any system of law which involves less than perfect humans, our system required reinforcement. We developed a grade system which rewarded positive behavior and we included in our ethical system the principle that if someone has a problem, they need help rather than punishment.

In our class, we discussed the idea of rehabilitation versus the idea of punishment. The result of our discussions was a fairly clear understanding of our penal system and a class decision that punishment may deal temporarily with a symptom, but it does nothing to solve the problem. In our class we had several students test the rules in one way or another for the first few weeks. In every case, class was immediately stopped and the class tried to find out what was wrong and help if possible.

This could easily have degenerated into a version of pop group psychology. It was my job to avoid that and keep the discussions on the relatively simple turf which included straight forward questions and some basic discussion and suggestions. For instance, when a student put his head down and appeared to be asleep, class was stopped and the student was asked why he was sleeping. About half an hour

of discussion revealed that he had a job and worked late, that this was his choice and not required for the welfare of his family, and that after work he had gone out on a short date. The class discussed again why it was important for everyone to participate in class. Some of the suggestions included having the student figure out his priorities, and adjust his hours and spending habits accordingly. It was not a very deep or philosophical discussion, but it was honest and non-threatening. I said very little. We wasted a class period but since everyone heard the arguments, everyone was able to

> *I found that when given the freedom to decide what kind of behavior they wanted in the class, virtually every student voted for a system which would be most teachers' dream.*

> *If you weren't there, you did not get the credit. If you were there, you were participating, and you got credit.*

think about his own priorities and make his own adjustments. There were several situations that came up, but after the class realized that I meant what I said and consistently stopped class while we dealt with problems, the behavior problems disappeared.

The second half of our reinforcement came from the grade system we developed. In our class, we decided that the process of learning was more important than testing. We felt that the skills gained were more important than the grade received. We felt that the general methods used in school involved fear-based learning. You tend to study because you are afraid of failing rather than because you want to learn. For these reasons, we developed a system which rewarded students who tried to do every assignment with full credit whether the quality of their work was high or low. Before you jump on this, let me explain our thinking a little more clearly.

During our discussions, we decided that everyone is of equal worth as a human being. We accepted as fact that some people know more words or have quicker reflexes or better families or genetic differences. We felt that one of the major problems in our society was that despite what it says in the Declaration of Independence, the Constitution or the various laws of the United States, all people were definitely not treated equally. It was a fact of life in the public school system that athletes were given special privileges, people who cheated got better grades than people who didn't and students who were verbally skilled got better grades than students who didn't talk a lot in class.

In order to have our classroom society treat people equally and reward effort rather than results at any cost, we created a system which awarded 30% of the grade for class participation, 30% for homework, 30% for test scores and 10% for participation in the class project. To earn the 30% class participation grade, students were required to be in class every day, behave according to the class standards, and participate in all classroom activities such as role playing, group discussion, free-writing and sustained silent reading. (Remember, the class rules said the student had to be there, listen, and be alert. The rule did not require students to talk unless they wanted to.) Since we accepted nothing less than full class participation at any time without stopping class, every student could get full credit if they missed no classes. We deducted 5% of this grade for each absence from class. No excuses for absence were accepted because we decided it didn't matter why students were gone. It was a fact that if they were gone they didn't participate and we were simply hard or honest enough to recognize this without making value judgements about reasons for being absent. If you weren't there, you did not get the credit. If you were there, you were participating, and you got credit.

Our homework assignments were based on the methods of learning the students wanted to use. We did things like watching television commercials and writing about what the commercials taught our society about sex roles. We would divide the class into groups and assign each group to prepare a short presentation on a major religion or on different sides of political issues such as the draft or the justice system. We might have everyone in class produce a list of the ten most important things a person needed to study in a sociology class, and pick the most popular questions for study. We frequently did assignments using dictionary definitions. Whatever we did, if the student made an attempt, the student was given full credit for the assignment. If the student attempted every assignment they would receive 30% credit. For each assignment missed, a number of percentage points was subtracted. No value judgements were ever made which praised students who thought or spoke or wrote a certain way. Our decision was that everyone had something of worth to say and it was not the job of a teacher to decide which student (which person) was of more worth than another. This appears to fly against the letter grade system, but that was not the truth. The students ended up deciding their own grade (or worth) based on how

Our decision was that everyone had something of worth to say and it was not the job of a teacher to decide which student (which person) was of more worth than another.

hard they tried. Their grades were based on the percentage points they earned and the grade was not based on the subjective judgement of the teacher.

The tests we had in class were worth 30% of their grade. The students decided that they wanted tests which included different kinds of questions. They felt that some people did better on true-false and others did better with multiple choice. Others liked the matching questions. They did vote to include one essay question per test, despite the fact that essay questions are open to subjective grading by the teacher. They decided they trusted my ability to grade at least one question fairly and, just in case, we decided all grades were subject to review by a group of peers if there was any problem that could not be worked out between the teacher and the students. No problems ever developed. On tests, students did not get full credit for trying to answer the questions. They had to get the correct answer to get credit.

We stressed the fact that this was a covenant and not a contract. The difference is that a contract is enforceable by law, or from without. Our covenant was a form of moral agreement. It was an agreement relating to principals of right and wrong in behavior and was enforced only from within the group. This made all the difference.

You can see that under our system, a student who tried to do everything and came to class every day could get no lower than a 70% or a grade of C. If they missed a day of class or failed to try an assignment and failed all the tests, their grade would fall below 70% and they would get either a D or an F grade. On the other hand, if the student tried to do everything and missed no classes and got even 30% of the test questions correct, that student would then get 10% for the test grade, 30% for homework, 30% for class participation and 10% for participation in the class project. The total would be 80% and a grade of B for the class. We were very proud of our system. We felt it allowed for human differences in communication skills, genetic make-up, etc. and still ended up with students earning grades which accurately reflected their abilities. I still like the system and hope to use it again.

I have tried to describe in some detail what we did in our attempt at having a class where the students learned by doing. It was, in my opinion, a classic example of experiential education which was easily applied in a public school situation without any extra cost or problems. I would like to spend a few pages reflecting on the experience and try to draw from the class some ideas which may help other teachers who want to use experiential education in the public school system.

First, I would like to stress the fact that the teaching method I have described is based on trust. I built this trust with the students by the simple means of doing what I said I would do and by holding them to their word as well.

Everything that we decided on in the class was written down in our class covenant. A covenant is a formal, solemn, and binding agreement between people for the performance of some action. Our covenant included a statement of why we were in school, how we would learn, how our learning would be evaluated, and the specifics of what acceptable class behavior was. We all signed the document and many arguments were quickly settled with the words "because it's in the covenant." Our covenant was reached by consensus, that is, by unanimous group agreement and not by majority rule. If one person was not satisfied, we hammered it out until we could all agree. Again, we based this on the idea that everyone was of equal worth and in our society there would be no angry minority. It worked in the class, even though we agreed it could never work with more than a small number of people.

Another important element was that, in my class, students were encouraged to make mistakes. I would tell them over and over that if they were doing or saying

something and if they made no mistakes; they already know how to do it. If that is the case, they should be trying to master something else. I tell the students not to be hesitant in class. Class is their opportunity to learn how to be adults. If they try new activities, behaviors, and ideas, if they make their mistakes in the classroom, they may not make the same mistakes in adult life. The older they get the more responsibility they will have and the more serious will be the repercussions if they make a mistake. I feel it is better to have a little chaos early in the class, rather than people getting hurt or having bad lives because they make mistakes as adults.

I don't believe that you become familiar with self-control, group behavior or the restrictions of our society by passing a lot of tests. I believe that students learn these social skills through practice.

My last observation is really a word of caution. We live in an industrial/hierarchical society filled with bosses or government or teachers or television telling our young how to think, what to do, what to eat, what to wear, etc. Then, we come unglued when they make bad judgement calls. Our school system typically consists of a teacher telling students what to memorize, then telling them to spit it out on a test and then telling them they are an A or an F person. The school system tells them how to act and how to talk and what is ok to think.

Like any system, we included in our ethical system the principle that if someone has a problem, they need help rather than punishment.

If you plan to use a system which lets students think and lets students experience learning first hand, you must be aware that many of your students will have had no previous experience in the free use of the mind. They may not have even the most rudimentary skill at analysis and abstract thought. I encourage you to be patient. Go slowly. If you give them a lot of thinking in too abstract a way too quickly, they will rebel. Gradually increase the scope of what you give them to think about. It is a skill they are learning just like rock climbing or ice climbing. It will take some time before they will be graceful doing it. I encourage you to help them because it is the most important skill they can learn.

The sad ending? I tried this method when I was a student teacher. My supervising teacher was what I call a straight row man. By this, I mean he likes the students in their seats, the seats in straight rows, the knowledge in the notes, the notes memorized, and the answers in the tests. He needs absolute control. This type of teacher is not uncommon in the public school system.

When I first met this man, he told me he was burned out. He said he was sick of teaching and sick of "wise-ass kids." He said that he was glad I had some ideas and that I could do anything I wanted with the class as long as I had good lesson plans and could tell him what I was going to do before class. He was tired, but he was afraid he would get in trouble with the principal if I made any mistakes.

This man became more and more unstable as the class became more and more self-actualized. As I think back, I suppose he began to wonder what good he was if the students were able to do the thinking and were doing the doing. It was the final breakdown of this man during class that provided the sad ending.

When the class decided to have a free car wash as a class project instead of something like helping old people or the mentally retarded, this man panicked. He was certain that if the class had a free car wash, he would get in trouble with the principal. I tried to calm him down and help him understand that it wasn't all that bad and besides, he had approved the covenant and it was part of the covenant that they could choose their project. That was a major part of our basic trust, and I told him I couldn't break the trust and violate the covenant. He said that he was the supervising teacher and he could and would.

It was a twisted, angry, and confused man who took over the class, vetoed the covenant, and told the students to take their chairs out of the circle and put them back in rows. It was a frightened man who told the class that from now on he would do the teaching and they had better get used to doing some real work for a change. It was a tired and brutal man who told the class that from now on there would be no more group discussion, no more sharing of personal experiences, no more voting, no more reading in class, no more freewriting, and they had better score well on his tests or they would fail the class. It was a hard time for me and it was a hard time for the class. I had failed. I had not failed with the students, but I had failed to communicate with and help the one person in the room who apparently had needed it most. It is not a mistake I ever hope to repeat.

So now you know the story and the sad ending. I had to leave that school and finish my student teaching at another school. I did finish, and I got my certification and my paper and my freedom to try again in another class. Working from within the public school system for positive change is a tough game. There is much risk. You will always find a principal or other teachers or parents who really don't feel good about you teaching their children to think freely and trust their own judgement. But, I believe that unless the young in our society learn to think, learn to do, learn to trust their own judgement; we will end up with a society filled with incapable, fear-filled, small minded human beings. I urge you to take the risk.

"Look To This Day"

Look to this day
for it is life
the very life of life
In its brief course lie all
the realities and truths of existence
the joy of growth
the splendor of action
the glory of power

for yesterday is but a memory
and tomorrow is only a vision
But today well lived
makes every yesterday a memory
                              of happiness
and every tomorrow a vision of hope
Look well, therefore, to this day!

(Lines from a sanskrit poem)

Last June, I was driving my small pick-up truck out of the school parking lot. A senior student of mine was walking across the pavement and I stopped to chat, my truck straddling one of those monstrous speed bumps. He laughed and commented, "Looks like you're hung up on one of those traffic mountains. Playing seesaw?" I smiled, knowing full well that I was "hung-up" thinking about students and learning and teaching, but I changed the subject and asked: "Hey, are you going to graduate?" The student laughed not too confidently, replied, "Yea, I'm making it! I'm going to make it!"

The student in the parking lot responded that he was "making it." What did he mean? Did he mean that he was indeed making himself, creating and forging himself, emerging unique and productive? Or did he mean that he had made it through—he had survived, he had persevered. He had stuck out the tedium. More often than not, tragically, "making it" means primitive survival. For us as educators, however, "making it" now and in the future means that we will utilize some very specific living skills that need to be taught and developed.

"Making it" in the future, as in the present, will demand much from us. The future with its complexities and imminent crises will challenge the best in us. It will demand personal and community flexibility, the ability to integrate bodies of knowledge and experience, a sense of community, spiritual courage, self-confidence, and love. As a teacher and a parent, I ask myself countless times, "Am I helping to nurture mature students who, above all else, will 'make it' in the future?" Are our educational systems daily asking questions of us and of our students — difficult human questions that demand complex human answers? If our students who

graduate from high school are confident in their future, a bit cocky and a bit idealistic, if they have a bit of divine discontent for inequalities and social shortcomings, then we can rest, with some assurance; but if they answer with a No, if they are not confident, then we must respond honestly. And truthful we must be. Largely, our schools have not prepared or helped young people to mature. We as educational professionals constantly hide behind the current demons of "accountability," budget cuts, conservative whiplash. Our responses to the realities of the learning-teaching situation demand that we expand our efforts in the area of EXPERIENTIAL EDUCATION for this mode contains the best potential for honest and mature relationships between teacher and student; we must expand our own concept and the community's concept of what experiential education really entails. It is more than wilderness adventures.

For ten years I taught in and guided an alternative high school program named by the students: O.T.O. — "Opportunities To Teach Ourselves." We were (and still are) an "integrated-day" experiential program for heterogenous high school students. I saw real learning, the mastery of skills, and I experienced magical, human moments, as we utilized wilderness exploring to penetrate the meaning of our State and the meaning of learning and sharing and surviving. The self-contained classroom allowed us time and

---

Bob Gillette *teaches English at Andrew Warde High School in Fairfield, Connecticut. An avid hiker, canoeist, and cyclist, he also teaches teachers at the Graduate School of Education at Fairfield University. He is currently writing a book about experiential education entitled, "Look To This Day," A Teacher's Faith in Experiential Education.*

241

flexibility of scheduling. Teaching in such a setting was utopian. But after ten years, I felt a need to move on and explore, once again, the potential for experiential learning in the traditional classroom, within the 50 minute hour. It has been three years since my re-entry into the "real world" of teaching and I am not dismayed nor discouraged, and I am ever more committed to experiential learning.

How can one incorporate experiential learning into the traditional setting? It can be done. First of all, we need to transform our classrooms into places that literally shout with human experience. Graphically, every nook should contain student art that relates how students and others perceive aspects of reality. The key words in every lesson must always be REALITY, EXPERIENCE, and MEANING. All the humanizing techniques that we use in experiential learning work successfully anywhere. Surely, there is more need to compress and structure technique within the traditional setting because of the restrictions on time, but every technique that aims to humanize and clarify experience works.

Many experiential programs gain momentum and dynamism from their goal-setting, especially in terms of wilderness trips; so it can be within the traditional classroom. All we need to do is scale down our activities. Instead of a week-long canoe trip down the Connecticut River, we can help our students experience the magic of the canoe on a nearby pond for an afternoon. Instead of a lengthy back-packing trip, we can introduce the students to the immense possibilities of a day hike close to home. We can meet before school for a breakfast at dawn, or share our thoughts under the moon at the shore. We can help students by giving them structured assignments that require that they experience for themselves, in addition to their experiencing vicariously through the printed word. Let them discover their own "listening points" and during class, help them communicate what they heard or saw or felt. Let us help the students to learn the technique of retrospecting experience and finding meaning in what was.

If the moon is full, help the students notice it. If there is a fog on the way to school, examine it. If the weather changes, exploit the occurance with questions and readings that constantly ask students to "make meanings," to make connections with experience. For what, ultimately, is experiential teaching? It means that we urge and cajole and pressure students to ask questions of their own lives and the lives of others. It means actively intensifying and focusing and connecting on the human situation. It means our insistence that together, teacher and student, we ask **What Does It Mean?** It means that we help by leading students through as many opportunities as possible that are living experiences. It is, after all, the teacher's enthusiasm and faith in the fullness of life's potential that is the contagious spirit of experiential education. It is our human gift to students, our saying — "Look To This Day." And that can be done within the restrictions of the traditional classroom setting.

A LOOK AT THE LIFE OF
AN OUTDOOR EDUCATOR

For an outsider taking a quick glance, the life of an outdoor educator seems ideal, even prosaic. But maybe there is more that lurks beneath the surface.

by Alan S. Kesselheim

At a recent dinner party I was introduced to a new aquaintence and in the process of making conversation we discussed our vocations. It turned out that he is an electrician in town and is able to make a comfortable living at his trade. When the conversation turned to me and I began explaining my job as an outdoor educator, I noticed his eyes lighting up, glowing from the fire of his romantic imaginings. This wasn't a new experience for me. Often I encounter people who are largely ignorant of the outdoor education field and who conjur up images of scaling peaks, running white water, living out of doors and incredibly, making money to boot! What they don't see is the extent to which I envy them their stable 9 to 5 lives with predictable parameters when the not-so-romantic aspects of my job press upon me.

I must admit that as a novice, I too had a rather less than real vision of this profession. As a matter of fact, I never expected to be able to make a living as an outdoor educator. At best I hoped to work summer courses for a few years while supporting myself by means of some more traditional employment. As it turns out, I have become an outdoor educator by profession and although the rewards and challenges of the life make it worthwhile, the romantic sheen of the profession has certainly become tarnished to a more realistic hue. I find myself from time to time weighing the pros and cons, toting up the balance sheet and seeking out the issues and conflicts that confront me in this profession.

To begin on a concrete level, I want to round out the romantic pictures of lush alpine meadows, roaring white water and untrammelled winter vistas. We should remember those meadows in June when the mosquito population is so thick that you can make bug puree with a single swat. (I shudder at the thought of the black fly population in the north country). Considering another season, I'm reminded of a winter camping trip

in northern Michigan on which the temperature plummeted to -35°F for two nights running. Trees popped around us, the stoves wouldn't work and we needed to move constantly during the day to avoid frostbitten appendages. This weather was followed by a day of drizzling sleet which instantly coated everything in a sheet of ice. And when we finally arrived at the roadhead at the completion of our trip, we found our van solidly packed into the parking slot by a pile of heavy snow deposited by a passing snow plow.

At first glance, the outdoor education field may seem free from boring routine and mundane working conditions, but we should perhaps mention the topic of food in this context. I am forcefully confronted by this realm of work routine every time I face another bag of GORP, my umpteenth one-pot stew made with whole wheat elbow macaroni as the main ingredient, or one more cup of oatmeal that would more profitably be put to use as wallpaper paste. To take another example, consider the number of times an outdoor instructor packs and unpacks his or her backpack in their career or has to tear down and fix yet another stove that for some reason refuses to work. In short, the postcard panoramas and exhilarating activities are only the obvious aspects of the employment picture, but one can't avoid for long the other career parameters, of which I have mentioned a few.

On a more serious plane, there are a number of issues that inevitably surface and provide fuel for conflict for people who spend any significant time working in this field. For instance, I think fairly frequently about the evolution of my feelings about wilderness. The first time I came out of the wilderness after an extended stay I felt confined in rooms, was surprised by my "different" face in the first mirror I encountered, had to supress a compulsion to burn my toilet paper and throw dirt into toilet bowls, and struggled to regain the images of a soaring eagle or the deep blue of the

243

morning Utah sky as we drove into the land of billboards and tater tots and beehive hairdos. In other words, I suffered from a sort of culture shock and was faced with the problem of assimilating the things I had seen and learned in the wilderness into my life in society.

As I have spent more time in the wilderness, both on my own and as an instructor, I have experienced this sort of culture shock less and less acutely. When I emerge from the wilds now it rarely causes me much discomfort to hop back into a car and drive away at 55 mph towards a cold beer and bath. In considering this rather disturbing desensitizing process, two root causes appear to be dominant. First and most obvious, I have gotten used to making this transition from the out-of-doors to society and back. In the same way I am only momentarily disoriented when I walk out of a movie theater, it is only infrequently an adjustment of any major consequence for me to enter or leave wilderness areas after having done it so many times.

However, there is a second factor in this case, and it is one that should perhaps command some attention. My own experience as an instructor has revealed that it is simply impossible to experience the wilderness as fully and personally as I would on my own trip when I am working with a group. The sense of responsibility for a group's safety, the task of providing an educational experience for students and the burden of individual and group counseling all mitigate against my own uninhibited interaction with an environment. Many times when I'm in the field with a group I wish I could be alone or not feel obligated to prepare a lesson plan when I would rather be fishing or climbing a peak. In a very real sense, if I were able to enjoy the environment as fully and intimately as I would on my own, I wouldn't be working effectively. What it comes down to is that this is a job and it is frought with many of the same demands and constraints as other jobs (with a few extras thrown in that electricians never have to think about).

Another wrinkle in this career exploration appears when the subject of student motivation comes up. When I first started in this field I never very realistically considered the possibilitiy that some people wouldn't be turned on and tuned in to the "wilderness experience". The outdoor education approach, in my rather naive estimation, would bypass the problems of motivation that plague classroom teachers. Then I ran into the first student on a trip who for physical or emotional or psychological reasons had no wish to be in the wilderness and let me know this in no uncertain terms. There I was in the Grand Canyon with someone who didn't want any part of it. . . This is a particularly common problem for instructors working with special populations such as juvenile delinquents who literally and somewhat frequently attempt to escape from the wilderness; but it is an issue for any program. Students must be motivated on some base level in order for a course to be safe, successful and educational.

One of the foundational themes in the outdoor education field has to do with the notion of risk. Not only does wilderness travel imply certain objective dangers due to weather or accident, but outdoor programming uses risk as a vehicle to encourage growth and change in students. We consciously plan activities and itineraries which involve students in stressful and strenuous activities. To be sure, student's perceptions of the dangers are likely to be inflated beyond reality and safety precautions can be followed carefully, but the fact remains that an element of risk and a statistical probability of accident are realities for outdoor programs.

This can be a wearing tension for an instructor. As the years go by and the number of trips led increases, one begins to wonder when the bad accident will happen in your group. As near misses occur — a loose rock whizzes down a talus slope narrowly missing students or someone falls during a stream crossing - you see just how quickly and irrevocably a serious accident can happen even with the best of safety precautions. After a while this builds a certain sense of paranoia and makes veterans in the field wonder if it isn't time to step out before the statistics catch up. At best this tension makes for a seasoned and safety-conscious ability to make sound judgments without losing sight of the need for perceived risk on a course. At worst, an instructor can get so caught up in this worry that he/she loses any ability to infuse a course with the sense of adventure and risk and exhilaration that is an essential ingredient for success.

And for me there is yet another conflict that I battle with. I am confronted with the fact that I am actually leading students into the wilderness, encouraging their involvement in a distressingly dwindling resource. I know how much I value solitude in the out-of-doors, guarding the location of my own secret spots zealously, and I inwardly wince when I take students out and more or less fill up an area. In striving to justify this I tell myself that I'm training and educating students to be responsible and knowledgeable in the environment and in this sense, actually am working to preserve the wilderness. When I worked for a program that dealt with juvenile delinquents, I told myself that the theraputic benefits of that type of counseling outweighed the environmental impact that our groups had on wilderness areas. You can minimize impact by not taking toilet paper or wearing tennis shoes in fragile ecosystems, but the fact remains that just the sheer numbers of footprints in certain areas has created an astounding impact and as an outdoor educator, I must deal with the ramifications of that situation.

Many of the reasons for which I entered this field are still operative. Outdoor education is a relatively new and exciting approach to growth and learning. One feels as if one is exploring new frontiers with exciting opportunities and stimulating companionship. Many jobs offer variety, flexibility, an informal atmosphere, room for growth, the chance to spend time in beautiful areas and perhaps a somewhat holistic blend of lifestyle and career. At the same time, the next time I'm at a party and someone says to me, "You mean you get paid for that!?", I'll be tempted to say, "Hey listen, you got a minute? Have a seat. There may be more to this than you think."

Alan Kesselheim is a former wilderness instructor for the Santa Fe Mountain Center in Santa Fe, New Mexico. He currently coordinates the Outdoor Education program for Northland College in Ashland, Wisconsin.

The Creek Still Sings:

REFLECTIONS ON AN INTERNSHIP

by Gale Warner

Jan. 3, 1983

It is enough. Out my door is a clear graceful stream, a squirrel's raucus face above me in a bay tree, three mountains furred in muted greens and browns, five warm Guernsey cows set against cool green, new green, January green grass. Enough. Within, a writer's retreat: a table that shudders beneath a typewriter, a dictionary spread open on the headrest, hot water for tea, Degas and Turner prints on the walls -- a space small enough to be amply lit by candles, and large enough to think. At night, I hear a coyote caterwaul, and the constant hum of the creek, measured, unhurried, well-mannered. The stars are blue-bright, piercing. More than enough.

I may be less sanguine after the first rain, when the bits of sky I see in the hatch above me become spigots, and a trip to the bathroom across the valley becomes a muddy expedition in galoshes and slicker. Or after the mice move in for my peanuts and crackers and begin to, as the kindly gentleman owner of this tiny trailer put it, "rearrange the insulation." Perhaps. Perhaps I will tire of busloads of city children unfurling cramped legs and voices every morning, or of thoroughbreds galloping in the arena ten steps from my door. But it doesn't seem likely now. It seems, instead, as through I have landed here propitiously from another planet, and have, by some kind of grace, been allowed to stay awhile.

Hidden Villa. Even its name evokes an air of rural gentility, with a dash of mystery

---

Gale Warner is a freelance writer who is currently traveling through Western Europe writing articles on the eco-political and conservation scene and serving as a "voluntary warden" at Minsmere Nature Reserve, Suffolk, England.

thrown in. It is called a ranch, but that is a concession to its location in California, for there are no crossed spurs above the doors, no thousands of bawling dogies, no dudes. It is a farm. It is hard to imagine it as anything else. Even in its days of wildness, when Ohlone Indians lived by its streams, caught salmon, and feared grizzlies, the small green valley must have seemed a welcome haven, hospitable to human life in a way that the damp bay laurel canyons and steep chaparral slopes surrounding it could not have been. Humans have always lived here -- that breathes from the land. Here the struggle has been for co-operation with land rather than conquest of it, and it shows. The land is as open and trusting as a child who has never been beaten, and who never expects to be.

I came to Hidden Villa in late December 1982 for a six-month internship with the Hidden Villa Environmental Project (HVEP) on the strength of fond memories of volunteering with the project a few years before. When I arrived, I had no idea that I would become absorbed, immersed, and converted into an environmental educator. After travelling for some time, I was looking for a place to root, and from 3000 miles away the serenity at Hidden seemed to call out a welcome. I was a writer, and I knew I could write there; the children, I thought, would be a pleasant diversion. Not long out of college, I was in that exhilarating and perplexing stage when what I *wanted* to do was clear enough, but *how* to do it was the probem; when creative fulfillment and practical survival seemed utterly contradictory; when part of me urged "settle down, find a job" while the other urged freedom and exploration. For such a stage in life were internships wrought.

Hidden Villa began as a family affair and owes much of its flavor to the blend of generations and perspectives created by one remarkable family and those they have managed to draw into the ranch's activities

> ## "When I arrived, I had no idea that I would become absorbed, immersed, and converted into an environmental educator."

over the years. At age 96, Frank Duveneck is still the benevolent patriarch of Hidden Villa. He and his wife Josephine moved to California's Bay Area during World War I and bought Hidden Villa's original 1000 acres a few years later. They built a house and moved there with their four children in 1929, but the ranch quickly became more than simply a home for the Duveneck family. As their neighbor Wallace Stegner once remarked, "they could not own a home without sharing it." Hidden Villa became a mecca for those sharing the Duvenecks' humanitarian, conservation, and educational ideals.

The Duvenecks helped found the Peninsula School for Creative Education in Menlo Park, and a variety of programs at the ranch soon followed: the Pacific Coast's first youth hostel in 1937, a multi-racial summer camp in 1945, farm tours for pre-schoolers, and the Environmental Project, launched in 1970 with three young teachers and a sense of mission. Since then HVEP has brought about 3000 elementary schoolchildren a year to Hidden Villa to learn ecological concepts, farm facts, and caretakership ethics through creative, experiential strategies, many of which are described in HVEP's acclaimed curriculum guide, *Manure to Meadow to Milkshake*. The classroom is the working farm and the 1800 acres of chaparral slopes, grassy ridges, and forested canyons that the Duvenecks have succeeded in preserving amidst the urban sprawl of the Silicon Valley.

Although a relatively recent addition to HVEP, interns have been described as the "meat" in a sandwich between the four part-time staff members and volunteer guides from the community and local colleges. The deal is symbiotic: Hidden Villa gets inexpensive, enthusiastic help, and we get $10 a week, housing in small cabins or trailers, fresh milk, butter, and vegetables, credit if we need it, and invaluable training and experience. In addition to guiding children with HVEP, interns assist in the hostel, garden, animal care, maintenance, and administration, as well as carrying out individual projects. Interns are also on call to pick up the slack when volunteers contract final exams or when overworked staff members cannot be in three places at once. All this proved plenty to juggle, and weekly scheduling meetings were often hilarious when we booked our lives six weeks in advance. Yet the resultant variety of experience kept us from getting stale: on any given day we might teach children, arrange fund-raising picnics, make yogurt, dig garden beds, ride a horse, fix plumbing, prune blackberries, milk cows, pour cement, or perform puppet shows during the half-day classroom visits that staff members use to prepare the children for their Hidden Villa trip.

Sure there were times when I wondered what forking out packed sheep manure three feet deep had to do with environmental education. But all that scrubbing of toilets and digging of postholes, besides being necessary and tangible work, promoted the attitudes of self-reliance and community gumption that somewhere along the line become essential to environmental teachings. We became convinced, rightly or wrongly, that we could do almost anything, that phone calls for outside help were unnecessary when a roof leaked or a downed tree had to be cleared.

We discovered that what holds true for the children holds true for us, the teachers: the experiential educator's maxim, "Let me do it and I'll understand." After getting up at dawn for morning chores, we could begin to teach children about farm life from the point of view of the farmer. The garden became more than a handy educational station to us after hours of turning the compost pile, preparing beds, planting onions, and staking tomatoes. And as hikers on the wilderness trails in our free time, we were able to extoll its virtues more lustily because we lived so near it and loved it so well.

Jan. 28
As each wave on the beach shifts the sands in a new pattern, brings in new kelp,

247

stones, shells, and jellyfish to ogle at, and washes others away, so is each day here in these mountains. The night rolls in and leaves behind a slightly altered land: infinitesimally greener hills, brand-new wildflowers, a new fallen tree, a new hue and cry of the creek. Each day begins afresh, washed clean, glistening, never to be repeated.

When the staff asked us, at the end of our time, if it would be possible to have as rewarding an internship without living on the ranch, we were emphatic that it was not. Living here allowed us to be part of the ranch community. Our work lives and our personal lives were united; our friends -- ranch hands, secretaries, volunteers, hostel managers, gardeners -- were also our co-workers. The camaraderie engendered by spontaneous get-togethers after a full day of clearing downed trees or shoveling trenches to combat mudslides was an irreplaceable part of the experience. We had the rare opportunity to teach about our home, not some place segregated from the rest of our lives. By tilling the garden we were putting into practice exactly what we were trying to inspire: taking care of the earth and its creatures. The sweat and muscle required to maintain the farm, animals, and facilities deepened our understanding of the notion of being connected to land and responsible for its well-being.

March 29

Home again after a week away. The lambs are bigger, and Lee has had her calf. The miner's lettuce is huge: the once heart-shaped leaves have grown around the stems, come full circle, and created collars of Elizabethan splendor. The maple near my trailer is putting out clusters of purpled-red leaves -- surprise! At twilight, as Ross drove the cows home from pasture, his full baritone echoed in the canyon: "How Can I Keep From Singing?" How, indeed.

Some of the children who come to Hidden Villa grew up in the inner city and have never before seen a live cow or taken a walk in the woods. A few are as petrified of walking down a sunny trail in the hills as I would be walking around their neighborhoods at night, and for similar reasons: unknown dangers lurking behind the bushes. They tend to associate wildness with hardship, hidden precipices, and lions and tigers and bears (oh my!). Other chil-

Frank Duveneck and great grandchild.
Photo by Gale Warner.

248

dren sport Sierra Club badges on their backpacks and can relate tales of their most recent expedition to the mountains with aplomb. For some of these children, however, exposure to nature has been so frequent that they almost take it for granted, and often they are more difficult to keep alert ("so there's moss on the tree -- so what?") than the uninitiated underprivileged children, who view their day at Hidden Villa as an enormous once-in-a-lifetime adventure.

They come from grades one through six, public and private schools, a rainbow of ethnic backgrounds, and a medley of socioeconomic situations. Their parents include Vietnamese and Cambodians fresh off a boat, millionaire Silicon Valley executives, Hispanic residents of barrios, Stanford University professors, and a large measure of middle-class suburbanites.

"Sure there were times when I wondered what forking out packed sheep manure three feet deep had to do with environmental education."

Whatever their previous experience, all the children come with something to learn. The affluent and middle-class children may be veterans of junior nature expeditions, but they have little awareness that anything they do in their lives could have any effect on the environment around them. They tend to be prissy about sitting on the ground, intolerant of animal odors in pens, afraid of getting dirty, and, in general, more interested in competition than in cooperation with their peers. Those from less advantaged backgrounds tend to have lesser reading and writing skills and to be more fearful of the large animals and long hikes, but they are also more curious, more cooperative, and more eager to learn. Of course, such generalizations are inherently problematic and exceptions common; a great deal depends on the individual classroom teacher and parental environment.

But one of the most valuable aspects of my internship was being able to work with such a diversity of cultural attitudes toward nature, forcing me to re-examine some assumptions about human relationships to the natural world that I had cherished for a long time.

April 12 -- Josephine Duveneck's birthday
"Becoming aware of the relationships of all living things to other living things is the key to knowing ourselves. It is the basis for understanding the intricate web of life. By what means can such experience be brought about? The challenge for the teacher is to set the stage so that this kind of learning can take place."
--Josephine Whitney Duveneck
(1891-1978)

I have a lot of reasons to feel as happy as I do now. I have been acutely aware, all day, of other people around me and my relationship to them -- in that order. Often, the relationship of the moment, with a ponderous "me" on one end, tends to overwhelm my awareness of the other person: but today I moved freely amid dozens of persons, able to see each clearly and to do something to amuse, comfort, or gladden them in some tiny way. I can do this, I realize, because this is home -- because I am so firmly rooted to this place, so planted and secure (though my season here is short), and thus able to view the kaleidoscope of people around me calmly and with the affection for them that I feel within.

Today I created a string of grand adventures and memories for four children with learning disabilities -- bright, personable children, wonderful to be with. I was "on" today, really teaching, and balancing it with plain friendship and fun. I can feel the growth in them after just this one day -- what a precious treat for a teacher! My self-confidence and ability with children is steadily growing. I have armfuls of tricks up my sleeves now. Enthusiasm, good spirits, and a hells-bells attitude smooth over just about anything, I'm discovering, though a hefty repertoire of techniques, and sufficient composure to be able to make them up on the spot sure helps.

I have discovered so much about myself here. When I'm rich and famous, will I sleep as well as I do on these old cotton covers, in this endearingly tacky trailer? I fold the same clothes over and over again after laundry with genuine affection, not boredom. How many skins do I need? My shoes have more holes in them than intact surface; it matters little when they finally rip. I have bought almost no material goods except staple foods for months. I eat simply and healthily, and like to cook for myself. I love the morning air on my face, the wake-up tapping of a woodpecker in my tree, the chill dew igniting the grasses in early sun, the sheep and cows bellowing, the creek's song. These are constant, dependable, cherished things -- things that are now irrevocably part of how I choose to live. I know now a little more clearly how I do and do not want to live. And this -- is close. Very close.

There are some pitfalls to live-in internships as well. At times the mixture of work and home grew too intense and I needed to get away; also, after awhile it was tempting to believe that the world revolved around Hidden Villa. It is easy to over-extend just because one is physically *there* all the time.

But the staff was always sensitive to this, quick to work out any difficulties, and supportive of the need to take time off. When the chips were down and phone calls had to

---

"I fold the same clothes over and over again after laundry with genuine affection, not boredom. How many skins do I need?"

---

be made, a mailing had to go out, or extra guides were needed, the interns were expected to come through. Yet the care and interest the staff showed for us prevented

The creek on a hot day. Photo by Liz Dana.

us from feeling used. Our crew of five was rewarded with frequent kudos from the staff and enrichment sessions with visiting speakers on jobs, resumes, grants, and setting up non-profit corporations. We were told directly and indirectly that we were being trained to be leaders in the field, capable of setting up our own programs in the future.

One of the keys to Hidden Villa's success is the staff's credo that the guides and interns must be treated with the same care and solicitude as the children. An hour before the classes arrive, guides share "values" in a circle to prepare themselves mentally for the day. After the children go home, a "debriefing" session, with edible treats, gives each guide a chance to share the day's ups and downs with a sympathetic audience, and tips for next time are passed around. Potlucks, folk dances, and other social gatherings impress on the volunteers that the staff takes a personal interest in their growth and learning as well as that of the children.

"Not long out of college, I was in that exhilarating and perplexing stage when what I *wanted* to do was clear enough, but *how* to do it was the problem."

May 26

Because of a teacher's mix-up yesterday, some children from Palo Alto missed their three-mile hike across Rhus Ridge and had an hour to get fidgety and bored before we discovered where they were. Their energy level was so high that all of Mike's magic couldn't transform the experience from an exuberant outdoor slumber party, soon forgotten, into a memorable, illuminating night under a full moon. Since the children were so intelligent and potentially so receptive, it was frustrating that they were so rowdy and uncooperative. But we

did what we could. I played some penny-whistle tunes for them after they were all in their sleeping bags, as the fog rolled in over the hills.

The next morning I woke in a field of flowers and hiked off the ridge to meet the next day's children. They could not have been a greater contrast: black, Hispanic, and Asian sixth-graders from San Jose, enthused, curious, sensitive, bright -- a joy to be with in every way. My five children were active and willing for any adventure, yet also capable of being quiet and mature. But I ached inside when I read their heartfelt, grammatically disastrous writings about their feelings for Hidden Villa. No one can tell me that these kids are not as intelligent, if not more so, than the super-privileged Palo Alto fourth-graders. They couldn't spell or construct correct sentences, or divide one fourth in half to get an eighth, but their creativity and sensitivity for each other and for the wild things we encountered have me inspired as an educator. They have never been prodded to read, to write, to stretch themselves to learn, to listen and think, to consider exploring all their potentialities away from San Jose's east side. I had to hold back the tears when they told me they didn't want to go to junior high school "because you get beat up all the time." Gifted and sweet Jesse? Adorable Isabel? We are sending lambs to the altar. Dear children, there must be something we can do.

June 3

Partings. The taste, full and pungent, slides down the throat to the chest: a tightening. Familiar enough, though always before felt for a person, a loved one. Not this generalized ache for a place, something that I cannot embrace -- not all of it at once, firm and warm within my arms. It is elusive. A group of people, some low brushy mountains, a dwindling clear creek still singing through my door, so hushed, so gentle. How can I describe my feelings when the folks tonight after dinner spoke of this summer, next year ... it will all go on without me. This morning I lingered in the parking lot, hoping I would be needed to guide. I wanted kids -- more and more kids. I wanted it to go on. So those huggable first-graders yesterday were

Playing Blob Tag. Photo by Gale Warner.

the last? No more new games, decomposer dance, calves, rangers, planets, riddles, rump-bump, stories, writings, alone walks, tree hugs, lambs? No more feeding the chickens, holding the snake, hunting for bones in dry coyote scat, playing in the creek? No more music?

June 16
Wherever I go, whatever I do, I will have Hidden Villa with me. Within me. I am leaving temporarily and bodily so that others may take my place, may alight, root, grow, and seed here as I have. Dana, today, was already touched by the glow. Another counselor lay quietly by the creek and did not hear me as I returned from a last hike. The camp children arrive Saturday; Matilda is about to have her piglets. It is all as it should be. I have had my time here.

BOOK REVIEWS

Books in Review

Ascent: The Spiritual and Physical Quest of Willi Unsoeld

Laurence Leamer
New York: Simon and Schuster, 1982

Reviewed by Jasper S. Hunt, Jr.

Editor's Note:
Willi Unsoeld was a leading experiential educator who served as a mentor to many people presently in the field. He was very involved in AEE in its beginning years. Willi was one of the first four Americans to reach the summit of Mt. Everest, and he served as director of the Peace Corps in Nepal and executive vice president of Outward Bound, Inc. He held degrees in physics, theology, and philosophy, and was a professor at Evergreen State College in Olympia, Washington until he was killed in an avalanche on Mt. Rainier in 1979.

His daughter, Devi, who is also mentioned in this review, died while on a climbing expedition with her father to Nanda Devi, the peak in the Himalayas for which she was named.

***

That how an actual entity becomes, constitutes what that actual entity is; so that the two descriptions of an actual entity are not independent. Its 'being' is constituted by its 'becoming.' This is the 'principle of process.''
Alfred North Whitehead, Process and Reality.

As a process philosopher it is impossible for me to write a review of Laurence Leamer's *Ascent: The Spiritual and Physical Quest of Willi Unsoeld,* without paying considerable attention to the process whereby this book came into being. The content of this book must be seen against the background from which it emerged.

Willi Unsoeld died on March 4, 1979. Willi's wife, Jolene, was besieged by writers and filmmakers. Knowing her own lack of expertise in the professional publishing world, Jolene was put in touch with Laurence Leamer, a professional writer and former Peace Corps volunteer. Because Leamer impressed her, Jolene responded favorably to his request to do the writing and opened up her materials about Willi to Larry. As Jolene told me in a letter of February 15, 1980, "I was elated at the prospect of a biography that would reflect the joyful spirits that were Devi and Willi. For several months I worked collecting and organizing the reams of material and tapes to make Larry's research easier." Then Leamer wrote a draft of the book. Jolene's response was to recoil in horror. She wrote, "The hopes I had for this book and the confidence I had in this author have been dashed to bits. I find the 120 page proposal which Larry says he has submitted to a number of publishers unbelievably ugly, tawdry, and evil." Jolene did not like the direction the book was taking and tried her best to dissuade Leamer from pursuing the project. Many of Willi's closest friends agreed not to aid Leamer in his research for the book.

What is vital to know here is that Leamer had been given complete access to Willi's materials. Although Jolene held (and still holds) the copyright to Willi's materials, nevertheless Leamer physically retained possession of some of them. One might well think that, as a matter of common human decency, Leamer would respect Jolene's wishes and stop the project. This did not happen. Even though Leamer was completely in Jolene's debt for his access to the Unsoeld materials, he refused to modify or stop his project. As Jolene has written, "Although I begged Larry to accept a financial settlement and give me on the first anniversary of Willi's death the gift of release from the additional suffering that his writing was causing our family, he said he had a 'moral' obligation to finish the book." In a letter to Jolene Leamer wrote, "Willi's story is too important not to be told. In the light of his direct impact on my life over a decade ago and my concentrated exposure to his work and to his family these last months, I continue to believe that I am the person to write that book." Finally Leamer told Jolene, "But whether or not I have your support and cooperation I want to assure you that I will

not violate any of your legal rights in any book that I may write." The man had the audacity to tell Willi's wife and family that Willi's life was too important not to write about... as if the Unsoeld family was not completely aware of the importance of Willi's life!! On top of that the threat is made that the book will be written regardless of the families' wishes and that he would watch out about legal rights. The key word here is legal rights. Any claim that Jolene may have had to moral rights was nothing to Leamer. As any freshman ethics student knows, legal and ethical goods are often very different things. In this case they had nothing whatsoever to do with each other.

"To relegate Willi to the classification of a fuzzy-minded nature mystic is completely to ignore the rigor with which Willi approached mysticism and nature."

Process comments aside, what is objectionable about this book in terms of content? As a scholar I am always bothered by lengthy quotations and passages lifted directly from copyrighted materials without a single footnote or acknowledgement of copyright. Reading this book, one never knows where the lengthy quotations came from and the context in which they were found. If one of my graduate students did a similar thing in a thesis, I would charge him or her with plagiarism.

The implication throughout the book that Willi harbored an unconscious death wish borders on the bizarre. In my own 13 years experience as a climber I have had to confront the possibility of death many times. Every climber must deal with this issue and Willi's dealing with it was no more unusual than many other mentally healthy climbers I have known. Leamer's fascination with depth psychology completely distorts this issue.

Leamer implies that Willi's teaching at The Evergreen State College was sloppy and totally oriented towards his own self agrandizement. I did several independent study projects with Willi and found him the most academically rigorous teacher I encountered in 4 years at Evergreen. As a graduate student in philosophy at the University of Colorado, I found that the preparation in the history of Western philosophy I received from Willi was adequate, even above average. Willi did not take kindly to sloppy philosophy and I even found him a bit harsh at times on my own sloppiness. It is true that Willi thought that process is as important as content in education. Just because he sought to rectify an imbalance between process and content in traditional education, it does not follow that he, therefore, held content in low esteem.

The presentation of Willi as a philosopher is brief, superficial, and shallow. Leamer makes no attempt to present the philosophical problems Willi wrestled with and how he solved them. To relegate Willi to the classification of a fuzzy-minded nature mystic is completely to ignore the rigor with which Willi approached mysticism and nature.

Leamer's attempt to psychoanalyze the Unsoeld family left the most bitter taste in my mouth. In the name of interpersonal sanity, what large family does not have intense interpersonal issues to deal with? Leamer implies that the Unsoeld family had abnormally conflict ridden relationships. Leamer illustrates this by relating a story of Devi swallowing her own vomit in class when she was a child. I wonder how many school age children have not done exactly that same thing in order to avoid embarrassment in the classroom. I know I

did. This mundane episode is supposed to convey deep conflicts within Devi and within the family. I saw it as a normal child doing what normal children do routinely.

"The implication throughout the book that Willi harbored an unconscious death wish borders on the bizarre."

In summary, I find this book to be a biographical aberration. In terms of process, it emerged from a morally bankrupt atmosphere. It was written without the input of many of Willi's closest friends and against the express wishes of his wife and family. It presents Willi and his family in a light that is historically highly questionable. I think readers of the experiential education Journal should be aware that purchasing this book will fill the financial coffers of people who care nothing about the sensitivities of those who loved Willi the most - his family. In conclusion, I urge readers of the Journal to look elsewhere for information about Willi Unsoeld, a man who had a profound impact on the development of experiential education in the United States.

Jasper S. Hunt, Jr. is Assistant Professor in the Department of Experiential Education at Mankato State University in Minnesota.

Outward Bound, USA
Learning through Experience in Adventure-Based Education
By Joshua L. Miner and Joe Boldt

William Morrow and Co.
New York, New York, 1981
$17.95 Hardcover
$8.95 Paperback

Editor's Note: This book will be of special interest to AEE members since many of its past and current members are mentioned in the book as well as the beginnings of the association itself.

By James L. Elder

This is a book that should be in the library of every experientially oriented teacher and program.

The current experiential education movement was spearheaded by Outward Bound, and Joshua Miner was among those few on the point. Miner spent over ten years learning from Kurt Hahn (Outward Bound's creator) and experimenting with his concepts at Phillips Academy. He directed the first United States Outward Bound courses; he helped found the Colorado Outward Bound School; and he led Outward Bound as its President and Chairman through the critical beginning ten years of its operation.

OUTWARD BOUND, USA is a chronicle of Miner's own twenty year long O.B. course—his successful "expeditions" with others towards a goal of influencing the mainstream education. As a collection of warm and personal anecdotes, **OUTWARD BOUND, USA** introduces the reader directly to Hahn and his compassion for young people. It shows how Hahn's visionary synthesis of educational methodologies were imported and modified by Americans. It tells the story of the founding of each of the six U.S. Outward Bound

Schools as well as some of the major offshoot programs such as Homeward Bound and Project Adventure.

The creation of a new institution is always a fascinating interplay of creative and committed people, dynamic societal forces, and good timing. In Outward Bound's case Miner is one of the few with a full perspective and involvement in these terms, and the only one to tell the story to date. His inspiring narrative style walks the reader through the highlights of the Outward Bound movement, some of which include the Peace Corp's involvement, and Dewitt Wallace's first $1 million gift, and attempts to broaden the influence of Outward Bound's ideas such as the founding of the Association of Experiential Education.

The trials and tribulations, the faith and dedication—many of the lessons here are translatable to our own efforts. This is one caring adult's story of his efforts to provide young people with a healthy environment in which to grow; to empower them with the ability to learn. As Douglas Heath pronounces in the preface: "it is a case study of hope".

James L. Elder, *Director, The School for Field Studies, Boston, Mass.*

FUTURE OF EXPERIENTIAL EDUCATION

Educational Communities:
The Future of Experiential Education

by Anne Leonard, C.N.D.

The following was originally delivered as a paper at the Seventh Annual Conference on Experiential Education in October 1979. The author envisions a changed dynamic in the educational environment of the future.

During my days here I have been deeply touched and moved. I go away a richer person and, I hope, a more committed person. I come to you from experience in what you would regard a formal setting, in an alternative system. I don't intend to say anything new, but I believe in what you are doing, and I come to encourage you to use your influence to make change possible, to extend your scope beyond your own programs so that the strength of your commitment will reach educators who do not share your philosophies or values. I believe that change comes from the individual and has to be internalized. It cannot be superimposed by external forces. During my time with you I have felt your commitment. I have sensed unity in your great diversity. I would challenge each of you to work toward creating an educational environment for the future that will provide for all children what you now provide for a fortunate but relative few. I come to you to share my vision for education, a vision that I work toward and believe in every day of my life.

Over the next fifteen years, life in our world will become increasingly complex. The energy situation, already serious, will become desperate, affecting our overall lifestyle and forcing the development of alternative resources. We will be forced to recognize the delicate balance of the environment and adjust our technology to protect it, or face inevitable destruction. The inequitable distribution of goods will continue to result in mass starvation for segments of the world's population. The third and forth worlds will grow stronger, demanding and getting a greater share of wealth and power in exchange for their natural resources, which the more developed countries have squandered.

In response to these pressures, America will gradually phase out the throw-away society and thoughtless consumerism. The larger work force created by extend-

ed retirement age, more working women, and continued immigration, coupled with the accelerated trend toward a limited number of technical, highly skilled jobs, will cause radical changes in our concept of work and leisure. There will be increasing isolation from nature, less capability for self-sufficiency, an increased interdependency on technological satisfaction of needs, and on the government aid programs. People will feel more powerless, more helpless and more desperate.

What do these probably conservative predictions say to us? What qualities must persons possess to cope, to change, to experience happiness, security, and personal fulfillment amidst this rapid impersonal change and external turmoil? What things must we, as educators, do? What services must we provide to help create whole, healthy people, to neutralize the happenings that will dehumanize them, blind them, hamper their growth and strip them of their dignity and rights?

Certain human qualities must be recognized and developed in order to enable people to work cooperatively together toward solutions or toward decision — making processes that are shared, human, and respectful of their rights and the rights of others. Therefore, education will be supremely important in the future. Perhaps, as people become disillusioned with the conventional schooling of the 1970s and early 1980s, this will provide the impetus to try real education, true education. We see signs right now of the disintegration of the old in the pressures on the schools to be all things to all people, to meet everyone's expectations and seemingly to place education at the source of every problem. While that could be true, education can also be the solution if it is education that moves toward the full development of the individual and toward his or her identification with an ever-widening concept of social and cultural responsibility. Out of the shambles and seemingly destructive forces operative today, I see that a goal emanating from a White House Conference on Education held in the 1970s will have a chance to be reborn, to take on flesh and become imbued with life. That goal, a little paraphrased to eliminate sexist language, is:

Sister Anne Leonard, C.N.D. is currently serving as Superintendent of Elementary Schools in the Archdiocese of Chicago.

261

We have to strive toward helping the person of the 21st century become one with a strong sense of self and his or her own humanness, with awareness of thoughts and feelings, and the capacity to feel and express love and joy and to recognize tragedy and real grief. For the educated person of the next century will be one who, with a strong and realistic sense of his or her own worth, is able to relate openly with others, to cooperate toward common ends, and to view mankind as one, while respecting diversity and difference. This person will be a being who, even when young, somehow senses within himself or herself the capacity to become more than he or she is now, the capacity for life-long spiritual, emotional, and intellectual growth. This person will challenge that vision of what he or she is capable of becoming and will cherish the development of the same potentiality in others.

Notice the description of such a person includes no reference to possession of strong academic knowledge and skills, a competitive nature or job preparation that will make for materialistic and societal success and advancement. It does excite me as a possibility, attainable and real - a vision that, from what I see of you and have experienced with you, closely parellels your aspirations. That this statement is not taken seriously

---

Education will be supremely important in the future. Perhaps, as people become disillusioned with the conventional schooling of the 1970s and early 1980s, this will provide the impetus to try real education, true education.

---

and examined by educators today, to ascertain if programs and practices parallel the words, is indeed a tragic commentary on the professionalism, and perhaps the understanding of what a teacher is and should be, and the sense of purpose allowed, or should I say denied teachers in what we think is academic freedom.

A study of this goal and its implications could indeed provide an impetus to depart radically from the purely cognitive connotation we have attached to educational endeavors, and the lip service we now give to development of the affective domain.

Because of the pressures on the school today, and the increasing pressures on the world of the future, I see us moving into an era of emerging "educational centers" or "communities". Helped by the beliefs and struggles

of a nuclei of persons as yourselves, these centers will be infused with life - grow and develop. Their hallmark will be true learning. Their vitality will spring from relating, serving and committed persons—persons who are developing their talents and ever renewing themselves—persons who have a sense of their being, identity, and worth, and who are always learning how to learn.

Helped by the beliefs and struggles of a nuclei of persons as yourselves, these centers will be infused with life - grow and develop. Their hallmark will be true learning.

In an educational community, of which one dimension is learning, each person is uniquely important. The learning environment, consequently, is rooted in love and concern for the individual student based on the conviction that each student has talents to be developed and that each one has to feel good about himself or herself, have a realistic sense of abilities and be encouraged to share his or her gifts with others. In such centers, it is no longer "schooling", but an education for self-awareness and self-esteem that is provided, a vision of a lifetime of growing - a lifetime of learning that is deliberately chosen - an everyday ongoing process leading to significant changes in behavior and attitude.

In the educational community, learning is seen as a mystery that is unfolding everyday, a process seasoned and tempered by, with and in time. It is an integral part of every life—and goes on as long as one lives. Therefore, everyone feels at home in these new communities. Formal education remains essential to the processes of lifelong learning, but equal recognition is given to all the experiences of persons as they develop, adjust and live.

In such communities, the boundaries of formal education give way to merger with the existing realities of life. Curriculum experiences are integrated vertically in terms of time. They are past, present and future oriented, and are constantly being scrutinized and reassessed. Early childhood is recognized as more than just a waiting period prior to readiness for schooling. These educational centers extend resources downward to assist parents as their young children develop language skills, thought processes and a sense of identity. They also extend to the other end of the continuum —to adults who need continuing education at all levels of skill and training—who need the opportunities to become flexible, to adjust to new roles—employer, employee, parent or retiree to that of a student, a teacher who needs to find ways of sharing the richness of their experience with others.

In the horizontal dimension of learning, these communities address the reality that every learner is a private and a public person, one who relates to home and society, to the worlds of recreation and work, to private thoughts and mass media. Therefore, curriculum is designed to help youth make sense of and find meaning and connections in their social, intellectual and religious experiences. Experiences are provided which address the development of the total person—spiritual, intellectual, emotional, social, aesthetical and physical; experiences that are ongoing and that prepare for rapid change, for coping with that change, for decision-making and for a fulfilling use of leisure time.

The programs offered in such communities are intellectual experiences, yes, but they are coupled with action programs which are personalized, and where students move at their own pace and take responsibility for their own learning. There is the ongoing assessment of students and the matching of teacher and student learning styles. There is team and cooperative learning and teaching so as to provide a variety of learning experiences. These communities influence and are influenced by the total experiences of the learner. They expand the idea of instruction to include every variety and range of learning experience that enables a learner to become a person in a community.

In such communities, the boundaries of formal education give way to merger with the existing realities of life.

In these learning communities, content experiences support and strengthen self-awareness. Experiences enable the learner to become self-directed, curious, able to solve problems and motivated to continue to learn. The experiences are futuristic because they enable students to act on their values, to recognize and defend positions, to be comfortable with change and to think in terms of alternatives. Content experiences help expand the learner's social awareness and responsibilities, as do work experiences sponsored by business, agencies and institutions of the wider community.

Evaluation in this community is ongoing. It is designed to help students assess their quality of learning, motivation and competence in terms of intellectual, character and personal goals. There is a place for failure, for frustration, for successes and for beginning anew. Contrast this with evaluation and its meaning today—the stress on marks, grades, labeling. As students become involved, there is freedom to identify new situations, to deal with them and to adjust behavior

according to new insights. Such experiences lead young learners to the awareness that to be an adult doesn't mean you don't have to learn anything any more, but rather what you learn will be more complex and potentially more rewarding. They work toward gaining an intellectual, emotional and physical inner strength through experiences of reflection, self-discipline, self-assessment, self-respect and the courage of deep inner convictions. Ongoing, open, nonpersonal evaluations develop their own confidence so eventually they direct their own growth—a growth that reflects their uniqueness and adds to the strength they need to keep on growing.

In the horizontal dimension of learning, these communities address the reality that every learner is a private and a public person, one who relates to home and society, to the worlds of recreation and work, to private thoughts and mass media.

Besides learning, there is a value placed on **service**, on being responsive to the needs of others. Realizable goals then become:

1. The creation or sustaining of a community where staff needs are matched with parent-adult-student needs to bring about growth.
2. Sensitivity to the existence of the problems of justice, weakness, breakdown in our systems, suffering, racism and respect for all life is promoted and encouraged through limitless experiences and opportunities.
3. All actions and experiences witness that the educational community is a community living out its pledge to be a center of service which reaches out to individual and surrounding community needs.
4. Ongoing deepening of the sensitivity of each group to the needs of the other and encouragement and facilitation of individual and group response, where possible, is present through many opportunities to both give and receive help.
5. People resources are tapped in articulating the potential of being helped—of being the helper so as actually to experience the pros and cons of each one.
6. Problem solving is valued—the difficulties of service orientation and the difficulty of growth in such a conviction are lived out.

Besides learning and service, a rather high priority is placed on coping skills. There is on-going preparation in the skills of human relations, in dealing with uncertainties, in learning to choose wisely among alternatives, in communicating concerns, hopes and aspirations. Since members of an educational community are open to all human experience, forming relationships is not a simple process, nor a goal to be reached in a day. It is a reality that is among other things, dynamic, difficult, painful, rewarding, stretching, growing, satisfying and often even annoying. People change, and so do circumstances. Some days are better than others. Each day provides new experiences to sharpen awareness of new ways and means to build relationships, to better the quality of living by developing skills of listening, reflecting, discerning, responding, celebrating. The focus in the educational communities is never on a building or an institution, but on people—people acting together responsibly and humanly in building quality relationships. With shared responsibility comes shared decision making and shared wisdom. When people who are affected by a decision are actively involved in the experience of the decision-making process, they claim ownership for the end results and there is greater hope for the quality of the outcome.

Therefore, parents and learners have a significant role in education, in problem solving—in being support. There must necessarily exist a greater climate of trust and love where people are free to express their fears, needs, hopes and vision. Accountability, enrichment, concern for one another, clear communication, sharing of resources—people-community-things— gives a feeling of belonging and reciprocal expectations and responsibilities.

When people who are affected by a decision are actively involved in the experience of the decision-making process, they claim ownership for the end results and there is greater hope for the quality of the outcome.

Lastly, an educational community provides time for its people to reflect, to ponder, to listen, to situate themselves in circumstances that afford those experiences not as luxuries, but as necessities. Time is given for persons to reflect on life, ponder it, wonder at it, celebrate it, integrate it with their own inner feelings and convictions. Individual differences are seen as a strength. All members show respect for each other in an atmosphere of open support and encouragement where values can be tried out, rejected, experienced and shared.

This is not so unrealistic a vision. Many dimensions of this educational community already exist in numer-ous programs and schools, and on many levels. I know they cut across several of your own individual interests and are representative of aspects of what you are already doing. There are seeds of this in Outward Bound programs, distributive educational programs, continuing education, mainstreaming, interdisciplinary programs and alternative schools; each exhibits characteristics of the community that I describe. I believe that all of us who understand and participate in this kind of learning must work toward making it a reality that can be lived and enjoyed by as broad a population as possible. If these ideals are to be attained, it is incumbent on you to work toward change in the formal educational establishment.

It can happen. These changes can come about because of people like you, because of your beliefs, because of your belief in yourself, because you are willing to risk, willing to assume leadership, willing to fail, then try again. They will come about because you are dissatisfied with schooling that is confined to a classroom and conducted in an information-bank manner. They will come to be because you see yourselves as life-learners, people persons, bridge builders, team members, educational leaders, facilitators of growth and change. They will come about because you are enthusiastic, caring, willing to make waves—waves that ensure philosophies of education that place the learner first become operative, and all other considerations assume a secondary position. They will come about because you are aggressive in trying to secure for a future generation philosophies and styles of living and learning that are rooted in conviction and are not always reactionary.

Such communities will come about because you have the courage of your convictions. Through the experiences you provide, you will demonstrate the belief that it is your mission to open young people and young adults to the world and to life, to the wonder and beauty of nature, to the diversity and richness of art, to the conquests of science and technology, to deep thought and reflection, to the variety of civilizations, to the joys of friendship and giving oneself to others. Such is not attained overnight, but it is your task and my task, for it is better to envision what has to be done and to orient ourselves toward this goal—to have tried, and perhaps failed, then never to have tried at all. Our task is ever to foster the growth and development of all persons—men and women truly present to their world, intelligently aware of the conditioning to which the human person is subjected and willing to face up to changing realities and operate responsibly within them. We know more and more that there are no ready-made answers. But while changes are deep, we can do our part by remaining committed to education — education in the broadest sense of the word, education for our times and for the future.

264

Futurology and Experiential Education

by John D. Haas

*"At a moment of ripeness,
the unseen will become visible,
the unthinkable thought,
the unactable enacted;
and by the same token,
obstacles that seem insurmountable
will crumble away."*

--Lewis Mumford
*The Transformations
of Man,* 1956.

No matter how probable future forecasts are or how likely the scenarios, *expect surprises.* This said, what can be gleaned from the future's literature that is pertinent to the endeavors of experiential educators? Two considerations precede a direct response to this question. One is a general statement staking out the ground peculiar to experiential education. Second is a range of perspectives one might use in envisioning the future.

John D. Haas is a professor of education at the University of Colorado in Boulder.

The Territory

It appears that historically "experiential education" is a term applied to at least three realms of educational thought and practice: 1) as a psychological learning theory (i.e. the reconstruction of personal experience based on a cycle of reflective thought), 2) as a philosophical theory drawing primarily on educational progressivism, but also borrowing some justification from educational reconstructionism -- both outgrowths of the tradition of pragmatism, and 3) as a potpourri of projects, programs, curricula, courses, methods, and practices.

A cursory look at the contemporary literature on experiential education suggests that educators in this field emphasize some or all of the following aspects:

1. out-of-classroom/school encounters or activities, which occur in a learning environment such as the community, nature/wilderness, or real-world workplaces,
2. learning by responding to a challenge or problematical situation, the outcome of which is some efficacious

form of personal or collective action,

3. the combination of affect, cognition and psychomotor activity in a context that promotes the development of personal and social coping skills,

4. learning under *optimal* stress, risk, ambiguity, dissonance, curiosity, and arousal, and

5. use of motivational techniques such as ritual, ceremony, myth, esprit de corps, membership, and group solidarity, in combination with personal existential techniques such as contemplation, introspection, mediation, journal reflections, and other "aloneness/at-one-ness" processes.

Perspectives on the Future

How one views the future is crucially dependent on one's sense of time, from past-to-present-to-future and on one's reading of history with respect to the continuum from continuity to change to discontinuity (as in a social revolution). From these factors, three perspectives on the future (i.e. three types of futurists) seem to emerge; the Extrapolationist, the Transformationist; the Transformationist.

The **Extrapolationist** sees present-to-future events and scenarios as the uninterrupted continuation of past-to-present trends. She/he is a momentum theorist, where past direction and momentum extend into the present and carry forward into the future, where the status quo is preferred over other visions, and where continuity through time is the norm.

A **Transitionist** views change as a very gradual process in which evolution rather than revolution is the rule. Significant changes in civilizations or ways of life take many decades or even centuries to occur, as for example, in the transition from agrarian society to industrial society.

Lastly comes the **Transformationist** who looks for the radical disjunctions in history, those dramatic and traumatic changes we call revolutions. A society rises and falls, peaks and wanes, goes through cycles from birth to maturity to crisis to death, to rebirth which is the transformed "new age" aborning, the phoenix bird rising from the ashes of the ancient regime.

Implications of Selected Futures for Experiential Education

I. The current popularity of the field of futurology owes much to the works of Alvin Toffler, especially his initial book, *Future Shock* (1970). In 1980 he came out with his most ambitious undertaking, *The Third Wave,* an analysis of three historical waves of change in Western societies: Wave I -- Agricultural Revolution, Wave II (now passed its crest) -- Industrial Revolution, and Wave II (just building toward its crest) -- Communications Revolution.

As Wave III rises and forms a new wave, the kind of education (not necessarily schooling) called for will be:
--less formal
--less expensive
--less wasteful
--more individualized
--more realistic
--more humane
--more fun
--lifelong

Much of today's school curricula will be handled by the new and emerging communication technologies, freeing teachers and other educators to coordinate student learning in a variety of contexts such as home, community, workplace, marketplace, museums, recreation sites, and of course, schools.

Because of such persistent problems as personal mental health, interpersonal conflict, and intergroup antagonisms, Third Wave educators will devote much time and effort to helping people learn intra- and interpersonal skills. These will include a variety of psychotechnologies (e.g. yoga, meditation, psychotherapy) as well as a number of social-psychological processes (e.g. conflict management, mediation, consensus strategies).

II. Elliot Seif at Temple University calls for a "new curriculum for a new age" and advocates ten emphases:

1. mastery of technology
2. cooperative living
3. basic survival skills
4. developing life options
5. self-directed learning
6. critical, creative thinking; problem-solving; decision-making

7. communication skills
8. nation/world citizenship: issues and skills
9. value-moral education
10. human dignity (people matter)

III. In a current bestseller, *Megatrends (1982)*, John Naisbitt describes ten broad shifts in American society, not all of which have important ramifications for education. In discussing the movement from industrial society to information society, he observes that "we are drowning in information but starved for knowledge."(24) The solution to this seeming paradox is selection coupled with synthesis.

Another shift is from forced technology to high tech/high touch. Here Naisbitt makes two points: 1) that industrial society is based on mass production of uniform products, and 2) that the new high technology is accompanied by a compensating concern for "high touch," the human response. For example, at the same time intensive care units in hospitals became high technology marvels, the hospice approach to death also gained momentum. In education, the shift to the use of computers (especially microcomputers) will be accompanied by high touch moves such as "being out in nature" and "teaching values and motivation, if not religion."(47)

There is a shift occurring from reliance on institutional help to self-help or self-reliance. Americans are beginning "to disengage from the institutions that had disillusioned them and to relearn the ability to take action on their own."(13) A companion change is away from representative democracy and toward participatory democracy. This is a grass-roots, "bottoms-up," radical approach to social reform, that affirms that "people whose lives are affected by a decision must be part of the process of arriving at that decision."(159)

Naisbitt argues that Americans are gradually abandoning hierarchical forms of organization in favor of networks. "The failure of hierarchies to solve society's problems forced people to talk to one another -- and that was the beginning of networks.... Simply stated, networks are people talking to each other, sharing ideas, information, and resources."(191-192)

IV. In a recent Club of Rome report, **No Limits to Learning (1979)**, the authors build a case for fostering human learning of the "Innovative Type."(10) They argue that today in all nations there exists a "human gap" which came about as the result of several factors: the rapidity of change, the growing complexity of social problems (a "crisis of crises"), and the inability of humans to cope with crisis and change due to a reliance on "Maintenance

---

"The new high technology is accompanied by a compensating concern for 'high touch,' the human response."

Type" learning. Maintenance learning "is the acquisition of fixed outlooks, methods, and rules for dealing with known and recurring situations..., the type of learning designed to maintain an existing system or an established way of life."(10) In contrast, "Innovative" learning is more suited to "long-term survival, particularly in times of turbulence, change, or discontinuity,... It is the type of learning that can bring change, renewal, restructuring and problem reformulation..."(10) The two key features of innovative learning are anticipation and participation. Anticipation, in contrast to adaptation, is "an orientation that prepares for possible contingencies and considers long-range future alternatives."(10) Participation is an attitude of seeking to maximize the sharing of decisions by cooperation, dialogue, and empathy.

V. In his provocative *An Incomplete Guide to the Future (1976)*, Willis Harman forecasts a "learn-and-planning society" which would promote 1) "individual growth in awareness, creativeness, adaptability, curiosity, wonder, and love" and 2) participation "as a partner with nature in the further evolution of the human species on earth."(125) He urges "replacement of the

Protestant compulsive work ethic with a ... work-play-learn ethic."(125) Harman argues that "citizens cannot develop or participate fully in a society unless they have opportunities to grow intellectually and emotionally," and that such opportunities must be provided "by all institutions -- by the home and place of employment as well as by schools and the government."(131)

VI. Probably the best known educational futurist is Indiana University's Harold Shane who has written a number of books and articles on the future of education and whose current work (with M. Bernadine Tabler) is *Educating for a New Millenium*. (1981) In this work it is assumed that the overarching goals of "a curriculum that anticipates tomorrow" are basic survival skills and development of human potential both intra- and interpersonal. As one aspect of the proposed curriculum, Shane and Tabler recommend "incorporating real world experiences," by which they mean "extending learning into the real world with its present and future problems,... (involving) genuine student participation in society's problems and processes."(88) This they suggest is appropriate at all grade levels and for all learners -- children, youth and adults.

VII. Finally, on the basis of extensive reading in the futures literature, this writer has gleaned the following short list of high-mileage concepts for designing educational futures:

1. spatial/temporal holistics: the study of time and space dimensions of reality and existence; that is, past, present and future in local to global to outer and inner space environments

2. psychotherapeutic and human relations skills: these are the necessary elements in creating peace -- in heart, home, workplace, and world

3. systems orientation: everything and everyone is related to and interacts with everyone else and everything else

4. multiple options: of teaching methods, of learning modes, of educational environments

5. communications media: technology as servant of human need, software and hardware, personal and communal modes

6. living is learning: cycles, evolution, growth, the continuous reconstruction of experience in individual and collective consciousness

Clearly, then, there is both a considerable fit as well as a degree of incompatibility between the field of experiential education and selected futures. Perhaps the way to envision the future social roles of experiential education is a complement to certain trends and as a necessary compensatory element for other forecasts. For example, experiential education seems consonant with and complementary to such trends as providing individuals with multiple living/learning options or with less formal, more realistic, more humane educational programs. Similarly, experiential education's emphasis on getting people out of institutions and out of routines would seem to be a useful balance and compensating factor to such trends as greater use of technology and the tendencies toward passivity and spectatorship in many leisure pursuits. In either case, experiential educators can view the future as both challenge and opportunity, while yet allowing for those inevitable, unexpected occurrences.

References

- Botkin, James W., Elmandjra, Mahdi, and Malitza, Mircea, *No Limits to Learning,* New York, NY: Pergamon Press, 1979
- Harman, Willis W., *An Incomplete Guide to the Future,* New York, NY: Simon and Schuster, 1976, p. 125
- Naisbitt, John, *Megatrends,* New York, NY: Warner Books, Inc., 1982.
- Seif, Elliot, "Dare We Build a New Curriculum for a New Age?" (mimeo), Paper presented at Education Section Conference, World Future Society, Minneapolis, MN, October 18, 1979.
- Shane, Harold G., with M. Bernadine Tabler, *Educating for a New Millenium,* Bloomington, IN: Phi Delta Kappa, 1981.
- Toffler, Alvin, *Future Shock,* New York, NY: Random House, 1970.
- Toffler, Alvin, *The Third Wave,* New York, NY: William Morrow and Co., 1980.

Editors Note:
Several times, this editor has been in the difficult position of reporting on what happened at the annual AEE conference. This time, my job has been made easy. Kathryn

Nelson of St. Louis was asked to close the conference with a synthesis of what had occurred there. The following was what she read aloud at the closing ceremony on Sunday morning.

The Legend of the 11th Annual Conference - AEE

And the people of Experiental Education
    did come together
Singing people, laughing people
  Searching people, thinking people
    Working people, studying people
      Strong people, talented people
        Thoughtful people, planning people
          Healthy people, running people
            Eating people, swimming people
              Climbing people, speaking people
                Creative people, stretching people
Dancing the dance of love in the sunshine
    And they did study and ponder
    And reflect and share
And the air was filled with music and talking and
    laughing
    And with hoping and growing and touching
We sang songs of joy and hope and faith
    But we never forgot the clouds of fear
    that gathered around us and threatened our
    very being
There were some who were inspired
    Some who challenged
Some who stored in their pockets
    precious ideas to be nurtured and adapted
    and tested
Some made new resolves - to sing more, to write
    more, to study more, and to be more political
To spend more time doing the things they love,
    promises to take time to take the gifts a
    child has to give ...to keep the magic alive.
And there was much swapping of "How to"
    "How come" and "What for"
And hours did bubble and boil and simmer
    with new ways 'a borning from those
    daring to come close to the "Creative Edge"

And notebooks were filled and pamphlets
    squirreled away and cards were exchanged
New friendships made and networks expanded
We had looked back to our roots
    celebrated the here and now
    and strained toward a vision of the future
    as we moved toward the frontiers
    of creativity
Those back home will ask
    "What was it all about?"
What shall we tell them?
Shall we say, "It was about Growth and Hope
    and Love and Celebration"
"It was about music and movement
    and thinking and striving"
"It was about change and new directions"
"It was about creativity and yeast"
"It was about healing and making things new"
"It was about connectedness and wholeness"
"It was about images and symbols and
    powerful words..."
Or perhaps just say...
    "It was about love and reconciliation;
    empowering and renewal
About strength and weakness - About
    life and trust and faith
About dedication to our Causes"

And so we came - and now we will go
Tomorrow Williams Bay and George Williams
    College will look the same

But we who came will never be quite the same

           Halleluja and Amen.

INTERNATIONAL PERSPECTIVES

Experiential Learning in Revolutionary and Post-Revolutionary China

by Richard J. Kraft

"All genuine knowledge originates in direct experience," wrote China's most important education theorist, Mao Tse-Tung in his famous essay *On Practice* in 1937 (Mao Tse-Tung, 1968:8). One year later, Mao's American educational counterpart, John Dewey, wrote *Experience and Education* (Dewey, 1963), his treatise on learning through experience as opposed to learning only from texts and teachers in the classroom. Both the People's Republic of China and the United States of America have experimented with various forms of experience-based learning in the forty years since those essays were written, but without question, the lengths to which this "progressive" movement went were vastly greater in China than in the United States.

Traditional Chinese Education

Traditional Chinese education was an elitist system largely based on Confucian classics. Difficult examinations, following long years of study, effectively limited it to the upper classes. Contact with the West in the mid-19th century and the defeat by the Japanese in 1895, followed by the founding of the Republic in 1911, led to modifications in the traditional educational system as the Chinese saw the increasing need for skilled government officials to run the country. John Dewey and Bertrand Russell both

Dick Kraft is a professor in the School of Education at the University of Colorado, Executive Director of AEE, and a member of Colorado State Board of Education.

visited China in the early part of this century and many Western ideas were adopted, but the system remained basically elitist, with the vast majority of the population (upwards of 90%) remaining illiterate and without any formal education whatsoever.

Early Communist Experiments

The Chinese Communists did not wait to gain control of the whole nation to begin experimentation with a new system of education. Following the Long March in 1934 and 1935, the Communists structured the new educational system in North Shensi province. The system was to be for the masses, and although there were primary and middle schools as well as higher educational institutions, a whole range of non-formal educational processes were set in motion during those years. It is these non-formal educational processes, which I have labeled experience-based learning, that will be addressed in this paper.

In *Red Star Over China* (1972), his classic work on the Long March, Edgar Snow comments on the search for and sharing of knowledge among the soldiers not on front line duty. Everyone was a teacher and everyone a learner, prompting observers in Yenan to comment that the area seemed like a big elementary school. Many of the non-formal schooling processes experimented with in the Cultural Revolution of 1966-76 were first begun in the late thirties and early forties around Yenan. Wall newspapers and posters, classes in the factories, drama groups in the countryside "educating" the peasants, discussion groups in the fields, factories and homes, and special literacy classes were but a few of the non-formal educational activities started at Yenan.

Mao's Education Theories

It was also during this time that many of Mao Tse-Tung's most important educational works were written in his cave home in Yenan. Perhaps his most important work was his essay, *On Practice*, referred to at the start of this paper. In it, Mao lays down the basic thesis that practice takes precedence over theory, a position which was to be accepted and rejected in regular swings of the pendulum for the next forty years in the formal and non-formal educational systems.

The location of where learning should take place was also a major theme in the essay, with Mao once again sounding like John Dewey in his emphasis upon the need to escape the confines of the classroom and enter into the real world.

"Whoever wants to know a thing has no way of doing so except by coming into contact with it, that is, by living (practicing) in its environment." (Mao Tse-Tung, 1968:7)

This point became not only the basis for the initial experiments in Yenan to break away from the formal, traditional school structure, but continued to serve as a basis for many of the reforms of the Cultural Revolution in which, at times, it appeared that "education" occurred only outside the classroom, and that anything done in the schools was but "mere intellectualism."

"One cannot have direct experience of everything; as a matter of fact, most of our knowledge comes from indirect experience...what is indirect experience for me is direct experience for other people. Consequently, considered as a whole, knowledge of any kind is inseparable from direct experience." (Mao Tse-Tung, 1968:8)

It is a matter of emphasis, however, throughout Chinese educational history as to which, direct or indirect, experience should be emphasized, with Mao and the radicals emphasizing the direct, and the revisionists or conservatives emphasizing the indirect.

The great Brazilian educational philosopher, Paolo Friere, in his *Pedagogy of the Oppressed* discusses the importance of a praxis in which to "speak a true word is to transform the world." (Friere, 1973:75) Mao makes a similar point that

"The world's largest nation effectively 'deschooled' itself several years prior to Ivan Illich coining that phrase."

not only was knowledge to be directly experienced, but it was also to lead to revolutionary practice. Friere put it this way: When action occurs without reflection it becomes mere activism, and when reflection occurs without action, the word becomes an "alienated and alienating blah." (Friere, 1973:76)

Mao and the Gang of Four as representatives of the radical educational faction recognized this contradiction, but chose to emphasize action, at what the revisionists regarded as a severe cost to reflection, while Liu Shao-chi and Teng Hsiao-Ping chose an emphasis upon reflection at great cost to revolutionary practice. It was during the Cultural Revolution that the emphasis upon "doing" in the Marxist dialectic reached its zenith, and it has been since Vice Premier Teng's April 22, 1978 speech on education that the emphasis has dramatically shifted to "knowing." But that is getting ahead of the story.

Education and the "Great Leap Forward"

The "two lines" in education were present in the earliest days of the Chinese communist party and struggle between them has continued unabated up to the present day. However, it wasn't until the Great Leap Forward in 1958, that substantive, experiential modes of learning once again became the focus, as they had some twenty years earlier in Yenan. The Central Committee of the Party issued an important document in June of 1958, titled *Education Must be Combined with Productive Labour*, which was the first post-liberation educational document directly dealing with experience-based learning for the formal and non-formal educational systems of China.

"We insist on the educational principle of all-round development. We consider that the only method to train human beings in all-round development is to educate them to serve working-class politics and combine education with productive labour...The chief mistake or defect in our educational work has been the divorce of education from productive labour...Because the principle of combining education with productive labour is beginning to go into operation, with schools setting up their own factories and farms, and factories and agricultural co-operatives establishing their own schools on a large scale, the phenomenon of students who are at the same time workers and peasants, and of workers and peasants who are students at the same time is beginning to appear." (Fraser, 1965: 293-297)

This was also the time that the beginnings of decentralization were to be observed in the Chinese educational system, and the attack on "professional" teachers, which was to reach violent proportions ten to fifteen years later was started. Half-work, half-study schools were begun, affirmative action programs for children of peasant families were started at the universities, and students became involved in all kinds of industrial activities, including the famous or infamous "back yard blast furnaces." From a foreign capitalist perspective, the Great Leap Forward was an unmitigated disaster, but from the perspective of Mao and other revolutionaries, it helped to bring about a raised level of consciousness on the part of peasants, who for the first time had some of the veil of mystery ripped away from the processes of modernization and industrialization. This process is what has come to be known as "conscientizacao," or critical consciousness, in which the peasant comes to understand himself and his society. Friere and his followers have capitalized on the lessons learned during the Great Leap Forward in their work with peasant cultures in other Third World countries.

Experience-based learning suffered in the early sixties, as revisionists led by Liu Shao-Chi attacked the economic failures of the Great Leap Forward, and branded the various experimental educational programs started as second-class, inferior institutions, while at the same time exploiting their existence to create a dual system, with full-time schools on the Soviet model for the elites, and half-work, half-study schools for the proletariat. The revolutionaries were increasingly concerned that the young people who had not grown up in the revolutionary period, but had only known comparative security and better living standards, would lose or had never gained

a revolutionary zeal, and that the "revisionists" with their continued emphasis upon a Soviet elitist educational model were helping to perpetuate these problems.

The Cultural Revolution

The Great Proletarian Cultural Revolution was the result of numerous internal and external forces, which have been dealt with in great detail by numerous Chinese and foreign scholars. We shall only concern ourselves here with those documents and actions which affected non-formal approaches to education during the critical period of Chinese educational history. The date May 7, 1966 has become one of the most important dates in Chinese history. On that date Mao gave one of his most important speeches, in which among other things he stated:

"While their main task is to study, they should, in addition to their studies, learn other things, that is, industrial work, farming and military affairs. They should also criticize the bourgeoisie. The period of schooling should be shortened, education should be revolutionized, and the domination of our schools by bourgeois intellectuals should by no means be allowed to continue." (Mao Tse-Tung, 1966)

By mid-1966 almost all schools, colleges and universities had stopped offering formal instruction, and the buildings were turned into centers for the discussion of politics and revolutionary practice. Thus the world's largest nation effectively "deschooled" itself several years prior to Ivan Illich's coining that phrase. (Illich, 1970) Whether the political, economic and educational chaos, which was wrought by the Red Guards in the next few years could be called experience-based learning is a matter of some debate, as it appears that most of what went on was in the nature of intellectual posturing and political rhetoric, rather than actively involving young people in the ongoing work of the society.

One aspect of the Red Guards' activities presaged Maurice Gibbons' idea of a "Walkabout" as a rite of passage for American youth. Gibbons took his idea from the Australian film, Walkabout, and suggested that contemporary youth in developed societies desperately needed a meaningful rite of passage, and that this could best be achieved through five basic challenges which students would be re-

"It is, no doubt, stretching the comparison too far to say that the Red Guards were on their own Walkabout, but the excitement of moving outside the classroom walls, trips to Peking for political action, working in the countryside,... and perhaps for the first time having a real sense of political and personal power is very similar to the excitement caused by Gibbon's ideas when they first hit the American press."

quired to complete before High School graduation. These challenges were:

1. **Adventure:** a challenge to the student's daring, endurance, and skill in an unfamiliar environment.
2. **Creativity:** a challenge to explore, cultivate, and express his own imagination in some aesthetically pleasing form.
3. **Service:** a challenge to identify a human need for assistance and provide it; to express caring without expectation of reward.
4. **Practical Skill:** a challenge to explore a utilitarian activity, to learn the knowledge and skills necessary to work in that field, and to produce something of use.
5. **Logical Inquiry:** a challenge to explore one's curiosity, to formulate a question or problem of personal importance, and to pursue an answer or solution systematically and, wherever appropriate, by investigation. (Gibbons, 1974)

It is, no doubt, stretching the comparison too far to say that the Red Guards were on their own Walkabout, but the excitement of moving outside the classroom walls, trips to Peking for political action, working in the countryside, writing wall-posters, conducting political action in the factories and communes, and perhaps for the first time having a real sense of political and personal power is very similar to the excitement caused by Gibbons' ideas when they first hit the American press. The major difference, however, between the two societies is that the Red Guards had the political power structure on their side in their attempt to break down the walls of the school and deschool the society, while American students found only a few national commissions on their side, and the vast majority of the political, economic and educational

establishments firmly opposed to much change in the status quo. Thus, while Chinese adolescents were taking power into their own hands, American youth were being forcefully herded back into their schools, and if the message didn't get through clearly enough, the National Guard was called out to deal forcefully with the threat. When the excesses of the Red Guards became too great for even their revolutionary elders, they too were returned to their classrooms, but not until one of the most interesting, and possibly disastrous, educational experiments in history had been conducted.

Experience-based Learning

As part of the continuing process at breaking down the school walls, the three-in-one alliances of workers or peasants, Liberation Army members and teachers and students were formed in 1967 to work out the new educational system. At this time, many schools formed their own factories or established direct links with factories. University students went out to factories and construction projects to carry out research and investigations, resulting in proposals for mergers of factories and universities into a new communal arrangement, which would effectively break down the ivory-tower nature of academia. It was also at this time that the decentralization moves reached their peak, with attempts made to adapt the curriculum to the needs of each local school. In addition to decentralizing the curriculum, it was also made simpler, with a stress placed on a combination of theory and practice. Courses were merged or

276

abolished, with the following five courses remaining at the primary level: productive labour, military training and physical culture, revolutionary literature and art, arithmetic, and politics and language. At the secondary level, in addition to productive labour, military training, and revolutionary literature, Mao Tse-Tung Thought and agriculture were added. These latter two courses were to combine all of Chinese history and political thought in the case of Mao's Thought, and in the case of agriculture, the course was to be a practical application of mathematics, physics, chemistry and economic geography. All other courses were dropped from the curriculum.

It was also during this time that Mao revived his phrase, "Serve the People," with the resultant campaign to send city youth to the countryside. Students soon learned that the correct response as to where they would like to work was, "wherever I am needed," and with that, tens of thousands were sent to the frontiers and into the poor rural areas to work with the peasants. This caught on with the young, somewhat in the same manner as the Peace Corps ca__red the attention of American youth, but ___ riots in Shanghai in 1979, and the fact that l__ numbers of youth secretly returned to t__ ity are evidence that, in spite of the initial e__ _ment over the change to combine education __ productive labour and put one's theoretical __ _ning into practice, a large portion of the students were not wholeheartedly involved in this non-formal schooling effort.

Two institutions were started during the Cultural Revolution, which were specifically geared to out-of-school, non-formal, experience based learning. The first of these was the May 7 cadre schools in which the initial emphasis was upon "thought rectification" and political study, and the attendance was seen as somewhat of a punishment for inappropriate bureaucratic behavior and attitudes. In recent years, the schools have taken on more of an in-service training function in which hard physical labor is meant to give the bureaucrats an empathy and understanding of the problems of the Chinese peasant population.

Mao Tse-Tung, in his directive of July 21, 1968, praised the Shanghai Machine Tool Plant No. 1 for their attempts at combining theory and practice in what was to become known as the July 21st Worker's University. These institutions

of "higher education," operate in a factory setting to provide full-time training in the classroom and on-the-job to prepare engineers and technicians. Students are selected by their fellow workers, and many classes are taught by workers, not just "stinking intellectuals." All students have work experience before receiving the advanced training, and all continue to receive their full pay and benefits while attending school. The reason the university title could be applied to this unique job related institution is the fact that scientists and engineers from the universities collaborated directly with the worker-teachers in planning the curriculum and in teaching. (*China Reconstructs,* 1973)

Some 67 polytechnic institutes or universities established contacts with 2,825 factories, mines and people's communes during the Cultural Revolution. It wasn't just technical and engineering subjects which were taken outside the traditional classroom setting. The humanities also used society as a workshop, with students going out among the people to carry out their research projects. At Tsinghoua University in 1974 alone, "worker-peasant-soldier" graduates carried out 360 projects in practical work and according to the reports, "Achieved better results than any intake of students of the former, pre-cultural revolution university had ever been able to obtain." (Houa in *Prospects*)

At the middle school level, factories run by schools produced a broad range of products. At the Yehkochuang village middle school, the students produced an insect lamp which was a boon to farming because it destroys dozens of insects. Students learned not only basic theories, but in addition, they learn the "practical needs of the countryside."(Hsueh in *Prospects*) Accountancy is taught in the marketing of the products, mechanics are trained on the farm machinery, and all kinds of mathematics are taught in the fields of the commune.

Graduation examinations also took on a practical side during the Cultural Revolution with students from Peking University being sent out to solve practical problems, rather than taking final examinations.

"Formerly the students racked their brains to write graduation papers in the library or study rooms. But after graduation their papers were pigeonholed in the library...The topics now come from scientific research tasks set by government departments, from urgent problems in socialist construction and research items raised by the university's own factories." (Yi in *Prospects*)

These are but a few of the many types of practical, on-the-job, non-formal, experience-based types of experiments carried out during the Cultural Revolution. In the final section of this paper, we shall turn our attention to what has happened to these reforms since Mao's death in 1976, the arrest of the Gang of Four, and more particularly since Vice-Premier Teng's address on education on April 22, 1978.

Education under Teng

With the "Revolution of the Superstructure" in 1976, dramatic changes were begun in the society and the educational system. Clark Kerr has outlined the major contradictions between the two lines, and the current position of the government on each.

- "Red" versus "expert," with the current emphasis on the expert and thus on meritocracy.
- Modernization versus egalitarianism, with the current emphasis upon modernization but not without an ongoing "tug of war."
- Rural versus urban, with the current emphasis on urban and industrial development.
- Discipline versus constant mass participation (even mob rule), with the current emphasis upon discipline.
- Trained intellect versus political spirit, with the current emphasis on the training of intellect.
- The blooming of a "hundred flowers" versus the single correct "line," with the current emphasis on a carefully and cautiously chosen "hundred flowers."
- Bureaucrats versus "the people," with the bureaucrats again in an enhanced position.
- Academic versus revolutionary (social justice in admissions, creation of the "new man," politics triumphant) models of education, with the present emphasis almost totally on the academic model.
- Hard work versus revolutionary politics, with "hard work" and "promote production" the current themes. (Kerr, 1978:3)

Kerr has captured the major changes in the educational system, changes which have been documented by countless other observers of the Chinese educational system in the past few years. Vice-Premier Teng's speech at the National Educational Work Conference was given at the time of Kerr's visit (1978), and about one month prior to our own visit. That speech is a classic attempt to redefine Mao Tse-Tung thought along obviously revisionist lines, and it was widely reported to us to have been received with great joy and even tears on the part of teachers, who had suffered greatly under the Cultural Revolution.

Teng once again reiterated the fundamental principle of Mao that "education must serve proletarian politics and be combined with productive labour," but went on to claim that the Gang of Four had "willfully distorted and trampled" the principle, causing grave damage to the educational system. He roundly condemned the Gang of Four for not making strict demands on students, and then reiterated another of Mao's dictums, that the students' main task is to study, and as almost an afterthought, said that they should, of course, not just learn book knowledge, but industrial and agricultural production. His emphasis, however, was on "studying," and learning "book knowledge."

A second major area of Teng's concern in his speech was the need to "strengthen revolutionary order and discipline," adding once again that this would lead to a new generation with a socialist consciousness and revolutionize the society. The Gang of Four were accused of making not only "illiterates" but "hooligans," and that the schools under the new period of the "four modernizations" should inculcate a style of "learning diligently, observing discipline, loving physical labour, taking pleasure in helping others, working hard and daring to fight the enemy."

The egalitarian ethic of the Cultural Revolution also took a beating, as Teng stated that "we have to admit the disparity in the abilities and moral qualities of different people, which will surface in the course of their development." From now on, only students who are outstanding on their "moral, intellectual and physical levels" would be permitted to go on for further education, an obvious move towards being "expert" rather than "red" under the new regime.

Of greatest concern to our topic in this paper was Teng's call for a reevaluation of the experience-based learning programs which had

"University students went out to factories and construction projects to carry out research and investigations, resulting in proposals for mergers of factories and universities into a new communal arrangement, which would effectively break down the ivory tower nature of academia."

become such an important part of the education system in the previous decade. He did not directly call for their abandonment, but stated that schools should rethink their time schedules for combining labour and teaching, and the times spent in the rural areas and factories.

Needless to say, this was all that the teachers and administrators needed for one of the most rapid abandonments of an educational reform movement in history. By the time of our visit to China in May and June of 1978, stiff examinations had been reinstituted for university entrance, youth in the countryside were beginning what has turned out to be a mass return to the cities, young people were no longer required to work for two years prior to university attendance, much of the production work in the schools appeared to us to be insignificant or busy-work, and the curriculum had been changed so that considerably less time was spent in agricultural work or production work. "Back to the Basics" was the theme, and although we never heard that exact phrase, teachers and administrators told us time and again of the need for basic reading and computational skills on the part of the "lost generation."

How much of the educational revolution really took hold in the sixties and seventies and how much of it was but a paper reform is difficult to judge, but it does appear that the educational system of the People's Republic of China in 1979 more closely resembles that of many other Third World countries with an emphasis on dictation, discipline and basics, than it does the revolutionary ideals of Mao, Lenin or Castro.

References

- *China Reconstructs,* Peking, July, 1973.
- Dewey, John. *Experience and Education.* New York: Collier Books, 1963.
- Fraser, Stewart (ed.). *Chinese Communist Education.* Nashville: Vanderbilt University Press, 1965.
- Friere, Paolo. *Pedagogy of the Oppressed.* New York: The Seabury Press, 1973.
- Gibbons, Maurice. "Walkabout," *Phi Delta Kappan* (May, 1974), pp. 599-600.
- Houa, Souen. "Combining Theory with Practice," *Prospects* (Vol. 5, No. 4), p. 488.
- Hsueh, Fang. "Visit to a Village Middle School on Peking Outskirts," *Prospects* (Vol. 5, No. 4), p. 496.
- Illich, Ivan. *Deschooling Society.* New York: Harrow Books, 1970.
- Kerr, Clark. "The Great Chinese Cultural Reversal: Education," *Observations on the Relations Between Education and Work in the People's Republic of China.* Berkeley: The Carnegie Council on Policy Studies in Higher Education, 1978.
- Mao Tse-Tung, May 7, 1966 (speech).
- Mao Tse-Tung. "On Practice," *Four Essays on Philosophy.* Peking: Foreign Language Press, 1968.
- Snow, Edgar. *Red Star Over China.* New York: Penguin Books, 1972.
- Yi, Tung. "A New Type of University Graduation Examination," *Prospects* (Vol. 5, No. 4), p. 497.

THE SLOPES OF KILIMANJARO:
Teaching Experientially in Tanzania

by Graeme E. Donnan

Immortalized by Ernest Hemingway, the snows of Kilimanjaro offer Tanzania its greatest claim to fame. Rising abruptly to 19,340 feet, this volcanic massif intrudes upon the neighboring flat and arid plains of the Maasai Steppe. The great bulk and height of Kilimanjaro forces rain from the sky to irrigate its fertile soils where the local WaChagga tribe grow their crops of maize, bananas and vegetables. Within this setting lies the International School Moshi, nestled on the lower slopes of Kilimanjaro amidst coffee plantations and small farms called kihamba.

Northern Tanzania attracts tourists from all over the world. The towns of Moshi and Arusha have become the focus points for these tourists who, armed with cameras, reels of film and a Kiswahili phrasebook, migrate across the national parks and conservation areas like Serengeti and Ngorongoro Crater. Many have saved their nickels and dimes over months or years to

Graeme E. Donnan is a teacher at the International School Moshi in Tanzania.

pay for the holiday of a lifetime in East Africa. For some, the main attraction is a wildlife safari whilst others seek a greater challenge and aspire to climb Kilimanjaro, the highest mountain on the African continent. For the students and teachers of ISM, this rich setting is their backyard, both an adventure playground and a huge classroom for environmental studies.

"The attractions of northern Tanzania read like a catalogue of geographical features clustered together for the sake of convenience."

Disillusioned with the stultified education system in England, I came to Tanzania two years ago ready to commit myself to a thriving private school in a poor socialist

country. It soon became obvious to me and other new teachers that Tanzania was not a land flowing with milk and honey; the country faced acute shortages of food and other basic necessities of life, a problem that was accentuated by a lack of foreign exchange and other economic difficulties.

In spite of the harsh reality of life in Tanzania, expatriates usually live in comparative luxury, with the means to enjoy the recreational opportunities that Tanzania can offer rather than devoting each day to a subsistence style of living that is common to many people of this land.

The majority of students who attend ISM are expatriates supported by an increasing number of Tanzanians who now account for about forty percent of the student population. In all, some thirty-five nationalities are represented within the school but these are predominantly British, American and Scandinavian.

ISM is one of many hundreds of international schools spread across the globe. These schools, and a small number of United World Colleges, tend to cater to an expatriate community who are involved in foreign aid projects, missionary work, or perhaps attached to the diplomatic services. The children of these expatriate workers provide a cosmopolitan enrollment to the school which serves them.

The curriculum of these schools is intended to reflect the international community it serves, but more often than not it is western in its orientation. Because there are so many international schools, their aims and courses of study do vary considerably, but academic assessment usually culminates in the International Baccalaureate Diploma or Certificate. In keeping with a general philosophy that seeks a wholesome rather than purely academic education, those schools which are suitably located usually offer outdoor pursuits in some form.

When I arrived as a new recruit in August 1982, it required no imagination to realize that ISM's location provides a unique potential for pursuing outdoor education through adventure activities and environmental studies. Having been involved in outdoor pursuits for several years I was fully aware of the rewards that mountaineering and wilderness travel can offer the growing adolescent. "Great things are done when men and mountains meet," wrote William Blake (Gnomic Verses), and I have always been inclined to agree. Initially however, I devised an outdoor pursuits programme for each semester based mainly on mountaineering activities with

ISM students and staff rest at Gillman's Point near the summit of Kilimanjaro.

the occasional wildlife safari for added variety. In those early days I did not seek to combine this programme with any aspects of the school's academic work. The physical challenge of a climb on Mount Meru or Kilimanjaro seemed to offer sufficient reward without the need for incorporating practical field studies. Later I was to realise the importance of extending the students' knowledge of their natural environment.

One of the most popular mountain trips at ISM is a five day climb to Uhuru Peak, the summit of Kilimanjaro at 19,340 feet. Each day of the climb becomes progressively harder owing to the effects of altitude which of course makes physical effort an exhausting business. Only rarely do all the students in a group actually reach the summit, despite having participated in other mountain trips. Only the more fit and determined

students complete the final ascent from Kibo Hut at just over 15,000 feet.

All the students on the trip learn skills like navigation and weather forecasting and view features of geomorphology that we discuss in the classroom and those who reach the top also view the summit icefields and the crater of Kibo. Each time I have taken students to the top they have been smitten with a kind of euphoria to know they have climbed the highest peak in Africa by enduring hardships and forming a close relationship with students of other nationalities.

Organizing any activity divorced from the usual school routine presents a number of problems. In Africa, Tanzania in particular, these problems become magnified and often result in the cancellation of what might have been a very worthwhile venture. Obtaining suitable food for a long mountain trip is a major headache as prepackaged and freeze-dried foods are not available. Apart from importing foodstuffs, all items of equipment like boots, rucksacks and sleeping bags have to be bought from abroad and are then subject to over one hundred percent Import Tax. In recent years the weather in East Africa has been quite unreliable with an absence of long rains creating dustbowls reminiscent of Nebraska in the 1920s. Even when the rains do come, the once dusty roads become a quagmire of sticky clay. An essential factor on any excursion whether by foot to the remote parts of the mountain or by vehicle to the national parks, is self-reliance. Assistance of any kind ranging from gas stations to a mountain rescue team is difficult to find. "There is a gas station, but there's no gas. There is a breakdown truck, but it's brokendown. There is a rescue team, but..." To organize outdoor activities of any kind you need an ample share of initiative — a charmed existence also helps.

With any overland safari there is always the element of the unknown in terms of the practical difficulties that are encountered. Acute fuel shortages, road blocks (official and otherwise!), impassable roads, rainy seasons, lack of food, and the vagaries of Tanzanian bureaucracy all conspire to hinder progress. Any activity that requires more than the simplest degree of organization is inevitably beseiged with problems that would be unknown in somewhere like America. Excursions into the remote conservation areas in northern Tanzania may take a party over fifty miles away from the nearest settlement, necessitating total independence with regard to the provision of food and self-help for vehicle breakdown. Even the drive itself is an exercise in endurance over miles of unkept dirt roads, choking passengers with red dust and subjecting them to a roller-coaster ride over ruts and bumps.

With a variety of complexities that are likely to befall even the most well organized activity, it is not surprising that the occasional safari does not go according to plan. On a wildlife safari to Tarangire National Park, apart from the annoyance of being assailed by numerous tetse flies, viewing the abundant game was cut short by a slight mishap with the school's four-ton truck which left it inextricably wedged in a deep sand-drift. Such incidents however, are the bread and butter of a journey in Africa. The students took the event in their stride. With barely a word of complaint, they rallied together to pile stones and sticks in front of the truck's wheels. Whilst pondering over the problem that had befallen us, I briefly recalled a previous occasion when plans were rudely interrupted by a vehicle breakdown. At that time I was in England taking a party of thirty comprehensive school students on a geography trip to the Geological Museum in London. Owing to the gross neglect of our driver, our

The author collects water on the way to Uhuru Peak.

coach ran out of diesel fuel. Despite being marooned for only one hour, these sixteen year old students were quite uncooperative, humorless and impatient. In sharp and pleasant contrast, hardened to the ways of Africa, the students from ISM viewed our plight as an amusing challenge. Several miles from the nearest assistance, amidst lions and elephants, with a tropical sun emptying its 95 degrees of heat upon us, our situation was altogether more serious.

Before continuing the discussion, perhaps I should explain the ending to this story. After six hours of fruitless endeavour, we had only progressed some eight feet or so across the sand drift. Many schemes to move our four tons of truck had been tried and had failed ranging from jacking up the wheels and placing rocks beneath them, to cursing and blasphemy. With darkness soon to descend on this pantomime with usual tropical abruptness, we felt the time had come to summon assistance. Accustomed to the ways of the wilderness, the biology teacher was elected to run the gauntlet of assorted four-legged carnivores and hike the five miles back to the Lodge to find a breakdown truck. Our brave saviour only encountered one pride of lions on his walking safari (fortunately they were not hungry!), and soon returned driving a suitable vehicle to pull us out of the sand.

Any programme for outdoor education will inevitably be unique to some extent as no two environments are exactly alike and the ideas and ex-

The school truck is used to take students on safari.

periences of the teachers involved will always differ. Even so, the attractions of northern Tanzania read like a catalogue of geographical features clustered together for the sake of convenience. The Gregory Rift Valley is probably the dominant feature with its associated landforms like Ol Doinyo Lengai, Ngorongoro Crater and of course Kilimanjaro lying to the east. Having just taught in a large school in an urban environment, arriving in Moshi was like being dropped into a geographical Disneyland. I did not imagine for a moment that I would need to convince other teachers in the school that we should allow students to explore and learn from this rich environment. Aside from organizational problems in terms of transport, fuel shortages and accessibility, the negative attitude of my less enlightened colleagues became an unforseen and unnecessary stumbling block. With a few notable exceptions amongst

the staff, particularly in the biology department, I spent a considerable amount of time trying to persuade teachers that at least for biology and geography, the classroom was not the classroom.

"...as wide as all the world, great, high, and unbelievably white in the sun, was the square top of Kilimanjaro." Captured in these words by Ernest Hemingway, Kilimanjaro is a geographical oddity. Soaring over 16,000 feet above the surrounding plains, the mountain could easily have been built with students in mind to provide mountaineering activities and a cross section of world climatic and vegetation zones. At every height, from the tropical vegetation of the lower slopes up to the lifeless Nival zone, the flora and fauna occupy their own ecological niche, adapting to the harsh conditions.

Realizing that the geography syllabus for my senior students lay all around

Students enjoying the cramped but warm luxury of a hut on Kilimanjaro.

the school just waiting to be used, I set about organizing a combined geography and biology field trip to Barranco Valley on Kilimanjaro. Lying at an altitude of 13,000 feet, this impressive, deeply glaciated valley possesses an abundance of features that bring life to the dull and staid diagrams in textbooks. The logistics of the exercise were not easy. Arranging for porters and carrying food and equipment for eighteen people up a steep, thickly forested ridge over a period of several days can be a headache in more ways than one. But the end result was justification. Students were able to experience a condensed climatic and ecological transect from Equatorial through to near Arctic conditions. Once in the valley, the sky was the limit. Soil profiles, river channel studies, til fabric analysis, weather recordings — a veritable paradise for practical studies in a remote area, rarely if ever frequented by a similar expedition. The amount of knowledge students gained from this experience was only limited by the expertise of the teachers.

At ISM, I have found great benefits in students being able to witness at first hand the features and events of our natural world, and to combine this with practical environmental studies. Addi-

tionally, experience of school safaris to the mountainous regions of northern Tanzania instills in students the desire to preserve our environment so that generations to come will be able to enjoy the mountains, forests and plains of East Africa.

And finally, the benefits that accrue from outdoor education in terms of preparing students for adulthood are enhanced when students are from many cultures and parts of the world. With careful leadership, any group of students that is composed of several nationalities can be woven into a team. The group goal, the one single aim of successfully completing a climb or safari, tends to unite individuals and overcome any personal differences whether social, religious or cultural. This is not to say, however, that each nationality shows equal desire to participate in adventurous exploits, nor does there seem to be equality in terms of physical prowess and sheer determination. As an observation and not a point of criticism, students of African origin generally show little interest in the mountain environment; students from the Indian sub-continent show interest but lack the relentless capacity for endurance and adventure shown by Scandinavians and West Germans. On the whole, I have found Americans and British to be a rather mixed bunch, about whom I cannot easily make such generalizations. Whatever the unique cultural and social background of the students, after a successful trip a feeling of achievement is usually common to all.

ENGLAND'S SCHOOL CONCERN PROJECT:
A Humane Application of Knowledge

by Richard O'Connell

Memories tend to get dulled by constant innovation — especially when the innovations were largely the result of unforeseen circumstances and the fumblings of an insensitive bureaucracy. Because of this tendency, project workers often assume that the point that they have reached was indeed the point that they had originally planned to reach by that time.

Take, for example, the so-called School Concern Project which, six years ago, started up with high hopes and a team consisting of two professional teachers, a youth and community worker, and an Occupational Therapist, backed up by an eager, if inexperienced team of eight full-time able-bodied volunteers. Add on a budget, quite a big budget by British standards. Six years later, the project is healthy, but the professionals have disappeared, the budget is minimal, and the volunteers who now run it are all physically disabled. An accident? Not really, but then it wasn't planned either — though to hear me talking sometimes you would think that we had worked out every little detail from day one to now, and had predicted the exact composition of the 1984-1985 academic year team back in 1978.

The Task

Until 1978, I was employed as the Head of a Unit for children with special learning and behavioural needs which was integrated into a

Richard (Fitch) O'Connell is secretary of the Salford, England Council for Voluntary Service.

Secondary School (11 to 18 year olds) in Oxfordshire, England. I was attracted by an advertisement in one of the national specialist papers which stated that Community Service Volunteers, the national volunteer agency, were looking for a team leader to run their new idea, the "School Concern Project" — a scheme which would aim to investigate the link between craft and design work in schools and the designing and making of aids for physically handicapped people; observe the effect that this would have on the schools; observe the effect that this would have upon the community. Truly, this was to be a "learning through doing" scheme, or as Alec Dickson — founder of CSV put it "a humane application of knowledge."

The Setting

There were a few problems to be sorted out when I was offered the post, not least the fact that the scheme was to be based in the City of Salford. Apart from the fact that in England the distance of two hundred miles — from where I lived to Salford — involves at least three changes of culture and four major changes of regional accent, amounting to a change of dialect — the Salford community appears on first sight to give a new meaning to the word "apathetic." Sadly enough, their new meaning was underlined on second and third sights also. It seemed that the idea was that if it could succeed in Salford, it could succeed anywhere. And there lies the knub of the tale. The project had to be seen not as a seven day — or even two year — wonder, but as a viable model for development in a whole variety of habitats.

To repair some of the damage to the reputa-

"To bring a pioneering educational project into such an environment was either foolhardy, or inspired."

tion of Salford that I have incurred, I should say a little about the city, and to put it into some kind of context. It grew as a result of the boom in trading during the nineteenth century with North America, and was a principle part of the Lancashire cotton industry. The river that runs through the city spawned the World's Industrial Revolution, and the wealth that resulted from the British Empire was largely accrued in industrial cities like Salford in the northwest of England. Unfortunately, the rich people lived on the other side of the river, in Manchester, Salford's rival.

When the British stopped raping and pillaging the rest of the world, and started to face up to the problems of being an overcrowded collection of islands that was now dominated by a world economy that it no longer controlled, cities like Salford — never the prettiest places in Britain, (but then which discarded engine room ever is) — crumbled and fell in on themselves. By the 1950s Salford had the onerous reputation of possessing the worst slums in Europe — and this while Berlin, Cologne, London and Liverpool still had acres of bombed rubble from World War Two. Today, some areas of Salford — including the one in which I write this — have a male unemployment figure in excess of 70% of the population, with female unemployment raising the figure to over 80% overall. The city has little pride in its inner areas. To bring a pioneering educational project into such an environment was either foolhardy, or inspired. It turned out to be inspired. Inspired because the environment was challenging to the point of being hostile, when it wasn't too busy being apathetic. Inspired because the City Authorities, for all their caution, recognized a need to support something which, while perhaps being a little radical, could bring kudos to the City's endeavors nationally. Tragically, the inspiration that also helped towards the final success of the scheme was the simple fact that industrial towns

have a large number of physically handicapped people, industrial accidents accounting largely for the fact that Salford has the highest proportion of *registered* disabled people of any area in Britian. So while there was a tremendous amount against the outcome of the project being successful, there were hidden advantages.

Sample Accomplishments

To document the project in terms of success statistically is a boring and probably unproductive affair; suffice to say that in the first two years over 300 schoolchildren were involved in the production of nearly 250 items of novel design and construction in conjunction with 500 physically handicapped people. Many of the designs were totally original, and some displayed lateral thinking that shamed one or two professional engineers. For example, a small group of professional engineers had been (voluntarily) looking at the problem of total inclusion of blind people playing the game "Bingo" alongside sighted people for a number of years. A somewhat aggressive city councillor challenged our project to solve the problem that the "professionals" hadn't managed in two years. Mischievously I chose a junior group of nine to ten year olds, who solved the problem - quite successfully - in two and a half hours of class time. Their success? They weren't hampered by concepts of technology. They merely saw a problem, and solved it using the materials that were familiar to them (in this case cardboard, paints, scraps of cloth and velcro). The "professionals" had failed by introducing in their designs new techniques to be learnt by the (largely elderly) blind people with which they weren't able to cope. The children approached the problem at their own level which assumed a level of knowledge which *all* the potential users already possessed.

Designing with the Disabled

A further lesson to be learnt from this example, perhaps, lies in the participation of adults other than the teacher in the gaining of experience by the youngsters. During the initial

286

"problem solving" period - the first two and a half hours - it appeared important to part of the solution that someone with knowledge of Braille as well as other scripts for blind people became involved. A local society for the blind was contacted, and the school never got beyond the telephone receptionist, who, having understood the needs of the school, volunteered himself to bring along his Perkins braille typewriter and show the kids its basic functions. This he did with some success, enough in fact, for the schools Parent Teacher Association (PTA) to buy the school its own Perkins Brailler. The children became adept enough to write letters, and consequently developed a school wide 'pen friendship' with a school for blind children in Yorkshire, an adjacent county. More importantly, profound changes of attitude occurred amongst the children because the scheme had brought them into direct contact with blind people; the learning process had occurred at a very direct level, and was never of a second hand nature. This contrasted with the teams' first experience in the project, when it was considered quite proper for the team to suggest problems that disabled people *might* come across, and for the schoolchildren to work out the problems in the comfort of their own classrooms without actually having to come into contact with handicapped people. One teacher, in fact actually forbade that her pupils should meet a physically handicapped person as she thought "That it would be rather macabre." After about two years, it had become apparent that the original description of the scheme, in which school kids were envisaged as "designing aids for disabled people" had become "designing *with* disabled people." And as much as people like me, who can now cheerfully observe from the sidelines, will say "But of course we designed it that way," reason dictates that it was not designed so — otherwise it would have been built into the original working model. Luckily, the original model, with all its imperfections, was flexible. That became a critical factor for it meant that while we were allowing children to participate directly in experiential learning, we were also able to do it for ourselves.

So although we were well aware that we were in a vanguard of radical education within certain fields, we were in fact being taught by the children we purported to teach! Easy enough for us, perhaps, as outsiders, or, at best, catalysts or

"Over 300 schoolchildren were involved in the production of nearly 250 items of novel design and construction in conjunction with about 500 physically handicapped people."

enablers. But how far could this experience develop beyond our direct involvement as a team.

"If it worked in Salford..."

The original scheme was set up as a pilot project. As such we had a limited amount of time to complete our work and to come up with some ideas which, at the least, would satisfy the Government Department that had funded us, and at the best provide a working model that would inspire other groups, possibly even as far away as Scotland, to indulge in the scheme. Direct funding had ceased at the end of 1980, just in time for the beginning of the UN International Year Of Disabled People, which seemed a suitable point to appeal for more funds. Private Enterprise provided another eighteen months of funding which was aimed exclusively at disseminating the information gathered, and in setting up similar projects but without the backup of a local team as had been the case in Salford. I found myself playing on the origins of the project: "Come on", I would say, "if it worked in Salford, of course it will work here!" Some people even believed me!

The immediate benefits educationally were clearly all related to the direct experience of the children in a learning situation that demanded real solutions to real problems. It was this "learning through doing" process that made its impact when we tried to move the idea from the immediate environs of Salford, and started to develop the pilot scheme in other areas - rural areas and the special problems that they faced, and urban developments of a different nature

287

> "The deterioration in direct involvement by disabled people always heralded the demise of a scheme, the result of non-involvement, apathy, or just plain reaction soon resulted in patronisation and a lack of ideas."

than the inner city complexities of Salford. Even while remaining within the British Isles we were able to experience a number of different administrative and interpretive educational systems: the Welsh are more examination orientated than their English counterparts, the Scottish education system is significantly different than the English or the Welsh, and in Ireland the education system of the six counties is different again. Meanwhile the Republic of Ireland presents us with yet another model. Within two hundred miles of Salford all of these different approaches towards providing the schooling needs of children can be experienced, and within urban, suburban and rural areas; within poor communities and within rich ones. The period of dissemination which followed the pilot saw the scheme develop in Wales, Scotland, both sides of the border in Ireland and in many other places in England. Over fifty projects emerged within a year and, though not all lasted for more than one academic year, it was immediately obvious that the scheme was highly adaptable, and could be grafted onto a whole variety of environments. Visitors from other European countries came to observe, notably from France and Germany. A Japanese film crew took the message home with them for young viewers in schools. Inquiries flooded in from many countries, the result of two being invitations to me to help set up similar schemes in Denmark and Sweden. The uniquely simple nature of the exercise seemed to be universally adaptable. Even so, there was a flaw.

Leadership by the Disabled

Left by themselves, some of the schemes appeared to drift quite rapidly away from the mutual participation between able-bodied and disabled people. The deterioration in direct involvement by disabled people *always* heralded the demise of a scheme; the result of non-involvement, apathy, or just plain reaction soon resulted in patronization and a lack of ideas. The exercise soon became, once again, classroom based and, all too often, academic.

One plan was to set up "cells" of interested disabled people in various places who would respond to the inquiries received from their area. Once they had made contact and had started the process, they could be recognized as the organizers - the people who were doing something. They would guarantee their own involvement by organizing it, and would be able to sustain the correct balance between the involved parties. A fine theory! And something, it must be added hastily, which did happen. But not without a great deal of work. In fact, the development of this kind of self-motivated support service proved to be far more complicated and involved than the initial School Concern Project, and had to confront complex issues surrounding unemployment, bereavement and self-esteem. While the information needed to set up a successful school based project by teachers only required the publication of a teaching kit ("Design With Disabled People"), the involvement of disabled people as the instigators has so far produced a handbook, a national pilot study leading to a full scale inquiry, and the production of a video tape aimed at school children but made by disabled people, which gets across a serious message in an amusing way. The two parts of the overall scheme work well together: they actually demand each other.

The following is an extract from the handbook intended for use by disabled people who wish to explore direct participation in school based education, and serves to illustrate the relationship between the involvement of disabled people and experiential learning.

Experiential Education for Survival:
AN IDEA FROM THE THIRD WORLD

by R.M. Kalra

My experience and contacts with educators from various developing countries has led me to believe that formal education does not offer a meaningful solution to the daily life problems of the students in the school system, especially those from the weaker sections of the society. Because the curriculum in the schools as it now exists presents a world which is alien to these students, their disinterest, resulting failure and eventual "dropping-out" should not come as a surprise. A student's interest is aroused only when he perceives something of value in the educational system or sees practical application of the knowledge to be gained.

Functional Education

Education in democratic societies is meant for the benefit of all people and it must be ensured that they become aware of the advantages which education can bring to their lives. The education needed to make democracy work effectively is not just any kind of education, but a system of education that will enable young students to develop skills and acquire knowledge which has a higher probability of producing a better understanding of their environment. Education should also acquaint students with the process of discovery of knowledge. Furthermore, a school curriculum in this context would not lay emphasis on theoretical knowledge that is unrelated to the students daily life, but rather the emphasis would be placed on the application of knowledge to improvement of living condi-

Dr. R.M. Kalra is a Professor in Education at the National Institute of Education, New Delhi, India.

tions and to other aspects of everyday life. It may be called "Functional Education." This concept of Functional Education should not teach peasant cultures of the Third World that their entire past life has been a lie and their value systems must entirely be replaced by one from an alien culture. Rather, "Functional Education" means bringing an extended dimension to their own ways of thinking and building upon what is already there. Only then can the people of developing countries be free to accept the idea of a functional education and not fear domination by it. Functional education thus has to make an attempt to find meaning in the lives of the learners, formulate long range goals to free the individual from the fear of livelihood and grow towards the goals that somehow sustain us during difficult times. Understood in this way, the concept of functional education includes different dimensions of realities of life.

An Example of Functional Education

Taking the above convictions into consideration, I have developed a learning material entitled "Setting up a Small Business" under the project CAPE (Comprehensive Access to Primary Education) financially assisted by UNICEF. This project is an experimental approach and is a sort of alternate system of non-formal education being developed by the National Institute of Education, (Ministry of Education) India.

The booklet narrates a venture of unemployed young boys (14-15) years old - Ram and Shyam - to make a meaningful living as well as learning 3R's by setting up a small business. The booklet is based on discussion with Ram and Shyam about their future prospects. During discussions they decided themselves to open a tea stall as discussed in the capsule 1-1-1. To achieve their objectives, they learn about 3R's in a functional manner. The learning material contains steps such as getting help from various people, learning basic mathematical processes, obtaining a loan from the bank and preparing tea.

The following is an outline of some suggested activities which Ram and Shyam had to take to achieve their objective which was opening a tea stall.

Package 1 - Setting up a small business.
Module   1-1   Ram and Shyam Open a Tea Stall
Sub-Unit 1   Opening a tea stall
Sub-Unit 2   Ram and Shyam learn to add
Sub-Unit 3   Ram and Shyam learn to subtract
Sub-Unit 4   Ram and Shyam learn to multiply
Sub-Unit 5   Ram and Shyam learn to divide
Sub-Unit 6   Calculation Profit and Loss
Sub-Unit 7   Getting a loan from the bank
Sub-Unit 8   Preparation of tea
Sub-Unit 9   Disposal of waste material from the tea stall
Sub-Unit 10   Getting a loan from the bank for new purposes
Sub-Unit 11   Expansion of the Tea Stall

The learning activities related to self-employment have functional literacy as the most important component. In this self-employment episode, "Ram and Shyam Open a Tea Stall," literacy is not imposed on the learner in a formal manner, but a need-based environment has been created so that the learner is motivated to know about the 3R's and develop skills to set up a tea stall. Similarly, some persons may be interested in opening a cycle repair shop, grocery store, vegetable stall and a barber shop, etc. In all the above self-employment ventures, functional literacy is a built in component and may be taken as a motivating factor (hooking device). The decision to establish a small business is that of the learner.

Opening a Tea Stall

As an example, the first sub-unit "Ram and Shyam Open a Tea Stall" is presented. It is a programmed material with EBOs (Expected Behavioral Outcomes), overview and feedback questions.

Ram: Shyambhai, it is 10:00 a.m. You are still sleeping. What is the matter? Haven't you found any job yet?

Shyam: Rambhai, what job? I am still unemployed. Nobody gives me a job. I am poor. Who cares for me?

Ram: Shyambhai, true, but don't lose hope. I am also without a job. If we haven't got a job it is not the end of the world. Let us start some business. We could open a shop.

Shyam: What shop?

Ram: We have some general provision stores in our locality, but it is strange that there is no refreshment stall. After a day's hard work people may like to chat and have a cup of tea. How about opening a tea stall?

Shyam: It is true that we don't have any tea stall in our locality. But, Rambhai, it requires money. Who has got the money? Also I don't know to handle money.

Ram: Shyambhai, let us go to Keshavbhai (who teaches adult classes). He may help us in getting some money and in handling money matters. (Shyam and Ram visit Keshav at his home).

Keshav: What is your problem?

Shyam: Keshavbhai, we are frustrated as we are unemployed. We want to open a tea stall. We need your guidance in handling money matters.

Keshav: Ram and Shyam. It is good that you want to open a tea stall in our locality. Before we discuss matters related to handling of money, I would suggest, you both go to Mohan's tea stall which is not far away and study the pros and cons of opening a tea stall. After your visit please come to me.

Ram: It is a good idea, Shyambhai. Let us go to Mohan's tea stall and benefit from his experience (Shyam and Ram go to Mohan's Tea Stall)

Shyam: Mohanbhai, we are planning to open a tea stall in our locality. We would like to have the benefit of your experience about opening a tea stall. We need your help and guidance.

Mohan: I would be glad to guide you in this regard. In order to open a tea stall, you will have to consider the following points. 1. Is there any other tea stall in your locality? 2. Have you selected a site? 3. Have you got a wooden frame? 4. What articles are needed for opening a tea stall? 5. Are you going to have cash sale only?

Shyam: Let me answer your points one by one. 1. We don't have any tea stalls in our locality. The nearest stall is yours which is about two kilometers from our place. 2. We have selected a site which is located at the entrance of our mohalla. 3. We can ask Chandu, our village carpenter, to make a wooden frame for us. 4. For articles, we need milk, tea, sugar, coal, oven, cups and plates, spoons, biries, poles and tarpaulin. This is what comes to my mind. But you can guide us better. 5. I would suggest cash sale only. But we might have to have both cash and credit.

Mohan: Well, you have answered very well the first three items. But, concerning the fourth item you may sit and enjoy a cup of tea. As regards the fifth, supply tea on credit to customers whom you know fairly well. But, I suggest sale on credit should be given with great care. It should be mostly cash sale. To discourage sale on credit you may sell tea at an increased rate i.e. 31 paisa per cup instead of 30 paisa. Another thing you need to know is how to estimate the quantity of articles. How much milk would you need a day? How much coal? For all these activities, you will have to know some arithmetic.

Ram: Thank you, Mohanbhai.

Shyam: Now let us go to Keshavbhai. We have got some information about opening a tea stall. But we

---

"A student's interest is aroused only when he perceives something of value in the educational system or sees practical application of the knowledge to be gained."

---

still don't know the handling of money matters. (Both go to Keshavbhai).

Keshav: Come in, Ram and Shyam, how was your visit to Mohan's tea stall?

Ram: It was quite good. We have learned quite a few things. But we still do not know about handling money and getting a loan from the bank.

Keshav: I am glad that your visit to Mohan's tea stall has been helpful. In order to know about handling money and getting a loan from the bank, it is necessary to understand some arithmetic. If you want to learn some arithmetic let us do some activities which are found in capsule 1-1-2.

The text of the brochure leads thus into a new context of learning. In the actual booklet, feedback questions and learning guides complete the uncomplicated text.

Conclusion

My experience with culturally different pupils around the world especially in the Western Hemisphere (Canada and U.S.A.) with Afro-Americans and native Indians for more than a decade suggests that this experimental approach comprised of the functional learning package, may be one of the attempts which may be taken into consideration for linking education with socio-economic issues of our disadvantaged pupils. In this process of functional education, teaching and learning becomes a sharing and meaningful experience for a student which is an important step to increase participation in development.

The author has received quite favorable comments concerning this experimental idea to "Functional Education" from various developing countries. However, no formulative evaluation has been conducted. Also, it is worth mentioning here that the most important contribution of the facilitator, teacher or field worker must always be his ability to make interpretations, innovations, invent his own study units and make them come to life by adopting opportunities in the living environment. He must be inventive in demonstrating examples of an idea from the resources at hand in specific situations based on their life experiences. Thus, the functional learning package mentioned above, is concerned with one aspect of every day life and can be applied in its methods to other similar aspects leading to development activities with conscious learning processes.

To conclude, let us think, organize and strive together as a profession, so that young boys and girls, especially disadvantaged ones in the third world, can discover for themselves the value of logical inquiry, tested intuition, and the general process of innovation, for both themselves and their community and also make effective contribution in the participation of the development process of their respective countries.

Outdoor Leadership "Down Under"

by Simon Priest

New Zealand and Australia have each evolved independent schemes of outdoor leadership development based upon the British Mountain Leadership Certificate System. This article examines these unique model programs and makes some comparisons and contrasts between the two methods of training.

AUSTRALIA

Of the seven Australian states, three actively involve themselves in the training of outdoor leaders. South Australia, Victoria and Tasmania all offer certification programs in "Mountain and Bushwalking Leadership." The Victorian program was the first of the three to be created in response to concerns that the heavy use of outdoor teaching environments might lead to accidents and fatalities. The South Australian program is very similar to that of Victoria, but concentrates primarily on training school teachers to care for children involved in outdoor adventure activities. The Tasmanian program takes the Victorian system one step further by incorporating a unique experimental component and is aimed more at commercial adventure tourism operators than at school teachers.

Historically, the Australian outdoor leadership development movement began with the first Victorian course offered in May of 1969. The program format at that time was heavily predicated upon the British Mountain Leadership Certificate scheme currently used in the United Kingdom. Training materials were ob-

---

Simon Priest recently completed a study tour of New Zealand and Australia and is presently pursuing doctoral studies at the University of Oregon.

tained from the U.K. advisory training boards and adapted in some content areas to suit local bush settings, such as those which might be encountered in the Snowy Mountains region. Over the years which followed, many alterations occurred as it became apparent that there were a few shortcomings to the British system of leadership development. These changes have included the application of advisor and assessor panels and the introduction of preliminary appraisal sessions.

Today, a typical program for leadership applicants begins with an initial week long residential course, during which the technical and safety skills of each applicant are appraised and recommendations on their potential for leadership ability is made. If the applicants are lacking in any major skill areas they are refused acceptance to the training program and additional experience or outside training are suggested. Should they lack only one area of competence, such as first aid, they are accepted on probation to the candidate stage and told to improve that skill area with the appropriate training.

Once they have been recommended for leadership candidature, the candidates are assigned established and experienced leaders as advisors for one or two years. During this interim training period, the candidates experience a wide variety of leadership roles, with many different groups and in a range of settings. These intensive and extensive experiences are recorded in a log book. The candidates meet often with the advisor to discuss this log. Once the candidates have collectively logged a minimum number of days as experienced apprentice leaders, they are once again appraised and recommended for advancement to an assessment stage.

The assessment stage begins with individual four day trips under the full leadership responsibility of each candidate. The advisor attends as a back-up leader and members of an assessment

"[In Australia] candidates [for the outdoor leadership certificate] experience a wide variety of leadership roles with many different groups and in a range of settings."

panel attend to critique each candidate's leadership performance. If satisfactory performance is demonstrated on this trip, the candidates are advanced to a final week long residential assessment course. During the final assessment a panel of advisors and assessors observe and evaluate the leadership performances of several candidates under a wide selection of actual and simulated situations. At the conclusion of the assessment period, candidates who meet the criteria for advancement are recommended for a leadership certificate. At any stage of this process, any candidate who fails to meet an assessment criteria has the option of withdrawing from the program or returning to repeat an assigned stage of training.

Both the South Australian and Tasmanian programs follow this scheme with a few exceptions. The South Australian program, being oriented toward outdoor education teachers, concentrates heavily on the instructional capabilities of their candidates. The program focuses on teaching strategies, instructional aids and lesson planning.

Tasmania, the rugged island state which lies south of Victoria, concentrates more on the safety skills such as accident response, route finding, weather interpretation, and search and rescue. The Tasmanian program also has more stringent application prerequisites than the other two programs. Applicants must be very experienced in bush and mountain travel before they will even be considered as a candidate. The result is a leadership candidate group of advanced technical skill level, providing an opportunity for the trainers to concentrate on the more critical aspects of leadership development, such as group dynamics, decision making and problem solving.

All three states make use of the manual

Bushwalking and Mountaincraft Leadership, published by the Victorian Bushwalking and Mountaincraft Advisory Board (1978). The manual details six areas of concern for the leadership candidate: The Leader, Trip Planning, The Walk, Food, The Elements, and Emergencies. Appendices list further readings, equipment, food menus, outdoor shops, outdoor clubs, leadership skills and knowledge. As the program evolved, organizers realized that there was more to leadership than the technical skills covered in the manual. So in time a series of information papers specific to each state were prepared to compliment the course notes. These information papers cover such topics as Conflict Resolution, Party Morale, Leadership Style, Group Dynamics, Decision Making and Environmental Ethics.

One unique experimental component of the Tasmanian program is an attempt to adapt present leadership theories from the worlds of education, the military, and business to the situation of leading groups in the outdoors. Currently, the program looks closely at the Vroom & Yetton Decision Making Tree (Vroom and Yetton, 1974), the Fiedler Contingency Theory (Fiedler, 1971), and several models proposed by Blanchard & Hershey (1980), Valenzi & Bass (1975), and Green & Mitchell (1979). Participants in these study sessions are given written theories to read and assimilate. These theories are then demonstrated through simulated practise cases. Actual experience is gained by attempting to apply the theories on field trips. The course organizers feel the models presented by Fiedler and Vroom & Yetton have greatest application in outdoor leadership situations. However, their investigations are quite new, and they are the first to admit much more study is needed in this area.

NEW ZEALAND

In 1977 a provisional Outdoor Training Advisory Board (OTAB) was formed to examine a national outdoor leadership training system for New Zealand. The "Hunt Report" had recently been published in the U.K. advocating sweeping alterations to the British Mountain Leadership Certificate Scheme. OTAB's recommendations for outdoor leadership development at home were based heavily upon the changes occuring overseas.

After lengthy and difficult discussions, OTAB prepared a policy to approach outdoor leadership training from a new and fresh perspective. They agreed to adopt an open-ended development scheme which did not present a certificate, thus implying a candidate should continue to seek life long learning opportunities in outdoor leadership training. A modular approach was used, allowing the system to be flexible enough to meet an individual's unique needs, to be applicable at many levels of skill or experience, and to be available to potential leaders from many outdoor pursuits areas and organizations. In addition, OTAB decided upon self assessment rather than evaluation by a panel of board members as a means to encourage leaders to take the responsibility for their own training and development.

OTAB is designed to be an advisory agency. Their present aim is to assist other outdoor associations with outdoor leader training prorams at the "grass roots" level, rather than dictating a mandatory series of courses for all leaders in general. They operate a resource and information clearing house based in the capital city of Wellington, and have two major publications of note: a self assessment *Logbook* (1981) and an *Outdoor Training Guide (1980)*.

The Logbook is quick to state that any entries should not be interpreted as a guarantee of leadership competence and that the responsibility for useful accuracy lies with the owner. The log has space for personal particulars, equipment checklists, training sources, and further information. Three categories exist for recording new experiences: Course Experience for noting any new learning which has occurred, General Experience for listing personal trips, and Experience of Leading for entering the details of trips where a role of responsibility was held. The section on Self Assessment provides the opportunity to evaluate one's leadership capacity in fourteen core modules adapted from the *Outdoor Training Guide*. Assessment, made from time to time, is suggested on a scale of 1 to 5, and *Logbook* owners are cautioned to be wary of overestimating their skills and knowledge.

The *Outdoor Training Guide* (interim edition 1980) suggests suitable guidelines for leadership development and assessment. It details fourteen areas of leadership knowledge and skill including: Leadership Theory, Human Growth and Development, Environmental Issues, Planning and Organization, Legal and Moral Issues, Finance and Administration, Food and Hygiene, Clothing and Equipment, Weather, Land Navigation, Interpreting the Environment, First Aid, Emergency Procedures and Water Safety. It is designed to provide a means for leaders, instructors and course coordinators, to analyze their personal strengths and weaknesses, and to respond by seeking an appropriate educational source. The publication lists reading references and resource associations as sources available to all leaders.

REFERENCES

- Blanchard, K.H. and Hersey, P. "A Leadership Theory for Educational Administrators" *Education* 90:4, p. 303, 1980.
- Fiedler, F.E. *Leadership*. Morristown, New Jersey: General Learning Press, 1971.
- Green, S.G. and Mitchell, T.R. "Attributional Process of Leadership in Leader-member Interactions" Org. Beh. Hum. Perform., 23:429, 1979.
- New Zealand Outdoor Training Advisory Board. *Logbook*. Auckland, New Zealand: Private Bag, Symonds Street, 1981.
- New Zealand Outdoor Training Advisory Board. *Outdoor Training Guide*. Wellington, New Zealand: Box 5122, 1980.
- Valenzi, E.A. and Bass, B.M. "The Bass-Valenzi Management Styles Profile" *Proceedings of the Academy of Management,* 1975.
- Victorian Bushwalking and Mountaincraft Training Advisory Board, *Bushwalking and Mountaincraft Leadership*. Melbourne, Victoria: Youth, Sport, and Recreation, 570 Bourke Street, Melbourne, Victoria, 3000.
- Vroom, V.H. and Yetton, P.W. *Leadership and Decision Making*. New York: Wiley and Sons, 1974.

People interested in more information about the assessment instruments mentioned in this article, should write directly to:

New Zealand OTAB P.O. Box 5122 Wellington	BMTAB of Victoria 570 Bourke St. Melbourne 3000	BMWLTB of Tasmania Kirksway House Hobart, 7000

Oh, Those Missed Opportunities!

by Dr. Alec Dickson

On April 22, 1977, a sheet of flame erupted out of the North Sea in the Ekofisk-Bravo oilfield, well over 100 miles east of Aberdeen. A blow-out in mid-ocean, in some of the roughest waters of Northern Europe, was not only a totally new problem for the operators, it could portend disaster for Britian's efforts to establish its own dollar-earning petroleum industry.

Later that day the Rector — that is President — of Aberdeen University convened an emergency meeting of Faculty Heads. "Professor Erskine — Mechanical Engineering — what do we know of the containment of liquids under high pressure? Professor Chambers — Chemistry — where are we in regard to fire extinction at sea? Professor Mackintosh — Marine Biology — what will be the impact on our rich fishing beds of an unchecked flow of thousands of barrels of oil? Professor Elphinstone — Environmental Economics — how will the summer holiday season, starting next month, be affected by polluted beaches all along the coast?"

"Well, gentlemen, let us meet tomorrow to pool our ideas and see what contribution we can make to this crisis. Oh, by the way, do please alert all your students, for they may have a crucial role to play."

Thus an ancient seat of learning founded exactly 500 years ago, reacted to this emergency, determined to place its combined intellectual

thrust and students' energies at the service of Scotland, indeed of the United Kingdom.

Of course, I'm fooling. Only the first paragraph of this piece is factual. No such meeting was called. The atmosphere on the campus was as serene that April day as on any other. This was something for the oil companies or drilling firms to deal with — or the Royal Navy, the Department of the Environment or the Minister for Energy in London. Anyhow, practical solutions were more the concern of Colleges and Institutes of Technology: the University's concentration of study in this respect was in the realm of research (and teaching) in Pure Science.

In this event, nobody in Britian or Western Europe knew how to handle such a crude oil problem, if that is the right description. Long-distance calls to Texas resulted in those two daring and practiced desperados, "Red" Adair and "Boots" Hansen, flying in to deal with the crisis: the blow-out was extinguished and capped. So a chance to mobilise a great university and apply its resources to an emergency of national significance was lost. Why?

****

Grafton Street lies off Piccadilly, in the heart of London's West End. There, in late June (1984), some two dozen Administrative Officers in their mid-twenties assembled at the London office of the Hong Kong Government. All graduates of the University of Hong Kong, of Chinese race but speaking polished English, hand-picked by rigorous selection for the highest echelon of Hong Kong's Civil Service, they had just completed a year's special course in Political Science and Administration, most at Oxford, others at Cambridge. I had been brought in from outside to speak to them on "The Meaning of Service" — an address which might have been more timely had it come when they first arrived

---

Dr. Alec Dickson is founder of Voluntary Service Overseas and Community Service Volunteers in Great Britian as well as founder of an Outward Bound school in Nigeria.

"I do not share the view that it is harder to transmit... vision and imagination... than academic knowledge or technical skill."

in Britian rather than the day before they returned to the Far East. I spoke as follows.

"I'm assuming that you will all have spent a brief period in Northern Ireland, staying some nights in the homes of Republican Catholics and some with Protestant Loyalists, as well as discussing with local officials the problems of how to administer a Province which seems ungovernable and the implications of trying to reconcile two apparently irreconcilable ideologies.

"Presumably you will have each worked the beat beside some young policeman, white in colour, whilst he has been on patrol in an area like Brixton in South London, with its high percentage of blacks, and sensed his personal tension in streets where serious riots took place two years ago.

"Of course you will have visited Piccadilly and Soho (with its relatively high ratio of Chinese workers), only three hundred or so yards from where we now are, to discover for yourselves how youngsters who've left home to make their way to London now find themselves jobless, homeless, exposed to sexual advances and the dangers of drugs. And you will have

considered their plight against your own experience, since your own parents may have immigrated from the Chinese mainland to Hong Kong, a place where drug addiction is not unknown.

"And because the Hong Kong Government generously finances your travel on the Continent during vacations — so that your experience of British ways of thinking can be broadened by acquaintance with the lifestyle and governmental measures of other European countries — naturally some of you will have visited the Netherlands to contrast how the Moluccans, who came as Christians from the old Dutch East Indies to Holland in the late 1940s, rather than live under an Islamic and radical Indonesian regime, are coping in the 1980s — and you will have pondered why some of their Dutch-born second generation now feel so alienated that they have highjacked trains and held passengers for ransom. And how the Turkish 'guest-workers' or Gastarbeiter whose labour was so welcome during West Germany's Economic Miracle feel, now that there is unemployment and they are being pressured to return to their Turkish villages. How does the record of the three countries — Britian, the Netherlands, West Germany — compare in this respect?"

There was a good deal more to say: the main theme of service had not yet been touched upon. But this seemed an appropriate moment to pause. Dead silence. Then one young Hong Kong Administrative Officer remarked defensively but justly: "But we did not design this course, that was the responsibility of Senior Lecturers in the Political Science Departments at Oxford and Cambridge." And the British civil servant concerned with organizing things at the London office observed quietly: "Senior Lecturers at Oxford and Cambridge have never themselves had the kind of experience you've been describing."

Yet on the shoulders of these indubitably intelligent, well-motivated Hong Kong Ad-

> "...One perceives what might be called the Schweitzer syndrome — of noble-hearted characters...who may stir the conscience of the rest of humanity but fail to impart their commitment to those nearest to them."

ministration Officers will fall the awesome burden in a few years' time, as the British withdraw, of negotiating the handover of power to representatives of the Chinese People's Republic or at least striving to reach a political/economic/social *modus vivendi*. What if their training has concentrated on the theory of political/administration — perhaps punctuated by visits to Local Authority Planning Departments in Britian and possibly some simulation exercises — but virtually ignored exposure to the terrible forces of human passion?

••

The scene changes to Mashi, a large village (or small town) in Northern Nigeria. Passing through the outskirts one notices a board, "Government Secondary Vocational Training School." "Can we look in here?" I ask, and the answer is "Yes, of course." But by this time the car has entered the market-square. As the driver swings the wheel round, one catches sight of village women laboriously lowering buckets by hand down the well: evidently the pumphandle is fractured. And as we sweep up the drive to the school, there is a glimpse of a crippled boy lying beneath the shade of a tree.

We are shown round the workshops and subsequently a small staff meeting is called — most courteously since we have arrived quite unannounced, on a hot late afternoon. The Principal is away — a pity, for his background is interesting: he had first come to the country as a black American in the Peace Corps — and then taken Nigerian nationality and become a Muslim. Most of the staff are African but there are some 'expatriate' technical instructors (principally British). They describe the syllabus of training. Then I ask whether the students are encouraged to apply their skills in metalwork and carpentry to community problems and human needs. For example? Well, the broken

handle of the village pump. "But that's the responsibility of the Public Works Department at District headquarters!" How about the lame youngster at the entrance, then, who could benefit from an adjustable Canadian-style crutch? "Oh, that would come under the Medical Department's regional centre!"

I plead that, since these needs are apparently not being tackled by the appropriate authorities, would they not provide opportunities for their students to relate what they are learning in the classrooms and workshops to real-life situations? "Ah, but the Education Department barely gives us enough wood and metal to train our students with." At this point I exclaim that they are living in a country with perhaps the largest open-cast mineral deposits and timber resources in Africa — the abandoned remains of trucks smashed in accidents, which litter the roadsides throughout the region, which they could legitimately plunder for material. This must be a very odd visitor, with such impractical, eccentric ideas, comes across during the silence which follows my statements.

••

So what conclusions can be reached? Surely that opportunities for students to engage in experiental education, in service-learning, are being missed time and again. And not principally through the reluctance of students to jeopardize their grades by leaving the lectureroom or lab to do something of positive value in the neighborhood — but through the inability of experienced educators to relate theory to practice or to link courses and curricula to concern for the community.

Some would argue that we are talking about vision and imagination — harder to transmit, so it would seem, than academic knowledge or technical skills. I do not share this view: it *is* possible to open eyes so that they see opportunities of service and to move hearts so that they want to respond to human needs. But the resistance of institutes of training to make such provision in the preparation of teachers or lecturers for the role of catalysts, "animators" or Pied Pipers is, admittedly, enormously difficult to overcome. So one finds those with the power to inspire leaving or avoiding the mainstream of the educational system: I think of Robert Burkhardt, directing the San Francisco Conservation Corps or James Kielsmeier pioneering the National Youth Leadership Council — and the whole development of the Outward Bound movement — outside the structure of formal schooling.

Quite in the opposite direction one perceives what might be called the Schweitzer syndrome — of noble-hearted characters who devote themselves to the welfare of the sick or bruised, but somehow limit their effectiveness by ignoring the critical multiplication factor: they may stir the conscience of the rest of humanity but fail to impart their commitment to those nearest to them. Every generation has need of saints, whose sacrificial lives reach pinnacles of perfection. Yet each time Mother Teresa's name is mentioned, one asks oneself what the twelfth graders in Calcutta's high schools, the undergraduates at Calcutta University, the students of social work training in that city are doing to share or indeed assume altogether the responsibility for their abandoned and dying.

But it is a disservice to end on a note of pessimism, even if the examples quoted come not from the mainstream but the fringes, thereby reinforcing the conclusion already described earlier. I think firstly of the multinational students from the United World College of the Adriatic who regularly visit patients in a semi-abandoned psychiatric hospital in Trieste. Across the barriers of language and mental confusion how can a bridge be built? Well, Trieste is famous — like Venice, Rio de Janeiro and Trinidad — for its annual carnival. So the patients have been helped by the students to prepare costumes and masks. And when the whole population of Trieste explodes into a world of fantasy, they, too, join without stigma in the revelry. No close connection with the curriculum — but surely a flash of genius on the part of 16/17 year-old students.

And then a visit to a training school, or 'Efterskole,' for youngsters from disturbed and troubled backgrounds, on the coast of southeastern Denmark. It was at a time when the Solidarity movement in Poland had just been declared illegal by the Government in Warsaw. Suppose things got worse, these Danish teenagers reasoned, perhaps some Solidarity members might endeavour to get away by sea. If that happened, the escapees might even land on the shore not far from their school. A thrill of hope went through the school, to the extent that staff members, who might otherwise have been skeptical, said nothing to dash their expectations. So the youngsters began to store some of their own food which could be preserved: to discuss how they should learn of a landing and what they could do to welcome them if or when they actually arrived. Without expressing it in words, they began to see their school as a resource centre to tackle human needs. Would that every school and college thought in similar terms.